THE GUIDE FOR BROWNIE GIRL SCOUT LEADERS

Girl Scouts of the U.S.A.
420 Fifth Avenue
New York, N.Y. 10018-2702

GIRL SCOUTS OF THE U.S.A.

B. LaRae Orullian, *National President*
Mary Rose Main, *National Executive Director*

Inquiries related to *The Guide for Brownie Girl Scout Leaders*
should be directed to Program, Girl Scouts of the U.S.A.,
420 Fifth Avenue
New York, N.Y. 10018-2702.

CREDITS

Authors
Karen Unger Sparks
Chris Bergerson
Sharon Woods Hussey
Judith Brucia
Martha Jo Dennison
Carolyn L. Kennedy
Robyn J. Payne

Illustrators
Don Morrison
Michael Hostovick

Designer: The Antler & Baldwin
Design Group

Design Coordinator
Kristine Schueler

ISBN 0-88441-280-6
10 9 8 7 6 5 4 3 2

Contents

Introduction

Welcome to Brownie Girl Scouts! If you are new to this age level in Girl Scouting, this book will be a helpful guide and source of information. If you are a "veteran" Brownie Girl Scout leader, you will find some fresh ideas and an affirmation of your efforts.

Your basic resource as a Brownie Girl Scout leader is this book. The complete edition of the girls' book—the *Brownie Girl Scout Handbook*, which includes all of the Brownie Girl Scout Try-Its—is printed in Part II of this book. Each page is reproduced exactly as it appears in the girls' handbook. Your version includes safety tips, helpful hints, and program links in the "wrap-around" text bordering each page.

Part I of this leaders' guide contains information that cannot be found in the girls' handbook. The first chapter, "About Girl Scouting,"

Welcome to Girl Scouts

"Okay, girls, I'll see you next week. Please remember to bring your permission slips for the camping trip," Mrs. Carreras said as we left the school cafeteria.

Later that night . . .

"I can't wait to go camping!" I said as I climbed into bed. "My first overnight trip! I know I'm going to have a great time!"

Oh, hi! My name is Jessica and I am a Brownie Girl Scout. At our meeting tonight, we had a party. We sang songs, played games, and listened to a story! After we listened to the story, Mrs. Carreras, our leader, told us she knew a woman who loved stories and Girl Scouting as much as we did. She was born on October 31, 1860.

The Story of Girl Scouting

covers basic information about the Girl Scout program, including the Girl Scout program standards. The second chapter, "Planning for the Year," contains ceremonies, songs, tips for planning meetings and trips, and a troop-year calendar for your own notes. The third chapter, "Working with Brownie Girl Scouts," offers advice for leading activities with girls ages six through eight and covers group management, conflict resolution, and sensitive issues. The fourth chapter, "Adapting Girl Scout Program Activities," will assist you in varying activities to meet the individual needs of girls. "Help You Can Expect," the fifth chapter, includes diagrams and descriptions of the support Girl Scouting provides for leaders and an annotated bibliography of resources.

Throughout your leaders' guide you will find real situations that lead-

ers have faced in their Brownie Girl Scout troops. These sample dilemmas and suggested resolutions will help you decide how to manage your troop or group. You have plenty of room to write, take notes, plan, and create in these pages.

Brownie Girl Scouts have many other resources available to them. An annotated list is included in Chapter 5. Your *Girl Scout Leader* magazine and *Girl Scout Catalog* are additional valuable resources. Your local Girl Scout council representative will keep you up-to-date on other new Girl Scout program materials. You and the girls in your troop or group can use the Brownie Girl Scout resources to create a set of activities that uniquely fits your interests, needs, and circumstances. Your innovative ideas and individual contributions are what keep Girl Scouting exciting and growing.

Girl Scout Program: An Overview

Key Aspects of Girl Scouting Fit Together to Form the Design for Girl Scout Program

The Girl Scout Promise and Law:
The Foundation of Girl Scouting

The Four Program Goals:
Our Goals for Girls

Five Worlds of Interest:
Activity Areas

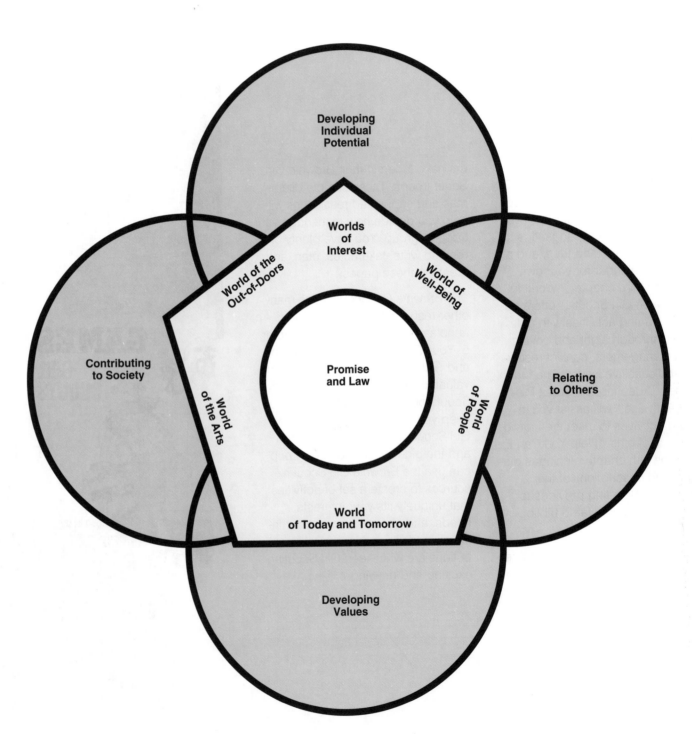

About Girl Scouting

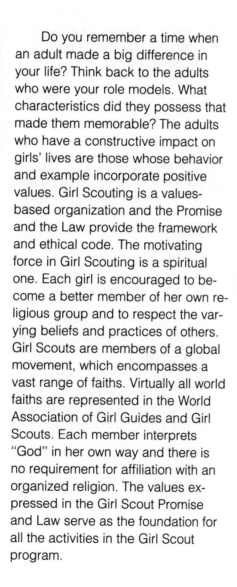

CHAPTER 1

Do you remember a time when an adult made a big difference in your life? Think back to the adults who were your role models. What characteristics did they possess that made them memorable? The adults who have a constructive impact on girls' lives are those whose behavior and example incorporate positive values. Girl Scouting is a values-based organization and the Promise and the Law provide the framework and ethical code. The motivating force in Girl Scouting is a spiritual one. Each girl is encouraged to become a better member of her own religious group and to respect the varying beliefs and practices of others. Girl Scouts are members of a global movement, which encompasses a vast range of faiths. Virtually all world faiths are represented in the World Association of Girl Guides and Girl Scouts. Each member interprets "God" in her own way and there is no requirement for affiliation with an organized religion. The values expressed in the Girl Scout Promise and Law serve as the foundation for all the activities in the Girl Scout program.

The Girl Scout Promise

On my honor, I will try:
To serve God and my country,
To help people at all times,
And to live by the Girl Scout Law.

The Girl Scout Law

I will do my best:
to be honest
to be fair
to help where I am needed
to be cheerful
to be friendly and considerate
to be a sister to every Girl Scout
to respect authority
to use resources wisely
to protect and improve the world
*   around me*
to show respect for myself and others
*   through my words and actions.*

More About Girl Scouting

Brownie Girl Scouts are one of the five age levels in Girl Scouting: Daisy Girl Scouts, Brownie Girl Scouts, Junior Girl Scouts, Cadette Girl Scouts, and Senior Girl Scouts. Often you may hear people say, "I was a Brownie, but I was never a Girl Scout!" Brownie Girl Scouts are Girl Scouts ages six, seven, or eight or in first, second, or third grade. They are part of a worldwide movement that has members in more than 100 nations all belonging to the World Association of Girl Guides and Girl Scouts (WAGGGS). The age levels are:

Daisy Girl Scout
(grades K–1 or 5–6 years old)
Brownie Girl Scout
(grades 1–3 or 6–8 years old)
Junior Girl Scout
(grades 3–6 or 8–11 years old)
Cadette Girl Scout
(grades 6–9 or 11–14 years old)
Senior Girl Scout
(grades 9–12 or 14–17 years old)

As a Brownie Girl Scout leader, you are also a member of an organization that is expressly for girls, all girls who make the Girl Scout Promise. The all-girl setting of Girl Scouting is of primary importance in helping girls achieve the goals of the Girl Scout program. Research has shown that girls often receive less attention and fewer opportunities when in groups with boys. Brownie Girl Scout activities give girls the opportunity to experiment, create, challenge, and grow in a nurturing and supportive environment.

The Four Program Goals

The Girl Scout program has four goals for girls. These goals describe the ways girls will grow and develop through their Girl Scout experiences.

1 Develop to her full individual potential.

- Foster feelings of self-acceptance and unique self-worth.
- Promote her perception as competent, responsible, and open to new experiences and challenges.
- Offer opportunities to learn new skills.
- Encourage personal growth.
- Allow girls to utilize and practice talents and abilities.

2 To relate to others with increasing understanding, skill, and respect.

- Help each girl develop sensitivity to others and respect for their needs, feelings, and rights.
- Promote an understanding and appreciation of individual, cultural, religious, and racial differences.
- Foster the ability to build friendships and working relationships.

3 Develop values to guide her actions and to provide the foundation for sound decision-making.

- Help her develop a meaningful set of values and ethics that will guide her actions.
- Foster an ability to make decisions that are consistent with her values and that reflect respect for the rights and needs of others.
- Empower her to act upon her values and convictions.
- Encourage her to reexamine her ideals as she matures.

4 To contribute to the improvement of society through the use of her abilities and leadership skills, working in cooperation with others.

- Help her develop concern for the well-being of her community and its people.
- Promote an understanding of how the quality of community life affects her own life and the whole of society.
- Encourage her to use her skills to work with others for the benefit of all.

As a Brownie Girl Scout leader, you will find it helpful to keep the four Girl Scout program goals in mind when planning activities with the girls. Remembering the goals of Girl Scout program will help you build a complete experience for girls.

Another way to achieve a balance of activities is to guide girls in selecting activities from each of the Girl Scout worlds of interest. These five broad interest areas provide a simple structure for varying activities. By periodically checking that you have done activities in all the worlds of interest, you can be certain that girls are experiencing variety.

Most activities in the *Brownie Girl Scout Handbook* relate to more than one world of interest. For example, the chapter "People Near and Far" contains a song from Peru. This relates to the World of People and the World of the Arts. The sensory nature hike activities in the "How and Why?" chapter relate to the World of Well-Being (hiking), the World of the Out-of-Doors (being outside—learning about nature), and the World of Today and Tomorrow (using your senses). Though many activities are based on more than one interest area, drawing activities from each of the five worlds of interest is a helpful way to ensure that troop activities are not drawn too heavily from just one or two topic areas.

The World of Well-Being includes activities that focus on physical and emotional health: nutrition and exercise; feelings and self-discovery; personal relationships; sports, games, leisure-time activities; as well as home, safety, consumer awareness, and careers.

The World of People includes activities that focus on developing awareness of the various cultures in our society and around the world, and on building pride in one's heritage while appreciating and respecting the heritage of others.

The World of Today and Tomorrow includes activities that focus on discovering the how and why of things, exploring and experimenting with the many technologies that are encountered in daily life, dealing with change, looking to future events, roles, and responsibilities.

The World of the Arts includes activities that focus on enjoying and expressing oneself through art forms, appreciating the artistic talents and contributions of others, and learning more about the visual, performing, and literary arts.

The World of the Out-of-Doors includes activities that focus on enjoying and appreciating the out-of-doors, living in and caring for our natural environment, and understanding and respecting the interdependence of all living things.

Brownie Girl Scout Try-Its

There are 40 Brownie Girl Scout Try-Its. They are designed to encourage girls to attempt new things. The emphasis is on new experiences, not gaining proficiency. The themes of the Try-Its are based on the five worlds of interest in Girl Scouting, though many could fit in more than one world of interest. Each Try-It has six activities to select from. When girls complete four of the activities, they may receive the Try-It patch to wear on their sashes or vests. When possible, encourage girls to try all six of the activities.

The illustration of the vest and the sash show where to place the Try-Its.

The activities in the Try-Its are ideally done as group activities; however, the activities are flexible enough so that it is possible for a girl to work on a Try-It by herself or with just one other person. Some activities may require adult assistance. Before introducing any Try-It to the girls in your troop or group, make sure you have "tried it" yourself so that you know just what materials you will need, how long the activity will take, and what results you can expect.

Earning Try-Its is only one aspect of the Girl Scout program for Brownie Girl Scouts. It is important to help girls have fun in what they do and not feel that every activity must end with some type of patch or award. Earning Try-Its should not become the primary structure of meetings.

One of the most important things to remember when working on Try-It activities with girls is that Try-It activities have not been designed primarily so that girls can develop measurable skills or proficiencies in one particular area. Girls are not so much mastering a skill as learning about things new to them. Girls may choose to do one or two activities in a Try-It and then move on to another one. Girls should not feel pressured to complete a Try-It they really do not want to finish. Also, girls should not feel that having more Try-Its than someone else is a measure of who has done better. However, you do want girls to try a variety of activities. Encourage them to sample Try-Its on themes about which they may not initially be enthusiastic. You determine when a Try-It has been earned. Remember each activity counts only once. An activity completed for one Try-It may not be counted for another. It is also best not to apply activities that have already been done to a Try-It started at a later date.

When special circumstances make it difficult or impossible to complete an activity—for example, if a child has a disability, or distance or geographic location poses problems—activities may be adapted. Sometimes the adaptation is as easy as choosing one activity over another. Sometimes, though, you and the girls may need to figure out an alternative way of completing a requirement. For example, the activity may require a number of books about children in different countries. The nearest library is 50 miles away! Instead, girls may exchange family stories that illustrate their backgrounds and family histories. Tips for adapting particular Try-It activities appear in Part II of this book. Just remember that four activities are needed to earn a Try-It.

Girls may receive their Try-Its at a Court of Awards, a ceremony to recognize a girl's achievements. It may be held periodically throughout the year or at the end of the year. You can work with girls to decide when and what type of ceremony they would like to hold.

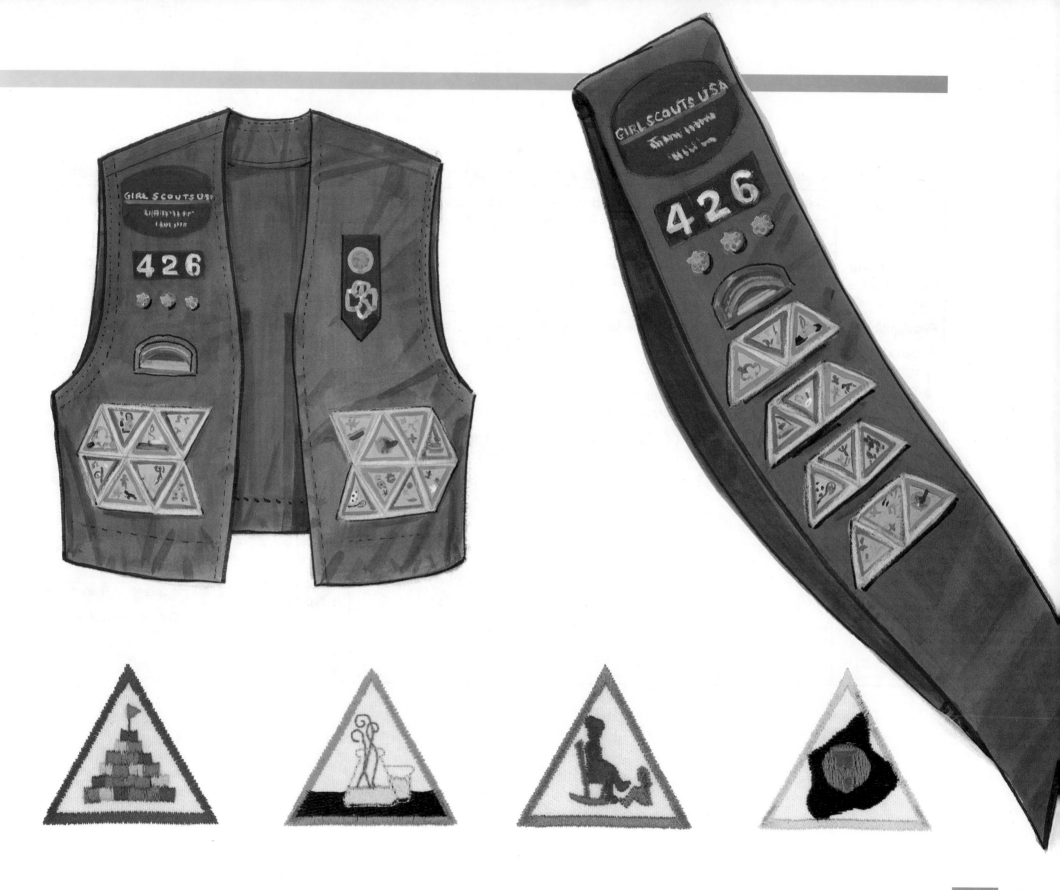

Girl Scouting at the Five Age Levels

	Daisy Girl Scouts	Brownie Girl Scouts	Junior Girl Scouts	Cadette Girl Scouts	Senior Girl Scouts
Age or Grade	5–6 years old or kindergarten or first grade	6–8 years old or first, second, or third grade	8–11 years old or third, fourth, fifth, or sixth grade	11–14 years old or sixth, seventh, eighth, or ninth grade	14–17 years old or ninth, tenth, eleventh, or twelfth grade
Form of Troop Government	Daisy Girl Scout Circle	Brownie Girl Scout Ring or Brownie Girl Scout Circle	Patrol system, town meeting, or executive board	Patrol system, town meeting, or executive board	Patrol system, town meeting, or executive board
Recognitions	Bridge to Brownie Girl Scouts patch	Brownie Girl Scout Try-Its Bridge to Junior Girl Scouts patch Badges earned as part of bridging activities Religious recognitions	Badges (Dabbler, white, green, tan) Signs (Rainbow, Sun, Satellite, World) Junior Aide patch Bridge to Cadette Girl Scouts patch Religious recognitions	Interest Project patches Tan badges Leader-in-Training pin Counselor-in-Training pin From Dreams to Reality patch Religious recognitions American Indian Youth Certificate and Award Cadette Girl Scout Challenge pin Cadette Girl Scout Leadership Award Girl Scout Silver Award Bridge to Senior Girl Scouts patch	Same as Cadette Girl Scouts, except no tan badges, Cadette Girl Scout Challenge pin, Cadette Girl Scout Leadership Award, and Bridge to Senior Girl Scouts patch Ten-Year Award Girl Scout Gold Award Bridge to Adults Girl Scouts pin Senior Girl Scout Challenge pin Apprentice Trainer's pin Career Exploration pin

	Daisy Girl Scouts	Brownie Girl Scouts	Junior Girl Scouts	Cadette Girl Scouts	Senior Girl Scouts
Basic Resources	*The Guide for Daisy Girl Scout Leaders* *My Daisy Girl Scout Activity Scrapbook* *Daisy Girl Scout storybooks*	*Brownie Girl Scout Handbook* *The Guide for Brownie Girl Scout Leaders*	*Junior Girl Scout Handbook* *Girl Scout Badges and Signs* *Junior Girl Scout Activity Book*	*Cadette and Senior Girl Scout Handbook* *Cadette and Senior Girl Scout Interest Projects*	*Cadette and Senior Girl Scout Handbook* *Cadette and Senior Girl Scout Interest Projects* *Girl Scout Gold Award Booklet*
Supplementary Resources	*Sing-Along Songbook and Cassette* *Games for Girl Scouts* *Exploring Wildlife Communities with Children* *Contemporary Issues booklets*	*Sing-Along Songbook and Cassette* *Brownies' Own Songbook* *Sing Together—A Girl Scout Songbook* *The Wide World of Girl Guiding and Girl Scouting* *WAGGGS Brownie uniform and badge posters* *Games for Girl Scouts* *Exploring Wildlife Communities with Children* *Outdoor Education in Girl Scouting* *World Games and Recipes* *Trefoil Round the World* *Contemporary Issues booklets*	*Sing-Along Songbook and Cassette* *Sing Together—A Girl Scout Songbook* *The Wide World of Girl Guiding and Girl Scouting* *WAGGGS Girl Guide/Girl Scout uniform posters* *Games for Girl Scouts* *Exploring Wildlife Communities with Children* *Outdoor Education in Girl Scouting* *World Games and Recipes* *Trefoil Round the World* *Contemporary Issues booklets*	*Sing Together—A Girl Scout Songbook* *The Wide World of Girl Guiding and Girl Scouting* *Games for Girl Scouts* *Outdoor Education in Girl Scouting* *World Games and Recipes* *Trefoil Round the World* *Contemporary Issues booklets*	*Sing Together—A Girl Scout Songbook* *The Wide World of Girl Guiding and Girl Scouting* *Games for Girl Scouts* *Outdoor Education in Girl Scouting* *World Games and Recipes* *Trefoil Round the World* *Contemporary Issues booklets*

Brownie Girl Scout Uniform

These illustrations show the Brownie Girl Scout uniform components and the proper placement of insignia. While girls are encouraged to wear the uniform, wearing it is not a requirement for belonging to Girl Scouts, nor is it a requirement to have all the components. The needs and interests of girls always come first.

Safety-Wise

All Girl Scout program activities should meet the program standards and guidelines as stated in *Safety-Wise*. Every Girl Scout leader receives a copy of *Safety-Wise*. One of your major responsibilities as a Girl Scout leader is to provide for the safety and security of girls. Using *Safety-Wise* as your guide for planning and implementing activities is a sure way to do this.

Girl Scout Program Standards

There are 35 Girl Scout program standards. As a Girl Scout leader, you need to be familiar with these standards because they list the necessary elements of a quality program experience and the basic levels of health, safety, security, and well-being that must be provided for the girls in your troop or group. Program standards describe how to put the principles of the Girl Scout program into practice. The guidelines provide examples and details that more fully illustrate what must be done in order to meet each standard.

Here are some typical incidents that have occurred to Brownie Girl Scout leaders. How could they best be handled? The answers may be found in one or more of the 35 program standards (and on pages 19–20).

What would you do in this situation?

A The attendance in your troop has been steadily declining. You started off the year with 25 girls and now never have more than ten at a meeting. You ask two of the girls after the latest meeting if they know why fewer girls have been coming. One mumbles something about "only doing crafts stuff" and runs to her waiting father. You have been doing the activities the girls have chosen themselves and are a bit surprised by this answer.

B Sally is very active. She never seems to sit still and wiggles and twitches some part of her body all the time accompanied by almost non-stop whispering or talking. Three of the older girls have heard that a ballet touring company will be in town and have convinced the majority of the girls in the troop that a great way to spend the extra troop trip money would be to attend a matinee performance of "Swan Lake." You think that some would enjoy it, but that others would be bored and Sally could be disruptive.

C You have mentioned a number of ongoing neighborhood beautification projects to the girls as possibilities for service projects they could join. They ask you what kind of patch they'd get if they did.

D You have never gone camping and hate to consider waking up without access to a blow dryer and an indoor bathroom! The girls in your group want to earn the Outdoor Adventurer Try-It including the activity on sleeping out. What do you do?

E You love to camp—you started as a Girl Scout and spend your vacations camping. You are eager to pass along your love of the out-of-doors to the girls in the group. They either yawn or tell you how much they hate bugs!

F You started with one Try-It. Now that is all the girls want to do. They love getting the triangles and spend a lot of time plotting which Try-Its are the quickest and easiest to earn so they can fill up their sashes and vests. They definitely seem happy, but . . .

G Your local mall is more than willing to give you the space for a booth to sell your Girl Scout cookies. One of the girls tells you that she must bring her younger sister, a Daisy Girl Scout, on that day because her mom is working and no one else can baby-sit.

H At your council shop, you bought a copy of *Caring and Coping: Facing Family Crises*. A lot of the information in the booklet and the activities pertain to the girls in your troop. One girl's grandmother has recently died; a few of the parents are recently divorced or separated; one girl has been living with her grandmother for a year with limited visits from her mother. How do you go about using the activities in this booklet with your troop?

I You are the leader of a Brownie Girl Scout troop that meets in a local church. All the girls in the troop are of Hispanic origin, mostly with Puerto Rican and Dominican backgrounds. The community is also composed of Asians—people with Korean and Taiwanese backgrounds, and some recently arrived Russian Jewish immigrants. You have heard a few of the girls use ethnic slurs, obviously imitating words they have heard at home, on the street, on television, or somewhere outside the troop setting.

J You are the leader of a Brownie Girl Scout troop made up of girls from the same ethnic, cultural, and socioeconomic background. In fact, as far as you know, everyone in your community is fairly homogeneous. You have never heard anyone making any bigoted remarks; in fact, the topics of race, racism, or prejudice rarely seem to be mentioned.

K Your Girl Scout council has scheduled an Earth Matters activity day at a local Girl Scout camp. All the girls in your troop want to go and you can take all of them if they ride in the back of your pickup truck.

L One of the girls in your group has informed you that her mother will not let her sell cookies this year. Two other girls overheard her and start saying that if she doesn't sell cookies, she shouldn't go on troop trips.

Read through the following 35 Girl Scout program standards. How would the information here help you in the situations just described? (The complete set of standards and guidelines may be found in your copy of *Safety-Wise*.)

**1
Girl Scout Program—
Foundation and Goals**

Program experiences and activities should meet the needs and interests of girls, be based on the Girl Scout Promise and Law, and enable girls to grow and develop, as described in the four Girl Scout program goals.

**2
General Activities**

Program activities should include a balance of subject and interest areas. The types of activities should be determined in partnership by the girls and their leaders and reflect the girls' needs and interests, physical and emotional readiness, skill level, and preparation. The activities should provide for progressive learning experiences, both at the current age level and in preparation for the next one.

**3
Health, Safety, and Security—
Activity Planning Implementation**

At all times, the health, safety, and security of girls should be paramount. All activities should be planned and carried out so as to safeguard the health, safety, and general well-being of girls and adults. Girls and adults should follow proper safety practices at all times.

**4
International**

Girl Scouting is part of a world-wide movement, and program activities should emphasize this international dimension.

**5
Service**

Service is inherent in the Promise and Law and is given without expectation of payment or reward. All girls should take part in service activities or projects.

**6
Experiences Beyond
the Troop/Group**

Girls should have experiences that broaden their perspectives and enable them to interact with individuals beyond their immediate group. Program activities should provide girls with opportunities to have experiences beyond regular troop/group meetings.

**7
Outdoor Education**

Activities carried out in outdoor settings are an important part of Girl Scout program for each age level. The leader should receive the appropriate training from her council to help her guide preparation for and implementation of the outdoor activities.

**8
Girl Scout Camping**

Girl Scout camping should provide girls with a fun and educational group living experience that links Girl Scout program with the natural surroundings and contributes to each camper's mental, physical, social, and spiritual growth.

**9
Girl Scout Recognitions**

Girl Scout recognitions should acknowledge a girl's accomplishments and attainment of specified requirements. Leaders should work in partnership with girls to decide when recognitions, such as badges, patches, or awards, have been completed. At all times, adults should play a key role in stressing the quality of the program experience over quantity of recognitions.

10
Parental Permission

Written permission from a parent or legal guardian should be obtained for participation in Girl Scouting. Leaders and girls are responsible for informing parents or guardians of the purpose of Girl Scouting; of the date, time, and place of meetings; and of the type of activities included in troop plans. When activities take place outside of the scheduled meeting place, involve travel, or focus on sensitive or controversial topics, parents and guardians should be informed and asked to provide additional written consent.

11
Girl Scout Membership Pins and Uniforms

All Girl Scout members should wear the membership pin when participating in Girl Scout activities. Since Girl Scouting is a uniformed organization, girl and adult members should be informed, at the time they become members, that they are entitled to wear the Girl Scout uniform appropriate for their age level. Although the wearing of the uniform is encouraged, it should be clearly conveyed that the wearing of the uniform is not required for participation in Girl Scouting.

12
Girl/Adult Partnership

Girls and their leaders should work as partners in planning and decision-making. Tasks should be sensitive to girls' developmental maturity and commensurate with their abilities, with each girl encouraged to proceed at her own pace. With each age level, the girls' opportunity to act independently and handle responsibilities should increase.

13
Troops/Groups

Each troop or group should have at least one adult leader and one or more assistant leaders. Because the female role model is essential to fulfilling the purpose of Girl Scouting, at least one member of the leadership team must be an adult female.

The adult leaders must be at least 18 years of age or at the age of majority defined by the state if it is older than 18. Leaders should have training as specified by the council. In addition, an active troop committee of registered adult members should provide ongoing support to the troop.

14
Health, Safety, and Security— Adult Supervision and Preparation

Proper adult supervision and guidance for each activity are essential. Adults with requisite expertise are part of the adult leadership when implementing activities. Adequate training and preparation for girls and adults precede participation in any activity.

15
Council Support to Adult Leadership

All adults within the Girl Scout council work in concert to ensure the highest quality program experience for girls. Communication and cooperation are essential for providing training, giving ongoing support to troops and groups, and obtaining appropriate activity approvals.

16
Program Consultants

The regular adult leadership of any Girl Scout group should be complemented by program consultants who possess technical competence and the ability to share specialized skills.

17
Program Centers

All centers and facilities used for Girl Scout program activities should have present at least one adult with appropriate qualifications and competencies to guide girls in the type of program conducted at the facility. Additional adults trained for their particular roles should be present in numbers required to provide adequate adult guidance for the ages of the girls, the size of the group, and the nature of the activity.

18
Adult Leadership— Girl Scout Camps

All Girl Scout camps should be staffed by adults who possess the qualifications and necessary competencies for the positions held.

19
Pluralism and Diversity of Troops/Groups

Girl Scout troops and groups should reflect the diversity of socioeconomic, racial, ethnic, cultural, religious, and disability groups in the community. Whenever possible, troops and groups should include girls from different age and grade levels.

20
Size of Troops/Groups

Girls should be able to participate in groupings large enough to provide experience in self-government and in groupings small enough to allow for development of the individual girl.

21
Meeting and Activity Planning

Troops and groups should meet often enough to fulfill the needs and interests of girls and to maintain continuity of their program experience.

22
Meeting Places/Camps/Sites

All meeting places, camps, and other sites used for Girl Scout program activities should provide a safe, clean, and secure environment and allow for participation of all girls.

23
Girl Scout Camps

All Girl Scout camps should be operated in compliance with local and state laws for maximum protection of campers' health, safety, and security, and with regard to protection of the natural environment.

24
Overnight Trips, Camping

All sites and facilities used for overnight trips or camping should be approved by the Girl Scout council.

25
Private Transportation

Private passenger cars, station wagons, and vans may be used during Girl Scout activities. They must be properly registered, insured, and operated by adults with a valid license for the type of vehicle used. Any other form of private transportation may be used only after council approval has been obtained.

26
Public Transportation

Public transportation and regularly scheduled airlines, buses, trains, and vessels should be used whenever possible.

27
Travel Procedures

All travel procedures and preparations should make provision for adequate adult supervision and maximum safety.

28
Activities Involving Money

Troops/groups should be financed by troop/group dues, by troop money-earning activities, and by a share of money earned through council-sponsored product sales. Daisy Girl Scouts may not be involved in handling any money, including troop dues and proceeds from troop money-earning activities and product sales.

29
Troop Money-Earning Activities

Money-earning activities should be a valuable program activity for girls. Daisy Girl Scouts do not participate in troop money-earning activities.

30
Council-Sponsored Product Sales

Troops/groups may participate in no more than two council-sponsored product sales each year and only one of these may be a cookie sale. A percentage of the money earned through product sales should be allocated to participating troops and groups. Daisy Girl Scouts may not sell cookies or other products.

31
Product Sale Incentives

Participation in a council product sale incentive plan should be optional for troops and individuals. Incentives, if used, should be program-related and of a type that will provide opportunities for girls to participate in Girl Scout activities.

32
Council Fund Raising

Fund raising or fund development to support the Girl Scout council is the responsibility of adults and this responsibility should not be placed with girls. Girls may provide support to these efforts through voluntary service.

33
Fund Raising for Other Organizations

Girl Scouts, in their Girl Scout capacities, may not solicit money for other organizations. Girl members may support other organizations only through service projects. (See national policy on solicitation of contributions in the *Leader's Digest: Blue Book of Basic Documents.*)

34
Collaborations with Other Organizations

When collaborative relationships or cooperative projects are developed with other organizations, all Girl Scout program standards are followed.

35
Political Activity

Girl Scouts, in their Girl Scout capacities, may not participate directly or indirectly in any political campaigns or participate in partisan efforts on behalf of or in opposition to a candidate for public office.

Here are sample solutions to the incidents discussed on pages 15–16.

A *Standards 1 and 2:* You probably should do a needs assessment. Ask all the girls, including the ones who haven't been coming, what's wrong. Your role as a leader is to make all the girls aware of the variety of options available in Girl Scouting and present these options as being equally attractive. The girls might have chosen the crafts-type activities because those were the activities with which they were most familiar.

B *Standards 2, 6, and 14:* There are two issues here—a few girls seem to have more influence than others in choosing activities, and Sally may not be capable of attending a ballet. One way to deal with the first issue is casually to introduce a confidential vote after a brief brainstorming of some of the ways the troop could spend the trip money. The other potential issue, concerning Sally, could be dealt with by having an extra adult go on the trip. This adult can sit with Sally and go into the lobby or some other area if Sally is disruptive. Before the trip, have a talk with Sally about what she can do if she feels restless. Make the rules of the trip and the expectations about her behavior clear to her.

C *Standards 5 and 9:* Service is done without payment. The

girls might need to review the Girl Scout Promise and Law and discuss the intrinsic value of certain activities such as service.

D *Standards 2, 6, 7, and 8:* Turn to your council. You will find that the training the council provides could make you quite comfortable, even enthusiastic, about your camping experience. Also, someone who has prior outdoor experience and who can convey her love of camping to the girls should accompany you. The girls' interests do come first, and the Brownie Girl Scout age level is the perfect starting point for progressive experiences that encourage girls to enjoy the out-of-doors.

E *Standards 2, 7, 8, and 16:* Maybe this is an example of your moving a bit too quickly for the girls. The girls could use some advanced preparation to spark their interest. Activities in the out-of-doors in Girl Scouting follow a clear progression. Start simply, maybe with some environmental or nature awareness activities, and move forward from there. Taking the readiness of the girls into account and moving slowly may foster a lifelong love of the outdoors rather than a dislike.

F *Standards 2, 6, and 9:* This can happen very easily. Maybe you need to repeat the purpose of the Try-Its and then suggest some other activities the girls would enjoy; trips are usually one activity that Brownie Girl Scouts are eager to do. Also, think of some physical things: dancing, sports, singing, and games can

help move the girls' attention past the Try-Its and into other areas.

G *Standards 28, 29, and 30:* "Tag-alongs" are children for whom no specific supervision is being supplied while the Girl Scout activity takes place for the girls. The parent will need to be informed that the younger sister cannot participate and cannot "tag along." Many situations arise when decisions are made that younger sisters (and brothers) cannot be permitted to accompany a girl or adult on a trip or activity. Sometimes there are insurance or safety reasons, but at other times the quality of the experience for the other girls or a program standard would be diminished.

"Tag-alongs" are not covered by the Activity Accident Insurance, even if they are members of some other troop or group. If it is decided to have dedicated supervision for such children, it is possible for the council to help arrange for optional insurance for them at a small fee as a supplementary supervised unit. The decision to have or not have nonparticipating children should not center on whether or not these children are insurable, but on the ability to provide adequate supervision, the ability to comply with standards, and the effect that the presence of these extra children may have on the quality of the experience.

H *Standards 1, 3, 10, 15, and 16:* You need to be familiar with the guidelines your council has set for the use of the Contemporary Issues booklets. Your Girl Scout

council office or your local council representative could also have this information. Is training provided for leaders? Are program consultants available who have been trained in this subject? Are outside consultants available whom the council has recommended as resources?

I *Standards 1, 6, and 19:* You do have a responsibility to address this issue immediately. Disrespect for others is not tolerated and you will need to educate the girls as to why these expressions are unacceptable. Ask for help from the Girl Scout adult to whom you report or your council service center. They could help you with using the *Valuing Differences: Pluralism* Contemporary Issues booklet, activities in the handbook, community resources, or program consultants.

J *Standards 1, 6, and 19:* The Girl Scout Promise and Law and the above program standards require that girls do activities that promote respect and understanding of differing cultures. Girls will need these experiences to prepare them for a society that is becoming increasingly pluralistic. Moreover, have you really looked around your entire community to see who is a part of it? Again, ask the Girl Scout adult to whom you report or your council service center for assistance in utilizing any appropriate program or outside resources. Some councils do have "sister troops" comprised of linked troops of girls from different parts of the council.

K *Standards 3, 15, 25, 26, and 27:* It is always better for the girls to miss the activity than to put their health and safety in jeopardy.

You can ask your council for help in transporting the girls or ask your troop consultants and parents if they can provide assistance.

L *Standards 1, 29, and 30:* Selling Girl Scout cookies is a voluntary activity. There may be other ways that a girl could participate and assist the troop besides actually selling the cookies. She could help count the boxes, make posters, or keep track of the orders. You might also check with the mother concerning all the facts.

· ·

Religious Recognitions

Through Girl Scouting, each girl is encouraged to become a stronger member of her own religious group, and every Girl Scout group recognizes that religious instruction is the responsibility of parents and religious leaders. Religious recognition programs are always developed and administered by religious groups themselves. The following list of religious recognitions is periodically updated and revised. For more information, write to Religious Recognitions, GSUSA, 420 Fifth Avenue, New York, N.Y. 10018-2702.

Religious Recognitions for Girls and Adults in Girl Scouting

	Brownie	Junior	Cadette	Senior	Adult	Where to Get Information
Baha'i	Unity of Mankind	Unity of Mankind	Unity of Mankind	Unity of Mankind		Baha'i Committee on Scouting Baha'i National Center Wilmette, Ill. 60091 (708) 869-9039
Buddhist	Ages 6–8 Padma Award	Ages 9–10 Padma Award	Ages 12–14 Padma Award	Ages 15–17 Padma Award		Buddhist Church of America National Headquarters 1710 Octavia Street San Francisco, Calif. 94109 (415) 776-5600
Christian Science		Ages 9–10 Christian Science God and Country	Ages 11–14 Christian Science God and Country			P.R.A.Y. P.O. Box 6900 St. Louis, Mo. 63123 (800) 933-PRAY (7729)
Eastern Orthodox		Ages 9–10 Chi-Rho	Ages 11–14 Alpha Omega	Ages 15–17 Alpha Omega	Prophet Elias	P.R.A.Y. P.O. Box 6900 St. Louis, Mo. 63123 (800) 933-PRAY (7729)

	Brownie	Junior	Cadette	Senior	Adult	Where to Get Information
Episcopal	Ages 6–8 Grades 1–3 God and Me	Ages 9–10 Grades 4–5 God and Family	Ages 11–14 Grades 6–9 God and Church	Ages 15–17 Grades 10–12 God and Life	St. George Award Adult mentor programs for each Girl Scout age level are available	P.R.A.Y. P.O. Box 6900 St. Louis, Mo. 63123 (800) 933-PRAY (7729)
Hindu	Ages 6–8 Grades 1–3 Dharma Award	Ages 8–11 Grades 3–6 Dharma Award				North American Hindu Association 46133 Amesbury Drive Plymouth, Mich. 48170 (313) 453-5049 or 981-2323
Islamic	Ages 5–8 Bismillah Award	Ages 8–11 In the Name of Allah Award	Ages 11–14 Quratula'in Award	Ages 14–17 Muslimeen Award		Islamic Committee on Girl Scouting 31 Marian Street Stamford, Conn. 06907 (203) 359-3593
Jewish	Ages 6–9 Lehavah Award pin + certificate	Ages 9–11 Bat Or Award	Ages 11–14 Menorah Award	Ages 15–17 Menorah Award	Ora Award	National Jewish Girl Scout Committee of the Synagogue Council of America 327 Lexington Avenue New York, N.Y. 10016 (212) 686-8670
Lutheran	Ages 6–8 Grades 1–3 God and Me	Ages 9–10 Grades 4–5 God and Family	Ages 11–13 Grades 6–8 God and Church	Ages 14–17 Grades 9–12 Lutheran Living Faith	Lamb Award and Servant of Youth Adult mentor programs for Brownies, Juniors, and Cadettes are available.	P.R.A .Y. P.O. Box 6900 St. Louis, Mo. 63123 (800) 933-PRAY (7729)
(Mormon) Church of Jesus Christ of Latter-day Saints		Ages 10–11 Gospel in Action Award	Ages 12–13 Young Woman of Truth	Ages 14–15 Young Woman of Promise Ages 16–17 Young Woman of Faith Young Womanhood Recognition		Salt Lake District Center Church of Jesus Christ of Latter-day Saints 1999 W. 1700 South Salt Lake City, Utah 84104 (801) 240-2141

#2
Maryann Yarin
446 Vector Way
Wycoff 07481
891-4768

	Brownie	Junior	Cadette	Senior	Adult	Where to Get Information
Protestant and Independent Christian Churches	Ages 6-8 Grades 1–3 God and Me	Ages 9–10 Grades 4–5 God and Family	Ages 11–13 Grades 6–8 God and Church	Ages 14–17 Grades 9–12 God and Life	God and Service Recognition Adult mentor programs for each Girl Scout age level are available.	P.R.A.Y. P.O. Box 6900 St. Louis, Mo. 63123 (800) 933-PRAY (7729)
(Quakers) Society of Friends	Ages 6–8 Grades 2–3 That of God	Ages 8–11 Grades 4–6 That of God	Ages 11–14 Grades 6–9 Spirit of Truth	Ages 14–17 Grades 10–12 Spirit of Truth	Friends Emblem	Friends Committee on Scouting c/o Dennis Clarke 85 Willowbrook Road Cromwell, Conn. 06416 (203) 635–1706
Reorganized Church of Jesus Christ of Latter Day Saints	Age 8 Light of the World	Ages 9–10 Light of the World Age 11 Liahona	Ages 12–14 Liahona	Ages 15–17 Exploring My Life and World	World Community International Youth Service Award	Youth Ministries Office The Auditorium P.O. Box 1059 Independence, Mo. 64051 (816) 833-1000
Roman Catholic Church	Ages 7–9 Family of God	Ages 9–11 I Live My Faith	Ages 12–14 Marian Medal	Age 15 Marian Medal Ages 16–18 Spirit Alive	St. Elizabeth Seton Medal and St. Anne Medal	National Federation for Catholic Youth Ministry 3700-A Oakview Terrace, NE Washington, D.C. 20017 Attn: Orders Clerk (202) 636-3825
Unitarian Universalist		Ages 9–11 Religion in Life	Ages 12–14 Religion in Life	Ages 15–17 Religion in Life		Unitarian Universalist 25 Beacon Street Boston, Mass. 02108 (617) 742-2100
Unity Church	Ages 6–8 God in Me	Ages 9–11 God in Me	Ages 11–13 Light of God		Distinguished Youth Service Award Miniature Pin	Association of Unity Churches P.O. Box 610 Lee's Summit, Mo. 64063 (816) 524-7414

Planning for the Year

CHAPTER 2

Girl and Adult Planning

Brownie Girl Scouts are very capable individuals who can take an active role in choosing and planning their Girl Scout activities. Girls need the experience of making choices and plans to mature and develop their competence and self-esteem. Girls who are encouraged to be actively involved, who develop leadership skills, and who accept responsibility are also more likely to enjoy their Girl Scout program activities and stay with them longer.

In girl/adult partnerships, the level of planning and authority assumed by each partner is not constant. An adult might take on a stronger leadership role when safety issues arise or when girls are doing something for the first time. Girls who have had prior experiences in camping with their families, for example, may be able to lead the group in planning an overnight camping outing.

Troop Government

For Brownie Girl Scouts, the traditional form of troop government and decision-making is the Brownie Girl Scout Ring. In a Brownie Girl Scout Ring, the girls all gather in a circle and each girl shares in planning, problem-solving, and decision-making in her troop or group. Girls take turns expressing their opinions and ideas. A large troop might need to break into smaller Brownie Girl Scout circles, which then may select one girl to represent them. These representatives can then meet in their own circle. Pages 119–120 in the *Brownie Girl Scout Handbook* contain more information on troop government for girls.

A Brownie Girl Scout Ring is an effective planning tool, if the following guidelines are followed:

- Girls must listen to one another. No ideas are "dumb" ideas.
- Everybody has something to contribute and everyone should have a chance to speak.
- All girls should be encouraged to participate, though shy girls may need a bit longer to feel comfortable speaking in a large group.
- Time limits should be set and followed. Young girls cannot sit and listen for long periods of time, especially if it is the end of a school day.
- Pictures, charts, and other materials can help girls explain things and help girls make quicker decisions.
- Girls should know what choices are available to them. The *Brownie Girl Scout Handbook* and other resources are very helpful to use. Girls may choose activities from more than one resource.

The Brownie Girl Scout Ring can work for choosing and planning activities and trips, making up rules and assigning jobs and tasks, naming committee members, setting budgets for activities, and other occasions when group work and decisions are needed. In larger troops, some or all of these tasks might be done in the smaller Brownie Girl Scout circles.

Some Brownie Girl Scout troops and groups may elect leaders for special jobs such as treasurer or secretary. Keep terms short. These jobs should be rotated so that all the girls in the troop/group have a chance. Duties should be simple and clear. Some jobs for girls to handle are taking attendance or reporting on how much money is in the troop/group account. Try to avoid cliques and popularity contests if elections are held.

Holding elections for jobs is not necessary. Girls can sign up for jobs on a chart or roster, or you may find that in your particular troop it is best for you to assign jobs. If you do decide to have an election, discuss the qualities that are needed to do each job before holding any type of election. Emphasize that everyone will have a chance as a leader and that everyone is capable of leadership. Then, remember to adhere to some sort of rotation.

Kaper Charts

A kaper chart is a Girl Scout way of organizing activities. Kaper charts are a visible reminder of the tasks that need to be done. Girls may sign up individually for tasks; Brownie Girl Scout circles can volunteer for tasks; you may assign tasks; or you may choose a variety of ways for tasks to be assigned. A sample kaper chart is shown below.

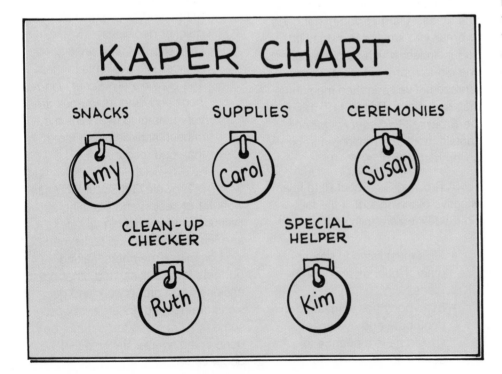

Tips for Planning Troop Activities

Some activities can be done with very little planning. Look through the *Brownie Girl Scout Handbook*, the Contemporary Issues booklets, the *Games for Girl Scouts* book, *Girl Scout Leader* magazine centerfolds, and other Girl Scout program resources. Activities vary greatly in the amount of time needed to complete them, in the amount of materials that are required, and in the complexity of the activity itself. The variety makes it possible for all Brownie Girl Scouts to do activities that are right for them. Girls need to know what activities are in these books so that they may choose those of greatest interest. Sometimes the entire group may choose to work on one activity together. At other times, girls may work on activities in smaller groups or individually. You might need to encourage girls to explore activities new to them, and you may need to explain what is involved and what can realistically be accomplished.

- Use the Brownie Girl Scout Ring to discuss any projects or plans. Divide work evenly.
- Agree on what you as the troop/group leader will do and what the girls will do.
- Decide whether you need help from other adults or people in your Girl Scout council.
- Evaluate the project. Ask why you and the girls are doing this particular activity.

- Set a realistic time frame for the activity with the girls. Sometimes, you might need to work with the girls to simplify a project. At other times you might need to show the girls where a project could be expanded or what could happen next.
- Break all activities down into sequential, simpler steps. Leave plenty of extra time for planning.
- Raise the practical points of planning. Think of costs, logistics, transportation, and so on.
- Make a chart or charts or a time line. Include the jobs or tasks, time needed, equipment and materials, assignments, costs, special reminders.
- Be aware of girls' capabilities. Do not move too fast for the group.
- Remember that abilities and development among girls of the same age vary significantly. Some girls may be able to move ahead much more quickly than others. Some girls may have the fine motor coordination necessary to create neatly printed and artistic posters. Other girls may have difficulty printing and drawing.
- If individual girls or the group becomes frustrated, evaluate the activity. Girls can modify their plans and change activities. Sometimes they may just need a break. Sometimes they may need to try another activity. Girls do not need to finish

every activity they have begun. All activities do not need to be perfect. Sometimes, the best learning comes through mistakes and trial and error. Girls need to have fun and need to move at a pace comfortable for them. A Girl Scout leader is judged a success not only by how well an activity is accomplished or how much is done on schedule, but by how much planning is done and choices made by the girls.

- Be prepared for everything! Be creative in handling surprises and outcomes different from what you expected. Always have something to do, a song, a game, a story, if activities finish early or something else is needed. Girls can often be a source for new songs and games to teach to the group.
- Emphasize the qualities that make each girl unique. Recognize and applaud all successes. Be generous with praise. Encourage girls to find ways to show acceptance and to support one another.

What would you do in this situation?

The girls are looking through their handbooks. They start telling each other about all the Try-Its they are going to get this year and all the pages in the book they will finish. You know they cannot possibly do all that work.

Here's one thing you could try:

Ask the girls to think about the things they enjoy doing the most. Then, point to a calendar and show them the number of troop meetings they will have. The girls can think about how much time the activities would take. They can make a list, as a part of their activities in a Brownie Girl Scout Ring or in a Brownie Girl Scout circle, and then number the activities from the most favorite to least favorite.

A Checklist for Troop Activities

Once a month, review the statements in this checklist. If most of your answers are yes, your troop or group has a balanced Girl Scout program experience.

	YES	NO	SOMETIMES
Girls are having fun.			
■ The girls are active in planning and choosing activities.	_____	_____	_____
■ The girls talk about "our" troop and activities that "we" did.	_____	_____	_____
■ The girls feel free to express their opinions, their likes, and their dislikes.	_____	_____	_____
Your troop is meeting program standards.			
■ The girls know and understand the Girl Scout Promise and Law and can talk about the ideals expressed in them.	_____	_____	_____
■ The times of activities and meetings and the costs of activities are set so that all girls can participate.	_____	_____	_____
■ When you review the Girl Scout program standards, pages 16–18, you can point to specific troop/ group activities or girl behaviors that meet these standards.	_____	_____	_____
■ You follow the *Safety-Wise* guidelines for all activities you do with the girls.	_____	_____	_____
■ The girls show an interest in helping people in their communities and families.	_____	_____	_____

	YES	NO	SOMETIMES

The troop activities are balanced.

- The activities are varied, not too many on one topic and not too many of one type. For example, activities would not be varied if too many arts and crafts activities or too much Try-It work was being done. _____ _____ _____
- Wider opportunities, activities outside the regular troop meeting site, are part of the troop's activities. _____ _____ _____
- Girls choose activities that introduce them to a wide range of interests. _____ _____ _____

The group maintains good relationships.

- Girls listen to each other and respect each other's differences. _____ _____ _____
- All girls have opportunities to participate. The activities are not dominated by one or more of the girls. _____ _____ _____
- The girls feel comfortable. They express their opinions and ideas openly. _____ _____ _____
- Girls are prompt in arriving and the attendance is good. _____ _____ _____

Tips for Working with Arts and Crafts Materials

Your copy of *Safety-Wise* has a section on safe ways to use arts and crafts materials with girls. You must read that section in *Safety-Wise* before introducing any art materials to girls. Below are tips for using materials with younger Girl Scouts.

Many common art materials may contain dyes, pigments, preservatives, and other chemicals that can provoke allergies in girls. Girls who are physically or psychologically disabled, or who are on medication, may be at greater risk for toxic materials. Some materials have hazards that can make the user chronically ill. Since 1988, these materials have been required to carry a warning label.

Materials to avoid:
- Dust or powders that may be inhaled or gotten in the eyes.
- Organic solvents or solvent-containing products, including aerosol spray cans and brushes.
- Lead-based paints for toys and home interiors.
- Anything that stains the skin or clothing (or that cannot be washed out of clothing).
- Acids, alkalies, bleaches, or other irritant or corrosive materials.
- Any donated or discarded material for which the ingredients are not known.
- Any old or unlabeled materials.

Appropriate materials to use:
- Water-based paints and products, including felt-tip pens and markers. Scented markers are not appropriate.
- Crayons or dustless chalks rather than pastels or dry chalks, which create dust.
- Pre-mixed clay, not powdered clay.
- White glue and school paste are appropriate. "Instant" type glues should never be used.
- Blunt-ended scissors should be used.

When supervising the use of art materials, make sure:
- Any sharp tool is stored in a safe place and is not accessible to girls without adult supervision.
- Girls are taught basic skills and that safe use and care of equipment is demonstrated.
- Girls never mold a paintbrush tip with their lips.
- Girls wear appropriate protective clothing.
- Equipment and supplies are ample for the group and safely stored.
- Manufacturers' labels on paints, chemicals, and aerosol cans are read before use.
- Art materials are purchased from reputable sources, such as school-supply houses. Do not substitute less expensive materials to save money.
- Food and beverages are not consumed in the activity area.
- A first-aid kit is available.

Special Traditions in Girl Scouting

Girl Scouting has ceremonies, special days, and traditions that help mark the passing of the Girl Scout year. More is written about these special days in "Welcome to Girl Scouts" in the *Brownie Girl Scout Handbook*. Celebrating these special days helps foster a sense of belonging and historical understanding. Girls learn of the larger organization of which they are members. Special Girl Scout ceremonies and traditions are shared by Girl Scouts and Girl Guides worldwide and can be used in celebrations.

Girl Scout Ceremonies

INVESTITURE: A way to welcome someone into Girl Scouting for the first time.

REDEDICATION: Girl Scouts who have already been invested renew their Girl Scout Promise and Law. Many girls do this at the beginning and the end of the troop year.

BRIDGING: Girl Scouts move from one age level to another. Brownie Girl Scouts call bridging "flying up."

COURT OF AWARDS: Ceremony in which Girl Scouts receive recognitions (Try-Its) and other insignia.

GIRL SCOUTS' OWN: A quiet ceremony designed by the girls in which girls express their feelings about a particular theme.

FLAG CEREMONY: A ceremony that honors the flag of the United States of America.

CANDLELIGHTING: A candlelighting (or flashlight) ceremony that helps remind people of the words and meaning of the Girl Scout Promise and Law.

OPENING CEREMONY: A short ceremony to start a meeting.

CLOSING CEREMONY: A short ceremony to close a meeting.

During the year, the ceremonies you most likely will need to help girls plan will be an investiture or rededication ceremony, a fly-up ceremony, and a flag ceremony. A Girl Scouts' Own can also be an important personalized celebration in Girl Scouting.

The following sample ceremonies have been adapted from *Ceremonies in Girl Scouting*, available from the National Equipment Service of GSUSA or your Girl Scout shop.

Basic Flag Ceremony

Purpose: For opening/closing an activity or meeting.

Materials and participants: American flag, troop flag (if available), bearer for each flag, guard for each flag, flag stands.

Ceremony: The troop/group forms a horseshoe. The girls stand at attention.

The Girl Scout-in-charge says: "Color guard, advance." The color guard advances to the flags, salutes the American flag, and picks up the flags. The American flag is always picked up first. Then they turn together and face the troop. The guards stand on either side of the flag bearers. They are silent throughout the ceremony.

The Girl Scout-in-charge says: "Color guard, present colors." The color guard walks forward carrying the flags to the standards at the open end of the horseshoe.

The Girl Scout-in-charge says: "Color guard, post the colors." The color bearers place the flags in the stands. The American flag is placed last. The color guard remains at attention next to the flags.

The Girl Scout-in-charge says: "Girl Scouts, honor the flag of your country." The group salutes the American flag by placing their right hand over their heart.

The Girl Scout-in-charge says: "Girl Scouts, recite the Pledge of Allegiance." She may also lead them in a suitable song, poem, or the Girl Scout Promise.

If the flag ceremony is part of a larger ceremony, the Girl Scout-in-charge dismisses the color guard and the main ceremony follows.

Following the ceremony, the Girl Scout-in-charge will say: "Color guard, retire," and they carry the flags back to the place where they are stored. The ceremony is over

when the Girl Scout-in-charge says: "Color guard, dismissed." All girls stand at attention during the closing. Usually, girls who are not a part of the color guard are silent during the ceremony.

Brownie Girl Scout Pin   *World Trefoil Pin*

Brownie Girl Scout Investiture Ceremony

Purpose: To welcome someone into Girl Scouting for the first time.

Materials and participants: American flag, troop flag, flag bearers, Brownie Girl Scout "pool" (for example, a mirror edged with greenery), Brownie Girl Scout pins, World Trefoil pins, new Brownie Girl Scouts, troop members, and leaders.

Ceremony: Opening flag ceremony.

New Brownie Girl Scouts may go outside the room where the ceremony is being held or may stay with the troop. The troop forms a ring around the Brownie Girl Scout "pool."

The leader at pool says: "Who comes to the Brownie woods?"

New Brownie Girl Scouts answer: "We do!"

The leader at pool says: "What do you want?"

New Brownie Girl Scouts answer: "We want to be Brownie Girl Scouts."

The leader asks: "Why?"

The girls have prepared short responses beforehand. Each girl gives her response and sits or stands by the Brownie Girl Scout pool. Each girl says the Girl Scout Promise in turn. After each girl has said the Promise, the leader takes the girl to the pool and turns her around in a circle, saying, "Twist me and turn me and show me the elf, I looked in the pool and saw _____."

The girl says: "Myself (followed by name)."

The leader pins the Brownie Girl Scout pin and World Trefoil pin on each girl and welcomes her to the troop.

Girls who are already Brownie Girl Scouts may plan a rededication ceremony to follow or precede the investiture ceremony.

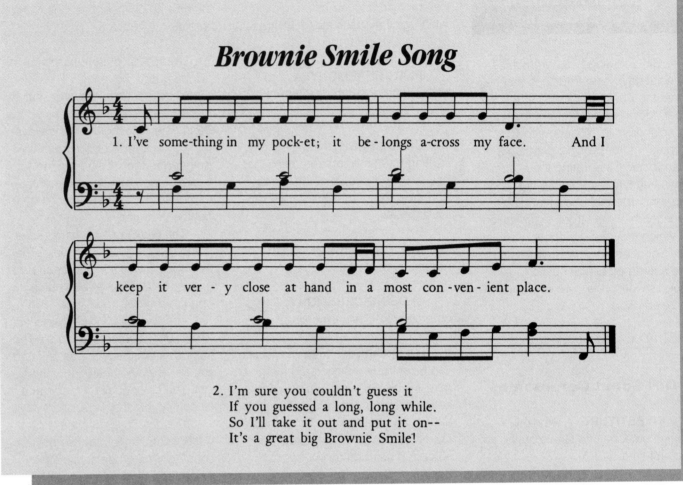

Brownie Smile Song

1. I've some-thing in my pock-et; it be-longs a-cross my face. And I keep it ver-y close at hand in a most con-ven-ient place.

2. I'm sure you couldn't guess it
If you guessed a long, long while.
So I'll take it out and put it on--
It's a great big Brownie Smile!

Used by kind permission of Harriet F. Heywood.

Brownie Girl Scout Wings

Brownie Girl Scout Fly-Up Ceremony (Bridging to Junior Girl Scouts)

Purpose: To recognize the Brownie Girl Scouts who are moving up to Junior Girl Scouts.

Materials and participants: Brownie Girl Scouts who are bridging, Junior Girl Scouts, Brownie and Junior Girl Scout leaders, and Brownie wings.

Ceremony: Open with "Brownie Smile Song" or other Girl Scout song.

Each girl steps forward and explains one of the special things she did as a Brownie Girl Scout. Or, she may explain one part of the Girl Scout Law in sequence.

All girls recite the Girl Scout Promise.

Leaders or Junior Girl Scouts pin the wings on the bridging Brownie Girl Scouts. Girls give the Girl Scout handshake, form a friendship circle, and sing a song.

Other Girl Scout Traditions

In "Welcome to Girl Scouts" in the *Brownie Girl Scout Handbook* you can read about many of the other traditions, such as the Girl Scout sign and Girl Scout handshake, that Brownie Girl Scouts share with other Girl Scouts. The "Brownie Smile Song," printed here, is a special song for Brownie Girl Scouts.

Singing is an important tradition in Girl Scouting. Songs can begin or end a meeting, can serve as a bridge to the next part of the meeting, and can introduce new themes and topics to girls. A song from another country is one way to introduce international games or some Try-Its from the World of People. The annotated resource list at the back of Part I of this book lists the titles of many Girl Scout songbooks. Here are some other songs you might want to sing with Brownie Girl Scouts.

Brownie Friend-Maker Song

Kathryn Templeton   Traditional (Israeli)

1. Your Brown-ie hand in my Brown-ie hand, and my Brown-ie hand in your Brown-ie hand.

Come a-long with me, and sing a-long with me! Yes, I'll come a-long with you and___

Chorus

sing a-long with you. Hi! Ho! Friend-mak-ers all. Hand in hand's the

Brown-ie style. Hi! Ho! Friend-mak-ers all Greet you with a Brown-ie smile.

2. Your Brownie hand in my Brownie hand,
   And my Brownie hand in your Brownie hand.
   We have Brownie friends in many lands,
   Across the seven seas, the mountains and
       the sands.
   Chorus (repeat)

3. Your Brownie hand in my Brownie hand,
   And my Brownie hand in your Brownie hand.
   On Thinking Day our love goes forth to ev'ry friend,
   A chain of Brownie hands reaching out, their help
       to lend.
   Chorus (repeat)

Do a Grand Right and Left as you sing.

The More We Get Together

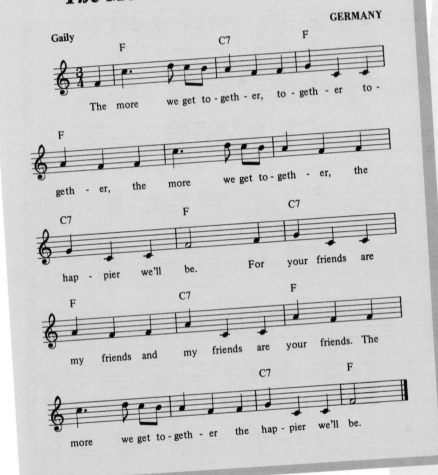

GERMANY

Gaily

The more we get to-geth-er, to-geth-er to-geth-er, the more we get to-geth-er, the hap-pier we'll be. For your friends are my friends and my friends are your friends. The more we get to-geth-er the hap-pier we'll be.

Make New Friends

TWO-PART ROUND

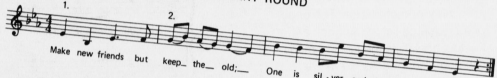

Make new friends but keep_ the_ old;_ One is sil-ver and the oth-er gold.

Whene'er You Make a Promise

TWO-PART ROUND

W. W. Shield, 1828

When-e'er you make_ a_ prom-ise Con-sid-er well its im-port-ance, And when made, En-grave it up-on your heart.

Planning Troop Meetings

There is no set length or frequency for Brownie Girl Scout meetings. Meetings should be scheduled to best meet the interests or needs of girls. For example, some groups of Brownie Girl Scouts may meet once every two months for three hours, while others may meet once a week for one hour.

There is also no such thing as a standard Brownie Girl Scout troop meeting. You will need to be flexible. Sometimes, one activity may take up the entire meeting. Other meetings may be filled with many different types of activities. Many Brownie Girl Scout meetings follow this outline.

- Start-up
- Opening
- Business
- Activities
- Cleanup
- Closing

For each section of the meeting, you will need to consider which girls should be in charge and what supplies or resources you might need.

Start-Up

Start-up activities occur before the regularly scheduled meeting begins. These activities give you time to greet and chat with the girls as they arrive and spend a few moments speaking with parents. Usually, these activities are self-directed. Girls can do the activity, alone or in pairs, with minimal supervision. The activity should not require a great deal of time to complete and should not cause a mess that would take a lot of time to clean up. Here are some suggested activities:

- Set out a number of song tapes and a tape recorder, so that girls may play and practice the songs.
- Have drawing paper and crayons or markers available, so that girls can draw what has occurred in their lives since the last meeting. A suggestion from the *Caring and Coping: Facing Family Crises* Contemporary Issues booklet is to make a poster on the theme "My Family." A suggestion from *Girls Are Great: Growing*

Up Female is to create a poster completing the sentence, "I like myself because . . ." A variation of this activity is to have each of the girls who arrives early write out her sentence. Then, a group poem could be created.

- Set out the Girl Scout program resources available for Brownie Girl Scouts. A list is on page 13. Girls can look through the books and try some of the activities.
- Provide materials for a simple game. Girls can learn some of the games from the *Games for Girl Scouts* book. Look especially at the chapter "Simple Games to Make and Play." Parachute Jump is a simple game from this chapter. To play, you will need:

  - A handkerchief or square cloth
  - 4 pieces of string about 8" long
  - A wooden thread spool

To make parachutes, tie one string to each corner of the handkerchief. Gather the opposite ends of the four strings together and thread them through the spool. Knot the four strings together so they are unable to slip through the spool, as shown. Girls can decorate the spools and the parachutes.

To play, girls can determine a parachute jump area and target. Toss the parachute in the air. The winner is the one whose parachute lands closest to the target.

- Prepare a set of index cards so girls can practice "acting." The cards can have the names or pictures of animals, types of jobs, different emotions, historical characters (fictional and nonfictional), names of objects, or other sorts of categories. A girl picks a card and mimes (acting without words) the word she has chosen. If other girls are present, the cards can be used to play a guessing game. The other girl or group tries to guess the

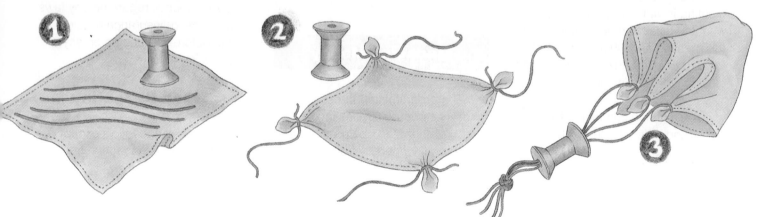

word on the card from the actions.

- Display a collection of children's magazines, books, encyclopedias, or other materials. These can provide some quiet start-up activities. School and community libraries may donate older books or sell them at a nominal cost.
- Provide a box with game boards and pieces of old and incomplete games. Using what is in the box, girls can create new games with different rules.

Opening

Opening activities should help the girls become focused on their meeting. This is the first activity of the meeting that the girls do as a group. Girls can take turns planning the opening activity. A simple flag ceremony is one suggestion. A Girl Scout song, such as "The Brownie Smile Song" or "Make New Friends," would also be a good opener. (See pages 28–30 for songs.) Or, the opening activity could be a "sharing time" for girls.

Business

Troop/group business could include making special announcements, taking attendance, collecting dues or fees, planning for trips or activities, or making up a new kaper chart. Girls can take turns conducting this part of the meeting.

Activities

Besides the *Brownie Girl Scout Handbook*, there are other resources full of activities for Brownie Girl Scouts. For example, see *Outdoor Education in Girl Scouting, Exploring Wildlife Communities with Children*, the Contemporary Issues booklets, and *Games for Girl Scouts*. Make sure the girls are aware of all the available choices. Try to do each activity yourself before doing it with the girls. Look at it from a girl's perspective. Also, consider your meeting place. Will this activity need to be adapted? Are there enough materials for each girl? Will you be able to clean up any messes?

Cleanup

The girls assigned to supervise the cleanup should have their names listed on a kaper chart. This assignment should be rotated among all the girls in the troop/group. It should never be used as a disciplinary tool, as girls need to know that cleaning up is a responsibility that all share. It is not a punishment.

Closing

The closing is the part of the meeting in which you emphasize what the girls have accomplished in this meeting and what they can look forward to in the next meeting. Good closing activities include:

- Gathering in a friendship circle and doing the friendship squeeze.

- Reciting the Girl Scout Promise and Law. Girls can take turns discussing the meaning of one part of the Girl Scout Law or describing something they have done that follows the Girl Scout Promise and Law.
- Girls stating one personal goal they would like to accomplish before the next meeting.

After the closing, be sure that each girl is met by a parent or adult and that you know each girl's arrangements for getting home.

The following page is available for you to use as a sample worksheet in planning your own meetings; you may copy it as needed. It is often easier to plan a meeting if you have a set goal or a special theme on which to base the activities. For example, if girls have expressed an interest in learning more about safety, your objective for the meeting may be to practice the fire safety procedures included in the *Brownie Girl Scout Handbook*. Your theme for the next meeting or so could be "safety" and girls would know to expect activities on safety, such as a field trip to a firehouse, a guest speaker from a child abuse protection agency, or creation of a first-aid kit.

Managing Money

The program standards and guidelines about activities involving money state that troops/groups should be financed by troop/group

dues, by troop money-earning activities, and by a share of money earned through council-sponsored product sales. Troop money-earning activities are activities planned and carried out by girls and adults in partnership to earn money for the troop treasury. Types of appropriate activities are listed in *Safety-Wise*. Permission is obtained in writing from a girl's parent or guardian before she participates in money-earning activities, and each girl's participation should be voluntary.

Girls need to have an active role in planning and carrying out all money-earning activities, including cookie selling. Cookie selling should enhance a girl's experience in Girl Scouting. It is part of the Girl Scout program and should be designed to increase decision-making, planning, and goal-setting skills. Page 122 in the *Brownie Girl Scout Handbook* has information on cookie sales for girls. Before you and the girls in your troop participate in any type of money-earning activity, you should do the activities on these pages together. You must also read the pertinent pages in *Safety-Wise* and obtain written permission from your Girl Scout council before starting money-earning activities. Be sure to check with your council regarding any laws, regulations, or insurance requirements before you decide on any fund-raising activity.

Troop Budgeting

Girls at all age levels except Daisy Girl Scouts engage in troop

Meeting Plan Worksheet

	What We Will Do	Who Will Do It	What We Need	Notes
Start-Up				
Opening				
Business				
Activities				
Cleanup				
Closing				

budgeting activities. For activities and guidelines on troop budgeting at the Brownie Girl Scout age level, see page 32. The girls take an active part in the decision-making process in determining troop dues and the uses of troop funds. Managing money is a progressive experience. All girls should have the opportunity to participate in the planning and decision-making processes, but you might need to play a more active role in teaching the girls responsible money management if they have not had these kinds of experiences. Girls can decide whether to save their money for a more expensive trip, to share their money with others through a service project, or to spend their money on troop/group supplies. Girls should also be given the opportunity to go to the bank to deposit group funds, go on shopping trips, or compare costs through newspaper advertisements or flyers before purchasing items and supplies. Older girls in your troop can be of great help in teaching younger girls how to budget and manage money. Although you handle the group funds, it is the girls' money. You should not add to it from your own money, nor should you remove money without the girls' knowledge and permission.

Planning Wider Opportunities

Wider opportunities are an important part of Girl Scouting. A wider opportunity is any type of activity that takes place beyond the usual troop/group setting.

Learning how to plan a trip should be a progressive experience for a Girl Scout, one that starts with an outing she is ready to handle. Girls themselves do the planning with guidance from adults, so taking a Girl Scout trip is an important way for girls to learn many skills. Every group that plans a trip starts with the same questions:

- Where are we going?
- Why are we going?
- When are we going?
- How will we get there?
- How much will it cost?
- How should we get ready?
- Will everyone be able to go?
- What will we do along the way?
- What safety factors should we take into consideration?
- What will we do when we get there?
- What will we do when we return home?

The girls answer these questions in the planning of their own trip. Through the planning process, they learn how to develop overall plans, make arrangements, budget and handle money, and accept responsibility for personal conduct and safety. Afterwards, they evaluate and share the experience with others.

Preparing for a Trip

Although Brownie Girl Scouts share in the planning of trips, Girl Scout adults need to take responsibility for guidance. For example, for travel of any distance, you must find out how long the trip will take. You must check on points of interest for Brownie Girl Scouts and make arrangements for finding places to eat and locating rest stops. You must check on whether or not the site is suitable for girls who may have disabilities. You must set arrival and departure times, schedule tours, arrange transportation, and obtain parents' permission. Troop committee members and older Girl Scouts may help with these pre-trip plans.

In preparation for the trip, you must lead Brownie Girl Scouts in a discussion about what they will see and do on the trip, what they need to bring, how much the trip will cost, and what is expected of them, particularly in regard to courtesy and safety. You should help the girls set up a "buddy system" so that each girl will know her partner's where-abouts at all times. If there is an odd number of girls, they may take turns being a buddy with you or another adult.

After the trip, in the Brownie Girl Scout Ring, have the girls talk about, dramatize, tell stories, or make paintings of what impressed them on their trip. Help them send thank-you notes, Brownie Girl Scout paintings, or poems to all the people who helped make the trip possible and memorable. Help girls make plans for future trips based on what they have learned, enjoyed, and need to improve.

Before going on any trip with girls, you must read the *Safety-Wise* chapter "Basic Safety and Security Guidelines." Also consult the "Planning Trips with Girls" section for more specific guidelines and tips that will make the trip successful and safe. You must also check with your council support person to discover what council procedures and guidelines have been developed for trips. Remember that parents must be informed and give written consent for activities outside the scheduled meeting place. For events, trips, and troop camping, there should be two adults to every 12 Brownie Girl Scouts and one adult for each additional six Brownie Girl Scouts.

The Progression of Trips

Trips should be planned progressively; that is, first trips should be simple and close to home, with subsequent trips longer in duration and farther in distance.

Meeting Time Trips

These trips are the simplest and start the progression. Girls visit points of interest in the neighborhood—for example, a walk to a nearby garden. Or, they may take a short ride by car or public transportation to visit a civic building, such as a firehouse or courthouse.

Day Trips

These are the next step. These are daytime excursions away from the troop meeting place and outside the regular meeting time. Girls might plan an all-day visit to a point of historic or natural interest, and bring their own lunches. They might go to a nearby city, and schedule time for a meal in a restaurant. They might travel to a Girl Scout council-sponsored or Girl Scout neighborhood-sponsored event.

Simple Overnight Trips

These usually involve one or two nights away. The destination might be a nearby state or national park, a Girl Scout camp, a historic site, or a city. The group may stay in a hostel, hotel, motel, or on campgrounds.

Extended Overnight Trips

These can range from three nights or more spent at camp to extensive travel within the United States. This is something that Brownie Girl Scouts can anticipate as they progress in Girl Scouting. Destinations may be a capital city, a national park, or a famous attraction. The group might use several different accommodations throughout the trips. The Girl Scout TREKKING Network is a nationwide network of council camps available for traveling groups of Girl Scouts. More information on the TREKKING Network is available from your Girl Scout council office.

International Trips

Girls who have progressed from overnight trips to trips across the border and across the ocean may be ready for extended international trips. Because of the special requirements of such trips, trips to other countries are dealt with in a special section of *Safety-Wise*.

Before planning any trips with girls, you must check with the appropriate persons in your Girl Scout council regarding local procedures for obtaining council permissions for trips.

Trips Appropriate for Brownie Girl Scouts

Some generalizations can be made about the types of trips and travel preparations appropriate to the Brownie Girl Scout age level. Brownie Girl Scouts will vary in their abilities according to the experiences that they have had in family or group travel.

Brownie Girl Scouts can go on discovery trips in the neighborhood or in nearby places, traveling by car, by public transportation, or on foot. The idea for taking the trip may come from the girls, or a discussion may be stimulated by a leader or older Girl Scout. In the Brownie Girl Scout Ring, the girls talk about what they would like to do; the leader helps them narrow down their ideas to those that are in line with their abilities and their budget. The girls can vote on the trips they would like to take or can make alternate plans.

Planning Calendar

The following pages may be used as a planning calendar for your troop-year activities. Mark in the days of the month and then the occasions for which you need to plan. Look through your Girl Scout program resources and make some tentative plans. Are there some activities that could be grouped into monthly themes? The *Brownie Girl Scout Handbook* is not written to be used in a sequential order. You and the girls may begin anywhere in the book, or with activities from other Girl Scout resources, and follow a plan that works best for you. Check with your Girl Scout council for dates of any special wider opportunities planned for Brownie Girl Scouts. Start penciling in some notes. Remember, the year should start with girls planning activities.

SEPTEMBER

Monday	Tuesday	Wednesday	Thursday	Friday	Saturday	Sunday

OCTOBER

Monday	Tuesday	Wednesday	Thursday	Friday	Saturday	Sunday

NOVEMBER

Monday	Tuesday	Wednesday	Thursday	Friday	Saturday	Sunday

The Guide for Brownie Girl Scout Leaders

DECEMBER

Monday	Tuesday	Wednesday	Thursday	Friday	Saturday	Sunday

JANUARY

Monday	Tuesday	Wednesday	Thursday	Friday	Saturday	Sunday

FEBRUARY

Monday	Tuesday	Wednesday	Thursday	Friday	Saturday	Sunday

MARCH

Monday	Tuesday	Wednesday	Thursday	Friday	Saturday	Sunday

APRIL

Monday	Tuesday	Wednesday	Thursday	Friday	Saturday	Sunday

MAY

Monday	Tuesday	Wednesday	Thursday	Friday	Saturday	Sunday

JUNE

Monday	Tuesday	Wednesday	Thursday	Friday	Saturday	Sunday

JULY

Monday	Tuesday	Wednesday	Thursday	Friday	Saturday	Sunday

The Guide for Brownie Girl Scout Leaders

AUGUST

Monday	Tuesday	Wednesday	Thursday	Friday	Saturday	Sunday

Program Trails

A program trail is a useful tool for planning activities. It is a diagram in which one idea sparks another. A program trail will take different paths and turns depending upon the interests of the girls in the group. Following are two examples of program trails, one based on activities in the *Brownie Girl Scout Handbook* and one based on some of the other Girl Scout program resources for Brownie Girl Scouts. What path would you and your girls take?

The blank pages that follow are for you to create your own program trails.

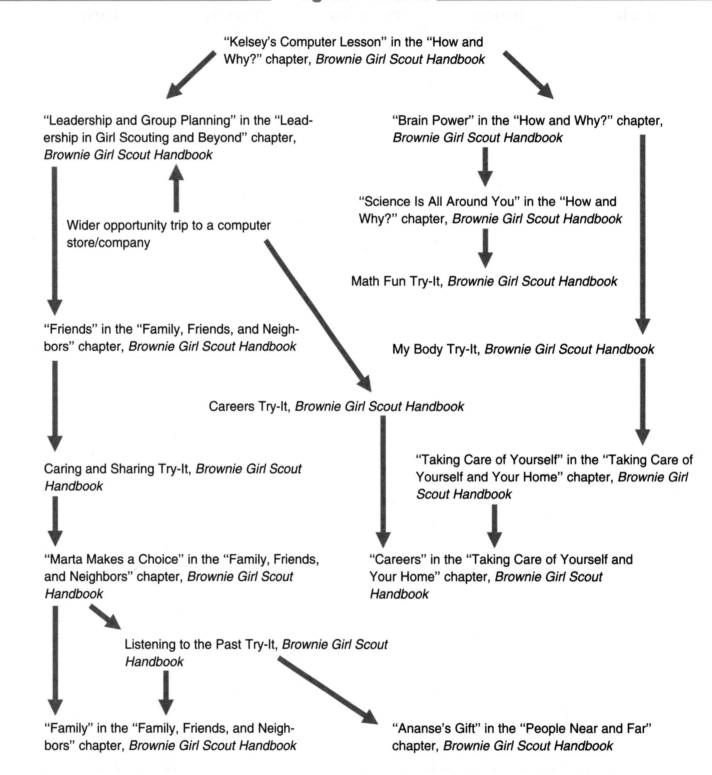

"Kelsey's Computer Lesson" in the "How and Why?" chapter, *Brownie Girl Scout Handbook*

"Leadership and Group Planning" in the "Leadership in Girl Scouting and Beyond" chapter, *Brownie Girl Scout Handbook*

"Brain Power" in the "How and Why?" chapter, *Brownie Girl Scout Handbook*

"Science Is All Around You" in the "How and Why?" chapter, *Brownie Girl Scout Handbook*

Wider opportunity trip to a computer store/company

Math Fun Try-It, *Brownie Girl Scout Handbook*

"Friends" in the "Family, Friends, and Neighbors" chapter, *Brownie Girl Scout Handbook*

My Body Try-It, *Brownie Girl Scout Handbook*

Careers Try-It, *Brownie Girl Scout Handbook*

Caring and Sharing Try-It, *Brownie Girl Scout Handbook*

"Taking Care of Yourself" in the "Taking Care of Yourself and Your Home" chapter, *Brownie Girl Scout Handbook*

"Marta Makes a Choice" in the "Family, Friends, and Neighbors" chapter, *Brownie Girl Scout Handbook*

"Careers" in the "Taking Care of Yourself and Your Home" chapter, *Brownie Girl Scout Handbook*

Listening to the Past Try-It, *Brownie Girl Scout Handbook*

"Family" in the "Family, Friends, and Neighbors" chapter, *Brownie Girl Scout Handbook*

"Ananse's Gift" in the "People Near and Far" chapter, *Brownie Girl Scout Handbook*

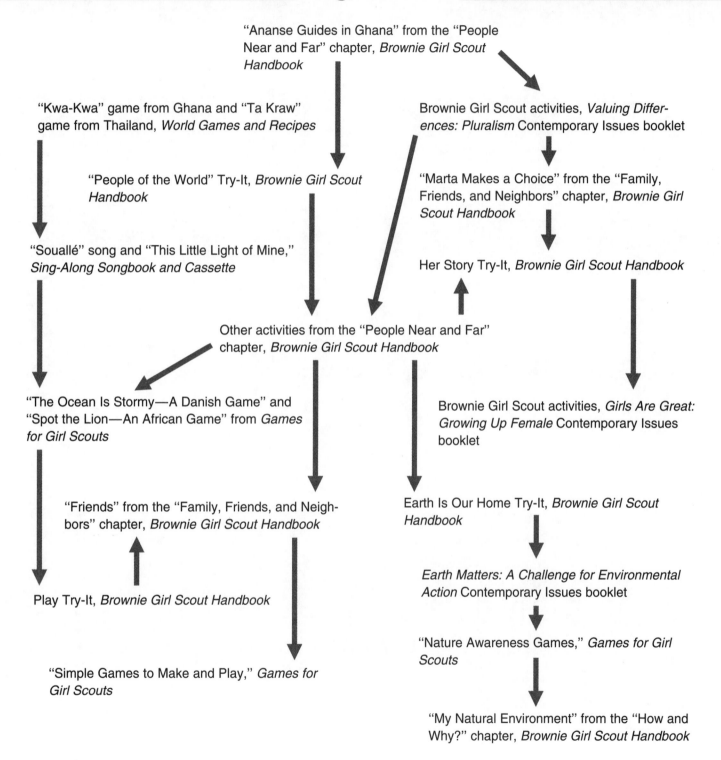

"Ananse Guides in Ghana" from the "People Near and Far" chapter, *Brownie Girl Scout Handbook*

"Kwa-Kwa" game from Ghana and "Ta Kraw" game from Thailand, *World Games and Recipes*

Brownie Girl Scout activities, *Valuing Differences: Pluralism* Contemporary Issues booklet

"People of the World" Try-It, *Brownie Girl Scout Handbook*

"Marta Makes a Choice" from the "Family, Friends, and Neighbors" chapter, *Brownie Girl Scout Handbook*

"Souallé" song and "This Little Light of Mine," *Sing-Along Songbook and Cassette*

Her Story Try-It, *Brownie Girl Scout Handbook*

Other activities from the "People Near and Far" chapter, *Brownie Girl Scout Handbook*

"The Ocean Is Stormy—A Danish Game" and "Spot the Lion—An African Game" from *Games for Girl Scouts*

Brownie Girl Scout activities, *Girls Are Great: Growing Up Female* Contemporary Issues booklet

"Friends" from the "Family, Friends, and Neighbors" chapter, *Brownie Girl Scout Handbook*

Earth Is Our Home Try-It, *Brownie Girl Scout Handbook*

Play Try-It, *Brownie Girl Scout Handbook*

Earth Matters: A Challenge for Environmental Action Contemporary Issues booklet

"Simple Games to Make and Play," *Games for Girl Scouts*

"Nature Awareness Games," *Games for Girl Scouts*

"My Natural Environment" from the "How and Why?" chapter, *Brownie Girl Scout Handbook*

Create your own program trail here.

Create your own program trail here.

Working with Brownie Girl Scouts

CHAPTER

3

Girls who are ages six through eight or in the first through third grades are growing and maturing at very different rates. Each girl is a unique individual with her own growth rate, talents, gifts, personality, intelligence, strengths, and weaknesses. The one definite statement that can be made about Brownie Girl Scouts is that they are growing and changing all the time. The following chart lists some broad generalities about the common characteristics of this age group.

Some Common Characteristics of Brownie Girl Scouts

Emotional	Can be inconsistent in behavior and moody, needs a lot of praise and encouragement, may react negatively to direction, interested in the difference between good and bad, may not like to try new things alone, likes working in groups, may like to help others, may be concerned about being accepted, often has a vivid imagination.
Social	Enjoys playing in groups, may start to demonstrate independence from family, may want to have lots of friends but may also have a "best friend," begins social telephoning to friends, can see different sides to an issue.
Physical	Is very active, can work or play in one place without fidgeting, may be able to do fine motor activities and has generally good eye-hand coordination, is eager to learn and become independent, has lots of energy, might be showing early signs of puberty (and may be quite self-conscious about it).
Intellectual	Is developing language and vocabulary: written, spoken, heard, may be reading, is interested in make-believe and fantasy stories, can attend to an adult-directed activity for 20–30 minutes or more but needs action.

What would you do in this situation?

Halfway through your troop year you notice that the third-year Brownie Girl Scouts have formed a tight clique. They often whisper to each other during the opening ceremony and share private jokes. The younger girls are just starting to mimic their behavior.

This is what one troop leader did:

One by one, she started asking the third-year Brownie Girl Scouts to take on more active roles in leading the troop activities, ceremonies, games, and planning. She asked them to plan a surprise scavenger hunt party for the rest of the troop to celebrate Thinking Day. They concentrated on that and their Flying-Up activities while the leader worked with the rest of the troop.

Multiage-Level Troops/Groups

Program Standard 19 states: "Girl Scout troops and groups should reflect the diversity of socioeconomic, racial, ethnic, cultural, religious, and disability groups in the community. Whenever possible, troops and groups should include girls from different age and grade levels." Brownie Girl Scout troops that include first-, second-, and third-graders and first-, second-, and third-year Brownie Girl Scouts provide the most benefits to girls and leaders. Younger girls learn from the older ones and look forward to progressing within Girl Scouting; older girls boost their self-confidence by sharing their expertise with younger girls and by being seen as role models. Leaders profit when girls are working with other girls. Leaders gain time when girls take on troop management tasks, such as attendance taking, record keeping, or activity planning. Leaders also benefit when girls can teach skills and share interests with others. The resources at the Brownie Girl Scout age level have such a wide variety of activities that girls who stay in Brownie Girl Scouts for three years do not need to repeat activities. Girls in their third year may also form interest groups and do some activities that differ from those of the rest of the troop.

If you have a multiage-level troop/group or if you have the possibility of working with a troop/group with more than one age level, you might consider the following:

- Make sure your Brownie Girl Scout circles (in a large troop) are mixed. You might want to start off the year with older girls taking a leadership role in troop government, but make sure the balance equalizes as the year progresses. Older girls should be encouraged to teach younger girls the duties and responsibilities of troop government.

- Find out what the older girls do well. Let them orchestrate a series of workshops, skits, lessons, or activities where they can show off their skills and abilities.

- Experiment with different types of meetings. Avoid meeting in one set pattern. Just as not all the girls need to be working on the same activity, neither do they need always to be working in small interest groups. Some activities might lend themselves better to large groups—certain games, songs, and demonstrations. Other activities work better with small groups—Try-It activities, decision-making, or repetitive work. Small groups can vary in size, and one girl or a pair of girls can also be working on an activity while the rest of the group does something different.

- Be sure to emphasize the positive in working with girls at different levels. First-year Brownie Girl Scouts have a lot to offer. While their interests may seem to differ or they may seem to require additional time for some activities, you may also discover that a first-year Brownie Girl Scout can be more mature than a third-year Brownie Girl Scout or may have a talent or skill that is more highly developed. Make sure that you and the girls in your troop project a positive atmosphere that welcomes everyone and that does not divide girls by older and younger. Encourage girls to look actively for opportunities to assist one another.

- Work together to adapt activities that need it. Games can be noncompetitive and use different skills—physical, such as walking and running, mental, such as strategizing and memorizing—so that every girl has a chance to shine. Some projects can be partially started and girls given the choice to work with those or to build their own from scratch. Girls can choose what suits them best. A girl may make a model or draw a picture. Even if you feel that a girl has the ability to make the model, but she chooses the "easier" method of drawing a picture, you have still given her the choice of how she wants to do her project. Giving her the opportunity to make these types of decisions is one of the most important things that you do as a Girl Scout leader.

Ten Tips for Working with Brownie Girl Scouts

These ten tips can help with the situations that arise whenever a group of girls gets together.

1 Focus on the talents and skills of each girl. For example, if a girl is very organized, but is very shy about speaking in front of others, try to give her tasks that use her organizational skills. Her confidence in a job well done will help build her confidence to speak up. You could also structure some activities in which she would need to speak in front of a small group of girls. A very active girl can be involved in tasks that require movement rather than more passive, "sitting still" types of activities.

2 Offer help in small doses. Girls often need less help than you think. Ask a girl the best way to do something. She usually knows. Make full use of the "buddy system" and rotate buddies so that everyone gets the chance to know one another. Brownie Girl Scouts may need some extra help in sharing and tak-

ing turns. If a girl becomes frustrated at not being able to use the materials she desires at that moment, suggest an equally attractive substitute.

3 Encourage respect for differing religious, racial, ethnic, and cultural backgrounds. Help each girl express pride in her own heritage and value the diversity of others. Be a role model in never using prejudiced words and in never taking prejudiced actions. Discover ways for girls to find accurate information and have positive experiences with girls and adults different from themselves.

4 Encourage girls to solve their own problems, to go to each other for support and assistance, and to take turns being the leader of the group. Intervene only if you are really needed. However, intercede immediately if a child's safety is at risk.

5 Girls learn best by doing. Encourage girls to discover things on their own and to try new things. Do not expect every Brownie Girl Scout to participate in every activity. If a girl does not wish to participate, suggest a quiet activity that will not disturb the group.

6 Girls need to feel positive about themselves. At this age, when girls are reaching beyond their families, getting positive affirmation from others is critical. Accept each girl as she is—strengths and weaknesses—so that she can learn to accept you and your guidance. Remember to use her name when speaking to her. Praise often; criticize never. Girls can understand that certain behaviors are unacceptable without being criticized. They need to be told clearly, and shown, which behaviors are acceptable.

7 Be supportive of and interested in the girls' ideas and interests, rather than being an entertainer for them. Rejoice with a girl when she achieves something important to her, no matter how small it may seem. Don't hold all girls to a uniform standard of performance. Vary the amount of help and support given in a situation according to a girl's physical, intellectual, and emotional status.

8 Keep directions simple and direct. Be sure the girl understands you. Try to meet at her eye level if giving complicated instructions or if working through a problem. Speak in quiet, pleasant tones. Girls listen better to someone speaking softly and calmly. Phrase directions positively: "Put your cup in the wastebasket, please" rather than "Don't leave your cup on the table."

9 Be reasonable about time with the girls. Start projects that the girls can finish. Give plenty of advance warning when an activity is going to end or begin. Brownie Girl Scouts may become frustrated or confused when hurried. Watch for signs of fatigue. Girls at this age can tire easily. Limits should be clearly defined and well maintained. Brownie Girl Scouts need consistency. They generally have a highly developed sense of fairness and will be quick to feel hurt if they believe you "play favorites." Be especially careful of this if your daughter is a member of your troop.

10 Involve each girl's family members as much as possible. Send notes home and spend some time speaking to family members who drop off or pick up the girls. Always be certain that any discussion you need to have with another adult about a girl is not within her hearing or that of any of the other girls. Share your successes with other leaders. Share resources and ideas.

What would you do in this situation?

Your Brownie Girl Scout troop is entering its second year. Last year, you never had enough time to finish all the activities you and the girls wanted to do. This year, though, is beginning quite differently. When you ask the girls what they would like to do, they shrug or reluctantly look through their *Brownie Girl Scout Handbook* and agree on the first thing someone mentions. You don't feel any enthusiasm and are not sure what to do about it.

Here's how one leader solved this problem:

She introduced the girls to the concept of brainstorming and spent a meeting brainstorming the types of things the girls enjoy doing—not only in Girl Scouting, but everything they like doing. Once she had a large list, she asked the girls to group activities that were similar and to select those activities they would like to do with one another as Brownie Girl Scouts. Using a large wall calendar, everyone began to plan the year. The girls took the lead as to which activities they preferred.

Managing Girls' Behavior

The recommended ratio of adults to Brownie Girl Scouts for meetings is two adults to every 20 Brownie Girl Scouts and one adult to each additional eight Brownie Girl Scouts. The leader, assistant leader, or other responsible adult designated by the leader or council is present during all troop meetings and related small-group activities.

Girls can learn to discipline themselves. They want to have a productive meeting. If the following are true of your troop/group, then the girls should be able to regulate their own actions and behavior.

- The girls feel secure, trusted, and valued.
- The girls understand the rules, know the rules are not arbitrary, and know why the rules exist.
- The girls are involved in planning their activities. Girls will not usually jeopardize an activity they want to do.
- The girls like each other and like you.

Conflict Resolution

Conflicts will occur from time to time. Girls will argue over whose turn it is to use the paint, or who likes whom the best, or which is the better brand of sneakers. Girls might argue because they are bored or restless or tired. They could be having a problem at home or at school. Sometimes, girls may disagree over more important issues that affect values and goals. Then it is particularly important to apply some conflict resolution techniques.

Conflicts can become larger or smaller. Conflicts will become smaller if the problem is recognized and if the focus is moved away from the participants and onto the problem and thinking of possible solutions. The point of conflict resolution is to discover a solution in which both participants win.

Conflict resolution techniques work well if the girls trust each other, trust you, and have positive feelings of self-esteem. The techniques might be harder to apply if the girls are competitive and use put-downs when speaking to each other. If this is true, you will need to work on the atmosphere of the meeting. Keep the girls busy choosing and doing activities while you begin work on changing the atmosphere.

Many activities in the *Brownie Girl Scout Handbook* and in other Girl Scout resources, such as *Girls Are Great: Growing Up Female* and *Valuing Differences: Pluralism* Con-

temporary Issues booklets, help girls build self-esteem and respect for others. If you see that the girls need help in those areas, start with those activities. There are more than enough choices to interest every girl.

The following techniques are some ideas for resolving conflicts. You may use different techniques for different situations and different girls.

Mediation. Each girl has a chance to tell her side of the story without interruption. The girl tells you what the problem was and what happened. Each girl tries to develop some possible solutions. The girls try to choose one.

Active Listening. You or one of the girls restates or paraphrases what each of the people involved in the conflict has said. You could use phrases such as "It sounds like you said . . ." or "You are saying . . ." or "Do you mean? . . ." or whatever sounds most natural. Often these phrases are used to discover the main reason for the conflict so that you can then go on to resolve it quickly.

Time Out. This can be used when you know the girls are capable of solving the problem themselves. You ask the girls to go off by themselves for a set period of time and return to you with their solution.

Role Reversal. This can help girls see another person's viewpoint. Ask each to state the point of view of another person.

Skillful Listening. The way you and the girls listen and speak to each other is also important for resolving conflicts. Listening is a skill. Do you look at a girl when she is speaking to you? Do you listen actively so that a girl knows you have heard what she said? Do you wait to give a girl a chance to answer you? Do you avoid interrupting her? Do your body language and facial expressions agree with what you are saying? Do the girls understand that put-downs are not allowed in the troop/group meeting? If the communication among the girls and between you and the girls is positive, then you have already taken a large step toward avoiding conflicts in your Brownie Girl Scout troop/group.

What would you do in this situation?

Every time you begin an active game or song Rasheena complains that Shauna bumps into her. You have not seen Shauna do this, but Rasheena never complains about the other girls.

What could you do?

Why not quietly ask both Shauna and Rasheena to stay a little later after the next meeting? Give each a chance to express her point of view, but set some ground rules first. No name-calling. No opinions. You only want to hear facts. You need to let them know that their behavior is unacceptable and that you are not in-

terested in being a judge, but you are willing to help them solve the problem between them. Often by listening to the "story" behind the story, you can discover the real problem. Perhaps Shauna has a new best friend and Rasheena feels left out. Maybe Rasheena has misinterpreted something that Shauna has said or done. The main thing is to try to discover a solution together, so that the girls really feel that they have solved their own problem. Girls will be much more likely to live by a solution they have worked out themselves.

Recognizing Signs of Distress

Divorce, poverty, death, homelessness, illness, violence, child abuse, and substance abuse are issues that many Brownie Girl Scouts may face directly or indirectly. Young people account for a large percentage of the nation's poor. Homeless mothers and their children are the fastest-growing percentage of the nation's homeless population. Nearly 1.5 million children in the United States are malnourished. Fifty percent of all children under the age of 18 have divorced parents. One in four girls has had a sexually abusive experience. Each year more than one million teenagers become pregnant. Each year approximately 12,000 children, ages 5 to 14, are referred to psychiatric hospitals for treatment of suicidal behavior, a figure that many experts believe is seriously underreported.

One very important way that you, as a Brownie Girl Scout leader, can help Brownie Girl Scouts is to be able to recognize some of the signs that a girl may show when she is in distress. The following is a list of some of the behaviors that may show that a girl is troubled. Keep in mind that these signs may be caused by many different emotional and physical problems or by simply growing up. The relationship and trust that you have developed with a girl will become critical in discovering more about a particular problem she may be facing, without your being overly intrusive. It is essential that you find out what procedures your Girl Scout council has set up if you suspect that any girl in your troop/group is in serious trouble.

Some Signs of Distress

- Increased secretiveness.
- A drop in the quality of the girl's work and abandonment of her goals.
- Changes in behavior—more disruptive and delinquent, or more quiet and uncommunicative.
- Chronic lying.
- Erratic mood swings or increased apathy and lethargy.
- Abrupt changes in friendships.
- Neglect of personal appearance and poor hygiene.
- Physical symptoms such as red eyes, sores, bruises, fatigue, drowsiness, loss or gain in appetite.

- Withdrawal from Girl Scout group and other school activities.
- Suddenly behaving in a more adult or sexually knowledgeable manner.

If you suspect that a child has been abused, follow your council's procedures for reporting the information. You may need to alert a council staff member, a child protection agency, or a law-enforcement agency. Since child abuse is a crime, an agency in every state is mandated by state law to receive and to investigate reports of suspected child abuse.

Tips for Helping Girls Cope

Girl Scouting can and does make a difference in the lives of girls. The skills a girl learns in her Girl Scout group and the support she receives can often help her deal with difficult situations.

Do:
- Provide an atmosphere of openness, freedom, and trust so that girls will feel comfortable when expressing themselves and when seeking advice from you.
- Listen seriously to what girls have to say.
- Be sensitive to the girls' ethnic and cultural backgrounds, religious beliefs, family traditions, and social customs.
- Be in touch with your own attitudes and behavior. Recog-

nize when your own beliefs may affect your judgment.
- Help girls become assertive and let them know it is okay to say no.
- Provide factual information in terms girls can understand.
- Help girls develop healthy ways to deal with stress.
- Take a preventive approach. Use creative methods like role-playing and games to discover what is on girls' minds and what they are experiencing in their own lives.
- Inform girls that they should always tell a trusted adult if they or someone they know is in distress. Know your council's guidelines and resources for girls who need special help.
- Be a positive role model of behaviors and attitudes.

Don't:
- Impose your own values and opinions on girls.
- Promise to keep information confidential if it might affect the girl's safety to do so.
- Leave a girl alone if the situation is life-threatening.
- Act judgmental, regardless of what you are told.
- Be afraid to seek help from others when you feel uncomfortable discussing certain topics.
- Provide information the girls do not want or need to know.

What would you do in this situation?

Janice, who had always been the first to try anything new, now expresses no interest in any of the activities. She chooses a seat as soon as she enters and rarely moves from that spot for the rest of the meeting. If you or the girls encourage her to participate in the activities, she becomes more withdrawn and unresponsive. You have noticed that her mother is often quite late in picking her up from meetings.

What signs of distress does Janice show? What can you do to assist Janice?

At the next meeting, ask your co-leader to work with Janice on an activity so you could wait outside for her mother. Mention to her mother what you have noticed about Janice's change in behavior. You discover that Janice's father has left the family; her mother has returned to work, and Janice has been feeling confused and neglected. Upon learning this, give her the name of a council staff member who has a list of community agencies and resources for women. You also speak to Janice with her mom present. You tell her you know she is going through a rough time and that you are there for her to speak to if needed. You mention that many other girls have experienced the same problem and you agree to respect her wish for privacy.

Adapting Girl Scout Program Activities

CHAPTER

4

Many occasions will arise when you will need to adapt or change an activity from the way it is stated in the *Brownie Girl Scout Handbook* or other Girl Scout resource. The activities are written to be flexible and easily modified depending on the needs of the group or an individual. Knowing the girls well—their strengths, weaknesses, and special needs—will help you know when an activity may need to be changed or even avoided. The following are some examples of adapted activities.

What would you do in these situations?

A The girls want to do the Sports and Games Try-It. Anne has juvenile rheumatoid arthritis. Her leg muscles in particular stiffen up and she often experiences pain in her fingers. You are not sure if she can do this Try-It.

After speaking with her mother, you find out that Ann's worst time is in the morning, but often by the afternoon she feels less pain. Ann often swims as part of her physical therapy. You schedule the activities for an afternoon and plan a play day utilizing a local park with a pool. You eliminate the skating activity, encourage Ann to shine as a helper for girls who cannot swim, and ask her to be a timer for the bicycle obstacle course.

B One of the girls suggests doing a service project for "those poor girls at the homeless shelter." What the other girls in the group do not know is that Mina, who just joined the troop, lives at the shelter and has asked you not to tell the other girls that she does.

The suggestion to do this service project was one suggestion of many. You add it to the list, commenting that "poor" should be used to describe the amount of money someone has, not her character or personality. You gently lead the girls to one of the other suggestions on the list.

You mention to Mina privately that you would like to discuss homelessness with the girls at another meeting and do some of the activities from the *Caring and Coping: Facing Family Crises* Contemporary Issues booklet. Mina tells you she doesn't mind as long as you promise not to tell the other girls where she lives. You agree. You contact your Girl Scout council support person who has a resource list of volunteer consultants and invite a consultant to join the next meeting. You also find out if your council has a fund to help subsidize activity fees for girls. At your next meeting, the consultant uses a large storybook to make a presentation about a homeless family and answers the girls' questions. If the cost of the uniform is an issue, you should be in touch with your council to see if they have a system for recycling uniforms or for buying uniforms.

C Your Girl Scout council has scheduled a science museum camp-in for a Friday night. Two of the girls in your group, Aisha and Layla, are of the Islamic faith and attend religious services on Fridays.

You arrange with the council that those girls from your group who wish to attend may join a group already going. Your co-leader and another parent agree to chaperone. About half of the girls in your group decide not to attend the council event. Those who went make a mini-presentation at the next meeting. You provide the girls with a list of upcoming Girl Scout opportunities and ask if there are any others they would like to attend. You also schedule activities for nights other than Friday.

D You suspect that one of the girls in the troop has a learning disability. She has a difficult time following directions. You have avoided suggesting some of the more complicated Try-Its and activities because you are afraid she cannot keep up and will be disruptive. Her mother has a very abrupt personality and you do not feel comfortable asking whether her child has a problem.

You ask your Girl Scout support person for assistance. In the mini-library is a copy of *Focus on Ability: Serving Girls with Disabilities*. In it you find advice for giving directions: Establish eye contact with the girl before you begin giving directions. Give directions in steps and number them. Present no more than three steps at a time. When these three have been completed, go on to the next three. Give directions orally and in writing when possible. After giving directions to the group, ask the girl with a disability to quietly repeat the directions to you or demonstrate that she understands. Ask the entire

group to repeat the directions from time to time. Restating the directions in a different way can also help. Do not embarrass the girl by giving her simpler activities or activities for younger girls. It is better to adapt the activity for all.

Girls with Disabilities

Many school-age children have some kind of disability. Many children without a disability may need special consideration due to economic or social problems.

Girl Scouting has been and continues to be a Movement for all girls and includes members with all kinds of abilities and disabilities. The disabilities may include physical, psychological, cognitive, or health needs that affect participation in daily activities. Intelligent and skilled intervention, in an atmosphere of understanding and acceptance, can help children with disabilities discover their strengths and gifts and realize their full potential. Focus on the girl as an individual. She can let you know what she is able and willing to do, and when and if she needs assistance. Be sensitive to the special needs she has, but involve her in all activities, adapting only when absolutely necessary.

For more information on disabilities, as well as specific tips for working with all girls, see *Focus on Ability: Serving Girls with Special Needs*, available from the National Equipment Service.

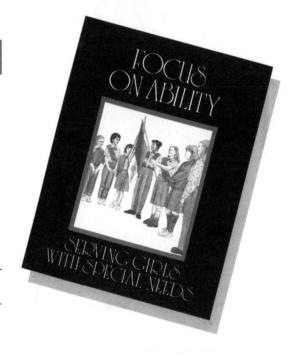

Help You Can Expect

Leaders and girls are the most important people in the Girl Scout Movement. As a leader, you make Girl Scouting happen; you keep the girls involved and interested, and you keep Girl Scouting dynamic and growing. Being a Brownie Girl Scout leader can be exhilarating and demanding. It should never be burdensome. That is why the Girl Scout organization has set up ways to make your job easier and to help you be an effective leader.

Other Volunteers

Working with other volunteers is one of the best ways to reduce the time-consuming odd jobs that arise and to add vitality to the troop/group meetings. The diagram below illustrates some of the volunteers who can make your life easier.

Parents and guardians can help by:

- Sharing special skills and knowledge.

- Helping with telephone calls, paperwork, and recordkeeping.
- Providing transportation.
- Providing assistance on trips and outings.
- Caring for younger children during meetings.
- Helping with money-earning projects.
- Helping write, type, or distribute a monthly troop newsletter for other parents/guardians.
- Keeping files of parents' and other adults' interests, hobbies, and careers that can be shared with the girls.

A troop committee, three to six women or men who are registered Girl Scouts, can help by:

- Assisting with special projects.
- Substituting for the leader when necessary.
- Recruiting consultants and other adults.
- Completing registration forms and other paperwork.
- Carrying out any of the duties listed under parents/guardians.

A program consultant is a volunteer recruited by the local geographic unit, the troop committee, or leaders to share her special interests or skills by:

- Participating in a service project.
- Acting as a consultant for a Try-It.
- Setting up a career exploration day or field trip.
- Teaching girls a new skill or craft.

Cadette and Senior Girl Scouts can help by:

- Teaching songs and games.
- Sharing special talents and skills.
- Planning and coordinating ceremonies.
- Helping with Try-Its and other activities.
- Participating as an extra assistant on field trips and at other events.
- Participating as Leader-in-Training, Counselor-in-Training, and/or program aide.

Sponsors, community organizations, businesses, block associations, social clubs, educational groups, churches, synagogues, mosques, temples, or other organizations whose aims for youth are compatible with those of Girl Scouting, can help by:

- Providing program consultants.
- Providing financial assistance.
- Providing recycled supplies and materials.
- Providing transportation and equipment.
- Providing a meeting place or a place for special events.
- Providing career exploration opportunities for girls.

The sponsor may further assist by ensuring that all girls in the community, regardless of racial, ethnic, or cultural background, religious or socioeconomic factors, have an opportunity to participate in Girl Scouting.

If a leader is approached by a local business or agency about becoming a sponsor, she should refer the group to the appropriate person in the Girl Scout council.

Your **local geographic unit**, which might also be known as a service team, neighborhood association, support team, or by some other title, is a group of volunteer workers who provide direct service to Girl Scout troops/groups within a neighborhood or other geographic subdivision of the council. The local unit

may have a chair or manager, one or more troop consultants, program consultants, trainers, and other specialists. The members of this unit can be your best resource and provide another link to your Girl Scout council. Some of the services provided by your council support team could be the following:

Organizing Groups of Girls. The service team could provide:

- Help in recruitment and placement of girls and adults.
- Help with membership registration.
- Help in finding suitable meeting places.
- Help in obtaining parental support.
- Help in promoting Girl Scout activities.

Offering Guidance with Program Opportunities. The service team could:

- Suggest ideas for local service projects and for field trips and community places to visit.
- Provide information on council-sponsored events and on camping opportunities.
- Provide ideas and guidelines for money-earning projects.

Providing Support to Leaders. The service team could:

- Help with management of troop/group.
- Act as a source of information for educational opportunities.

- Help find consultants for special activities.
- Help in utilizing various Girl Scout program resources, such as the Contemporary Issues booklets.
- Provide feedback and act as a sounding board.
- Help interpret national and local policies, standards, and procedures.

Who is in your local geographic unit? What are their phone numbers? What services can they provide for you?

Your Girl Scout Council

Your local council has been chartered by Girl Scouts of the U.S.A. to organize and maintain Girl Scouting in a certain geographic area. Your Girl Scout council has organized your local support team. You may receive some services locally and others may be provided by your Girl Scout council.

Your council may provide:

- Outdoor resources and facilities.
- Councilwide activities and projects.
- Opportunities for adult learning and sharing.
- Access to Girl Scout and other books, audiovisual materials, and resources.

- Interpretation of the council organization and operation.
- Opportunities for you to express needs and make suggestions.
- Interpretation and clarification of national and local policies, standards, and procedures.
- Bulletins and newsletters.
- Council-developed resources.
- Networking possibilities.

Whether you are new or experienced, you should feel comfortable seeking guidance from others in your council, who, like you, care about girls. Take advantage of training events. These events offer practical knowledge and skills that can help to make your Girl Scout leadership experience enjoyable and worthwhile. Many Girl Scout councils offer a wide variety of educational opportunities for leaders. Some are written modules that allow a leader to "self-study"; others provide brief evening opportunities or more in-depth day events. Many councils will also offer educational opportunities that introduce new Girl Scout program resources.

In addition, keep informed of other events scheduled by your council. Special events can broaden your experience, lighten your tasks as a leader, and provide girls with exciting opportunities. Your Girl Scout council has many ways of providing the support you need as a Brownie Girl Scout leader. Make sure you are familiar with the variety of opportunities offered and how this information is disseminated.

The staff organization charts show two different council structures. You also have space to record the name, address, and phone number of your Girl Scout council and the people there whom you might need to contact.

Staff Organization Chart, Council A

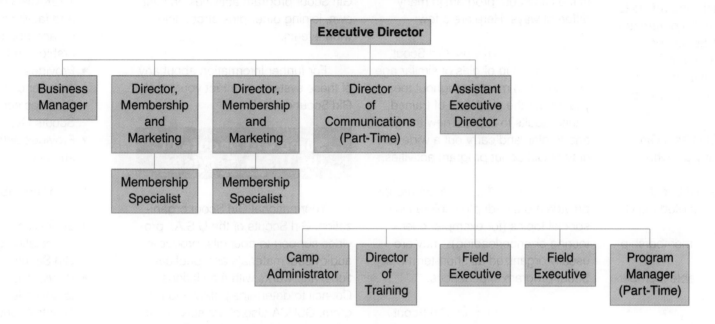

Staff Organization Chart, Council B

Membership in Girl Scouting

Membership in the Girl Scout Movement entitles girls and adults to participate in Girl Scout program activities and other Girl Scout-sponsored events, to wear the appropriate uniform and insignia, and to be covered by Girl Scout Activity Accident Insurance.

Active membership as a Girl Scout is granted to any girl who:

- Has made the Girl Scout Promise and accepted the Girl Scout Law.
- Has paid annual membership dues.
- Meets the applicable membership standards.

The membership standards for Brownie Girl Scouts are girls ages six, seven, or eight or in grades one, two, or three. Any girl who meets or can meet these membership requirements shall not be denied active participation in Girl Scouting because of race, color, ethnicity, creed, national origin, or socioeconomic status.

Active membership as a Girl Scout adult is granted to any person who:

- Accepts the principles and beliefs as stated in the Preamble of the Girl Scout Constitution.
- Has paid annual membership dues.
- Is at least 18 years old.

The Preamble of the Constitution of Girl Scouts of the U.S.A. is given in the *Leader's Digest: Blue Book of Basic Documents.*

Girls and adults can participate in the Girl Scout program in many different ways. Here are a few:

Girl Scout Troops. Girl Scout troop is a group of girls of similar age or grade who meet throughout the year under the guidance of trained, caring adults to explore new things and to plan and carry out a wide variety of Girl Scout program activities.

Interest Groups. Interest groups provide more in-depth exploration of special topics (for example, orienteering or cheerleading). They are usually organized as short-term Girl Scout program experiences.

Girl Scout Events. Girl Scout councils may sponsor wider opportunities for the girls in their own councils or in other Girl Scout councils. These events can be career days, exploration of topics in the Contemporary Issues series, camping weekends, trips, and tours.

Activity Centers. Activity centers are neighborhood facilities serving as sites for organized Girl Scout program activities. They operate at varying times during the year (after school hours, on weekend days, etc.). In some cases, the centers may accommodate girls of different age levels.

Girl Scouting in the School Day. Girl Scout program activities can be carried out as a part of the regularly scheduled school day.

Girl Scouts Registering Individually. Girls may register and do Girl Scout program activities on their own, joining other girls at council-wide events.

For further information about any of these systems, contact your local Girl Scout council.

Some Girl Scouts of the U.S.A. Services

Your national Girl Scout organization, Girl Scouts of the U.S.A., provides support to councils, produces audiovisual materials and publications, and works with the National Council to determine policy and program. GSUSA also offers services to adults and girls. For adults, GSUSA:

- Provides national educational opportunities at Edith Macy Conference Center.
- Operates the National Equipment Service and publishes the *Girl Scout Catalog.*
- Provides membership cards.
- Holds national meetings.
- Maintains the National Historic Preservation Center.

For girls, GSUSA:

- Selects girls for GSUSA-sponsored wider opportunities and provides travelships.
- Acts as a link for the International Post Box.

- Provides travel assistance, including cards of introduction for traveling troops, information for girls traveling across the border, information on the TREKKING network of camps and facilities, and information on and applications for scholarships and grants.
- Provides Gold Award certificates and lifesaving awards.
- Provides services to USA Girl Scouts Overseas.
- Provides activity accident insurance.

In addition, GSUSA:

- Serves as liaison to the World Association of Girl Guides and Girl Scouts.
- Provides consulting services to councils.
- Grants council charters.
- Maintains national centers.

The National Centers

Two national centers are owned and operated by Girl Scouts of the U.S.A. These centers, partially supported by membership registration dues, provide opportunities for girl and adult members to meet other Girl Scouts from across the country, to explore new places, and to gain new knowledge and skills.

Juliette Gordon Low Girl Scout National Center

Edith Macy Conference Center

Juliette Gordon Low Girl Scout National Center

Located in Savannah, Georgia, the birthplace of Juliette Low is part of the largest National Historic Landmark District in the United States. The Juliette Gordon Low National Center is a program center and public museum where visitors can learn about her childhood and her life's work in Girl Scouting.

For more information, write to Juliette Gordon Low Girl Scout National Center, 142 Bull Street, Savannah, Georgia 31401.

Edith Macy Conference Center

This center provides an environment for educational opportunities for adults. Located 35 miles north of New York City, the site also contains the John J. Creedon Center. Courses on such diverse topics as "Developing Older Girl Leadership Projects," "Workshops for Administrators of Council Day Camps," "Fun with Science in the Out-of-Doors," "Council Shop Management," "Making the Transition from Volunteer to Paid Staff," and "Recognizing the Importance of Pluralism" are offered. Many courses are designed especially for adults who work with girls. Any Girl Scout volunteer may attend these courses. You do not have to be selected. Some Girl Scout councils provide scholarship money for leaders to attend courses. Edith Macy Conference Center can also accommodate day tours or overnight stays by traveling troops.

For more information, write to the Training Registrar, Girl Scouts of the U.S.A., 420 Fifth Avenue, New York, N.Y. 10018-2702. Your Girl Scout council should have the current calendar listing training opportunities at Edith Macy Conference Center.

The World Association of Girl Guides and Girl Scouts (WAGGGS)

Girl Scouts of the United States of America is part of the international educational association for girls, the World Association of Girl Guides and Girl Scouts. All national organizations that are members of WAGGGS share a common history. Robert Baden-Powell, First Baron Baden-Powell of Gilwell, England, founded the Scouting movement in 1908.

In 1909, a Boy Scout rally was held in London. A number of girls turned up proclaiming themselves to be "Girl" Scouts! A separate movement, the Girl Guides Association, was formed in 1910.

A friend of the Baden-Powells, Juliette Gordon Low, was so enthusiastic about the idea of a youth organization for girls, that she founded Girl Scouting in the United States in 1912.

From these beginnings, WAGGGS has grown to 118 national Girl Guide/Girl Scout organizations with a membership close to eight million.

World Trefoil Pin

Common symbols are shared among all member organizations. The trefoil is the unifying symbol of WAGGGS and is used on the World Trefoil pin and the World Flag. The Girl Scout Promise, the motto "Be Prepared," the left handshake, the sign or salute, and the World Song are all essential parts of each national organization. These symbols remind all members that they belong to a worldwide organization.

Thinking Day is a celebration that all members of WAGGGS share annually on February 22, the joint birthday of Lord and Lady Baden-Powell. Girl Guides and Girl Scouts meet on this day to think of their sisters worldwide and to give voluntary contributions to the Thinking Day Fund. The money is used to promote Girl Guiding/Girl Scouting in isolated areas, to assist with training, or to support projects that deal with the problems of malnutrition, illiteracy, or people with disabilities.

The World Centers

The World Association of Girl Guides and Girl Scouts has acquired four world centers. Girl Scouts who are 14 years or older may stay at these centers and join special projects or events.

Our Cabaña, in Cuernavaca, Mexico, was founded in 1957. Here Girl Scouts and Girl Guides learn about Mexican culture, customs, and crafts and participate in special service and outdoor projects.

Olave Centre, located in London, England, was founded in 1932 and serves as the home of the World Bureau and as a world center. The center includes a new facility, Pax Lodge, where program and training events take place.

Sangam, in Pune, India, was founded in 1966. Sangam means "coming together," and girls from many cultures participate in activities and projects.

Our Chalet, located in Adelboden, Switzerland, was founded in 1932. A gift to WAGGGS from Helen Storrow of Boston, Massachusetts, the center is high in the Swiss Alps and focuses on the outdoors.

Annotated Resource List

The Girl Scout program contains many resources for Brownie Girl Scouts and Girl Scout leaders. Check with your Girl Scout council about borrowing resources or obtaining additional information.

Brownie Girl Scout Handbook. The basic book of activities for Brownie Girl Scouts. Brownie Girl Scout Try-Its are included in this book.

The Guide for Brownie Girl Scout Leaders. The companion piece to the *Brownie Girl Scout Handbook*, this resource contains tips and information necessary for leaders.

Safety-Wise. The basic guide to security and safety practices for Girl Scouts.

Leader's Digest: Blue Book of Basic Documents. Covers all the Girl Scout policies and includes excerpts from the Congressional Charter and the Girl Scout Constitution.

Contemporary Issues booklets. Contain information and statistics, tips for leaders, age-appropriate activities, and resource sections. The following booklets are available for Brownie Girl Scouts.

- *Tune In to Well-Being, Say No to Drugs: Substance Abuse*
- *Staying Safe: Preventing Child Abuse*
- *Girls Are Great: Growing Up Female*
- *Into the World of Today and Tomorrow: Leading Girls to Mathematics, Science, and Technology*
- *Reaching Out: Preventing Youth Suicide*

- *Caring and Coping: Facing Family Crises*
- *Earth Matters: A Challenge for Environmental Action*
- *Valuing Differences: Pluralism*
- *Right to Read: Literacy*
- *Developing Health and Fitness: Be Your Best!*

Outdoor Education in Girl Scouting. Contains ways to introduce outdoor activities to girls. This book includes information on camping, safety skills, and ways of evaluating the outdoor experience.

Exploring Wildlife Communities with Children. Helps adults explore the wonders of the environment with girls.

Games for Girl Scouts. Contains a wide variety of old and new games: travel games, outdoor games, wide games, quiet games, and simple games to make and play.

The *Sing-Along Songbook and Cassette.* Features old and new Girl Scout favorites.

The *Girl Scout Pocket Songbook.* Contains 60 international and U.S. Girl Scout songs.

Brownies' Own Songbook. Has 45 lively singing games and songs.

Sing Together: A Girl Scout Songbook. Includes over 140 favorites, and the *Sing Together Sampler* is a 40-minute audiocassette tape with helpful teaching tips.

Our Chalet Songbook. Songs compiled by the Our Chalet Committee of WAGGGS.

Canciones de Nuestra Cabaña. Contains 110 songs with lyrics in Spanish and English compiled by the Our Cabaña Committee of WAGGGS. The *Canciones de Nues-*

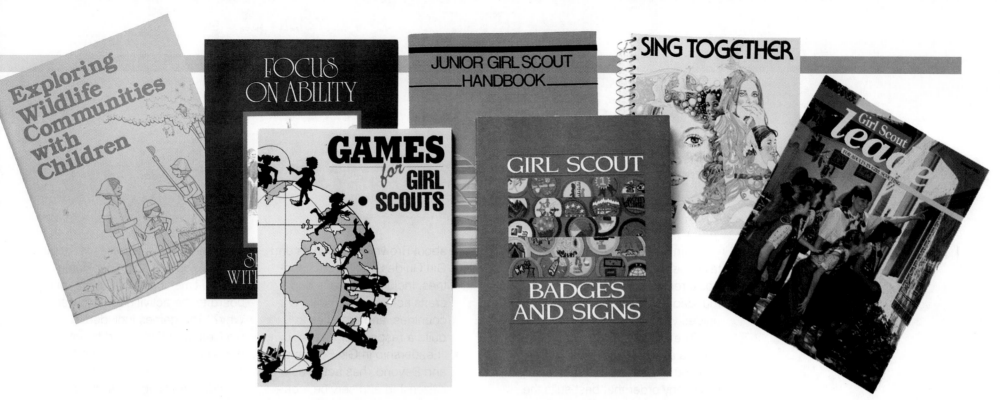

tra Cabaña Cassette has over 50 songs, most in Spanish.

The Wide World of Girl Guiding and Girl Scouting. Includes information on Girl Guiding/Girl Scouting activities in other countries.

WAGGGS Brownie Uniforms and Badge Poster. Shows Brownie Girl Guides and Girl Scouts in the uniforms of their countries.

Trefoil Round the World. Describes the history of Girl Guiding and Girl Scouting, including the basic facts on each country.

World Games and Recipes. Offers games and food from around the world.

Girl Scout Uniforms, Insignia, and Recognitions. Includes photos and information on uniforms and insignia for all age levels and adults.

Focus on Ability: Serving Girls with Special Needs. Provides information on various disabilities and ways to work with girls with special needs.

Ceremonies in Girl Scouting. Contains a compilation of popular ceremonies.

Troop Records and Reports. Preprinted forms and a binder for recording dues, attendance, and activities.

Girl Scout Leader magazine. Covers news and articles about events and activities in Girl Scouting. Received by all Girl Scout adult members.

Current Girl Scout Catalog and GSUSA Publications and Audiovisuals Catalog. Includes merchandise for sale through the National Equipment Service.

All of these materials are available through the National Equipment Service, GSUSA, 420 Fifth Avenue, New York, N.Y. 10018-2702. Check with your Girl Scout council first or your local neighborhood Girl Scout group to find out which books are available. Many Girl Scout councils also have a Girl Scout council shop that sells books, as well as other NES items. You may want to share the cost of some of these books with a group of your fellow Girl Scout leaders and set up a mini-lending library of resource materials.

If you contain the girls' experiences to those activities in the Brownie Girl Scout Handbook, you will be providing them with a quality and varied Girl Scout program, but you will not have explored the variety of materials available to you and the girls. Increasing the number of resources that girls use can help maintain their interest in Girl Scout activi-

ties. Certain topics, such as the environment, substance abuse awareness, or camping, require more detailed knowledge and activities than those in the handbooks. Some books on other subjects, such as The Wide World of Girl Guiding and Girl Scouting or Into the World of Today and Tomorrow: Leading Girls to Mathematics, Science, and Technology, can supplement the activities in the handbook. You may also want to add activities that you have used in teaching, for example, or that you have read about in an activity book. If you are using an activity that is not from a Girl Scout resource, ask yourself if it is compatible with the Girl Scout Promise and Law, four program goals, and safety standards.

Part II

INTRODUCTION

INTRODUCTION

Part II of this leaders' guide contains the *Brownie Girl Scout Handbook*, reduced in size and surrounded by wraparound text, which guides you with tips and resources.

The *Brownie Girl Scout Handbook* is a flexible resource. The girls and you may choose to do the activities in any order that best suits the needs and interests of the girls. The handbook is designed to be interactive; girls should feel free to color, write, and mark on its pages. A story introduces each chapter. Stories may be read aloud, acted out, used to start a discussion, or used to spark an activity.

Each of the chapters contains activities connected to a particular topic:

- "Welcome to Girl Scouting" contains basic information for girls on Girl Scouts and Brownie Girl Scouting.
- "Taking Care of Yourself and Your Home" has activities on health, home care, safety, and first aid.
- "Family, Friends, and Neighbors" has activities on family life, friendships, different types of people, and school life.
- "People Near and Far" gives information and activities

about Brownie Girl Scouts and Girl Guides in different countries. Included are arts and crafts activities from different countries, and activities to build a respect for diversity.
- "Leadership in Girl Scouting and Beyond" has activities on citizenship and service, goal-setting, troop government, selling cookies, and leadership.
- "How and Why?" offers activities on mathematics, science and technology, the weather, the environment, and the outdoors.
- "Brownie Girl Scout Try-Its and the Bridge to Junior Girl Scouts Patch" contains all 40 Try-Its, listed in alphabetical order, and bridging activities. The wrap-around text accompanies all of these chapters.

While the activities in the handbook do not repeat, similar themes may appear in different chapters. For example, "Taking Care of Yourself and Your Home" contains an activity in which girls are asked to draw a time line of their lives. The "How and Why?" chapter has sections on time and measurement. You and the girls could do the time-line activity and

continue with the activities in "Taking Care of Yourself and Your Home" or use the time-line activity as a springboard to the activities in "How and Why?" The games included in "People Near and Far" could be introduced when you are playing the games that appear in the "Family, Friends, and Neighbors" chapter or when learning about sports safety in "Taking Care of Yourself and Your Home."

The wraparound section that follows is printed around its corresponding handbook pages. The wraparound text contains two parts: "Tips," which will help you carry out program activities, and "Try-Its and Other Resources," which will help you find related activities within this book as well as in other resources.

The difficulty of the activities and the reading level of the text vary because girls at the Brownie Girl Scout age level not only differ widely in ability but also change and learn rapidly. What may have been too difficult and frustrating a month ago may now be an enjoyable activity. Build on the enthusiasm shown by the girls for a particular activity to chart your own course through the activities in this book.

Welcome to Girl Scouts

"**O**kay, girls, I'll see you next week. Please remember to bring your permission slips for the camping trip," Mrs. Carreras said as we left the school cafeteria.

Later that night . . .

"I can't wait to go camping!" I said as I climbed into bed. "My first overnight trip! I know I'm going to have a great time!"

The Story of Girl Scouting

Oh, hi! My name is Jessica and I am a Brownie Girl Scout. At our meeting tonight, we had a party. We sang songs, played games, and listened to a story! After we listened to the story, Mrs. Carreras, our leader, told us she knew a woman who loved stories and Girl Scouting as much as we did. She was born on October 31, 1860.

7

The cover of the *Brownie Girl Scout Handbook* has representations of many of the activities girls will do in Brownie Girl Scouting. Girls can see how many they can find. Also, girls could make their own cut and torn paper collages depicting their expectations of Brownie Girl Scouting or their experiences in Daisy and Brownie Girl Scouting. This can work as a main activity or as a "start-up" activity and may take several meetings to finish.

Tips

You have two stories, one within the other. The story of Juliette Gordon Low is being told by "Jessica," a Brownie Girl Scout who also gives information about Girl Scouting. Before reading the story with girls, you could find out what they already know about Girl Scouting. You could list the responses under the heading "What We Know" and when you finish reading the story, girls can make a new list: "What we'll do as Brownie Girl Scouts."

Do you know whom Mrs. Carreras was thinking of? If you do, you could write her name here.

_____

That's right! Mrs. Carreras was thinking of Juliette Gordon Low, the woman who started Girl Scouting in the United States in 1912. Mrs. Carreras said that "Miss Daisy" was just like us in many ways. And you know what? She really was! Here's her story. See if you agree!

The Story of Juliette Gordon Low

When Miss Daisy was born, an uncle said, "I bet she's going to be a daisy!" And Daisy became her nickname among her family and friends.

Daisy lived in Savannah, Georgia, with her mother, father, her older sister, Nellie, two younger sisters, Alice and Mabel, and with Willy and George, her two younger brothers. Daisy was born during the time of the Civil War and members

of her family fought on both sides.

As a young girl, Daisy liked to do many of the things you and I like to do. She loved to use her imagination to make up her own games. She enjoyed swimming, playing outdoors, making paper dolls, and acting in plays. She'd even write her own plays and star in them!

She wrote to her grandmother, "I never felt better in my life. My complexion has cleared up. I take so much outdoor exercise that I'm

never tired!" In the same letter, she wrote, "Wish Alice happy birthday. Tell her to look in my paper dolls, and choose five as my present to her!"

What are some of your favorite things to do?

_____

_____

Daisy had great adventures with her brothers and sisters! Once, Daisy was making a kind of candy called taffy at her cousin's house. One

The photograph on page 8 (center) is the youngest picture of Juliette Low that exists in the Girl Scout archives. The photograph on page 8 (right) is of Juliette Low when she was a teenager. The photograph on page 9 is the wedding photograph of Juliette Gordon and Willie Low. The photograph on page 10 is a photograph of an early Brownie Girl Scout troop. The photograph on page 11 is of Juliette Low and an early Girl Scout troop.

Some ways to read the story: Read aloud and ask girls to listen. Invite different girls to read different parts, taking turns playing the role of Jessica. Ask girls to read parts of the story silently while you read the other parts aloud.

As girls read aloud, try to avoid correcting them. Help them decode unfamiliar words by identifying sounds with which they are familiar. Also enlist the assistance of other girls in the troop.

cousin, named Rudolph, noticed that the taffy was the same color as Daisy's hair. "Let's braid some into her hair," he suggested, and Daisy, always willing to try something new, agreed. Can you guess what happened? Well, the taffy became very hard and sticky, sort of like chewing gum, and Daisy's mother had to chop all of Daisy's long, beautiful hair very short to get rid of the sticky mess!

Daisy loved animals. One time she was worried about a cow getting cold. In the middle of the night, she took her mother's bedspread to the stable and pinned it on top of the cow. Her mother was not very happy the next morning because the cow had stepped all over the bedspread when it fell off!

Studying was never so easy for Daisy, but she loved her drawing classes. Once she wrote her mother, "Dear Momma, Please let me stop school. I hate it so and I don't believe I learn a thing!" Her friends who went to school with her said that

she worked hard, but she also liked to have fun. Daisy's mother believed that education was really important. School stopped at the eighth grade in Savannah, so Daisy and her brothers and sisters all continued their high school educations away from home at boarding schools.

When Daisy finished school, she moved back home to Savannah. She went to a lot of parties and at one of these parties, she met an

Englishman named Willie Low. Daisy and Willie were married and moved to England. She became friends with famous people like Rudyard Kipling, who wrote the *Just So Stories*, and she spent a lot of time drawing and painting. She also made her own blacksmith tools and made a set of iron gates. Her arms got so strong that she had to make the sleeves on her dresses bigger!

Daisy did not have children of

 9

While reading, girls can think about the characteristics and personality of Juliette Low. What things did Juliette Low like to do that became part of Girl Scouting? How would you describe her? How would her talents and abilities help her start an organization like the Girl Scouts? In many ways she was ahead of her time. In what ways was she special or different?

her own but she always enjoyed doing things to help young people. She particularly liked to help kids who seemed not to get much help from other grownups. On her trips to places all over the world, such as Egypt and India, she would bring along one of her nieces or nephews. She always had wonderful stories to tell about her adventures and would bring home bags full of special presents for everyone.

What are some ways you could help kids younger than you?

_____

_____

But, like most people, Daisy had a life that was not always easy. She had many troubles with her health. Daisy had problems with her hearing. She had an accident that hurt her good ear and afterwards she was almost completely deaf. She also did not have a happy mar-

riage with Willie. When Daisy was 44 years old, Willie died. But Daisy refused to let her problems stop her from doing things with her life that she wanted to do.

A few years later, Daisy met a very interesting man named Sir Robert Baden-Powell. He told Daisy all about an organization he had started for boys called Boy Scouts. Six thousand girls also signed up, so, with his sister Agnes's help, the Girl Guides were started.

This idea of a girls' movement

really excited Daisy and she offered to start a troop in Scotland. Girls who were poor often did not have a chance to go to school. Usually, they would work in a factory. Factories were noisy, dirty, and very unhealthy. Daisy found a woman who could teach her and the girls in the troop how to spin cloth. They sold the cloth at a market in London and then used the money to start an egg business. The egg business was so successful that the girls could help their families with the money

Girls may want to know more about Juliette's deafness and may be concerned about an accident happening to them. You could mention that medical care at that time was not as advanced as today, which is one reason why Juliette's deafness worsened. You could also do the ac-

tivities on handbook pages 72–82 in "Family, Friends, and Neighbors."

Girls can look at the photographs of Juliette Gordon Low and discuss things that look different than they do today. Girls can bring in pictures of their grandmothers or other older relatives to compare to the pic-

tures of Juliette. Or they can share family stories from the past or present such as a special trip, a favorite memory from when they were younger, or a funny thing that happened to them and one of their brothers, sisters, or other relatives.

and not have to work in a factory. Daisy wanted girls everywhere to be part of this organization. She formed troops in London and then made plans to come to the United States.

On March 12, 1912, Daisy's dream came true! On this day, Daisy registered the first two troops of girls in Savannah, Georgia. That is why March 12 is the Girl Scout birthday. These first Girl Scouts found out that girls can do all sorts of exciting things. They went on hikes, formed basketball teams, and learned how to camp. These are some of the same things I do with my troop today. How about you?

Girl Scouting became a big hit all over the United States . . . and the world, too! Whenever a leader had a new idea, Daisy would always say, "Have you asked the girls?" Daisy continued to work very hard telling everyone she knew about Girl Scouting. When she died in 1927, there were 168,000 Girl Scouts in the United States. She had a special dream—and she made it come true!

She really was a lot like you and me because I know I have dreams that I hope to make come true. What are some of your dreams?

At the end of the story, girls can think about their own dreams. What do they need to do to make their dreams come true? What did Juliette Low do to make her dreams come true?

Here are some more things to try:

Ask girls to choose their favorite part of the story and act it out with a group of friends. Locate Savannah, Georgia, on a map. Ask girls if they have ever visited Savannah or the state of Georgia. Take girls on a journey into the past. What things did Juliette do that they think would be fun to try?

Try-Its and Other Resources

- Try-Its: Creative Composing; Her Story; Listening to the Past.

People around the world admire the wonderful work she did. The Juliette Low World Friendship Fund was started to help bring girls from different countries closer together. A ship, a United States postage stamp, and a federal government building were all named for her, and a sculpture of Daisy was placed in the Georgia state capitol. Her home in Savannah, Georgia, is now a national Girl Scout center called the Birthplace.

That's the end of the story that Mrs. Carerras shared with us. Just as I shared her story with you, girls everywhere get to share the special gift that Juliette Gordon Low gave us—Girl Scouts!

More About Girl Scouting

As a Brownie Girl Scout, you may be new to Girl Scouting, or you may have joined as a Daisy Girl Scout. Brownie Girl Scouts are six through eight years old or in the first, second, or third grade.

This handbook is for you to use during your Brownie Girl Scout years. Each chapter has fun activities and stories that will help you learn about Girl Scouting, yourself, family, friends, your community, and the world all around you.

The last chapter has 40 Brownie Girl Scout Try-Its. Try-Its are triangle-shaped patches that Brownie Girl Scouts can get for trying or learning about something new. The chapter "Brownie Girl Scout Try-Its" has lots more information about Try-Its.

Many parts of the book have places for you to write or draw. If you do not have enough space, add another piece of paper to the page. Then, you will have a record of all your Brownie Girl Scout adventures.

Tips

Girls who were Daisy Girl Scouts can share some of their experiences with girls new to Girl Scouting.

This is a good place to stop and ask girls what things they would like to learn about this year. This initiates the girl/adult planning process. Girls need to know the activities available to them as Brownie Girl Scouts in order to plan. If girls do not have their own handbooks, you will want to make sure that copies are available for them to look through before and after troop meetings.

There are many ways to plan. You and the girls can brainstorm a list and attach the list to their handbooks. The list can be updated as interests change. You could create a giant calendar of troop meetings or smaller calendars for girls to keep. Groups of girls can be assigned different sections and then tell the group about the fun things they have discovered in their sections. You may also want to check with your local Girl Scout representative about events and trips your Girl Scout council has planned.

You will also see Suzy Safety throughout the book. She is there to remind you to do things in a safe way.

Are you ready to begin your adventures as a Brownie Girl Scout? Let's find out more about Girl Scouting.

13

Suzy Safety. Girls can look through their books for pictures of Suzy Safety. Girls can share some things they know how to do in a safe way, for example, how to cross the street, use a knife to cut food, respond to a knock at the front door, or answer the telephone when home alone.

More information on safety can be found on handbook pages 48–62 in "Taking Care of Yourself and Your Home."

Try-Its and Other Resources

- Try-Its: Girl Scout Ways.

The Girl Scout Promise and Law

All Girl Scouts make the Girl Scout Promise. The words in this Promise are:

14

> On my honor, I will try:
> To serve God and my country,
> To help people at all times,
> And to live by the Girl Scout Law.

These words say a lot about being a Girl Scout.

Let's look at what a Girl Scout says she will do:

On my honor, I will try—This means that a Girl Scout promises to work hard to be her best at all times. The words that follow tell what a Girl Scout will try to do.

To serve God—There are many ways to serve God. Your beliefs are very personal. You may go to a church, a temple, a mosque, a special place indoors or outdoors. You may learn about your beliefs with your family. Every day you try to act in the way that your beliefs and your family teach you.

Tips

Girls can draw pictures or mime putting the Girl Scout Promise into action! Ask girls to show the different ways in which they serve God, serve in their communities, and help the environment, their families, friends, and neighbors.

Some girls may need help understanding some of the words in the Girl Scout Law. Assist girls in locating words they may find difficult, such as "considerate," "authority," "wisely," or "respect," in a children's dictionary.

And my country—A Girl Scout may serve her country in many ways. You can say the Pledge of Allegiance and be in a flag ceremony. You can obey the laws of your community and your country. You can learn more about your country. You can help your family, your neighborhood, and your community. What else can you do?

To help people at all times—A Girl Scout tries to help people. Helping someone carry packages is one small way. There are big ways to help, too. You could teach math to someone younger than you. You can fix something that is broken and you can plant trees to help the environment. What are some other ways to help people?

To live by the Girl Scout Law—The ten parts of the Girl Scout Law are ten ways that you can try to be the best person you can be. Try saying the Girl Scout Law aloud:

I *will do my best:* ~~Melissa~~ ✓
To be honest Kelly ✓
To be fair Jacqueline ✓
To help where I am needed Chelsea ✓
To be cheerful Laura ✓
To be friendly and considerate Kimberly
To be a sister to every Girl Meghan ✓
* Scout*
To respect authority Michelle ✓
To use resources wisely Karla ✓
To protect and improve the ~~Katie~~ Courtney ✓
* world around me*
To show respect for myself and Katie ✓
* others through my words*
* and actions.*

Why not draw or find pictures that show people living by the Girl Scout Law? Your pictures can remind you of what you can do to live by the Girl Scout Law.

15

The illustration shows some of the ways girls follow the Girl Scout Promise and Law. The actions of the girls are open to different interpretations. The girls in your troop or group can make up stories, tell before-and-after stories, or match the actions in the illustration to those in the Girl Scout Promise and Law.

The Worlds of Interest

Girl Scouts have five exciting worlds of interest to explore:

The World of Well-Being helps you learn more about how you are special and how to take care of yourself.

The World of People is about others—your family and your friends, people different from yourself, and people around the world.

The World of Today and Tomorrow has opportunities to discover how things work and how things happen, and how you can be ready for the future.

The World of the Arts has puppets and dance, music, pottery, weaving, painting, and much more.

The World of the Out-of-Doors explores the natural world surrounding your home, community, city, or camp.

When you do things in Girl Scouting, you will learn to be the best you can be. You will make new friends and learn about people from all different places, religions, cultures, and races. Girl Scouting will help you learn how to make decisions and decide how to act. You will do service projects that help other people or the community.

16

Tips

The worlds of interest provide a structure for activities. They are not rigid categories. They are a guide, however, to let you know if you seem to be doing too many activities with one particular focus: for example, too many art Try-Its or too many well-being activities. While girls are choosing the activities they would like to do, you will need to step in and point them in some other directions if their choices are lopsided.

The Brownie Story

Brownies have always been known for being honest, fair, and helpful. Have you heard about Brownies? Do you know how Brownie Girl Scouts were named? Here is one version of the story.

Mary and Tommy lived with their father and grandmother. Their father worked very hard all day and their grandmother was too old to do the housework.

Their father tried his best to keep the house clean. Mary and Tommy didn't help him very much. They just played all day long.

"Children are hard to care for," said Father.

"Children are a blessing!" said Grandmother.

"Not my children," said Father. "They do not help me a bit."

Just then, Mary and Tommy ran in, their shoes covered with mud.

"Wipe your feet outside!" said Father.

"What makes Father so angry, Granny?" asked Tommy and Mary.

"He is tired and you two do not help him. What this house needs is a brownie or two."

"What is a brownie, Granny?"

"A very helpful little person. She came in before the family was up and did all sorts of chores. The brownie always ran off before anyone could see her, but they could hear her laughing and playing about the house sometimes."

"How nice! Did they pay her, Granny?"

17

Tips

The Brownie story is a Girl Scout tradition dating back to Lord Baden-Powell, who adapted the original story written in 1865 for use by Girl Guides and Girl Scouts. Girl Guides and Girl Scouts in other countries also have a similar story, and in many countries Girl Scout leaders are called "Brown Owls." The story

Ananse's Gift on handbook pages 88–90 in "People Near and Far" is the traditional story of the Girl Guides in Ghana, West Africa.

Ask the girls if they can guess why they are called Brownie Girl Scouts. After some of the story has been read, see if the girls would want to guess again. The tips for introducing stories on page 69–70 of this book would also be appropriate here.

Some other ideas:

1. Write letters, write an advice column, or ask questions of the Wise Old Owl.
2. Create a poem or song about the ways Brownie Girl Scouts are helpful.
3. Make puppets and perform the story for a Daisy Girl Scout troop.

Try-Its and Other Resources

- Try-Its: Creative Composing; Listening to the Past; Puppets, Dolls, and Plays.
- Other Resources: *Right to Read.*

HOO! Hoo!
HOO HOO

"No, brownies always help for love. But the family left her some treats at night like cookies, fruit, and juice. She liked that."

"Oh, Granny, where are the brownies now?"

"Only the Wise Old Owl knows, my dear."

"Who is the Wise Old Owl, Granny?"

"I don't know exactly, my dear."

"Oh, I wish she hadn't gone away!" said Mary and Tommy together. "May we put out some juice and cookies for her? Maybe she will come back if we do."

"Well," said Grandmother, "she's welcome if she chooses to come. There's plenty of work for her to do here."

So Mary and Tommy put out some cookies and juice, and went off to bed.

That night, Mary could hardly sleep. She kept thinking about the brownie.

"There's an owl living in the old shed by the pond," she thought. "If it is the Wise Old Owl, she can tell me where to find a brownie. When the moon rises, I'll go look for the Wise Old Owl."

The moon rose and Mary hurried to the pond in the woods.

Everything was so still that Mary could hear her heart beating. Then suddenly, "Hoo! Hoo!" said a voice behind her.

18

"It's an owl!" said Mary. "Maybe it's the one I'm looking for."

The owl flew by her onto a beam that ran under the roof of the shed and said, "Come up! Come up!"

The owl could talk! Then it must be the Wise Old Owl! Mary climbed up the beam, and said, "Please, where can I find a brownie to come and live with us?"

"That's it, is it?" said the owl. "Well, I know of two brownies that live in your house."

"In our house!" said Mary. "Then why don't they help us?"

"Perhaps they don't know what has to be done," said the owl.

"Just tell me where to find those brownies," said Mary, "and I'll show them what needs to be done. There is plenty to do at our house!"

"Well, Mary, I can tell you how to find one of the brownies. Go to the pond in the woods when the moon is shining and turn yourself around three times while you say

this charm:

"Twist me and turn me and show me the elf.

I looked in the water and saw _____ ."

Then look into the pond to see the brownie. When you see the brownie, you will think of a word that ends the magic rhyme."

Mary reached the edge of the pond in no time. She slowly turned herself around three times while she said the rhyme:

"Twist me and turn me and show me the elf.

I looked in the water and saw _____ ."

She stopped, looked into the pond, and saw only her own face.

"How silly," said Mary. "There's no word to rhyme with elf, anyway. Belf! Helf! Jelf! Melf! I saw nothing but myself! Myself? That rhymes with elf! How strange! Something must be wrong! I'll go back and ask the Wise Old Owl about it."

19

Mary went back to the shed and told the Wise Old Owl she saw nothing but herself.

"And what did you expect to see?" asked the owl.

"A brownie," said Mary.

"And what are brownies like?" asked the owl.

"Granny says brownies are very helpful little persons. I saw no one but myself when I looked in the pond and I'm not a brownie."

"All children can be brownies," said the owl. "Couldn't you help out around the house and pick up your own things?"

"I don't think I would like it," Mary said.

"Would you rather be someone who makes work instead of doing it?" asked the owl.

"Oh, no!" cried Mary, "I don't want to be like that. I'll tell Tommy and we'll both try to be brownies."

"That's the way to talk!" said the owl. "Come on, I'll take you home."

Before Mary knew it, she was in her own bed. When daylight came, she woke up Tommy and told

him what had happened. Together they crept downstairs and did every bit of work they could find to do before their father woke up. Then they went happily back to bed.

When Father came downstairs, he looked around and rubbed his eyes. The table was set, the floor was clean, and the room was as bright and shiny as a new penny.

At first, Father could not say a word. Then he ran to the foot of the stairs, shouting, "Mother! Tommy! Mary! Our brownie has come back!"

One morning, Father woke up very early and heard laughter coming from the kitchen. "It must be the brownie," he thought. He went downstairs, opened the kitchen door, and saw Mary and Tommy dancing around the room.

20

"What's this?" he asked.

"It's the brownies! We are the brownies!" sang Tommy and Mary.

"But who did all the work? Where are the real brownies?"

"Here!" said Mary and Tommy as they ran into their father's arms.

When Granny came downstairs, Father told her how he had found the brownies.

"What do you think of it all, Mother?" asked Father.

"Children are a blessing," said Grandmother. "I told you so."

Just like Mary, there are many ways to show how you are a Brownie Girl Scout. Can you think of some? What are some things you'd like to do as a Brownie Girl Scout?

21

Special Girl Scout Ways

In a **Brownie Girl Scout Ring**, Brownie Girl Scouts get together to make their group decisions. Girls and their Brownie Girl Scout leader plan things to do in troop meetings, camping trips, and service projects.

The **Girl Scout sign** is made when you say the Girl Scout Promise. Hold your right hand like the picture shows you. The three raised fingers stand for the three parts of the Girl Scout Promise.

The **Girl Scout handshake** is the way Girl Scout friends greet each other. Shake hands with your left hand while giving the Girl Scout sign with your right hand.

In a **friendship circle**, stand in a circle and cross your right hand over your left. Hold hands with the people standing next to you.

A **friendship squeeze** is begun by one person in the friendship circle. When you feel your hand squeezed, you do the same to the person next to you. Everyone is silent as the friendship squeeze is passed. It stands for friendship with Girl Scouts everywhere.

22

Tips

Girls can practice the signs and talk about why they are useful to know how to do. A relay game or imitation-type game, like "Simon Says," could be a fun way to practice the signs.

Try-Its and Other Resources

- Try-Its: Girl Scout Ways.
- Other Resources: "Leadership in Girl Scouting and Beyond," handbook pages 115–117 and 119–122.

The **Girl Scout motto** is "Be prepared." Girl Scouts try to be ready to help when they are needed. They try to be ready for emergencies and be able to take care of themselves.

The **Girl Scout slogan** is "Do a good turn daily." What do you think this means? Even the smallest act can be very helpful.

The **quiet sign** is a way to let everyone know it is time to be quiet. Someone raises her right hand. She keeps her five fingers up to remind others of the fifth part of the Girl Scout Law, "I will do my best to be friendly and considerate." Each person who sees this sign stops talking and raises her hand until everyone is quiet. What are some good reasons to use the quiet sign?

Girl Scout Ceremonies

Girl Scouts hold ceremonies for many reasons. Some ceremonies celebrate a special day in Girl Scout-

ing and others are a way for a group to share their feelings. Girl Scout ceremonies can be short or they can be most of a meeting; they can take place indoors or outdoors.

Your Brownie Girl Scout ceremonies can include Brownie Girl Scouts, other girls in Girl Scouting, Girl Scout leaders, other Girl Scout adults, and special guests like family and friends.

In a ceremony, you can:

• Say the Pledge of Allegiance.

• Honor the flag.
• Say the Girl Scout Promise and Law.
• Light candles or hold flashlights.
• Sing songs.
• Recite poems.
• Read special sayings.
• Tell or act out stories.

In the ceremony opening, everyone learns the reason for the ceremony. The middle is the celebration, and the closing is the time to thank guests and say goodbye.

Try-Its and Other Resources

■ Other Resources: More information on ceremonies can be found on pages 27–28 in Part I of this book, and in *Ceremonies in Girl Scouting*. You will

also want to check *Safety-Wise* for the proper precautions to take.

The "Brownie Girl Scout Smile Song" is one of many songs that Brownie Girl Scouts may choose to sing at their ceremonies. More songs appear on handbook pages 24, 62–64, 95, 163, and 227 and on

pages 28–30 in Part I of this book. The annotated resource list on pages 66–67 in Part I of this book has other songbook titles. Remember that when girls are singing, enthusiasm and fun are much more important than hitting the right notes.

Songs and music are a special part of Girl Scout ceremonies. The "Brownie Girl Scout Smile Song" is the Brownie Girl Scouts' special song. The words and music are printed on this page. Why not try singing it?

Girl Scouting's Special Days

Do you celebrate some special holidays? Girl Scouts also have some special days.

October 31

Juliette Low's birthday (also known as Founder's Day).

You can honor Juliette Low on her birthday in many different ways:

- Use "The Story of Girl Scouting" to put on a play, skit, or puppet show about Juliette Low's life.
- Invite another troop to celebrate with you and have a party.

Brownie Smile Song

1. I've some-thing in my pock-et; it be-longs a-cross my face. And I keep it ver-y close at hand in a most con-ven-ient place.

2. I'm sure you couldn't guess it
If you guessed a long, long while.
So I'll take it out and put it on--
It's a great big Brownie Smile!

Used by kind permission of Harriet F. Heywood.

Tips

Mark the special days on your personal calendar. A few weeks before each date, remind girls that a special day is coming up and ask for suggestions for celebrations.

Try-Its and Other Resources

- Try-Its: Girl Scout Ways.
- Other Resources: *Trefoil Round the World*; *The Wide World of Girl Guiding and Girl Scouting.*

• Give money to the Juliette Low World Friendship Fund. Part of this fund is used to send Girl Scouts to other countries and to bring Girl Guides and Girl Scouts to the United States. The other part is used to help Girl Scouts and Girl Guides around the world.

February 22

Thinking Day is the birthday of both Lord Baden-Powell and Lady Baden-Powell, the World Chief Guide. This is the day that Girl Scouts and Girl Guides everywhere "think about" each other.

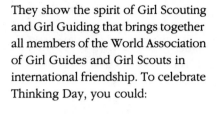

They show the spirit of Girl Scouting and Girl Guiding that brings together all members of the World Association of Girl Guides and Girl Scouts in international friendship. To celebrate Thinking Day, you could:

• Invite a Girl Scout who has traveled outside the United States to share her experiences with you.
• Make Thinking Day cards and send them to other Girl Scouts in your area.
• Give to the Juliette Low World Friendship Fund.
• Learn more about people who live in another country.

March 12

This is the day of the Girl Scout birthday, the date in 1912 when the first 18 Girl Scout members were officially registered. The week in which March 12 falls is known as Girl Scout Week. Some girls may celebrate a Girl Scout Sunday or Girl Scout Sabbath. These fall on the

weekend before the Girl Scout birthday. You could plan a special day with family and friends and with other Girl Scouts in your neighborhood and community. You might try especially hard to let others know more about Girl Scouting during this week.

April 22

Girl Scout Leader's Day is a special day to honor Girl Scout leaders all over the country. What are some ways you could honor your Girl Scout leader? Could you plan a party, write a poem, sing a song? What could you do with others?

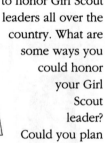

25

Brownie Girl Scout Uniform

The uniform and its different pieces let other people see that you are a Brownie Girl Scout. The pictures below show different styles of the Brownie Girl Scout uniform.

26

Tips

Ask girls to look at the pictures of the Brownie Girl Scout uniforms. Which items or combinations do they like best? You could also talk about the meanings of uniforms, the types of people who wear uniforms on their jobs, and why Girl Scouts wear uniforms.

Note: Uniforms are not required for girls to participate in Girl Scout activities. For more information, refer to *Safety-Wise*, Standard 11, and page 14 in Part I of this book.

27

Try-Its and Other Resources

- Other Resources: The illustration on handbook page 87 in "People Near and Far" shows Brownie age level Girl Scouts in other countries in uniforms.

Brownie Girl Scout Insignia and Recognitions

Girl Scout insignia are the pins and patches that you wear on your uniform that show you are a Girl Scout. Try-Its are recognitions you can earn as a Brownie Girl Scout.

Many religious groups have their own recognitions for girls of their faith who are Girl Scouts. If you are interested in the religious recognitions, you can find out about them from your Girl Scout leader or your religious group.

The **Brownie Girl Scout pin** tells others that you are a Brownie Girl Scout. It is shaped like a trefoil, which means three leaves. The leaves stand for the three parts of the Girl Scout Promise. In the middle of the pin is a brownie. You may wear your Brownie Girl Scout pin even when you are not wearing your uniform.

The **World Trefoil pin** shows that you are part of the World Association of Girl Guides and Girl Scouts. The three leaves represent the Girl Scout Promise. The flame stands for loving all the people in the world. The compass needle is to guide you, and the two stars are the Girl Scout Promise and Law. The outer circle is for the Worldwide Association of Girl Guides and Girl Scouts, and the golden yellow trefoil on a bright blue background stands for the sun shining over the children of the world. You may wear it on your regular clothes as well as on your uniform.

 28

Tips

Religious recognitions are not designed by Girl Scouts of the U.S.A. but by the religious organizations that provide the recognitions. A chart of recognitions is on pages 20–22 in Part I of this book. **More to Try:** Place the insignia and recognitions on a table, in a paper bag, or in a box. Girls can choose a pin or patch and put it on the Brownie Girl Scout sash in its proper place. With two or three sashes, you can have a relay game.

The **Bridge to Brownie Girl Scouts patch** is for girls who were once Daisy Girl Scouts and did special activities before becoming Brownie Girl Scouts.

The **Girl Scouts U.S.A. strip** shows that you are part of the family of Girl Scouts in the United States of America.

The **Girl Scout council strip** shows the name of your local Girl Scout council. Every Girl Scout **troop** has its own **number**. The number is given to your troop by your Girl Scout council.

The **membership star** stands for one year of membership in Girl Scouting. You get a star for each year you are a Girl Scout. The color of the circle behind the star tells the age level. The color green shows that you got the star as a Brownie Girl Scout, and a blue disc shows that you were once a Daisy Girl Scout.

Brownie Girl Scout Try-Its are patches, or recognitions, that show you have tried learning how to do many new things. You get a patch for each set of activities that you have tried.

29

Try-Its and Other Resources

- Other Resources: See pages 10–11 in Part I of this book, and handbook pages 161–165 in "Brownie Girl Scout Try-Its and Bridge to Junior Girl Scouts Patch" for more information on Brownie Girl Scout Try-Its.

Girl Scout Age Levels

All girls in kindergarten through the twelfth grade or five through 17 years of age can be members of Girl Scouting in the United States. Girl Scouting is for girls of all religions and traditions, of all races, and of all cultures. Girl Scouts of all ages in the United States do make the Girl Scout Promise and accept the Girl Scout Law, just like you.

The five age levels in Girl Scouting are:

- Daisy Girl Scouts—ages 5–6 or grades K, 1
- Brownie Girl Scouts—ages 6, 7, 8 or grades 1, 2, 3
- Junior Girl Scouts—ages 8, 9, 10, 11 or grades 3, 4, 5, 6

- Cadette Girl Scouts—ages 11, 12, 13, 14 or grades 6, 7, 8, 9
- Senior Girl Scouts—ages 14, 15, 16, 17 or grades 9, 10, 11, 12

Daisy Girl Scout *Brownie Girl Scout* *Junior Girl Scout* *Cadette Girl Scout* *Senior Girl Scout*

30

Investiture or Rededication

After you have learned the Girl Scout Promise and Law, you are ready to be invested. An investiture is a special ceremony in which you officially become a Girl Scout. As part of the ceremony, you make the Girl Scout Promise. If you were a Daisy Girl Scout, you have already been invested and you will be rededicated as a Brownie Girl Scout.

Investiture and rededication are important ceremonies in Girl Scouting. If you are being invested, you will receive your Brownie Girl Scout pin. If you are being rededicated, you will repeat the Girl Scout Promise and Law.

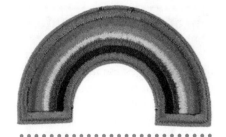

Bridging

Moving from one age level to another is called bridging. You will "cross the bridge" from Brownie to Junior Girl Scouting, the next age level, at the end of your last year as a Brownie Girl Scout.

Tips

After girls have attended a meeting or two, they are ready to plan their investiture. Girls can work in pairs, small groups, or as one group to plan different sections. Girls may want to invite their relatives or other significant adults. The planning tips on handbook page 123 in "Leadership in Girl Scouting and Beyond" and information about ceremonies on pages 27–28 in Part I of this book would be helpful. Girls who were Daisy Girl Scouts can share their investiture experiences, and second- or third-year Brownie Girl Scouts can discuss their ceremonies. A Junior Girl Scout can also talk about her investiture and her bridging ceremonies.

Girl Scout National Centers

Girl Scouts from everywhere in the United States can meet other Girl Scouts at two special places called "national centers."

The Juliette Gordon Low Girl Scout National Center, also known as "The Birthplace," is the home in Savannah, Georgia, where Juliette Low was born. People can visit this historic house museum and program center and learn about Juliette Low's life. Girl Scout troops can take part in many fun activities.

Edith Macy Conference Center is near New York City in Briarcliff Manor, New York. Adults learn more about Girl Scouting there.

Edith Macy Conference Center

Juliette Gordon Low Girl Scout National Center

World Centers

Our Cabaña (Mexico), Our Chalet (Switzerland), Pax Lodge (England), and Sangam (India) are four centers where older Girl Guides and Girl Scouts from all over the world can meet to get to know each other and share ideas, attend events, work on service projects, or learn something new.

Brownie Girl Scout Scavenger Hunt!

Leyla is new to Brownie Girl Scouting. Help her find in this book each of the items listed below. Circle each item you find. Look back through the chapter if you need help!

Girl Scout sign
Girl Scout handshake
Friendship circle
Girl Scout Promise
Girl Scout slogan
Daisy Girl Scout
Brownie Girl Scout Ring
World Trefoil pin
Brownie Girl Scout pin
Brownie Girl Scout Try-Its
Brownie Girl Scout Handbook
Girl Scout birthday
Membership star and disc
Junior Girl Scout
Girl Scout motto
Suzy Safety

Tips

Help girls locate the two national centers and the four world centers on a globe or a world map. If girls are interested in learning more about the world centers, write to: Program Group, Girl Scouts of the U.S.A., 420 Fifth Avenue, New York, N.Y. 100-18-2702. If they wish to know more about the Juliette Gordon Low Girl Scout National Center, write to: Juliette Gordon Low Girl Scout National Center, 142 Bull Street, Savannah, Ga. 31401.

Brownie Girl Scout Scavenger Hunt!: All the items on the scavenger hunt may be found in the "Welcome to Girl Scouts" chapter.

Try-Its and Other Resources

■ Try-Its: Around the World; People of the World.
■ Other Resources: *Canciones de Nuestra Cabaña; Our Chalet Song Book; Trefoil Round the World; The Wide World of Girl Guiding and Girl Scouting; World Games and Recipes.*

Taking Care of Yourself and Your Home

Marisol stretched her legs as long as they could reach and pointed her toes under the bed covers. She had danced across the stage, the star of the Ballet Folklórico. Everyone was standing and clapping and throwing red roses, until this B-Z-Z noise got louder and louder and louder. She was dreaming! The B-Z-Z noise was the alarm clock! "6:30 A.M." Across the room, she could see the curled-up shape of her sister, Lisa, pillow over her head. "I'm always the one to get up first," Marisol thought. "And I have to make sure Lisa gets dressed, and make breakfast for both of us, and

Marisol Starts a Club

33

Tips

Some Brownie Girl Scouts may have difficulty reading this story.

(1) You could read the story aloud.

(2) You could briefly summarize the story, and then read it aloud.

(3) Ask girls to take the roles of Marisol, Lisa, Raza, Tamara, and Carol with you or another girl as narrator.

(4) In small groups, girls could take turns reading the story or acting it out.

(5) You could read two or three paragraphs at a time and then ask girls to summarize what they have heard.

(6) Girls can prepare a skit or puppet show in advance and perform it for the group.

(7) You could give the girls some specific information to look for while they are reading: What is Marisol dreaming about? What do you think is Marisol's favorite thing to do? What are some of your favorite things to do? What are some of the ways Marisol, Raza, Carol, and Tamara help at home? What are some of the ways you help at home? Why is it hard at times to be responsible? What are some other ways you can be responsible? How will being responsible help Marisol achieve her dream of being a dancer?

find her missing homework. I'm the responsible one. I'm the oldest." She looked at the alarm clock—6:35. If she didn't have to get Lisa ready, she could sleep until 7:00—and dream some more about dancing. . . .

"Lisa, get up, get in the bathroom." Marisol pulled the pillow away from her sister's head.

"Oh, Marisol, please, five more minutes," Lisa begged.

"Not one more second! You have to get up now." Marisol watched her leave the room. "Every morning she asks for five more minutes. I don't have five extra minutes."

Marisol quickly made both beds. She chose her outfit—sneakers, jeans skirt, pink T-shirt, and an outfit for Lisa. She walked quietly down the hall. She knew her dad would be sleeping. He didn't get home from work until midnight.

She put two waffles in the microwave, poured some juice and some milk. She measured the coffee into the basket and started the coffee

maker. Her mom got home at 7:30 A.M. She worked the night shift at the hospital and was very happy to sit for a moment and have a cup of coffee when she got home.

Her mom had started working again last month. Her mom had talked with Marisol about doing more at home, especially in the mornings and after school. Marisol wanted her mom to be proud of her, but sometimes she wished she could be the younger one or her mom wouldn't go to work at all.

Lisa's homework was under the dog's bed. Lisa's sneaker wouldn't stay tied. Lisa couldn't find her lunch. Marisol found it in the bathroom. "Why did you bring your lunch to the bathroom?" Marisol looked at her sister and said, "Forget it, let's go." And she made sure she locked the door behind her as they left.

At lunch, Marisol sat with her very closest friends—Raza, Tamara, and Carol. She opened her lunch bag. "Oh, no, I have Lisa's lunch. She won't eat anything but peanut

butter and I hate peanut butter. Little sisters are such a pain!"

Raza looked up from her tuna fish and said, "Have half of my sandwich. I wish I had a little sister. Older brothers can be a pain, too."

"But, you don't have to be responsible," and Marisol told them all the things she did every day.

"Since my parents got divorced,

34

The theme of this story is the positive and negative aspects of being responsible—which ties into the chapter title: "Taking Care of Yourself and Your Home." Encourage girls to discuss the concept of responsibility. You can talk about personal responsibility—such as not taking drugs, not stealing, not cheating on tests, doing your best whenever possible. Social responsibility is also important—helping at home, helping your friends, being a good citizen, taking care of the environment. Brainstorm the benefits of being responsible—feeling good about yourself, making life better for yourself and others, learning more when you do things yourself—so that being responsible does not sound like a chore. Older girls may have no difficulty in pairs or small groups discussing why a person should be responsible. Younger girls may need more concrete questions and answers done with the entire group.

I do lots of things at home," Tamara said. "My Mom and I painted all the rooms in the house. I helped her put down tiles in the kitchen. I even help her take care of the car. She said if we can't keep it running, we'd be in big trouble. New cars are too expensive!"

Raza added, "My mom has always worked and lots of times she gets home late, so she makes a bunch of meals on the weekend and when she's going to be late, I get dinner ready. I never even think about it. I just do it."

Carol said, "I have two little brothers *and* a little sister. My mom always asks me to help her look after them. She says she doesn't know what she'd do without me. And I always feel good when she says that."

Marisol thought about all the times her mom told her what a big help she was. She thought about how good she felt when she made the coffee for her mom in the morning. "I feel really good, too, when I

do things around the house," Marisol said. "We're all very responsible. I have a great idea. Let's form a club—The Responsible Ones. We can call ourselves The ROS, for short. We can take care of ourselves and take care of our home and help our fam-

ilies and help each other—what do you think?"

Of course, it was such a good idea that Carol and Tamara and Raza agreed on the spot and their club, The Responsible Ones, was started that same day.

Try-Its and Other Resources

- Try-Its: Caring and Sharing; Food Fun; Her Story; Puppets, Dolls, and Plays.
- Other Resources: Handbook pages 36–47; "Leadership in Girl Scouting and Beyond," handbook pages 115–118. *Girls Are Great*. The following activity is from this booklet:

  With your troop or group, make a list of some of the things girls seem to be expected to do (for example,

play with dolls or wash dishes) and things boys seem to be expected to do (for example, play baseball or climb a tree). Talk about the reasons why some of these expectations may be unfair and what can be done to change them.

What responsibilities do you have? You probably have some responsibilities to take care of yourself. You need to keep yourself safe and take care of your body and your clothing. You need to eat food that is good for you and you need to feel good about yourself. Do you have responsibilities at home? Do you take care of your room? Do you do other things inside and outside your home? In this chapter, you will have fun learning about taking care of yourself and your home.

Taking Care of Yourself

You only have one very special body. Being good to yourself now will help you as you grow up.

Your Body Is One of a Kind

No one has a body just like yours. Bodies come in all shapes and all sizes. You have your own eye and hair color, hair texture, and skin color. Maybe you have freckles. Maybe you are tall. Maybe you are short. There is no one best body. How are bodies different? Try these four activities and find out.

1. Tape pieces of newspaper together to form a large sheet. Lie down on your back on it. Ask a buddy to take a crayon or marker and trace the shape of your body onto the paper. Draw in your face and clothing to complete this picture of you.

2. Try "Tracing Your Shadow" in the Me and My Shadow Brownie Girl Scout Try-It. Compare your silhouette with the others in your troop/group.

3. You could compare your body measurements with those of other people. You could also compare the measurements of different parts of your own body. Are different parts of your body the same length? Are the distances around parts of your body the same as the different lengths?

36

Tips

Many girls, even as young as Brownie Girl Scouts, have a negative self-image about their physical appearance. They are influenced by the media and by society and may well believe in a standard of beauty that is very different from their own appearance. The activities here can reinforce two very positive messages: (1) It is important to be healthy, to look your best, and to accept those aspects of your body that might not fit into the current "look." (2) Differences are what make people beautiful. How boring it would be if everyone looked the same! Differences in body type, hair color and texture, eye color, skin color, are what make people special. Valuing the differences among people is the first step in counteracting prejudices.

Note for Activity 3: The body parts chosen for measurement—neck, wrist, head, ankle—are those that would least embarrass a child who might feel self-conscious about being overweight or "too tall."

Get some ribbons, long strips of newspaper, or tape measures. Measure different parts of your body. Make a strip or ribbon for each of these:

• The distance around your neck
• The distance around your wrist
• The distance around your head
• The distance around your ankle

Which is bigger? Now measure the distance between your elbow and the tip of your longest finger. Measure the distance between your knee and the bottom of your foot. Which is longer?

4. Everyone has different fingerprints. Find out what yours look like. On a piece of paper, with a soft, dark pencil, make a spot about the size of a quarter. Press one finger at a time on the spot and then press your fingers in the outline here. You can put clear tape over your fingerprints to keep them from getting messed up.

Compare your fingerprints with other Brownie Girl Scouts in your group or with your family. What did you discover?

No one in the entire world has the same fingerprints as you. Scientists can identify people by their fingerprints. They can look at a set of fingerprints and find out whose they are. Scientists use computers to compare a person's fingerprints with the fingerprints they have in a computer file. Knowing someone's name through her fingerprints can help scientists find someone who is missing or find someone who has broken the law. Can you think of other uses for fingerprints?

Caring for Your Body

What do you do in the morning when you first get up to care for your body? What do you do at night before you go to bed? People care for their bodies in different ways. Some people need to wash their hair every day and some only once a week. You might need

37

Try-Its and Other Resources

• Try-Its: Me and My Shadow; My Body; People of the World; Senses.
• Other Resources: The measuring and finger-printing activities can be followed by more activities on measurement in the "How and Why?" chapter and in the Contemporary Issues booklet *Into the World of Today and Tomorrow*. Activities on valuing differences also appear in the "People Near and Far" chapter and in the Contemporary Issues booklet *Valuing Differences*. Activities on caring for your body follow in this chapter and also appear in *Girls Are Great* and *Developing Health and Fitness*. Information and activities on unrealistic body image and beauty also appear in *Developing Health and Fitness*.

to start using powder or a deodorant or you might not need to use a deodorant until you are much older. You might have oily skin that you wash often or you might have dry skin that you moisturize with cream or lotion. Maybe your skin is becoming oilier only in certain spots. You might want to use powder on your feet or in your sneakers or on your body when you know that you will sweat a lot. When you wash your hands and feet, take some extra time to make sure your nails are clean.

Changes in Your Body

These body care tips are important for your entire life. As you grow older, you will notice that your body changes. Parts of your body grow at different rates. You might notice that your nose looks bigger or your feet have grown. As you grow older, you may notice changes in your body that make you look more adult. These changes are called puberty and may start in some girls when they are eight, nine, or ten years old. Other girls may not have these changes until they are 16 or 17. Remember, every body is different! It is important to talk to a family member or adult you know and trust about these changes. Remember, change is a normal part of being a human being!

Try making a time line that shows how you have grown over the years. Here are some suggestions for your time line. What other things can you include?

My Time Line

_____

_____

Years   0   1   2   3   4   5   6   7   8   9   10

- When you lost your first tooth
- When you had your first birthday party
- When you said your first word
- When you went to school for the first time

38

Girls between the ages of six and eight are growing and changing at different rates. Some older Brownie Girl Scouts may show signs of entering puberty. Girls may be somewhat self-conscious about their size. Again, stress that each person grows and changes at a different rate. The time line activity can show the significant events and changes in each girl's life. Comparing time lines will clearly show differences. Time lines can also:

- Be drawn rather than written.
- Be projected into the future.
- Be used as a starting point for other activities. Girls can dramatize past events. Girls can discuss future goals and steps toward achieving these goals.

Body care will also differ for each child. The type of hair a girl has will affect its care. Some girls' skins will be oilier than others and need more frequent washing. It is important to emphasize cleanliness, regular doctor/clinic/dental visits, exercise, and good nutrition—the list of items under "Basics of Body Care for Now and Later." Field trips to a dentist or dental clinic or an invitation to speak at a troop meeting for a dentist, doctor, hygienist, nurse, or other

Basics of Body Care for Now and Later

Here is a list of the basic ways to take care of yourself. Follow these and you will look good and feel your best now and into the future.

- Exercise.
- Eat a variety of nutritious foods.
- Get a good night's sleep.
- Dress properly for the weather.
- See your doctor and your dentist for regular checkups.
- Learn to do things safely.
- Keep your body and clothing clean.

Eating Right

Think of all the different kinds of foods you eat. Some foods may taste better to you than others. You might like some foods that are good for you. You might also like some foods that are not so good for you. Your body needs lots of different

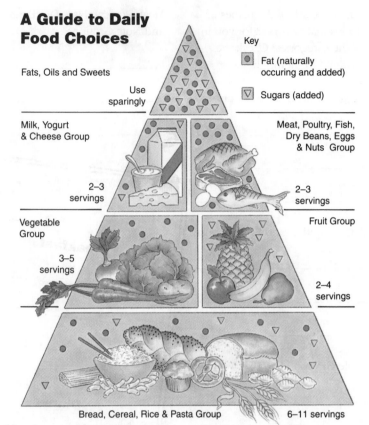

A Guide to Daily Food Choices

Key

⬤ Fat (naturally occuring and added)

▽ Sugars (added)

Fats, Oils and Sweets

Use sparingly

Milk, Yogurt & Cheese Group

2–3 servings

Meat, Poultry, Fish, Dry Beans, Eggs & Nuts Group

2–3 servings

Vegetable Group

3–5 servings

Fruit Group

2–4 servings

Bread, Cereal, Rice & Pasta Group   6–11 servings

kinds of foods to stay healthy and your body needs the right kinds of foods. The food pyramid is one way

of looking at everything you eat to make sure you eat the right food in the right amount.

39

health care worker would be a related activity.

Try this activity from *Developing Health and Fitness*:

Write and illustrate a good grooming booklet. A few girls can work on each section and you can make a troop/group booklet or each girl can create her own booklet.

Try-Its and Other Resources

- Try-Its: Art to Wear; Food Fun; Good Food; My Body; Safety; Sports and Games.
- Other Resources: *Developing Health and Fitness*.

Tips

The food pyramid is the revised basic nutrition guide from the U.S. Department of Agriculture. Foods are shown in the proportion that they should be consumed in the daily diet. Vegetables, fruits, bread, cereal, rice, and pastas make up over 50 percent of the recommended daily diet.

Can you think of the names of some foods that are good for you in each of the categories? Check the food pyramid for help.

Milk, Yogurt, and Cheese Group

_____

_____

_____

Bread, Cereal, Rice, and Pasta Group

_____

_____

_____

Vegetable Group

_____

_____

_____

40

Meat, Poultry, Fish, Dry Beans, Eggs, and Nuts Group

_____

_____

_____

Fats, Oils, and Sweets Group

_____

_____

_____

MENU

Breakfast

_____

_____

_____

Dinner

_____

_____

_____

Lunch

_____

_____

Snack

_____

_____

The menu is provided for girls to create their own daily healthy menu. They could try to develop a menu of foods in proportion to those listed in the food pyramid. They could also create a healthy restaurant menu.

Some other activities:

(1) Cut out or draw pictures of foods and make their own pyramids or pyramid puzzles.

(2) Take a field trip to a supermarket to decipher labels or to fill a cart with foods in the proportions of the food pyramid.

(3) Try some healthy recipes, especially salads or stews that combine bread, cereal, rice, or pasta with vegetables and fruit.

This recipe is from *Girl Scout Leader* magazine, Summer 1990:

Whole Wheat and Apricot Salad
4 ounces bulgur, quinoa, couscous, or brown rice
1 carrot, scrubbed and grated
2 scallions, chopped
2 ounces dried apricots, chopped, or cut up with scissors

When you are being good to your body, you are giving it nutrients—what it needs to grow healthy and strong. Fresh fruits, vegetables, whole wheat and grains, beans, and milk have lots of nutrients. Potato chips, candy, sodas, and cake are not good for your body. They don't help your body grow. You could gain too much weight or you could have problems with your heart. You need fruits and vegetables, a small amount of meat or other protein, milk or yogurt or cheese (low-fat is better), breads, cereals, rice and pasta (spaghetti and macaroni), lots of water—and just a little fat in your diet.

Think about the foods you eat each day. Are you eating healthy foods? Are you eating the right amounts? Think of what you can do to eat healthfully. Can you make a one-day menu (breakfast, lunch, dinner, and one snack) that follows the kinds of foods and amounts of foods from the food pyramid? Compare menus with those of other girls in your troop and group. You can see that there are many different ways to eat healthy foods.

Carrot, celery, or other raw vegetable sticks

Raisins

Fruit-juice popsicles

Fresh fruit mixed with low-fat cottage cheese or plain low-fat yogurt

Sliced bananas rolled in chopped nuts

Can you think of some healthy snacks? Make a list. A few are already written for you.

Try making this Food Pyramid Party Mix. You will need:

- 1/4 cup peanut butter or chocolate chips
- 1/2 cup dried banana or apple chips
- 1/4 cup sunflower seeds
- 1/2 cup raisins
- 1/2 cup air-popped popcorn
- 2/3 cup low-salt, low-sugar granola cereal
- 1/3 cup dry roasted peanuts

Mix well in a serving bowl. Serves three people, about one cup each. How much of each ingredient do you need to serve six people? twelve people? the people in your Girl Scout troop or group?

41

---

1 tablespoon low-fat mayonnaise
1 tablespoon low-fat yogurt
1 teaspoon freshly chopped parsley
Dash of black pepper

Cook the grains according to the package directions. Drain and cool. Mix in the apricots, scallions, and carrots; add mayonnaise and yogurt.

Sprinkle with parsley and pepper. Serves two.

Girls can also calculate how much of each ingredient they will need to serve more than two people.

Remember to remind girls to be careful whenever they are cooking or using knives and to always do so with an adult present.

Try-Its and Other Resources

- Try-Its: Food Fun; Good Food; My Body.
- Other Resources: *Developing Health and Fitness*. Recipes in "People Near and Far" and in *The Wide World of Girl Guiding and Girl Scouting*.

I'm Wise Enough to Exercise

Fitness is important. You can eat good food, but you also have to move your body to keep it strong. Many of the active games you like to play are good exercise. Swimming, running, skating, walking, bicycling, dancing, and jumping rope are all good ways to keep fit. Sitting in front of a television set won't even exercise your eyes! You need to

42

move every day. Here are some fun ways to move.

- Try the "Animal Moves" activity in the Dancercize Try-It.

- Pick some of your favorite music and make up some dance movements to it.

- Play follow-the-leader using as many different movements as possible.

- Invent your own exercise routine. Remember, exercise shouldn't hurt, so start slowly.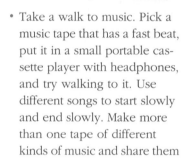

- Take a walk to music. Pick a music tape that has a fast beat, put it in a small portable cassette player with headphones, and try walking to it. Use different songs to start slowly and end slowly. Make more than one tape of different kinds of music and share them

with your family and friends.

- Form an exercise club. Plan on meeting at least three times a week. Take turns leading the exercises.

Caring for Your Clothes and Home

Taking Care of Your Clothes

It is important for your body to be clean and healthy. It is important to eat right and exercise. It is also important for your clothes to be clean. Imagine how your clean skin feels if you put dirty clothes on it? Think of your nice clean toes . . . in dirty smelly socks? Ugh! Keeping your clothing clean and neat is easy. Look at the pictures. The pictures will help you learn how to take care of your clothing. You can also ask an adult to help you learn:

- How to sew on buttons and make simple repairs.
- How to hand-wash clothing in a sink or basin.

Before introducing any exercise program, find out if it's all right for the girls to participate. Some girls may not be able to do every activity or may need adaptations. Girls can be timekeepers and spotters, or activities can be chosen in which every girl can participate.

- Try-Its: Dancercize; My Body; Play; Sports and Games.
- Other Resources: *Games for Girl Scouts*; *Developing Health and Fitness*. These activities and many more appear in *Developing Health and Fitness*:

Letters and numbers: Girls can form letters or numbers with their own bodies or with a partner. Try spelling words and doing calculations.

Circle romp: To the beat of music, girls form a circle and begin marching in place, slowly at first, then picking up the pace with more vigorous movements. Move around the

circle formation. Change movements as the leader calls them out: skipping, hopping, galloping. Vary the music.

Octopus: One player is the "octopus" who swims around in the ocean and tries to catch all of the "fish." When the octopus yells "Cross!" the fish have to try to cross the ocean without getting tagged by the

octopus. If they are tagged, they become the octopus's "tentacles" and help her catch the remaining fish. The "tentacles" can be instructed to be stationary and only move their arms to tag the fish, or they can swim around freely like the octopus for a more active game.

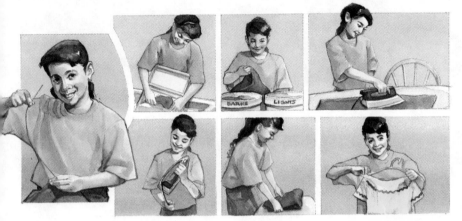

Write some of your favorite outfits here.

_____

_____

_____

_____

_____

_____

_____

_____

_____

_____

43

- How to operate a washing machine.
- How to sort clothing to be washed. Learn which temperature of water to use and which colors are washed together.
- How to use and store an iron.
- How to arrange clothes neatly in closets and drawers.

It saves lots of time in the morning if you spend a little bit of time the night before choosing the clothes you will wear to school. Then, fold them neatly or put them together on a hanger so you can get dressed quickly in the morning.

What are some of your favorite outfits to wear to school? (If you wear a uniform to school, think of your favorite outfits for the weekend.) What tops (blouses and shirts) and bottoms (skirts and pants) look good together? Can you mix and match to make some more outfits?

Tips

Girls will have differing levels of responsibility at home. Some might be caring for younger siblings while others may have few, if any, responsibilities. The tasks pictured and listed are a few essential life skills. Some girls at this age have difficulty getting ready for school in the morning. Setting up a morning routine can be very helpful. In the introductory story, Marisol has a number of morning responsibilities. Girls can discuss how to make getting ready for school easier.

Dressing for the Weather

What do you do if it is raining outside? If it is windy? If it is very sunny? How do you know what the weather will be like?

In some places, you can call to find out the kind of weather you will have that day. How else can you find out?

With permission, call the weather number in your area or look in a newspaper or listen to the weather report on the radio or on television.

Four types of weather are shown on these two pages. Draw pictures of the types of clothes you need for each, or cut out pictures from magazines or catalogs (get permission first) and paste them in the spaces at right.

Taking Care of Your Home

There are a number of things you should know how to do around your home. Ask an adult to show you:

44

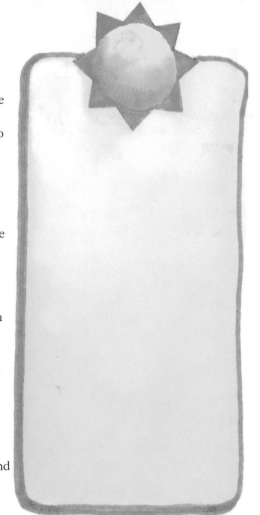

Try-Its and Other Resources

- Try-Its: Earth and Sky; Outdoor Happenings.
- Other Resources: More information on weather can be found in "How and Why?," handbook pages 137–143.

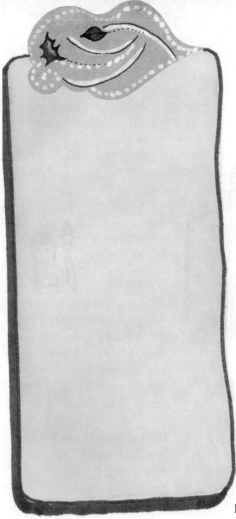

- How to put fresh batteries in a flashlight.
- How to program a VCR and how to clean it.
- How to install a water-saver shower head.
- What to do if you smell gas. Turn off any flames, open windows and doors, and leave immediately. Do not touch a light switch or pick up the telephone. Electricity can make a spark and cause an explosion. Never light a match! Call the gas company or fire department from a phone outside.
- How to warm up food for dinner in the microwave or on the stove or in the oven. Learn the right dishes to use, the right way to handle hot dishes, and the correct temperature and time to heat the food.

Learn what to do when the power goes out. Does your family

45

Tips

The skills in this section build on the life skills already learned by cooking and caring for clothing. Girls can brainstorm a list of things to know how to do at home. Check off the items as they are learned. Make sure safety rules are followed whenever girls work with tools or machines.

You might want to ask girls what they consider to be "girl" household jobs and "boy" household jobs. Then ask why they think some jobs are exclusively for boys or for girls. Remember to stress that jobs are "neutral" and that almost everyone can cook or mow the lawn.

In small groups, girls can mime the household tasks while others guess the action.

Some tasks, such as putting batteries in a flashlight, could be part of a relay game.

keep an emergency supply of candles, small cans of cooking fuel or a camp stove, batteries, and a portable radio? Unplug or turn off all appliances. When the power comes back on, a big surge of power can break them. Keep the refrigerator door closed. Keep your freezer door closed. A refrigerator can stay cold

46

inside for a day and a freezer for two days if it is not opened a lot. Fill the bathtub with water and fill some pots with water, too. Sometimes in a big storm when the power goes out, the water from your tap can become bad to drink. You will hear on the radio if this has happened.

Learn:
- How to put new rubber washer blades on a car windshield.
- How to check that the car has enough window washer fluid.
- How to use a vacuum cleaner.
- How to sort trash for things that can be recycled.
- How to make a bed.
- How to fix a chair or table that shakes or wobbles.
- How to clean the bathtub, sink, and toilet.
- How to repot a plant.
- How to unclog a drain.
- How to test a smoke alarm.

- How to plug and unplug a phone.
- How to use an extension cord properly.

Demonstrate some of these for your troop or group or friends and family. Try showing the others how to do these without using any words. Can they guess what you are doing?

Home Repairs
You need to learn how to use tools properly to take good care of your home. Some tools are simple. You can use them to make easy repairs. Have an adult show you how to use these tools:
- Hammer
- Common screwdriver
- Phillips screwdriver
- Sandpaper
- Pliers
- Wrench
- Level
- Tape measure

Tips

Be careful when girls are using tools, but do use real tools, not plastic or toy tools. Many tools, such as hammers and screwdrivers, are available in smaller sizes. You might want to have extra adults or Cadette and Senior Girl Scouts help with this activity, particularly if your troop or group is large.

Girls can make other projects too. They can screw hooks into a sanded and decorated board from which they can hang keys or utensils.

They can nail and glue wood scraps to make sculptures or doll furniture.

Now practice using these tools yourself. (Ask your family first.) Make sure you follow these rules:

- An adult is with you.
- You have space to work.
- The tools are in good condition.
- Use the right tool for the job.

Here are some examples of repairs you can make:

- Using sandpaper to smooth wood that has splinters.
- Hammering a nail in the wall to hang a picture.
- Tightening screws or bolts that have become loose.

Board Tic Tac Toe is a game you can make using simple tools. Make it for yourself or to give as a gift. You need:

- One square flat board
- 9 1" nails
- 5 large buttons of the same color
- 5 large buttons of a different color
- A ruler
- A pencil
- An ink marker
- A sheet of sandpaper
- A hammer
- 10 twist ties for closing plastic bags

Follow this diagram to make your board. Do the following:

1. Have someone help you make the board 12″ wide and 12″ long.

2. Draw lines like those in the drawing.

3. Hammer a nail in the top part of each box.

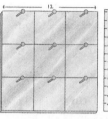

4. Poke a twist tie through each button.

5. You are now ready to play.

6. Each person gets five buttons of the same color. Take turns hanging buttons on the nails instead of writing Xs and Os. The first one to get three of her color in a row wins. Take the buttons down and start again.

47

Using heavier blocks of wood, they can sand the blocks and nail one perpendicular to the other to make bookends.

A carpenter, especially one who is female, could be invited to a troop or group meeting and lead the girls in building something.

Try-Its and Other Resources

- Try-Its: Building Art; Careers; Movers; Science in Action.
- Other Resources: Check with local unions, professional associations, high school or vocational school woodshop or mechanics courses, or businesses for additional resources and guests.

Staying Safe

You can take good care of your body by eating the right foods and by exercising. You can take care of your home and take care of your clothing. But, there is another very important way to take care of yourself—*staying safe*.

Safety Do's and Don'ts

Here are some Do's and Dont's. If a stranger approaches you,

DON'T go near his or her car, even if the person says your mother said it is okay. Get away!

DON'T even get in a conversation. Send him or her to the nearest adult.

DON'T believe any message he or she gives you.

DON'T take any candy, gum, or gifts.

DON'T enter any rooms, elevators, empty streets, or buildings with strangers.

If someone makes you feel funny or if you think someone will hurt you,

DO RUN FOR HELP. Drop everything and run quickly.

DO SHOUT FOR HELP.

When Walking:

DO walk with a friend.

DON'T take shortcuts through dark alleys, deserted buildings, or parks.

At Home:

DO hang up if someone you don't know asks you questions on the phone, even if he or she sounds very friendly.

DON'T tell anyone that you are home alone.

DON'T open a door to a stranger.

When you are in the house by yourself or when you are baby sitting for younger children, you should know some special rules to follow when you answer the phone.

DO call your parents, a close neighbor you trust, or the police if someone starts calling the house a lot when you are home alone. Tell them about the phone calls. Ask for someone to stay with you until the adults are home.

DO call the emergency number if you feel frightened or suspicious.

DON'T tell the caller that you are in the house by yourself. If he or she asks for your mom or dad or other adult, just tell the caller that your mom or dad cannot come to the phone right now.

DON'T give out any information. Just ask for the name and phone number and say that someone will

Tips

Activities on safety and first aid are often mentioned by girls as their favorite activities. These activities are designed to protect girls, not frighten them. Staying safe activities are one more way in which girls learn to care for themselves. The list of do's and don'ts may be acted out, turned into cartoons, or compiled in a safety booklet. Find out who in your community can visit the troop or group to provide additional safety activities.

Try-Its and Other Resources

- Try-Its: Safety.

return the call. Some homes have Caller ID service and you can see the phone number of the person calling you. Tell the person you have the number and have written it down. Ask for the name and say that someone will call back later. Be polite and then hang up.

In parks and play areas,

DO play where you can be seen by the person taking care of you.

DON'T play in deserted, out-of-the-way places, such as abandoned buildings, empty laundry rooms, storerooms, or rooftops.

DON'T leave school grounds during breaks or recess.

DON'T play around construction sites, mining sites, train yards, or any place with large trucks.

When you use public transportation,

DO wait at a busy, well-lighted transit stop.

DO run for help if you see someone you think is dangerous.

DO sit near the conductor or driver.

DO ask the conductor or driver for help if you are worried.

DO change seats if someone near you is making you worried.

When using public restrooms,

DO take someone you know with you.

DON'T talk to strangers or let them near you.

If you see something suspicious or a stranger approaches you, try to remember the following and tell an adult!

- What happened?
- Where did it happen?
- When did it happen?
- What did the person look like? How big was the person? Was he or she old or young, man or woman, boy or girl?

49

What were the person's hair color, eye color, skin color? Did the person wear glasses? A real or fake mustache? What kinds of clothing did the person wear? Did the person have any special marks or scars that you can remember?

- If the person was in a car, what did the car look like? Did the license plate look different? Did the car look

50

new or old? Was it scratched or dented? Can you remember the license plate number? How many people were in the car?

Safety with People You Know

Lots of people touch you. Parents hug you. Your brothers and sisters touch you when you play. Your baby sitter helps you get ready

for bed. Doctors and dentists touch you when you go for a checkup. Some touches are "good" touches. Adults and older children touch your body in ways that do not hurt you or make you feel uncomfortable. Some touches are "bad" touches. If someone's touch makes you feel uneasy or scared, you can say "No!" Practice saying "No!" You can say "No" to adults, even someone you know very well. You can protect

The majority of children who are abused are abused by someone they know. The Contemporary Issues booklet *Staying Safe: Preventing Child Abuse* has some excellent activities for Brownie Girl Scouts to increase self-esteem and assertiveness. It also contains helpful information and tips for leaders. Pages 55–56 in Part I of this book contain additional information on your responsibilities. If you suspect

that a girl in your troop or group has been or is being abused, consult *Safety-Wise* for the proper procedures to follow.

Try-Its and Other Resources

- Try-Its: Safety; Manners.

your body, especially the parts that are covered by a bathing suit. You can say "No" to any touch that makes you feel funny or uncomfortable. You can tell a parent, an adult you trust, a teacher, or a doctor, if you have been touched in a way that feels wrong. It is very important to tell someone.

Practice what you would say in these situations:

- A person you know won't stop tickling you and you don't like it at all.
- Your older brother pinches you very hard.
- A woman comes up to you on the playground and asks if you will show her the way to the closest grocery store.
- A neighbor invites you inside and offers you some cookies. The neighbor says or does something that makes you feel very strange.
- You are home alone and the phone rings. A man asks to speak to your father.
- You are separated from your mother at the shopping mall and a woman you don't know offers to help you find her.

Make a Safety List

You have already learned some safety rules. What does it mean to be safe? You are safe when there is nothing to harm you. What are some things that can harm you? Can you add to this list?

Fire _____

Drunk drivers _____

Poisons _____

_____

_____

_____

_____

_____

_____

_____

_____

_____

_____

_____

_____

_____

_____

_____

_____

What can you do to stay safe?

Emergency Who's Who

You can be ready for emergencies. Ask a family member to help you make a list of numbers to keep by the telephone.

Family Work Numbers _____

_____

Neighbor _____

Fire Department _____

Police _____

Ambulance _____

Health Department _____

Poison Control Center _____

Doctor _____

Dentist _____

What would you say or do if you had to make an emergency call? Follow the emergency guide below.

1. Use the emergency who's who list and dial the number you need.

2. Tell who you are. "Hello, my name is _____ ."

3. Tell where you are. "I am at _____ " (street, apartment, house number, city, state or name of park, trail, building, etc.).

4. Tell what the emergency is. "This is an emergency. I need _____ ."

Stay calm and follow directions.

Think of some emergencies and practice making pretend phone calls. One person can be the police or the emergency operator and another person can make the phone call.

On Your Own at Home

Sometimes you may be at home alone. You may be responsible for your younger sisters and brothers. On page 48 in this book are some basic skills that you should have when you stay alone. Know how to make emergency calls, what to do if there is a fire or if the lights go out, and how to answer the phone. These are good to know all the time, but especially when you are home alone. What can you do when you are by yourself?

52

Draw a map of your home in the space. Mark the emergency exits, the place where light bulbs and flashlights are kept, and the place where your family keeps its first-aid supplies.

Talk about the rules your family has made for the times when you are home alone. How do these rules help you stay safe?

Pretend that you are home by yourself. With your Girl Scout troop or group, or your friends and family, practice some things that can happen when you are by yourself and what you should do.

If you have a microwave oven at your Girl Scout meeting place, practice making some snacks in the microwave. Learn how to use a microwave safely. Learn how to make some snacks that don't need cooking.

53

Tips

In addition to the safety rules girls should follow, you could review some of the activities in the girls' handbook and look for those which would be good to do when girls are on their own. Girls can make a calendar, journal, or special "home alone" book of things to do.

Other things to do when you are by yourself:

- First, finish your homework and do any housework or chores you have.
- Try dancing. Dancing is a good way to spend the time. It is healthy and fun.
- Read a book. Visit the library so you have a supply of books to read when you are alone. Reading a favorite book again is also fun.
- Try making your own book. Write or draw a story. You can choose an autobiography, a mystery, a fairy tale, or a cartoon.
- List all the good things about being a girl. There are lots!
- Try a new hairstyle or different combinations of clothing.
- Make puppets. See page 248 for some ideas. Create your own play. Act out some real things that have happened to you.

54

- Write your name on a piece of paper. See how many new words you can make from the letters in your name.

- Write a letter to someone. Everybody loves to get letters.
- Make a greeting card to thank someone for doing something special or for being a special person to you.
- Try making up your own song. If you have a tape recorder, record your song. Or, try singing along to some of your favorite songs or try

listening to a radio station that plays a type of music different from the music you usually listen to.

Fire Safety

With your family and your Girl Scout group, prepare a plan for what to do in case of fire. In your home, the first part of your plan should be to make your home as safe as possible. Most fires can be prevented. Look for fire hazards. A fire hazard is anything that can cause a fire indoors or outdoors. Make a list of things to do to reduce the danger of fire. The second part should be a home fire drill. Know the best way to get out of your home, especially from the bedrooms. Plan a second way to get out of the house if the first way is blocked by the fire.

Smoke detectors can help make your home safe. Find out about smoke detectors. Does your home have one? How do you check that it is working?

Tips

Brownie Girl Scouts can save their own lives and the lives of others by knowing basic fire-safety rules. A trip to a fire station or a visit from a member of the local fire department can be fun if girls have an activity they can do.

Remember these three words:
stop, drop, roll.

Look at the picture above. Circle all the fire dangers.

What do you do if your clothes catch on fire?

1. *Stop.* Do not run or walk or jump around. Moving gives more oxygen to the fire and keeps it going.

2. *Drop.* Drop to the ground or floor. Cover your face with your hands.

3. *Roll.* Smother the fire by rolling over slowly.

▲ 55

List of fire hazards in the picture: smoking in bed, vase on television, paint, papers in attic and lightbulb on, turpentine and rags in attic, gasoline stored in garage, cigarette burning unattended, too many plugs in socket, space heater left on, iron flat on board, pot handle sticking out and pot left unattended, dish towel by stove, frayed cords.

What would you do if another person's clothes caught on fire?

1. Get the person to the ground.

2. Roll her over or use a coat or blanket to smother the flames.

3. Be careful that your own clothing or hair does not catch on fire.

56

Sports Safety

Sports are good for your body and your mind. Sports can help your body to be in good shape and can help your mind relax. If you start playing a sport now, you can discover a good way to spend your free time now and when you are older. Try some different sports. You might not like the first sport you try. Maybe you need to play it some more and get a little better at it, before you really enjoy it. Maybe there are some sports you just won't like. That's okay. You will usually find a sport that you like if you try a few. If you want to enjoy sports without having problems, you need to know some safety rules. Take this sports safety quiz. Check your answers. Are you a sports safety winner or loser?

Girls also need to know the proper ways to use sports equipment. Many sports, such as bicycling, roller skating, or horseback riding, require special safety equipment. *Safety-Wise* contains activity checkpoints that list the equipment needed for each sport. Also, *Safety-Wise* has a list of activities in which Brownie Girl Scouts should not participate.

True or False?

1. You should ride your bicycle against the traffic so you can see the cars coming toward you.

2. You should always wear a bicycle helmet when on a bike.

3. In a group of bicycle riders, always cycle in pairs.

4. Wear bright-colored clothing when bicycling at night.

5. If you skate outdoors, you need to wear a helmet, gloves, and knee protectors.

6. If you fall while skating at a rink, ask your "buddy" to help you get up.

7. It is never safe to ice-skate on a pond or lake alone.

8. Warm-up and cool-down exercises should be done when playing sports.

9. It is safe to swim without a lifeguard.

10. Sneakers are the best shoes for horseback riding.

11. Skiers only need sunglasses/goggles on sunny days.

12. Sandals are good shoes for soccer.

13. A street is a good place to jump rope because you have lots of room for the rope to turn.

Check Your Answers

1. False. You should always ride your bicycle in the same direction the traffic is going.

2. True.

3. False. Always cycle in a single file.

4. False. Wear bright-colored clothing when bicycling during the day. Wear light or reflective clothing at night. Make sure you have reflector tape on your bicycle fenders, handlebars, and helmet. Make sure your bike has a light that works.

5. True.

6. False. You should get up quickly on your own. If you use another person to help you, you can easily make her fall.

7. True.

8. True.

9. False. Always swim when a lifeguard is on duty.

10. False. You need boots or shoes with one-inch heels.

11. False. When skiing, you need sunglasses/goggles all the time to protect your eyes.

12. False. You should wear special shoes, kneepads, and a helmet.

13. False. You should play where no cars can hurt you.

Check Your Answers

12–13 right answers—congratulations! You're a safety winner!

9–11 right answers—You're on the first string of the safety team!

5–8 right answers—You're on the second string. Learn some more about safety.

4 and below—Practice, practice, practice! Find out lots more about safety and sports. You'll play better, feel better, and stay safe!

57

First Aid

First aid is the first help an injured or sick person receives. First aid may be washing a cut, saying things to keep someone calm, or getting a doctor.

You should have a first-aid kit in your home, in your family's car, and on Girl Scout outings.

Here are some things to put in the kit:

- First-aid book
- Soap
- Safety pins
- Scissors
- Tweezers
- Sewing needle
- Matches
- Adhesive tape and sterile gauze dressings
- Clean cloth
- Calamine lotion
- Anti-bacterial antiseptic
- Emergency telephone numbers
- Money for phone calls
- Rubber or plastic gloves
- Simple face mask
- Plastic bag

Infections

A simple cut can be very dangerous if it gets infected. An infection is bacteria growing in your body. This can happen if a cut is not taken care of properly. Signs of infection include swelling, redness, a hot feeling, pain, tenderness, fever, and pus.

If you get a cut, wash your hands with soap and water before cleaning the cut. Seek medical care right away. If you must help someone who has a cut, wear rubber or plastic gloves from your first-aid kit.

Bites and Stings

All bites need first aid because there are lots of bacteria in the mouth. Even small bites can be dangerous. Animal bites can be very bad because some animals carry rabies, a very dangerous disease. Never go near a wild animal or other animal you do not

58

Tips

It is essential that you follow the procedures in *Safety-Wise* before you or the girls administer first aid.

Girls can practice these first-aid procedures; develop skits, stories, posters, or songs; or create other activities about first aid.

Check with your local school, community health organization, ambulance or emergency medical service, or other local health organization for ideas for trips or visitors.

know. Do not go near an animal you do know if it is acting strangely. People bites can also be bad. People have germs in their mouths, sometimes more than dogs do! If you have been bitten, tell an adult immediately. If you know where the animal is, point it out to an adult. If the animal has run away, describe it to an adult.

If no one is nearby and you get bitten, you might have to give yourself first aid.

1. Wash your hands with soap and water.

2. Wash the wound with soap and water.

3. Rinse the wound well with clear water.

4. Blot the wound dry with a clean towel.

5. Apply a bandage.

6. See a doctor.

If you have to help someone who has been bitten, make sure you wear plastic or rubber gloves from your first-aid kit.

Most insect bites, like mosquito bites, are not serious. Your skin may get itchy and swell up, but the bite soon goes away—especially if you do not scratch it! A bee sting can hurt, but usually it is not dangerous. If you get stung by a bee and the stinger is in your skin, try to scrape the stinger out with a clean fingernail or needle. Don't squeeze the stinger. Press a cold washcloth or an ice cube on the sting.

Some people are very allergic to bees and other insects. If they get stung, they may have a hard time breathing. If someone who is allergic gets stung, she must see a doctor or get to a hospital right away.

Burns

A burn is an injury to your skin from heat or chemicals.

If you have a burn, run cool water, not ice water, over the burned area. Be gentle with your skin and don't break any blisters (the bubbles of skin) that pop up. Put clean cloth bandages over the burned part. Don't put butter or anything greasy on it! Find an adult to help you take care of the burn and to help you decide whether you need to see a doctor or go to a hospital.

Too Much Body Heat

Your body can get too hot. Doctors call this heat exhaustion or heatstroke. You can get sick from the heat if you stay in the heat or in the bright sun too long. Heatstroke

can give you a fever and red, hot skin. It can also make you feel faint or dizzy. An adult should help you cool off by wiping your skin with cool water, putting cold packs on your skin, helping you sit in cool water, and/or finding an air-conditioned place to lie down. Get medical help. Heatstroke is very serious and needs to be treated right away.

The signs of heat exhaustion are feeling weak or feeling like you

might throw up, feeling dizzy, having bad cramps in your stomach, fainting, and having skin that feels cool or cold and wet. Get out of the sun right away and tell an adult that you don't feel well. Put a cool cloth on your forehead and body. Take some sips of salt water. Lie down and raise your feet. If you don't feel better in an hour, see a doctor.

Too Little Body Heat

Your body can get too cold. This is called hypothermia. If you stay outside too long in cold or windy weather, or when it is wet outside, even on a day that's not so

cold, you can get hypothermia. Wearing the right clothes and a hat is very important. Hypothermia can make you shiver, your teeth chatter, your hands and feet feel cold. You need to get inside right away and slowly eat or drink something that is warm.

Frostbite

When it is very cold, the parts of your body that are not protected can actually freeze. This is called frostbite. Most frostbite happens in fingers, toes, nose, cheeks, and ears. The skin may be slightly red and then turn white or grayish-yellow. There is no pain in the frost-bitten part. You can get blisters and your skin feels cold and numb. Frostbite is dangerous. Go indoors and warm up. Don't rub the skin. Put the part in warm water between 102°F (39°C) and 105°F (41°C) or gently wrap it with a sheet and warm blankets. Find an adult to help. See a doctor right away.

Nosebleeds

Nosebleeds can happen when the air is very dry, if you have had a cold, if you have had too much exercise, if you are in a very high place, like the mountains, or if you hurt your nose. Try to stop the bleeding by sitting down and squeezing your nose firmly for about ten minutes. Placing cold towels on your nose may help. If the bleeding continues, get an adult to help you.

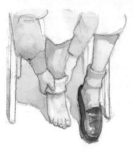

Bumps and Bruises

Put a damp, cold cloth on the area. If there is a lot of swelling, ask an adult to help you.

Choking

If the person can speak, cough, and breathe, do nothing. Otherwise, stand behind the person and grasp your hands around her, just under her rib cage. Press your hands into her stomach with four quick upward

moves. Do this until the person spits out the food or object.

If you are choking, move your hand across your throat to let others know. If no one is around, try pressing your hands into your stomach with four quick upward moves.

Poisoning

This is always serious and a big emergency. If you or someone you know has taken poison, or even might have taken poison, call the poison control center and your emergency first-aid number immediately.

Be very careful about what you put in your mouth. Check to make sure that the food and liquids that you buy are sealed and safety-wrapped. Food that needs to be in the refrigerator can spoil easily. Food can look and smell good and still be spoiled and make you sick. Make sure you keep this food cold.

Don't ever take any kinds of medications, drugs, or pills unless they have been prescribed to you

61

The section "Poisoning" includes drugs, cigarettes, and alcohol as poisonous substances. The Contemporary Issues booklet *Tune In to Well-Being, Say No to Drugs* has current information and activities for girls and leaders. Try this activity from the booklet: Act out what you would do if:

- Your friend's mother leaves a can of beer on the table.

- Your younger sister drinks a bottle of cough syrup.

What other situations can you act out? *Note: Safety-Wise* contains a section "Being a Health and Safety Role Model" that has essential information. The girls in your troop or group will often model their behaviors and attitudes after your own. Those considered unhealthy or inappropriate are listed in that section.

Try-Its and Other Resources

- Try-Its: My Body; Safety; Sports and Games.

by a doctor and an adult is present. Don't drink alcohol or try cigarettes because you think it is "grown-up." Alcohol and cigarettes can be very harmful to your body.

Are You Prepared?

Practice these first-aid techniques on each other. Practice with your family and friends, too. Remember the Girl Scout motto is "Be Prepared." You need to be prepared to stay safe.

62

Feeling Good About Yourself

Look at the pictures. They will help you sing this song.

This song is special. It is about you. Write the words or draw the pictures in the empty spaces that will complete the song.

_____'s SONG

My name is

_____.

I am _____ years old.

I have my own story

And here it's told.

Tips

Girls can follow the pictures for movements to each line of the song or they can create their own movements. Girls can also continue the song or make up their own songs. The song can be done to a "rap" or "sing-song" rhythm or put to music.

My name is (*girl's name*).
I am (*girl's age*) years old.
I have my own story
And here it's told.

_____ is where I live,

My nose is right here on my face,

My favorite food is

_____ .

I am _____ inches high.

And ____ is the color of my eyes.

And _____ is my favorite game.

(Girl's address or town/city name) is where I live.
I am (number) inches high.
My nose is right here on my face,
And (color) is the color of my eyes.
My favorite food is (name of food),
And (name of game) is my favorite game.

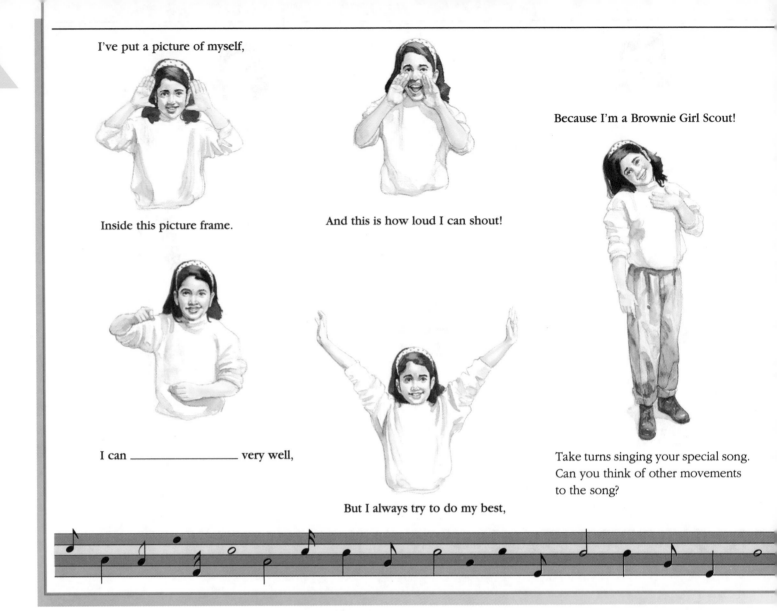

I've put a picture of myself,

Inside this picture frame.

And this is how loud I can shout!

Because I'm a Brownie Girl Scout!

I can _____ very well,

But I always try to do my best,

Take turns singing your special song. Can you think of other movements to the song?

I've put a picture of myself, Inside this picture frame.
I can (*talent, skill, hobby*) very well,
And this is how loud I can shout!
But I always try to do my best,
Because I'm a Brownie Girl Scout!

Try-Its and Other Resources

- Other Resources: See the annotated resource list on pages 66–67 in Part I of this book, for a list of some of the Girl Scout songbooks that contain other action songs.

You Are Special

You have learned many different things in this chapter. You have learned about staying safe and practicing first aid. You have learned about taking care of your body and taking care of your home. You can also take care of the person inside.

You are a very special person. No one in the entire world shares your feelings, your thoughts, your likes, and dislikes. No one looks just like you or can do all the things you can do. Even if you have a twin sister or brother, you would never be exactly the same.

Feelings

You do not feel the same way all the time. Sometimes you feel happy. Sometimes you feel sad. You can feel angry, scared, bored, excited, surprised. Why do you feel different ways at different times?

Often you can change your feelings. What are some things you can do when you feel scared?

Share your feelings with other people. Your family, your friends, your teachers, and your Girl Scout leader want to know about your feelings and your thoughts. Draw pictures or write a story about your feelings. Dancing, listening to music, playing a sport, walking outside, and reading a book are some good ways to change your feelings if you feel sad or bored.

You can show how you feel in many different ways. Show how you would feel if:

- You heard someone tease you about your clothes.
- You hit the winning home run in your softball game.
- Your younger brother used your best blouse to polish his bike.
- You forgot to bring your homework to school.
- You wrote a story on the computer at school and someone accidentally erased it.

65

Coping; Developing Health and Fitness; and *Reaching Out.* The following two activities have been taken from *Reaching Out:*

Ask girls to think about what they would do if a brother, sister, or friend said she was very sad and wanted to run away from home. Talk to them about not promising to keep a secret like that and telling a trusted adult as soon as possible. Have them discuss what they could do when they're feeling sad themselves.

Invite a mental health professional (psychologist, family therapist, psychiatrist, or social worker) to talk to your troop or group about feelings and what girls can do when strong feelings scare them.

This activity is from *Developing Health and Fitness:*

Stretch a long piece of string or yarn partway along one side of the room and to two chairs. Ask girls to draw pictures of things that make them happy. When they are finished, they can clip the pictures to the yarn and describe them.

Tips

Brownie Girl Scouts should feel positive about themselves and their abilities. Encourage girls to feel proud of their accomplishments and to feel comfortable sharing their accomplishments with others. A "sharing time" or other special part of the meeting can give girls the opportunity to talk about goals they have met or activities they have done.

Brownie Girl Scouts may have intense feelings, and while sharing feelings and emotions can be positive for girls, a Brownie Girl Scout leader, in her leader role, is not a troop psychologist or therapist and should be careful to maintain an appropriate distance. *Safety-Wise* contains procedures to follow if you suspect that a girl is having severe emotional problems or is suicidal.

Pages 55–56 in Part I of this book also contain tips for leaders.

Try-Its and Other Resources

- Other Resources: Other activities on feelings are in the Contemporary Issues booklets— *Girls Are Great; Caring and*

Talents and Interests

Interests are things you like, and talents are things you are good at doing. Sometimes, your interests and talents are the same. Singing is a good example. A professional singer is good at singing and likes it. Another person may like singing very much but may not be so very good at it. (She may have a lot of fun singing in the shower, though!)

Interests and talents can change as you grow older. You can work on talents that you know need improvement. You can also discover new talents. It is important to try many different types of activities so

 66

that you can find out what talents you have. Everybody has talents. Some people might have talents that are easier to see. Being good at sports is easier to see than being good at helping people to get along with each other, but both are very important talents!

What are some things that you do very well? Write them here.

_____

_____

_____

_____

_____

_____

What interests do you have?

_____

_____

_____

_____

_____

What are some things you would like to know how to do better?

_____

_____

_____

_____

_____

Tips

Girl Scouting is an excellent forum for girls to increase and practice their talents and interests. Almost every activity can spark a new hobby or develop a new skill. Make sure girls are aware of all the activities and opportunities available to them in the Girl Scout program resources and in wider opportunities available through your Girl Scout council.

Try-Its and Other Resources

- Try-Its: Art to Wear; Building Art; Careers; Creative Composing; Dancercize; Hobbies; Math Fun; Outdoor Adventurer; Science Wonders; Space Explorer.

What can you do with your wishes and talents?

_____

_____

_____

_____

_____

Careers

Talents and interests can lead to careers. A career is what you do as work. An interest in collecting rocks can lead to a career as a geologist, a person who studies the earth. A talent in drawing can lead to a career as a book illustrator or as an architect who plans and designs buildings. An interest in helping people might lead you to become a doctor or a teacher. A talent in sports could become a career as a coach or a sports announcer.

What possible careers match your talents and interests? Find out more about those careers. Try to find someone who is working in one of those careers. What would be some good questions to ask her?

Draw a picture of a scientist here.

67

While some women may choose not to work outside the home, many women may need to work to support their families financially. Many women also plan on working in a career that fits their interests and talents. Brownie Girl Scouts can look ahead to the career opportunities that will be available to them.

Brownie Girl Scouts can be encouraged to look beyond gender stereotypes in certain jobs and career paths, especially in the sciences and technological fields. Careers in the sciences and in technology will be expanding as today's Brownie Girl Scout matures and makes career choices. You can role-model the attitudes and language that help break barriers: police officer, not policeman; postal worker, not mailman.

Use "she" when speaking of engineers, scientists, astronauts, politicians, and bankers and invite women to tell their career stories to the girls in your troop or group. Try not to label certain behaviors as "girl behaviors," such as sitting quietly or not shouting. Girls are very attuned to your attitudes and actions. If they see that you are excited about the science activities in the "How and Why?" chapter, then they will catch that excitement—and positive attitude—from you. Give girls many activities in math and science and promote the fun and enjoyment these activities can provide.

Try-Its and Other Resources

- Try-Its: Careers; Citizen Near and Far; Earth and Sky; Her

Did you draw a woman? What kind of person do you think of when you think of a scientist? a firefighter? a lawyer? For a long time people thought women could not do those jobs. Now, along with those careers, women can and are doing many things that once only men did: astronauts, presidents of companies, politicians, and engineers. In fact, many of these women were Girl Scouts when they were young. What exciting career will you have?

Find out about someone who was the first woman to do what she does for a living. How did she feel? Was she treated the same way as the men who were working with her?

 68

Story; Math Fun; Movers; Numbers and Shapes; Plants; Science in Action; Science Wonders; Senses; Space Explorer.

- Other Resources: Two Contemporary Issues booklets are packed with activities that supplement this section: *Into the World of Today and Tomorrow* and *Girls Are Great*. The following activities come from the latter book.

Make a collage that shows the different jobs women hold. Look through magazines and newspapers. Do you think there are some jobs "just for women" and some jobs "just for men"? Why is this unfair?

Make a list of some things girls seem expected to do (for example, play with dolls or wash dishes) and things boys are expected to do (play baseball, climb a tree). How can these expectations affect girls as they are growing up? How can they be changed?

You could also move directly to the "How and Why?" chapter or try the leadership activities in the "Leadership in Girl Scouting and Beyond" chapter.

You could also check with your local Girl Scout council representative to see if there is a listing of women's organizations. Some of these might be resources for troop or group visitors or opportunities for girls to learn more about different careers.

Family, Friends, and Neighbors

Marta looked at the big clock again. 2:32! The hands were moving so slowly. At 2:40, school was over and today was Wednesday and on Wednesdays, she could barely wait for school to finish.

Marta jiggled her leg and tapped her pencil. Great, Ms. Liu was moving toward the front of the room. "Suki, what do you have to remember to do for tomorrow?"

"Write a story. About someone we admire. And why. I'm writing about Jackee Joyner-Kersee. I want to be in the Olympics, too, someday."

Marta Makes a Choice

69

Tips

This story introduces a chapter of activities on family, family history, friends, friends with different abilities, being a friend, school, neighborhood, and neighborhood workers. Through these activities, Brownie Girl Scouts gain skills in relating to others and develop increased respect for the people closest to them.

The theme of the story, respect and admiration for family members, can lead into a variety of activities and discussions. Two points to consider before beginning this chapter:

(1) The art running along the tops of these pages demonstrates some of the combinations of people that can constitute a family. The families were purposely drawn so that it would be difficult to tell exactly where one family ends and the next one begins. A family is a group of people who love and care for each other and can be two people (parent and child, older sibling and younger sibling, grandparent and child) or many people (extended families, foster families). A family can also be composed of people who are related genetically or legally (adoption) or in some other, less structured way.

(2) Some girls may not feel comfortable discussing their family situations, particularly if the family has undergone a recent crisis: homelessness, loss of job, death, or separation. If you have become aware of such circumstances affecting a girl or girls in your troop, you will have to decide whether it is wiser to skip these activities and only do those you feel will not have an adverse effect. On the other hand, girls may welcome a chance to express their feelings. You may have a troop in

Dr. Tamara Jernigan became an astronaut in 1986. She flew as a mission specialist in June 1991 and is scheduled for more space flights.

"You do run fast. That's a good choice," Ms. Liu said. "Has anyone else picked someone to write about?"

Michelle raised her hand. "I'm writing about Tamara Jernigan. I'd love to be an astronaut. I could float around my space ship, land on the moon, and jump 12 feet high!"

"That's also a good choice," Ms. Liu said. "Marta, what about you? Whom have you picked?"

Marta was staring at the clock as the hand clicked to 2:40. "I don't know. I really can't think of anybody." She looked at Ms. Liu.

"Well, if you think about it, I'm sure you'll think of someone you admire enough to write about. Any questions? No? Okay, see you all tomorrow."

Marta already had her backpack in her hand. She raced to the door, swung down the hallway, and down the front steps of the school. Her grandmother was waiting at the bottom step.

"Hi, Nana," said Marta as she gave her grandmother a big hug. She could feel Nana's bones through her sweater and dress. Nana had always been short and as she got older she got thinner and shorter, but much tougher, she told Marta.

Nana wasn't really a huggy kind of person, Marta thought. But, she was always there when she was needed. "Like when my parakeet, Mandy, died," Marta thought.

"I cried and cried, but Nana helped me get a box to bury Mandy in, and helped me pick out a song to sing when I buried her and let me spend the night in her room so I could sleep under the red and blue woolen quilt she had made when she was first married."

"That quilt is over 60 years old," Nana told her. "I made it when I married your grandpa. That was before we even came to this country."

And, Nana would tell her a story about when she was a child living on a farm that had goats and geese, or when she first was married and came to the United States with her new husband.

That was why Marta loved Wednesdays. Her mother went to school on Wednesday nights, and Marta and Nana had the apartment to themselves. Nana would cook something special for the two of them, always showing Marta what to do and what kind of spices or herbs would make each dish taste

70

---

which many of the girls are homeless or living with people other than their parents. Working on activities that reinforce the concept that family crises are not the fault of the child—or in many cases, the parent or adult— can help girls cope. For more information, see the Contemporary Issues booklet *Caring and Coping*.

Some story discussion questions:

Whom do you admire? What is special about that person? What are some unusual things this person has done? What can that person teach other people?

Note: Jackee Joyner-Kersee was a Gold Medalist in the 1992 and 1988 Olympics and has won many other events and races. She also has not let asthma stop her from competing.

Dr. Tamara E. Jernigan has flown missions on the space shuttle and has degrees in engineering, physics, astronomy, and space physics. She enjoys volleyball, racquetball, tennis, softball, and flying.

Both Jackee Joyner-Kersee and Tamara Jernigan were Girl Scouts. Some related activities:

Girls can interview former Girl Scouts in their communities.

Girls can interview a family member they admire and report about that person to the group, plan a special dinner or celebration for the people they admire, or create a "Person I Admire Most" award. The girls might also re-enact family stories or histories, create a puppet play of "Marta Makes a Choice," or take different parts and create their own plays, shadow plays, or shadow boxes.

extra good. As they cooked, Nana would tell stories and sing old songs, and the smell of the spices and the sounds of the stories would mix together as they traveled through Nana's past.

"It is strange. That quilt is so much older now than your grandpa." Marta had heard the story many times of how Grandpa had died when Nana was very young and Marta's mother was just a baby.

So, Nana had worked. In restaurants and people's homes, scrubbing and cleaning, and cooking and washing, until her hands were always red. Her hands were still red and the skin was rough, but no one's hands felt better than Nana's when Marta was sick or tired or sleepy.

"Weren't you ever scared, Nana?" Marta asked.

"Scared of what, Marta?" Nana asked.

"Scared of leaving your family and coming to a place where you didn't know anybody and you didn't speak English? And scared of being

alone after Grandpa died? Do you still miss him?"

"I didn't have time to be scared. I was always working. Well, probably I was scared at times and lonely, too. But, I also loved your mother very much and now I have you who asks me so many questions that I never have time to feel lonely—or even think!" Nana reached over and squeezed Marta's shoulder. "So, do you have homework?" Nana asked.

"I do, and I wasn't sure how to do it, but now I know exactly what I'm going to do," Marta said.

Whom do you think Marta wrote about for her story "The Person I Admire the Most"? That's right, she wrote about her grandmother. What do you think Marta admired about her grandmother?

71

The story does introduce the concepts of death in the family and feeling scared or lonely. The Contemporary Issues booklet *Caring and Coping* contains more information and activities and includes information on the loss of a pet—which in some cases is the first experience with death that girls have.

Try-Its and Other Resources

- Try-Its: Caring and Sharing; Her Story; Listening to the Past; Puppets, Dolls, and Plays; Space Explorer; Sports and Games.

- Other Resources: *Caring and Coping.* "Taking Care of Yourself and Home," handbook pages 52–54.

Family

hat is a family? Your family includes the people who take care of you, help you, teach you, and love you. In a family you learn how to get along with other people. Families are different. People in your family may live with you or they may live somewhere else. You may live with two parents or one parent or other people in your family. You could live with another family and become part of a new family. You might have sisters or brothers or be an "only child" with no sisters or brothers at all. You could live with your grandmother or grandfather, aunts or uncles, nieces or nephews, stepbrothers and stepsisters, stepmothers or stepfathers, cousins, godparents

. . . even pets! There are so many different kinds of people who can make up a family!

In this space you could paste a photograph of your family or draw

a picture of your family. You could write the names of the members of your family in a design that shows how everyone in your family is connected to each other.

In the Puppets, Dolls, and Plays Try-It, you can learn how to make many different kinds of puppets. Pick one type of puppet and make a set of family puppets. You can make the puppets like your own family or make puppets like a pretend family.

Use your puppets to act out these family situations:

- Something that made your family happy.
- Something that your family is planning to do.
- An activity that your family usually does together.
- Something funny that happened in your family.

72

Tips

If girls make a set of family puppets, they can use these puppets throughout this chapter. They can even add puppets that represent their friends for activities in the section on "Friends." Some girls may choose to make puppets of their own families, other families they know, or made-up families. Any of these ideas would be appropriate.

Girls can act out more situations than those listed, though too many situations can quickly become boring. Girls may want to set aside time at a number of meetings for playing with their puppets.

Activities on handbook pages 79–81 in the "Being a Friend" section are about conflict resolution. Resolving conflicts by looking for a solution in which everyone is a winner can also be applied to family situations. Additional information on conflict resolution is on page 55 in Part I of this book.

• Something that made your family sad.

Can you think of some others?

In a family, you learn how to get along with other people. Families can have a lot of fun together, but families can also argue. It is not so easy when people live together to get everyone to agree all of the time! Maybe you want to watch a program on television and your brother wants to listen to music and your mother wants to read the newspaper and wants quiet! What happens? Not everybody can have her or his own way. When you live with other people, you cannot always do what you want or get your own way. You have to cooperate with each other. Cooperation means working together. How could the family cooperate in the situation above?

Think of times when families disagree. Use your puppets to act out ways to cooperate with each other.

Make a "Help My Family" promise. What promise can you make for your family? Maybe you can promise to be ready for school on time so your mother doesn't have to remind you so often. Maybe you can promise not to argue with your older brother and he can promise not to argue with you!

Things Families Do Together

Families also do things together that are fun. Families can spend a lot of time together, but during the week, many families are busy doing things apart from each other, like working or going to school. Sometimes, families plan time on the weekends to spend together. Sometimes, different members of the fam-

ily are busy on the weekend, too. What are some things your family does together? What are some things you do with just one member of your family?

Think of a fun activity you can do with your family indoors. Maybe you could try a game or activity you learned in Brownie Girl Scouts.

Think of a fun activity you could do with your whole family or a member of your family outdoors.

Make a picture book, a poster, or a chart showing what an average weekday is like in the life of your family. Keep track of what is done from the time the members of your family wake up until the time you all go to bed. Share this with your family. Would you spend your time in a different way? Can you spend less time on some things and more time on others?

How does your family spend

73

Girls can compare the different types of activities families do together. These additional activities are from the Contemporary Issues booklet *Caring and Coping*:

(1) Share ideas about what you could do to help at home if your mother or father lost her or his job or was not able to work.

(2) Find pictures that show different kinds of families doing a variety of things. Make a family montage with the pictures.

When discussing holidays and celebrations, emphasize the diversity of holidays or even the different ways of celebrating the same holiday. Some cultures do not celebrate many holidays or birthdays, or may have quite subdued sorts of celebrations. Also note that some holidays, such

as Thanksgiving or Columbus Day, may have negative connotations for some groups of people. Care should be taken that religious holidays, such as Christmas or Easter, do not become the focus of crafts-type of activities that exclude girls who do not participate in those celebrations.

Girls can not only share their own traditions, but also invent some new traditions for their families. Why not create a "We're Glad We're a

Family" or "Our Family's Special" celebration?

Girls can refer to handbook pages 44–47 in "Taking Care of Yourself and Your Home" when talking about family jobs.

Saturday or Sunday? Choose one of those days and keep track of how your family spends time. Share your charts with your Brownie Girl Scout group. Did you find out something new to do with your family?

What are some family jobs? Make a list of the jobs that different people in your family do in the home. Who cooks? Who cleans? Who does the shopping? Try making a kaper chart for your family. What are your own family responsibilities?

Try making a special box or jar for family jobs. Write the names of jobs or draw small pictures on slips of paper and put them inside the box or jar. Family members can choose different jobs each week.

What are some special days you celebrate with your family? Talk about holidays and celebrations with your Brownie Girl Scout group.

Why not create a group holiday celebration? Each person can share a food, decoration, song, or tradition from her favorite holiday.

Families may also have times that are not fun. Sometimes parents don't live together. Sometimes parents get divorced. Maybe a grandparent dies. If you have a pet, you will feel sad if your pet runs away. Maybe your mother loses her job. These things may happen. Sometimes, girls your age worry about these things happening when they won't really happen. If you have worries like this, you should talk to people in your family and other people you love. Remember, you have people who love you very much and will listen to you if you are worried or sad.

Family History

Families celebrate holidays in different ways because families often have different backgrounds. Maybe people came from other countries. Maybe people came from different parts of the United States. Find out more about your family.

- Where were your family members born?
- Where were your ancestors (people like your great-grandparents, and their grandparents) born?
- How did your parents celebrate holidays when they were children?
- Are there any recipes, songs, dances, or customs from long ago that your family still shares?

74

- Try-Its: Caring and Sharing; Girl Scout Ways; Hobbies; Manners; People of the World.

Tips

Not every girl will be able to find out about her family's history. Some families do not or cannot keep a record, or they identify more with a particular region of the country than with an ethnic or cultural tradition. Some girls who have been adopted or who are living in foster homes may choose to use the history of their adoptive or foster families; others may not. Girls may decide to interview someone who shares their background or someone who has lived in the community for a long time.

This related activity appears in the Contemporary Issues booklet *Valuing Differences*:

A Brownie Girl Scout can gain pride in her family heritage by exploring her family history. She can draw a family tree on a large sheet of brown or construction paper. On the tree, she might include homes, pictures, or photographs of all the members of her family whom she can discover by talking to her relatives. She can include photos or drawings of places her family has lived or add pictures or drawings of important family events or traditions.

Girls can also create a "family time line," similar to the one on handbook page 38 in "Taking Care of Yourself and Your Home." The family time line would record family events.

If you can, think of questions to ask the oldest person in your family—or an older person who shares your cultural background or who has lived in the same place as you for a long time. Find a way to keep a record of this person's answers. You could use a tape recorder, a video recorder, or you could make a scrapbook.

Share your family history with your Brownie Girl Scout group. Can you make a story or a play? Can you re-tell a special story from your family? Can you act out something that happened to a person in the past?

Find out more about families which have the same background as yours and those which have different backgrounds. You could look for books in a library, visit a museum, go to an ethnic festival, or watch a movie or play.

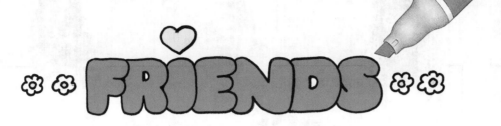

FRIENDS

Friends are important. Friends can act like a family. They can help you and take care of you. You go places together and you learn new things. You may have many friends, or you may have one or two friends. Sometimes you may get along and sometimes you may not. You may like people for different reasons. You can have friends who are a lot like you and you can have friends who are different.

Just as people in families may come from different places, so do friends. Maybe you have a friend who was born in a different part of the world, or who is older or younger than you, or who has different eye, skin, or hair color than you have. Having friends who are different

from you makes a friendship interesting. Think of how much you can learn from each other. Imagine how boring life would be if all your friends were just like you!

 What are three things I can learn from my friends?
 What are three things I can teach my friends?

Friends with Different Abilities

You and your friends have different abilities. An ability is something you can do. Maybe you can run faster than your friend, but she can read faster than you do. Everybody you meet has some things she does well and some things she

(*continued on page 77*)

75

Try-Its and Other Resources

- Try-Its: Her Story; Listening to the Past.
- Other Resources: *Valuing Differences.*

Tips

Encourage the girls to decorate the heading "Friends" with their own designs and colors.

Brownie Girl Scouts may be starting to experience cliques and peer pressure and most probably have begun to feel societal pressure to be "popular." You can help the girls in your troop or group build friendships and build their own feelings of self-worth by emphasizing the positive attributes of friends and friendships. An activity as simple as defining "What makes someone a good friend" or "How can I act like a good friend?" is a good starting point for other activities on friendship.

This section also touches on the diversity of culture, ability, ethnic and racial background, and other differences that can be found among friends. You may want to continue with the topic of diversity, so see handbook pages 108–110 in "People Near and Far." Or try some of the activities in *Valuing Differences* such as the following:

The slogan "We're the same/ We're different" can encourage an appreciation of differences. Assign partners and ask girls to sit or stand facing each other. Ask girls to think of three ways in which they are like their partners. Ask the partners to share their similarities and differ-

AUTOGRAPHS

This is a special space for your friends. You can have them sign their names here or write something special. You can put photographs of them in this space or draw a picture of your friends.

76

ences with each other and with the group. Here are some questions to discuss during this activity:

- In what ways were we different? How were we similar and different at the same time? For example, everyone has skin, but skin color can differ.
- What things could be noticed besides appearance?
- What differences and similarities are we born with? What can change as girls grow up?

Try-Its and Other Resources

- Try-Its: Around the World; Caring and Sharing; People of the World.

doesn't do well. Some of your friends may have a disability. Maybe you have a disability. A disability is something that may make it harder for a person to do some things.

A person who is blind cannot see. She may use her hearing or her touch to help her know more about the world. She may use a cane or a seeing eye dog to help move about. A person who is deaf may hear some sounds, but not very clearly, or may hear no sounds. She may look at the lips of people who are talking and figure out what people are saying. This is called lip-reading. If you are deaf, you may have a special machine for your television or telephone so you can read what people are saying.

You might have a disability that makes it hard to walk. You might need a wheelchair or crutches or a leg brace to help you walk. These disabilities are easy to see. You could also have a disability that is not easy to see, like a learning disability. A learning disability may make it hard

to learn how to read and write. You could also have a disability that makes it difficult to pay attention or to sit still.

Visit a place in your neighborhood that helps people who have disabilities or find out about a career working with people who have disabilities.

Learn more about some of the helpful tools for people with disabilities. Wheelchairs, hearing aids, walkers, leg braces, canes, artificial limbs, eyeglasses, reading machines, computers, talking books, and video machines are just some.

Here are some activities that will help you understand disabilities you might not have.

Blind walk. This activity will help you feel what it is like to be unable to see. Have a partner blindfold you and walk around with you slowly to make sure you don't get hurt. Stop to feel things. Use your senses of touch, hearing, and smell to learn about your environment. What happens to your other senses when you cannot see?

Learn a new language. Try wearing earphones or headphones for part of your Brownie Girl Scout meeting. How does it feel? How did you know what was being said? People who cannot hear often learn how to use sign language. There are different systems of sign language.

77

You may have girls in your troop or group who have a disability mentioned in this section or some other disability. Girls who have a disability may want to share the tools they use or stories about the difficulties they encounter. On the other hand, some girls may prefer not to be the focus of attention. Before introducing this section to the whole troop or group, you might ask any girls with disabilities of which you are aware if they would feel uncomfortable with the activities in this section. Also, the activities designed to increase sensitivity, such as the blind walk or the mirror image, should not be done as a game. Further, care should be taken that girls do not learn to pity someone who has difficulty reading quickly or buttoning a shirt easily. Rather than emphasize what cannot be done, encourage the girls to see what can be done.

HANDBOOK
Page 78

Use the sign alphabet chart to figure out the message on the facing page.

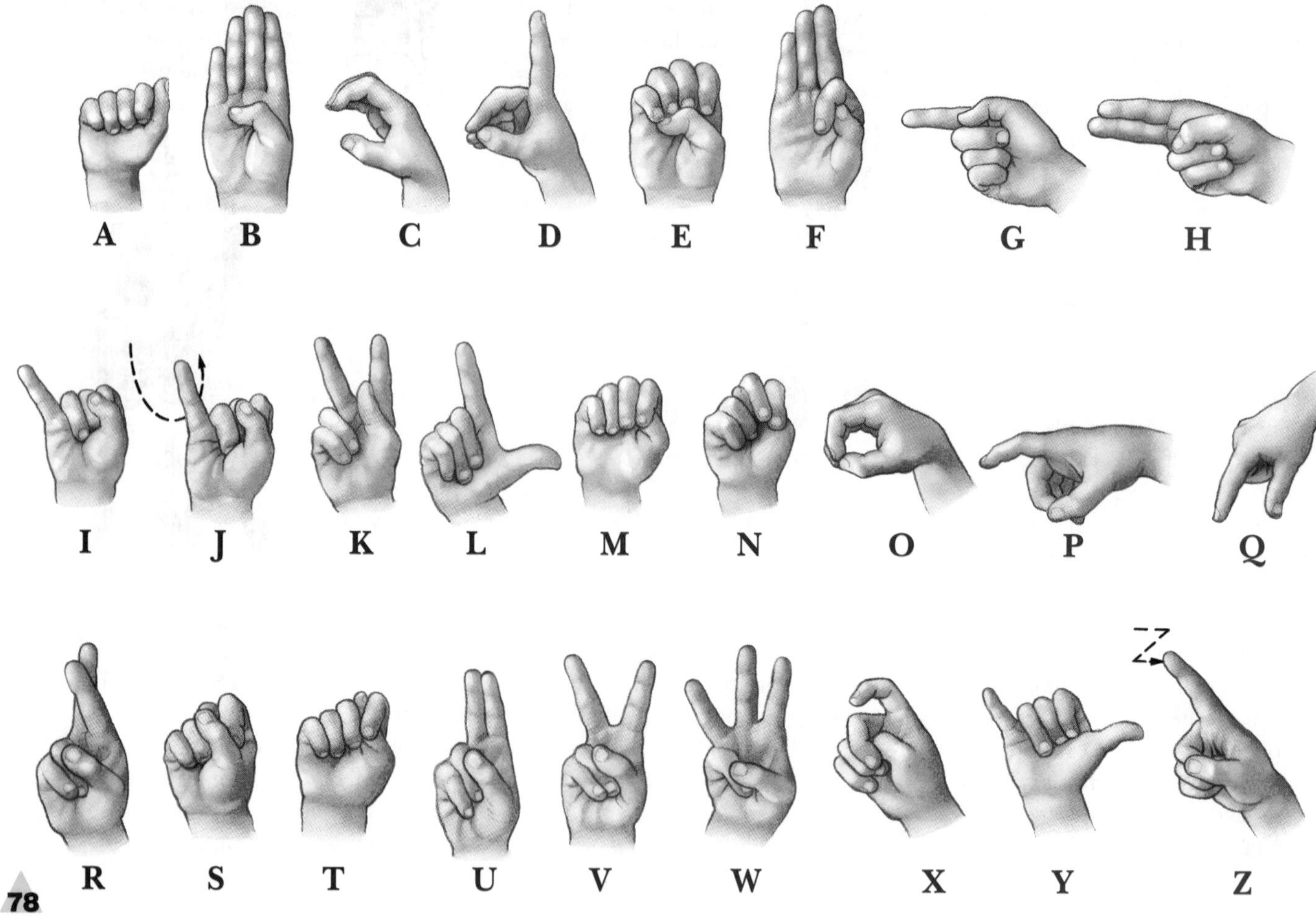
A
B
C
D
E
F
G
H
I
J
K
L
M
N
O
P
Q
R
S
T
U
V
W
X
Y
Z
78

Try-Its and Other Resources

- Try-Its: My Body; Senses.
- Other Resources: *Focus on Ability: Serving Girls with Special Needs* is an excellent resource filled with information and activities for Girl Scout leaders. See also "People Near and Far," pages 108–110, for more about different kinds of people, and pages 57–58 in Part I of this book on adapting activities.

Each hand position stands for a letter.

Practice making words with this new alphabet. If you meet someone who cannot hear, you'll be able to "talk" with her or him if she or he knows this alphabet.

Mirror image. Some people have trouble learning how to read. Letters may look mixed up to them. It's hard for them to make sense out of words on the page. This condition is called dyslexia (dis-lek-see-uh).

To see what this disability is like, try to read the message below.

THIS IS HARD TO READ

To figure out what this message says, hold the page up to a mirror. Imagine how it must feel to have to learn to read when everything looks so mixed up! However, most people who have reading disabilities can and do learn to read.

Dress yourself. Put on a man's shirt—unbuttoned. Put a pair of thick socks or very thick mittens on your hands and try to button the shirt. What happens? This will show you how someone who cannot move her body easily could have a hard time getting dressed. What kind of clothing would be easier to wear?

Being a Friend

Learning to be a friend is an important part of Girl Scouting. To have a friend, you must be a friend. How can you be a friend to someone? What do the Girl Scout Promise and Law tell you about friendship?

I am a friend when I _____

_____

_____

I am not a friend when I _____

_____

_____

_____

79

Tips

Communication and conflict resolution skills are necessary at any age. Page 55 in Part I of this book contain more information on conflict resolution. Girls can practice resolving conflicts that they have experienced with friends or in their families. Activities that promote active listening are also excellent communication builders.

Try this activity adapted from *Reaching Out: Preventing Youth Suicide*:

In a group, discuss what you would do if:

- Two friends wanted you to visit them on the same day.

- Your homework was not completed and you were told to go to bed.
- Your teacher said you were talking in class, but it was the girl sitting behind you.
- You want to sleep over at your friend's house on a Thursday night, but your parents want you to stay home on school nights.

When you are talking with your family, friends, or people you have just met, there are ways to make sure they understand what you are saying.

1. Be a good listener. Listen to every word the person says. Decide if the person is telling you something, asking you something, or just sharing what's on her mind. If you are not sure what the person is saying, try saying it back to her in a different way. You can say, "I think you said. . . ."

2. Think about what you say and how you say it. Does your voice sound angry? Do you give the other person a chance to speak? Do you treat your listener the way you would like to be treated? As a Girl Scout, part of the Law you are trying to live by is "to show respect for myself and others through my words and actions."

Here are some activities to help practice talking with people:

• Keep a diary for a day. Write how people acted when you listened carefully to what they said.
• Make a list of ways to show respect for others. For example: I show respect by not making fun of what someone said. I show respect when I listen carefully.

• When you and your friend do not agree about how to do something, what do you do? Think of a time that you and a friend didn't agree. What did you do? How did you make up?
• How would you solve the following problems?

1. You and two friends are in the playground and there is one jump-rope left.

2. Your friend doesn't want you to invite the new girl in your Brownie Girl Scout troop to your birthday party.

3. The older girls in your troop tease you because you cannot write well.

Sometimes our friends do things they should not do. They may think you should do it too. This is a time when being a friend is very hard. You must remember what is right and what is wrong, and then do what you know is right. Even if it means that you get teased or called

80

Girls may also be experiencing peer pressure to do things that they may consider wrong—for example, stealing, lying, being mean to a new girl in school. Some girls as young as six to eight have admitted to drinking alcohol, smoking cigarettes, taking drugs, or experimenting with sex.

Activities that help girls combat peer pressure or societal pressure

and that help them to say no can be found in the Contemporary Issues booklets *Tune In to Well-Being, Say No to Drugs*; *Girls Are Great*; *Developing Health and Fitness*; and *Staying Safe*. The following activity is adapted from the latter book:

Role-play with a friend. Learn how to say no when you are in a situ-

ation that may be harmful to you or when someone asks you to do something that you believe is wrong. What if someone asked you to take a puff of a cigarette? What if someone asked to copy your homework? What if someone you didn't know offered you a ride home from school?

names, you should never do something you know is wrong because other people want you to do it.

With friends or in your troop, think of some situations when people might ask you to do something you know is wrong. What can you say to them? Practice what you would say in each situation.

Things Friends Do Together

There are many things you can do with your friends. Playing games and sports are good ways to keep fit. Games and sports often have rules to follow. You should play fair and always try to do your best. Having fun is the most important thing, not who wins or loses.

Here are some games you can play with your friends. Can you think of some others? You can look in the *Games for Girl Scouts* book for more ideas.

Initials

Two or more players are needed. One player is chosen to be the "questioner" for the first round.

The questioner asks each player a question. The player must answer the question with an answer formed from the initials of her own name. If the questioner asks, "What is your favorite food, Rosa Carlo?" Rosa may answer, "Red cherries," or "Raisin cake." If the questioner asks, "How do you like to spend Saturday morning, Shelly Steinberg?" Shelly may answer, "Simply sleeping," or "Singing songs." The answers don't have to make sense. Actually it is more fun if they don't. If you repeat an answer or can't think of an answer, you are out. The last player becomes the questioner for the next round.

Invent your own games and play them with others. Try making a game in which everyone wins, like cooperative musical chairs. You still take a chair away in each turn, but everyone tries to sit on the chairs that are left, until you only have one chair and everyone tries to sit on it!

Here are some games that you can play with just one other person.

Make a Box

Draw 40 dots on a piece of paper. Each player takes a turn drawing a line between two dots that are next to each other. The first player to make a box puts her name or initials in the box. You keep playing until all the dots are connected or until one person gets ten boxes. The person who makes the most boxes is the winner.

81

- Try-Its: Art To Wear; Building Art; Colors and Shapes; Dancercize; Earth and Sky; Hobbies; Movers; Music; Outdoor Adventurer; Play; Science in Action; Sounds of Music; Sports and Games.

Brownie Girl Scout Try-Its encourage active play rather than passive activities, such as watching television. You can encourage girls to participate in a variety of activities in pairs or in groups and encourage new hobbies and interests.

- Other Resources: *Games for Girl Scouts* has many games

Brownie Girl Scouts would enjoy. The following are from this book:

Sticky Popcorn

Girls pretend to be popcorn kernels. They start out "popping" or jumping about slowly, and as the heat is increased— the game leader can shout "hotter"—girls hop faster.

Since this is sticky popcorn, when girls touch each other, they stick together, but they must continue to hop. They continue to hop until they've made one giant sticky popcorn ball.

Hug Tag

One girl is "it." Girls are safe only when they are hugging another girl—or three or four girls. Girls can't hug the same person twice in one round of the game.

Back-to-Back Tag

"It" can tag anyone not standing back-to-back with another girl. No one can stand by the same person longer than five seconds.

New Games from Old

Take out a chess or checkers set and invent a new game with your own rules. For example, you can make a rule that the checkers must be moved diagonally or two spaces at a time. Or, you can give the different pieces of a chess set different kinds of movements or give them all the same movements.

Your Friends and School

Many Brownie Girl Scouts spend a lot of their time in school. School gives you a chance to meet many friends and do fun things together. You can work on a class project, play an instrument in the school band, sing in the chorus, play softball, or put on a play together.

82

Tips

School is an important part of a Brownie Girl Scout's life. Girls may want to share their good and bad experiences. Discovering what girls enjoy most can give you more ideas of what they'd enjoy doing at troop or group meetings. Conversely, with schools experiencing cutbacks, the experiences in Brownie Girl Scouting may supplement a girl's school experiences and give girls opportunities they lack. Also, research has proved that schools traditionally favor boys. Girls find experiences in Girl Scouting—especially in math, the sciences, leadership, and decision-making—that they may not fully participate in in school.

MY SCHOOL STORY

Fill in the blanks below. Remember to add on pages as you move from year to year in Brownie Girl Scouting.

Name of my school

_____

Name of my teacher

_____

Names of friends in my class

_____

Number of grades or age levels

_____

Number of students in school

_____

Number of students in class

_____

My favorite school subject

_____

Draw a picture of or paste a photograph of your school, or describe it in the space above.

83

Your Neighbors and Neighborhood

Who are the people you see every day? The people who live near you in your community are your neighbors. A neighborhood is all of the people, all of the streets, all of the buildings, parks, and other places near your home.

Make a Neighborhood Map

Try making a map of a part of your neighborhood that you like. You can pick the streets near your home or near your school or near your Brownie Girl Scout meeting place. You can choose a park or an open space. How will you show the different buildings, streets, trees, and other special things in your neighborhood?

Maps have legends. The legend is the list of what different drawings

84

Here is the space for your map.

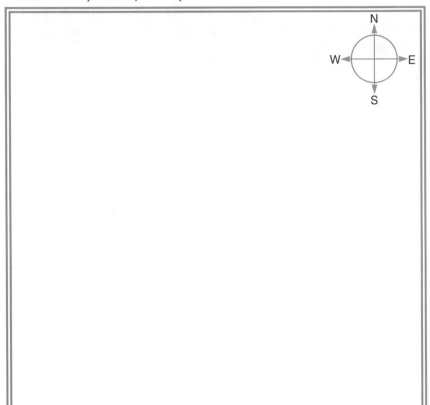

In this section, girls explore their surroundings. Field trips may greatly enhance learning, but you must first check with your local Girl Scout representative about field trip guidelines and safety procedures. See also *Safety-Wise*, and pages 34–35 in Part I of this book.

Some ideas for trips: park, library, cemetery, office building, government building, police station, firehouse, recycling plant, social services agency, women's shelter, museum, historical site, factory, dam or power plant, zoo, radio or television station, dental clinic. Your local Chamber of Commerce can provide other ideas for places to visit.

You can also invite neighborhood workers to speak to the troop. Since girls this age are naturally active, you will want your guest speakers to limit the amount of time they speak. They could also plan some "show and tell" or participatory-type activities.

mean on your map. Here are some examples.

 Tree

 House

 River

 School

 Office building

What kind of legend can you make for your map? Share your map with other people who know your neighborhood.

Explore Your Neighborhood

 Explore your neighborhood. Ask an adult or someone older than you to walk with you. Look for things that are:

Old _____

_____

New _____

_____

Made by people _____

_____

Natural _____

_____

Big _____

_____

Small _____

_____

People in Your Neighborhood

Who are the neighbors you could meet visiting places in your neighborhood? What kinds of jobs would these neighbors have? Do some of your neighbors have jobs where they can help people? How did they get these jobs? What school and training did they need? What else can you find out? Why not interview a neighborhood worker or ask her or him to visit your troop?

Be a Telephone Book Detective

Your telephone book can also give you a lot of information about your neighborhood. Find out if some people have the same last name as you. How many different names can you find?

85

What are the most common names? What can names tell you about the people who live in your neighborhood? If you can get to a library, find out if it has copies of old phone books. Compare the old phone books with the new ones. What information can you discover about your neighborhood?

Hidden Neighborhood Workers

The scrambled words on the right answer the questions about neighborhood workers on the left. First unscramble the words, then answer the questions.

1. Who makes sure that people obey traffic laws?

   a. gdo ccahetr

2. Who puts out fires?

   b. ehoteepln reptaoro

3. Who gives you health checkups and vaccinations?

   c. coliep

4. Who gives you the correct telephone number?

   d. bamanlecu vidrer

5. Who collects garbage and trash and cleans the street?

   e. blairarin

6. Who keeps stray animals from running loose?

   f. erfi fghitre

7. Who checks to see that your teeth and gums are healthy?

   g. tnidtse

8. Who will drive you to the hospital in an emergency?

   h. rapk greran

9. Who helps you find your favorite book?

   i. codrot

10. Who helps you discover more about parks and green spaces?

    j. nstiaonait krorwe

Answer key: dogcatcher, telephone operator, police, ambulance driver, fire fighter, dentist, doctor, sanitation worker, librarian, park ranger.

86

Try-Its and Other Resources

- Try-Its: Citizen Near and Far; Earth Is Our Home; Math Fun; Outdoor Adventurer; Outdoor Fun; Outdoor Happenings.

- Other Resources: See handbook pages 154–157 in "How and Why?" and handbook pages 115–117 in "Leadership in Girl Scouting and Beyond." *Earth Matters*; *Exploring Wildlife Communities With Children*.

People Near and Far

World Trefoil Pin

87

Brownie Girl Scouts are part of an international sisterhood. The illustration shows some Girl Guides and Girl Scouts the same ages as Brownie Girl Scouts from Korea, New Zealand, Israel, Zimbabwe, Brazil, Mexico, and Greece.

Also, this chapter contains activities in the World of the Arts, as arts and crafts are often woven into the cultural fabric of a particular country or group. If possible, invite someone who is from one of the countries mentioned in this chapter, or who has lived extensively in one of the countries, to speak to the troop or group.

When you became a Brownie Girl Scout, you became part of a very big family! Girl Scouts in the United States are members of the World Association of Girl Guides and Girl Scouts. In countries all around the world, you have sisters who are members of the world movement of Girl Guiding and Girl Scouting. The World Trefoil pin may be worn by all Girl Scouts and Girl Guides.

In this chapter are stories about Ananse Guides, Bluebird Girl Scouts, Alita Girl Scouts, and Grønsmutte Girl Scouts. The first story is about the Ananse Guides, which is what Brownie Girl Scouts in Ghana, West Africa, are called. Ananse is a spider. Why would you name Girl Scouts after a spider? Because Ananse is a very, very smart spider and many stories are told in West Africa about Ananse. Remember in "Welcome to Girl Scouts," you read a story about brownies? In Ghana, Ananse Guides read a story about Ananse the spider.

88

Ananse's Gift

In the middle of the forest there was a small house under an oil palm tree. A grandmother and two grandchildren, a boy and a girl, lived in this house. They were twins and named Abena One and Abena Two, which is how twins were named.

When Abena One and Abena Two were in school, the grandmother would walk to her farm and dig and weed and pick some vegetables for dinner.

One day, the children came home and saw an empty cooking pot. "Where's our dinner?" they asked.

Grandmother looked at the children. "I have worked hard, but now my back is bent and my arms are weak. I can't dig and I can't weed. Unless I get new arms and a new back, I can't bring home food anymore."

That night Abena One and Abena Two went to their beds, but they couldn't sleep. They waited until their grandmother was sleeping, and very quietly went outside.

Try-Its and Other Resources

- Other Resources: More information on the World Association of Girl Guides and Girl Scouts can be found on pages 63–65 in Part I of this book, and in *Trefoil Round the World.* The story of Juliette Gordon Low on handbook pages 8–11 in "Welcome to Girl Scouts" gives some information on the beginnings of this international Movement. The activities in "People Near and Far" explore four WAGGGS member countries in greater detail.

many feet that the children knew they had found Ananse and his wife.

Without getting up, Ananse waved the children into the room with two of his hands. At the same time, he used another two hands to pull up two chairs and put two mugs on the table with two more hands!

Ananse asked them what they wanted. Abena One and Two explained that their grandmother needed new arms and a new back.

Ananse folded two arms on the table. He used two more arms to scratch his head as he thought and then patted Abena One on the back with one arm and Abena Two on the back with another. He looked at his wife.

She spoke, "We are very clever, but even Ananse cannot give new arms and new backs. But, don't worry. I know a secret. The Good God has already answered your wish."

She took the children outside. "Close your eyes."

Ananse took Abena One's hands and put them on Abena Two's back. Abena One said, "That's a fine strong back for my grandmother."

"We must get our grandmother new arms and a new back. Let's go and ask the Wise One what we should do."

They walked into the forest where they saw a tiny house. From the house came two high, squeaky voices, singing this song, "Here they come, come one, come two. What's the good they want to do?"

Abena One and Abena Two looked in the doorway. They saw two small people with so many hands and so

Tips

The Ananse story is similar to the Brownie story on handbook pages 17–21 in "Welcome to Girl Scouts." Ananse is a common character in much of West African folk literature. Like the coyote in some American Indian tales or the fox in Aesop's fables, Ananse has many sides. Ananse can be very clever or even magical and work for good in some traditional tales, or be mischievous and sly in other traditions.

Many countries in the continent of Africa contain a large number of distinct ethnic groups, each with its own language, customs, and culture. "Ethnic group" is the preferred usage when referring to distinct groups of people. The word "tribe" is considered offensive by many people. These groups may live in more than one country. In addition, many residents of African countries are bi- or trilingual, speaking French, English, Arabic, and their own local languages.

Then Ananse's wife took Abena Two and put his hands on the arms of Abena One. Abena Two said, "Those are fine strong arms for my grandmother."

BOOOM! A big clap of thunder filled the sky and when the children opened their eyes, they were all alone. Ananse, his wife, and the little house had disappeared!

The next morning the children woke up early and walked to the farm. They weeded and raked. They picked just enough vegetables for dinner. When they got home, they swept the yard, started the cooking fire, and started a delicious soup. The smell of the soup drifted into the house and the grandmother woke up.

"What is that wonderful smell?" she said. Then she saw the soup

bubbling over the fire and the yard so clean and neat. She looked at the children. "We did it, Grandmother. We visited Ananse the Spider. We learned that we could be your arms and your back. Now you never have to worry."

Before they went to school each day, Abena One and Abena Two worked on the farm. Soon, they had the best farm in the village. They kept the yard and the house very clean—except for one small corner by the back door. In that corner was a shiny web and two small busy spiders who looked very much like Ananse and his wife.

Do you know any folk tales? A folk tale is a kind of story that shows you how to behave or how something happened. Maybe someone in your family knows some folk tales. Why not have a folk tale story hour in your Brownie Girl Scout troop or group meeting? Can you make up your own folk tale? It might be fun to make some new folk tales and act them out.

Some children may hold stereotypes of Africa because of old *Tarzan* movies and other common misinformation. Many newer books contain more current information and would be excellent reference tools for the activities in this chapter.

The theme of Ananse's gift is similar to the theme of the Brownie story—children learning to be helpful. The two stories can be compared, and both lend themselves to play-acting or puppet shows. Girls can think of a "moral" or lesson that they would like to convey and create a story. This story, with additional activities, also appears in *The Wide World of Girl Guiding and Girl Scouting.*

Ananse Guides in Ghana

If you were an Ananse Girl Guide, you would probably speak English and another local language. Most people in Ghana speak two or more languages. You could live in a city, a suburb, or the country. Wherever you lived, it would be hot most of the year. Half the year would have rainy weather and half the year would have dry weather.

In the country, you might live on a cocoa farm. Do you know what you can make out of cocoa? Chocolate! You might shop in a supermarket or an open market. On tables, you could see bananas, coconuts, peanuts, rice, mangoes and papaya, other foods, and things for the house, like soap, brushes, and dishes. Some fruits and vegetables would be hard to find in the United States, like soursop. It sounds funny, but it tastes cool and sweet and makes great ice cream! You could walk through the market, listening to people greeting

each other and buying their food, smelling all kinds of fruits and vegetables, and seeing so many bright colors. Maybe you would help your mother when you came home from school with her market table. In Ghana, women make much money for their families because they sell the food they grow or the things they make in the market.

At one time, Ghana had a marvelous empire, called the Songhai, with large palaces in which princesses and princes lived. People came from all over the world to sell and buy things. Many people would trade—give one thing to get a different thing. For example, a trader might want salt. He has iron. He would give the salt seller the iron and get the salt in trade. Today, Ghana is still famous for its markets.

Can you and your Brownie Girl Scout troop make a market? What could you bring in to trade? You could bring crafts you have made, food you have prepared, or other things that you think someone else

would like. What rules would you set up for trading? How would you set up the tables?

If you make some peanut or coconut cookies or some banana bread, or a fruit salad with bananas, oranges, and coconut, you could eat what Ananse Girl Guides like to eat. Hot chocolate would be a good thing to drink.

Adinkra Cloth

Ghana is famous for its beautiful cloth, especially a kind called Adinkra cloth. Stamps are made from a kind of gourd, a calabash. Each stamp has a different meaning. Different stamps make beautiful designs and tell a story.

91

Tips

Traditionally, stamps for making Adinkra cloth have been carved from calabashes. The stamp is pressed into black dye made from the bark of an African tree (badie tree) and then pressed onto the cloth in regular patterns. Adinkra is the name of the dye and means "good-bye." The cloth is

traditionally worn when guests are leaving or at funeral ceremonies. Each design has a different meaning, and one or more designs are stamped into squares making a distinctive pattern.

Many materials can be used for stamps—hard sponges, hard foam, pieces of foam trays used for meat or vegetables, or square art erasers. The stamps can be dipped into the

paint, or the paint can be brushed onto the stamp. Acrylic or fabric paint can be used if girls want to make a washable piece of clothing. Putting layers of newspaper under the cloth will help make a sharper impression and keep tables and floors clean! Girls can also use the stamps to make notepaper, book covers, or personalized stationery.

Adinkra cloth is usually divided into squares. You can make your stamps from hard foam or from a square eraser. Use a plastic knife to make your patterns. Traditionally, Adinkra cloth has black stamps, so you could use black poster paint. Press your stamps into the paint and then onto white construction paper or pieces of a white cotton sheet. If you want to wear the cloth, use acrylic or water-fast paint. Share stamps with your friends for different designs.

Bluebird Girl Guides in Thailand

Bluebirds are Brownie Girl Scouts in Thailand. Thailand is in Southeast Asia. Bluebirds go to Flock

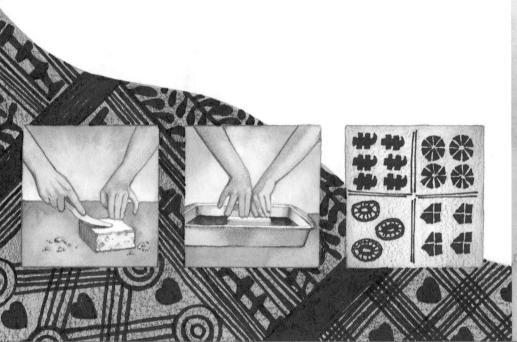

Tips

Thailand, in southeastern Asia, is a large country with a proud cultural history. Thailand means "land of the free," and Thais are proud that their country was never under foreign rule. The king and queen are the most respected people in the country. Dancing, music, and the arts are integral parts of the Thai culture, and Brownie Girl Scouts in Thailand, called Bluebirds, may play Thai musical instruments or do beautiful Thai dances using their fingers and hands to tell stories. Bluebirds also enjoy camping, protecting their environment, and working on service projects.

Another activity that a Bluebird might do is making a stone rubbing. Thailand has many temples decorated with raised stone designs. Prints are made by laying paper over the design and gently rubbing with a crayon or charcoal. Girls can make their own rubbings of interesting architecture or statues in their communities.

meetings with a Flock leader. If a girl wants to join a Flock, she is called a Fledgling, a baby bird. She has ten different things to do and if she does them, she gets a Blue Feather. Then she does ten more things—a little harder than the first— and gets her Silver Feather. And then, she can do eight more for a Golden Feather!

After three years in a Flock, just like your three years in Brownie Girl Scouts, a Bluebird flies away to Girl Guides, just as you would fly up to Junior Girl Scouts.

Thailand has mountains with forests and jungles, beautiful beaches, big and little cities, and many farms that grow rice. Elephants are common animals in Thailand and are used to help do work, like pulling logs or moving heavy things.

People in Thailand speak Thai and many people also speak French or English. The Thai language has a different alphabet than English and a different sound. The same word can have different meanings if you say it in a high voice or a low voice, so the language sounds very musical and beautiful. Here is the Bluebird motto, "Be Prepared," in the Thai language written with an English alphabet:

Chuey luer poo uen smer

Kite Festival

A very special holiday that Bluebirds look forward to is the Kite Festival. The Thai people make big and small kites in many bright colors and many unusual shapes. Some kites look like butterflies and some kites look like birds. Some even look like dragons! Imagine a sunny blue sky full of these kites!

Why not make your own kites? Look on pages 222–223 in the Movers Try-It. Decorate your kite with elephants or dragons or birds with bright feathers and you can have a kite that a Bluebird might fly.

93

Try-Its and Other Resources

- Other Resources: *Trefoil Round the World*; *The Wide World of Girl Guiding and Girl Scouting*; *World Games and Recipes*.

Crayon Resist

94

Batik

Silk is colored with beautiful patterns in Thailand. One way to make patterns on cloth is called batik. You put wax on cloth and dip it in different colors. When you take the wax off, the design you made appears!

You can use crayons to do something similar on paper. Crayons and paint together are called "resist." You will need white paper, white crayons, and different kinds of watercolors. Make a design on the white paper with your white crayon. Press hard so that the crayon sticks to the paper. Then, paint the paper with bright watercolors. Your "resist" design will show through the paint. Try using other light colors of crayons to make your designs.

Alita Girl Guides in Peru

In Peru, Brownie Girl Scouts are called Alitas, which means "Little Wing." Many people speak Spanish and some people speak two languages, Spanish and a local language. Alitas say their Promise in Spanish:

Tips

Batik. The art of batik is practiced in many countries, but is believed to have originated in southeastern Asia. Wax is applied to cloth, usually silk or cotton, in intricate designs, often of animals—fish, birds, butterflies—or of plants. Then, the cloth is dyed and some of the wax removed. Cloth can be dipped in dye a number of times, with a little bit of wax removed each time, to make a multicolored pattern.

Since hot wax would not only be difficult but also dangerous to use with a group of Brownie Girl Scouts, this crayon-resist substitution conveys the idea and method of batik without the risk and mess of hot wax.

Try-Its and Other Resources

- Try-Its: Art to Wear; Colors and Shapes.

Prometo hacer todo lo posible por cumplir mis deberes para con Dios y mi Patria.

Ayudar a otras personas, especialmente a los de casa.

Do you speak Spanish? Can you read the Alitas Promise in the Spanish spoken in Peru? Try singing this folk song from Peru that an Alita might sing.

Peru is a large country in South America. If you were an Alita, you could live in high mountains, the Andes, covered with snow, or near dry deserts, the rain forest, or near many beaches. Maybe you would live on a farm, or in the capital city, Lima. In the country, you would be able to see llamas and alpacas, members of the camel family. Llamas help carry heavy loads and alpacas have long, soft hair used to make beautiful clothing and blankets.

Los Maizales

Peru
Folk Song

Los mai - za - les bro - tan con pri - mor

ful - gu - ran sus ho - jas de co - lor; La tie - rra fer - til,

el sol be - só, su be - llo gra - no ger - mi - nó.

Tie - rra Pe - rua - na de _ho - nor te _em - bria - gas.

2. Después de la faena intelectual
vamos presurosos a jugar,
Cual nuestros padres al son de pan,
vamos el campo a cultivar.
Tierra Peruana, de honor te
embriagas.

This song describes the beauty of the cornfields and suggests that all Peruvians should help with the task of "growing their bread."

Tips

Peru is on the northwestern coast of South America and is almost twice the size of Texas. Peru has a coastal desert, lowlands with forests and jungles, and the mountainous Andes highlands. Several of South America's most advanced Indian cultures lived in Peru; the Incas were the last of these. The Spanish invaded Peru in 1523, and Peru declared independence from Spain in 1821.

"Los Maizales" describes the beauty of the cornfields and suggests that all Peruvians should help with the task of "growing their bread." The words roughly translate into English as follows:

- *Verse One:* The cornfields glow with beauty. The earth is fruitful. The grain is ready to be harvested. The soil of Peru surrounds itself with honor.
- *Verse Two:* After the work and the play of the day are done, come to the farm to help harvest the grain. The soil of Peru surrounds itself with honor.

Try-Its and Other Resources

- Other Resources: *Canciones de Nuestra Cabaña; Sing-Along Songbook and Cassette; Sing Together—A Girl Scout Songbook.*

Setting up
Loom

Diagonal
Stripe

Chevron
Stripe

96

Tips

Finger Weaving. The heavier weights of yarn are probably the easiest for Brownie Girl Scouts' fingers. A pencil or other short stick is needed that is longer than the width of the finished weaving.

Girls can tie the yarns onto the pencil or stick in any color arrangement that pleases them. Tie the tops of the yarns together and fasten the weaving to a table top, chair back, or doorknob to keep it steady. A piece of masking tape across the knot should be fine.

Start by taking the strand on the left and weaving it over and under until it comes out on the right. Always start from the left and always start weaving over the first strand of yarn. The strand used for weaving becomes the last strand on the right side and is woven into the design when the next piece of yarn on the left is woven into the design. Keep the yarns even, taut, and firm, but do not pull the yarns too tight.

Try-Its and Other Resources

- Try-Its: Art to Wear.

Finger Weaving

Finger weaving is one way to use alpaca yarn to make colorful belts. Follow these directions to finger weave your own belt.

You will need about 20 lengths of heavy yarn in one color and 20 lengths of heavy yarn in another color. (More yarn makes a wider belt. Less yarn makes a narrower belt.) You will also need a pencil. Measure your waist and cut the yarn long enough to go around your waist and make a fringe and a knot.

Tie the yarns on the pencil with enough left over for the fringe. Tie the yarns on top together and tie or tape to the back of a chair, a doorknob, a shelf, or something else to keep your weaving in one place.

Start with the piece of yarn (strand) on the left and weave it over and under until it comes out on the right side. Always start on the left. Always follow the over and under pattern. Keep the yarn even and straight, but don't pull it too tightly.

The Inca

If you were an Alita, you might be descended from the Inca. A long, long time ago, around 1500 A.D., a people called the Inca ruled all the lands around Peru. Many different kinds of people who spoke different languages were ruled by the Inca. The Inca built more than 10,000 miles of roads and many big cities made of stone. These cities were so well-made that some of the buildings are still there. Steps were cut into the high mountains so runners could travel faster. Runners would be

Tips

The Inca ruled most of the Andes mountain region and the desert coast of South America in the fifteenth and sixteenth centuries. They were excellent organizers, managers, and road builders. They built large stone cities where elaborate festivals and ceremonies were held and they made huge warehouses to store food and grain. A quipu was the device the Inca used to keep track of information, everything from food, animal herds, number of people living in a city, feast days and holidays, and valuables. Many strings of different sizes and colors were hung from a central cord. A system of knots could be used for counting. A quipu was a bit like a computer. It was used to store information, but it had to be programmed first so that the information could be filed and sorted in an orderly way. Only programmers, called quipucamayocs, who were trained at special schools, could plan how to make the quipu, picking the colors and amounts of yarns to match the information and quantities that needed to be recorded. How could the girls in your troop or group use colored string and knots to help them keep track of information? The colorful activity pages, "You and Computers," found in the Contemporary Issues booklet *Into the World of Today and Tomorrow* would be an

HANDBOOK Page 98

ready to run from city to city to spread news and carry messages. A team of runners could travel over 1,000 miles in one week!

Do you know how far 1,000 miles is? It is approximately the distance between Washington, D.C., and Savannah, Georgia! What city is 1,000 miles away from the place you live? What other cities are 1,000 miles apart?

The weaving that people in Peru do today was also very important to the Inca. Bridges that stretched high in the sky were made of woven rope! Accountants kept track of how much gold or how many potatoes were in a warehouse or how many people lived in a city on complex knotted strings called quipus. Clothing was woven to each person's exact shape. Reed plants were woven to make boats and another kind of reed plant was woven to make roofs for houses. Large woven fishnets were used in the ocean and in lakes. Incan soldiers

knew how to weave and could make their own woven armor. Armor is special heavy clothing worn by soldiers that makes it less likely they will be hurt.

Make a Simple Loom

Here are the directions for making a simple loom. Try weaving a purse that an Alita might carry with her.

You need cardboard, yarn, and a heavy needle for weaving or a long narrow piece of cardboard with a hole cut in one end (shuttle).

Cut two pieces of cardboard the exact size you want your weaving to be when you are done. Glue the two pieces together. Put a piece of tape over the top edge. Place an

even number of pins about one-quarter-inch apart. (You can put your pins closer together if your yarn is thin. Just remember to put your pins in evenly. Use a ruler to help measure.)

You will use two types of threads. Warp threads go up and down (vertically). Weft threads go from side to side (horizontally). Weft threads weave over and under, over and under. Warp threads stay fixed. The diagram shows you how to attach your warp threads.

Put your weft yarn onto your needle or cardboard shuttle. Start weaving over and under at the lower right-hand corner. When you are all the way across, turn the loom over

97

---

excellent supplement to this section as would Math Fun, Numbers and Shapes, and Science in Action Try-Its.

Weaving was very important to the Inca. Inca clothing was never cut, but woven to the exact shape of each person. The designs in the weaving identified the person's family group or a special festival. Everyone learned to weave: girls and boys, soldiers, royalty, and common people. Rope bridges were woven to

span high gorges in the Andes mountains. Some of these rope bridges are still standing. Reeds were even woven to make boats.

Simple Loom. By weaving on both sides of the loom, girls can make a purse. By weaving on one side, girls can make a placemat, potholder, bookmark, or book cover. The size and shape of the cardboard determine the dimensions of the finished weaving.

It is very important that the pins

be placed evenly along the top of the cardboard. Girls can mark the spots for pins by using a ruler. Warp threads (vertical threads) are the foundation of the weaving. They are fastened around the pins, up and around the first pin, going from left to right, carried to the bottom of the loom, and up again on the other side, hooking the thread over the same pin again from left to right. Bring the thread down the back and up the front around the second pin;

down the front and up the back around the same pin. Continue until all the pins are wound. Pin the warp thread about one inch in on the top right.

The woof thread on a needle or shuttle starts at the lower right-hand corner and goes over and under the warp threads. When the last warp thread is reached on one side, turn the loom over and continue weaving on the back until you are back where you started. Weaving continues this

and keep going over and under until you reach the place you started. Keep going around the loom until you are done.

A comb will help you keep your threads straight and your weaving neat.

If you weave on only one side and attach pins on the bottom of your loom, you can weave a placemat, a bookmark, or a wall hanging.

How can you make different designs in your weaving?

Grønsmutte Girl Scouts in Denmark

In Denmark, Brownie Girl Scouts are Grønsmutte, which is a wren—a small bird. They are also known as Brownie Girl Guides. Grønsmutte have the motto:

Vi vil sta sammen.
Vi vil gore vort bedste.

The poem is in Danish, the language spoken by many Grønsmutte. It means, "We will stick together. We will do our best." Grønsmutte speak Danish but also learn English in school. Here are some words in Danish:

Good day	God Dag	(Go-day)
Goodbye	Farvel	(Far-vel)
Thank you	Tak	(Tak)

Do you know how to say these words in another language? If you do, why not teach them to your Brownie Girl Scout troop/group?

---

way on both sides until the project is completed. Try to keep the threads straight. A comb will help keep the woof threads even.

Try-Its and Other Resources

- Try-Its: Art to Wear; Colors and Shapes.

Tips

Denmark is in northern Europe on the Jutland peninsula and has 483 neighboring islands. The island of Greenland is also Danish. Denmark is ruled by a king or queen and a parliament. Denmark is first in the number of books borrowed from public libraries and is one of the leading book-buying nations in the world. The literacy rate is 99 percent.

Brownie Girl Scouts in Denmark are interested in many of the same things as Brownie Girl Scouts in the United States, including camping, service projects, and protecting the environment. Instead of Try-Its, they have Interest badges, one of which is "Children in Other Countries." To receive this badge, they learn songs, games, and recipes from other countries and draw pictures and learn folktales.

"Davs" (pronounced dowse) means "Hi" in Danish. "Vare sa snill" means "please." Danes place great value on being polite when meeting and introducing people, while eating, or when visiting someone's home.

Hans Christian Andersen

Denmark is a country in the north of Europe. It is flat with lakes and woods and farms and ocean beaches. Denmark is famous for beautiful china and furniture, good food, and a very famous writer who loved children—Hans Christian Andersen. You probably know some of his stories—*The Little Mermaid*, *Thumbelina*, *The Ugly Duckling*, *The Wild Swans*, and *The Princess and the Pea*. The Danish people loved his stories so much that they put a statue of the Little Mermaid in the harbor of their capital city, Copenhagen.

The tales that Hans Christian Andersen wrote were usually about a person who has a problem and has to find some way, usually through wonderful adventures, to solve her problem. She might get help from others. She might learn something special. His stories almost always had a happy ending.

Here's room to write your own story:

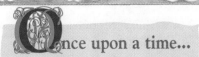 nce upon a time...

Why not try making up some actions to go along with your story? You could mime (actions without words) while someone else reads.

Things Danish Brownie Girl Scouts Like to Do

Danish Brownie Girl Scouts like to play games, just like you. If you were a Danish Brownie Girl Scout, you might play these games.

"Good Morning, Good Afternoon, Good Evening"

With your friends, make a circle. You run around the outside of the circle and tap one girl on the back as you pass. She runs the opposite way around the circle. When you meet, you each give the Brownie Girl Scout salute and say "Good Morning." Keep running until you meet again, give the salute and say "Good Afternoon." Run around one more time, stop, shake hands, say "Good Evening," and then run to the empty place on the circle.

Tips

Girls can write or draw their own story, create a play or skit, develop a radio play with a tape recorder or a "TV show" with a video camera.

Try-Its and Other Resources

- Try-Its: Creative Composing; People of the World.
- Other Resources: *Games for Girl Scouts* has a chapter on active games for indoors and outdoors. This Danish game— "The Ocean Is Stormy"—is included in that book.

You need: string or chalk to mark circles.

How to play: Girls form pairs. Every pair except one stands within its own small circle, which is marked on the floor or the ground. Each pair, with the exception of the odd pair, chooses the name of a fish. The odd pair are the whales and walk about the room calling out the names of fishes. When a pair's name is called, the girls leave their circle and walk behind the whales. After all the names have been called or after the whales have called all the names they can remember, the whales cry, "The ocean is stormy." The whales and all the fish walking behind rush to stand within one of the small

Fruit Salad

Sit on chairs in a circle. The apple-woman stands in the middle. She does not have a chair. Everyone else has the name of a fruit (orange, banana, pineapple, etc.) If the apple-woman yells "Oranges," all the oranges change places and the apple-woman tries to find a chair. If the apple-woman calls "Fruit Salad!" everyone gets up and finds a new place to sit.

Make a Danish Open-Faced Sandwich

Playing a game called "Fruit Salad" could make a Danish Brownie Girl Scout think of food. One of her favorites would be open-faced sandwiches. They are easy to make and so good to eat. Why not try some?

You will need:

• Thin slices of buttered bread (or margarine)
• Toppings:
   Thin slices of Danish cheese
   Thin slices of ham or chicken
   Sardines or herring
   Slices of hard-boiled egg
• Garnish (makes the sandwich look nice):
   Small slices/pieces of cucumber, tomato, lemon, radish, parsley, watercress, green pepper, dill

Your sandwich will have three parts: a slice of buttered bread, a topping, and a garnish. Mix and match to make many different kinds of sandwiches. Just remember not to put a piece of bread on top!

100

Games from Around the World

Not only do children in Denmark love to play games, but children all around the world love to play games, too. Many of the games that you play are played in other countries.

Rabbit Without a House (Brazil)

This Brazilian game is best when you have at least 11 people.

1. Pick someone to be "it" (the rabbit without a house) and someone to be the caller.

2. Divide the others into groups of three.

3. Each group makes a rabbit in a house by two girls holding hands (the house) and one girl (a rabbit) standing inside.

---

circles. Two girls left without a circle become the new whales.

Variation: When the whales cry "The ocean is stormy!" all fish must find a circle, but no fish should return to the same partner or circle as before.

Open-Faced Sandwiches. Open-faced sandwiches are simple for girls to make. *World Games and Recipes* and *The Wide World of Girl Guiding and Girl Scouting* also contain international recipes. You might want to find some simple recipes from Ghana, Peru, and Thailand for girls to try.

Games from Around the World. Find a way to adapt the games for girls who may have a physical disability that prevents them from participating in the game as written. Girls can often figure out how to adapt the game so that everyone is included. You can offer alternative activities so that all girls have a choice of quiet or active activities, and girls who may be physically unable to participate are not the only

4. The caller yells out "Find a house" and all the rabbits, including the one without a house, have to run to find another house.

5. The rabbit left without a house becomes it.

Jan-ken-pon (Japan)

You'll need two players.

1. Two players face each other with their hands behind them.

2. Together, they say "jan-ken-pon." On "pon," both bring a hand forward to stand for a stone (a fist), paper (flat hand), or scissors (V-shape with the index finger and middle finger).

3. Stone beats scissors because it can break them. Scissors beat paper because they can cut it. Paper beats stone because it can wrap up the stone.

4. A player gets a point each

time her hand beats the other's. The first player who gets seven points wins.

Mr. Bear (Sweden)

You'll need at least three people, a place for "home," and the bear's den.

1. One person is Mr. Bear. He is trying to sleep in his den.

2. The other players sneak up to Mr. Bear and whisper, "Mr. Bear, are you awake?"

3. Mr. Bear pretends not to hear them. Then the players yell, "MR. BEAR, ARE YOU AWAKE?" This makes Mr. Bear furious! He chases them all and tries to catch them before they reach home, which is the safe place.

4. Everyone tagged by the bear before reaching home becomes Mr. Bear's cubs. They go back to the den with Mr. Bear.

5. When the remaining players come back to wake up Mr. Bear again, the cubs help Mr. Bear catch them.

6. When everyone has been caught, Mr. Bear picks someone else to take his place.

Hawk and Hens (Zimbabwe)

You'll need at least four people and two safety zones.

1. One person is the hawk.

2. All the other players are hens.

3. The hawk stands between the safety zones and tries to catch the hens as they run back and forth from one safety zone to the other.

4. When a hen is caught, she sits on the side and watches the game.

5. The last hen to be caught by the hawk becomes the next hawk.

101

ones left out (or always set up as the timekeeper or judge).

Jan-ken-pon is a sitting game, and *Games for Girl Scouts* includes many quiet games that could be substituted for some of the more active ones.

Try-Its and Other Resources

- Try-Its: Around the World; Dancercize; My Body; People of the World; Play.

Art from Around the World

Just as you enjoy creating things, children all over the world enjoy drawing and painting, singing and dancing. You have already learned a little about art in Ghana, Thailand, Peru, and Denmark. The Brownie Girl Scout Try-Its on pages 166–277 have more kinds of artwork for you to try. Here are some more.

Clay Birds from Mexico

You will need some self-hardening clay, or clay that can be hardened in a low-temperature oven overnight.

People in Mexico have made clay figures for many centuries. One of the most popular figures is a clay bird. Other animal shapes are also made.

Try making your own animal shapes. Once the clay has hardened, try painting designs on the clay with acrylic paints or poster paints. Once the paint is dry, you can protect your clay with a special coating made for clay. An adult will have to help you with this step.

Greek Mosaics

In ancient Greece, tiny bits of colored glass and stone were cut and put into cement. Mosaics were often used to decorate the floors and walls of a home. Later, the art of making mosaics spread all around the world.

You will need different colors of construction paper and black or dark blue construction paper for the background.

With a ruler and a pencil, put a mark every half-inch along the short side of the colored construction paper. Then, do the same on the long side. Draw the lines. You will have one-half-inch squares. Cut them out. Keep all the squares of the same color in a dish or bowl.

Now, choose your paper tiles to make your mosaic and paste them on the dark paper in a design.

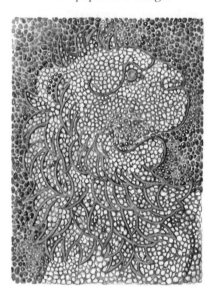

102

Tips

The clay birds, mosaics, and tie-dyeing are only a sample of the types of art activities that are derived from various cultures. Girls may be able to teach or show samples of art or crafts that are indicative of their own ethnic/cultural groups. In some cultures paper is cut and folded into intricate designs. In many cultures in Asia, Africa, and North America, masks are made. Puppets are made in many countries. Your local school or public library will have books about art projects from other cultures.

:

Tie-Dyeing

Tie-dyeing is a way of making cloth that has many colors. Tie-dyeing is done in many countries in South America, India, and China. It is also very common in the countries in West Africa, like Liberia, Senegal, Sierra Leone, and the Ivory Coast.

To tie-dye, you will need some plain white cotton cloth, different colors of fabric dye, some strong rubber bands, and basins of water or a sink for dyeing.

Tie the rubber bands around the cloth in different ways. You can dip the cloth in one color, undo the rubber bands, retie them in new places, and then dip the cloth again. Make sure the cloth is dry before you untie it. You may want to try different designs on small pieces of cloth first.

Do not take the cloth out of the dye until it is a little darker than the color you want it to be when it is dry. Rinse out the extra dye under running water or in a big basin. Change the water between rinses. Again, make sure the cloth is dry before you untie it.

To make a wall hanging, iron the cloth and then glue it to a long stick.

1.

Tie rubber bands or string around cloth in different ways.

2.

Dip the cloth into a pail of dye.

3.

Rinse the cloth twice in cold water and hang it up to dry.

4.

Make sure the cloth is dry before you untie it.

103

Storytelling

Almost every country has stories. Stories are often a way to pass along information or to entertain a group of people. Families have been sharing stories long before there was television or electricity. In West Africa, storytellers were called griots and passed down family histories from one generation to the next. Many American Indian groups have stories and folk tales that teach lessons and entertain. A famous character in some of the American Indian stories from the West is Coyote.

Coyote and the Moon

It was nighttime and Coyote was hungry. "I haven't eaten all day. What I would really like is a nice round corncake. I don't want to cook one. Maybe I can very quietly find a family cooking their dinner and quickly grab a cake!"

Tips

Most girls love telling and hearing stories. The coyote is a character that appears in Navaho and some other American Indian folklore. He is often tricky and sometimes lazy.

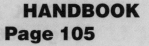

As you can see, Coyote was very lazy and not very nice at all.

Looking ahead, he saw a family sitting near their fire. They were just on the other side of the lake. He thought, "Good, I can almost taste that cake now."

He went along the side of the lake very slowly. He looked down, and there, in the lake, he saw a big, round shiny corn cake. "What luck!" he thought. "Those people left their corncake in the lake. I'll just help myself now."

So, he reached down for the corncake, but as he touched the water, the cake broke into many pieces and then disappeared. He tried again and again and the same thing happened. He sat back, very angry and very hungry, and looked up.

"Oh, no," he said. "How did that corncake get in the sky? Maybe the family wanted to keep it safe from me. Now I am really hungry." And he put his head back and cried.

That is why when you sometimes hear the Coyote crying at the moon, you know it's because he still wants his corncake!

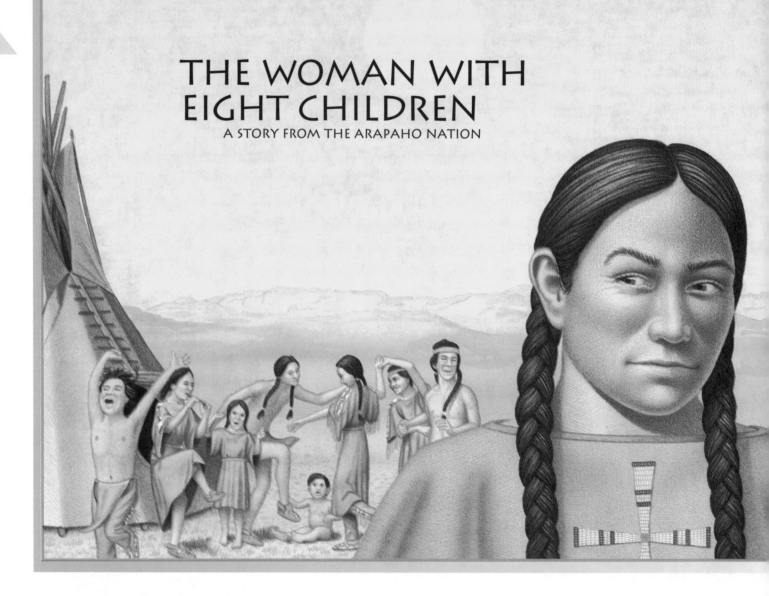

THE WOMAN WITH EIGHT CHILDREN
A STORY FROM THE ARAPAHO NATION

Tips

Many stories, including the one from the Arapaho Nation, are told to explain natural phenomena. This one explains how the Little Dipper was formed. Girls can invent their own stories that explain why things happen or why mountains or the moon or stars were formed. Girls may also be able to share stories from their own cultural traditions. A professional storyteller would be an excellent guest speaker. Your local library or school may be able to recommend someone.

"I'll hit you with my broom if you don't stop dancing," she shouted.

Whoosh! Up into the beautiful night sky rose the children. The woman tried to catch them, but she could only touch the foot of one boy with her broom.

The boy fell back to earth, but when he hit the ground he was turned into a tree! His arms and legs became tree branches and his fingers became the twigs.

Many, many years ago, in a large forest, a woman lived with her eight children. The children loved to sing and dance all day long, never stopping for a minute except to eat.

Well, the woman got angrier and angrier that all the children would do is dance and sing and never help her with cooking or cleaning or getting wood for the fire. So one day, when they were dancing in a circle, laughing and singing, she raised her broom and shook it at them.

The other children rose higher and higher, still laughing and dancing until they formed a shape like this in the night sky.

You may see them on a starry night, twinkling as they dance and sing.

More About Storytelling

Many stories were used to explain the things that happen in nature, like thunder and lightning, big winds, or earthquakes. Can you make up a story about nature?

Many communities have someone who is good at telling stories. Find out if she or he can come to a troop meeting.

Try telling some stories yourself. Telling stories is a little different than writing stories. Try to choose words and actions that are easy to see or easy to act out. Why not have a storytelling hour at home or at a meeting?

More About People

Now you know a lot more about different kinds of people. People are the same in many ways. Everyone needs food and water and a place to live. Most people want to love somebody else and want other people to love them. They also want to feel good about themselves and be the best people that they can be.

People are also very different. Your family background, your religion, your race, your culture, the place you live, your friends, and many, many other things make you unique. Unique means different from everybody else. Differences among people are what make the world an interesting place. When different people with different ideas get together, they discover better ideas and better ways to do things. There is no "right" way to live, look, talk, dress, eat, or act.

Just as the world contains many different types of people, so does the United States. In the chapter "Family, Friends, and Neighbors," you learned a little more about the people in your community. What did you find out? Even if you did not find so many different types of

108

Tips

The activities in this section focus on valuing differences, especially the different people who live within the United States and their traditions, customs, and culture. Valuing the differences among people is more appropriate than valuing the idea that "all people are the same," which really isn't true. Valuing the diversity of people shows respect for individual, cultural, ethnic, and racial uniqueness and contributions.

The information and activities in the *Valuing Differences* Contemporary Issues booklet would be a great resource to use when working with girls on this section. The activities below are from this booklet:

Ask girls to think of situations in which they or someone they knew was treated unfairly or not allowed to be part of the group. Choose one or two of these situations to role-play. Freeze the role-playing at a point where girls can develop a new ending that is positive. Discuss the different ways these situations could end. What can the girls do to help treat people fairly?

people in your neighborhood or community, you will find many different types of people in the United States. As you grow older, you may go to school in a new place or get a job in another place or marry someone who lives in another part of the country. You will meet many people different from you.

The United States of America

Your country, the United States of America, is special. It is a country of American Indians, Inuits and Aleuts from Alaska, Hawaiians from Hawaii, and other people who come from all parts of the world and bring their individual ways with them. The United States is like a mosaic made up of many different little pieces that come together to make a beautiful picture.

United States of America Montage

To make a montage of the United States of America, you will need to find pictures and drawings that show the different parts of the country. Look for pictures of mountains, forests, lakes, rivers, and deserts. Also look for pictures and drawings that show the many people who live in the United States. Make sure the drawings and pictures you find show how people really look and live. Sometimes, the pictures in books can be untrue.

Add your own drawings and words to show how we all live in the United States of America. You will also need poster paper, scissors, and glue.

1. Decide where to put the pictures on the poster.
2. Glue everything in place.
3. Show your montage to your friends.

People Different from You

When someone doesn't know a lot about people who are different from him, he may get afraid or confused and may even dislike these other people. Isn't it silly not to like someone you don't even know? This bad feeling is called prejudice. People are not born with prejudice. But often people learn to be prejudiced as they grow up.

You can be a prejudice fighter.

109

Girls can get very caught up in a role-playing "persona." You may need to stop or freeze a role-playing exercise that is getting too intense or out-of-hand. Also, role-playing is different from a skit or play in that role-playing is a problem-solving technique while a skit is entertainment.

Girls can think of a time that they were called a name. How did they feel? What did they do about it? Have they ever called someone else a name? Why? How did they feel afterwards? Almost everyone has participated in some form of name-calling at some time. What are some positive ways to express feelings?

If a girl utters an ethnic or racial slur during the discussion, it is extremely important to emphasize that these words are highly inappropriate and will not be tolerated in a Girl Scout troop or group.

Remember the Girl Scout Promise and Law. You promise to be a sister to every Girl Scout and to show respect for yourself and others through your words and actions. Can you think of ways you can show respect for others through your words and actions? What would you do if:

- You heard a friend make a joke about people different from herself?
- Your classmate at school called someone bad names because of the way she looked?

- Someone told you that you couldn't do something you wanted to do because you are a girl?
- You saw a group of kids making fun of someone wearing clothes in an old style?

Think of some times you heard about people being treated unfairly. What could you do to be fair? Talk about how you can really get to know someone. How can you find out more about other people?

110

Leadership in Girl Scouting and Beyond

"I'm so bored! I wish there were more to do around here."

"Kathi, if you say that one more time," Reema threatened, "I'm going home! You know what, I *am* going home. All afternoon you've been no fun at all. I wanted to watch a video. I wanted to play with dolls. I wanted to play soccer. Every time, you said you didn't feel like it. Now you're bored. Forget it—I'm going home!"

Ruth looked at both of them. "We could go to the library and get some new books . . ."

"Who wants to read all day?" Kathi said.

Brownie Girl Scouts Make a Difference

111

Tips

The activities in this chapter encourage the building of leadership skills within and outside of Girl Scouting. You might want to start the chapter by asking girls to describe or draw a "leader." What type of person is a leader (include Brownie Girl Scout leaders!). Encourage girls to think of some famous women leaders and to think of the various ways one can be a leader. The girls in the introductory story demonstrate different leadership styles. What are some of the different styles exhibited by the girls in your troop or group?

"You don't sound very nice," Mie looked at Kathi. "It's a good idea. It's better than sitting around here. Let's go."

So, they went, though Kathi made a face and kicked at everything she passed all the way to the library.

Ruth ran up the steps. As the other girls followed her down the hallway to the children's books area, they heard all this noise coming from a group of girls in one of the meeting rooms.

Ruth poked her head in the door. The other three piled up behind her and peeked in. They saw all these girls around a table—some kneeling, some sitting, some standing, some hopping up and down—and all were helping a woman fill in a big poster.

"What do you think they're doing?" Reema asked.

"I don't know, but they look like they're having a lot of fun," Ruth said.

Kathi said, "I know who they are—they're Brownie Girl Scouts. Remember, there was a poster up at school in September. I didn't know that they did stuff like this."

"There's Zora and Ashley—they're in the class across the hall from us." Reema looked at the others and said, "I'm waiting until they're done and I'm going to talk to that lady in the front. I want to learn more about what they're doing."

"I spend so much time here," Ruth said. "We all do. And, I hate looking at dirt and garbage everywhere and we should help make this place better."

"What about you, Kathi? Will you stay?" Mie asked.

"All right. I don't want to walk home all by myself," she answered.

The lady was a Brownie Girl

112

Ask girls if they ever feel bored. What are some positive things they can do to stop feeling bored? Why not plan an anti-boredom day or month with lots of different activities?

Service has always been important in Girl Scouting. How do the Girl Scout Promise and Law encourage girls to perform service? What are some reasons why people should help other people? Altruism and generosity can be abstract concepts for girls to understand, as can the idea of doing something for someone or a community without receiving a tangible reward. You might want to find out about people in your community who volunteer or perform service and present them as examples. One or two as guest speakers might be a good way to introduce this concept. Girls can share times when they or someone they knew helped others.

Scout leader. Her name was Mrs. DeAngelo.

"What were all of you doing?" Mie asked. "It looked exciting."

Mrs. DeAngelo told them a little bit about how Brownie Girl Scouts make plans. She also told them about the kinds of service projects Brownie Girl Scouts do. The Brownie Girl

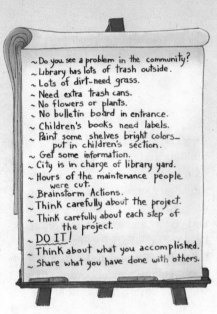

~ Do you see a problem in the community?
~ Library has lots of trash outside.
~ Lots of dirt-need grass.
~ Need extra trash cans.
~ No flowers or plants.
~ No bulletin board in entrance.
~ Children's books need labels.
~ Paint some shelves bright colors—put in children's section.
~ Get some information.
~ City is in charge of library yard.
~ Hours of the maintenance people were cut.
~ Brainstorm Actions.
~ Think carefully about the project.
~ Think carefully about each step of the project.
~ DO IT!
~ Think about what you accomplished.
~ Share what you have done with others.

Scouts in this troop had thought of many different problems in the community. They knew about people who were hungry and they had talked about collecting canned food and other ways to help hungry people. They knew that another Brownie Girl Scout troop was working on a community garden. They also saw that a local playground needed to be repaired, but after the girls had talked about all the different things they saw that their community needed, they decided to help the library where they had their meetings. They knew that lots of children loved using the library. Many older people spent the day there. And, so the Brownie Girl Scouts had thought of an Action Plan, a way to design a service project.

Mrs. DeAngelo also told them about all the other things that Brownie Girl Scouts do. They go on trips, sing songs, play special games, even do lots of different activities to earn patches called Try-Its, but, be-

ing a Girl Scout means doing service for your community and for other people.

"Ruth, you look funny with dirt on your nose!" Kathi was laughing as she put another coat of green paint on the trash can.

"Maybe, but you have paint in your hair!" Ruth put some more dirt around the roots of the flower and looked at Kathi. "You don't say you're bored so much anymore."

"That's right," Reema said. "I haven't heard you say you're bored in a long time."

"That's because I'm not!" Kathi said. "I'm glad we're doing this service project for the library and I like all the stuff that Brownie Girl Scouts do. Becoming a Brownie Girl

113

Make an Action Plan poster—a blank one is on handbook pages 116–117—and share it with girls when you reach that point in the story. You could brainstorm some community problems and solutions then, or wait until reaching the activities on pages 116–117.

After the part in the story where Mrs. DeAngelo has finished describing the work of Brownie Girl Scouts, ask the girls if there is anything else

they can share about being a Brownie Girl Scout with Kathi, Reema, Ruth, and Mie. What do they think are the very best things about being a Brownie Girl Scout?

Try-Its and Other Resources

- Try-Its: Creative Composing; Caring and Sharing; Girl Scout Ways.
Other Resources: *Right to Read*.

Scout was a good idea! I guess I said I was bored too much. I was kind of rude to you. But, we weren't doing things like this before. I promise you won't hear me say it again—cross my heart!"

"Okay," Ruth said, "You want to stop working on this project and go to my house and watch TV?"

 114

"No way," Kathi said. "We have lots more to do and TV would be too bor . . . . Ooops, sorry."

They were laughing so hard that they almost couldn't see how great the library looked. A new bulletin board hung in the entrance with a sign, "What's Going On?" along the top of it. Pink and red flowers

marched all along the border of the building and two new trash cans painted bright green stood next to the library steps. Through the window, shelves painted blue and red and yellow and green held children's books. The library looked great and the girls felt proud and bursting with good feelings inside, because they were the ones who had done the work.

Getting Involved in Brownie Girl Scouts

When you became a Brownie Girl Scout, you learned the Girl Scout Promise. You promised to serve your country and to help people at all times. The girls in the story were making their promise come true. They were helping their community. All the people who used the library or even walked past the library would feel happier. When people work together in a community, they make life better for everyone. A service project is a task or plan for helping other people, improving the community, or improving the world beyond the community.

Citizenship

A citizen is a person who lives in a certain country and who has the special rights that country gives, such as voting, being protected by

that country's army, and being able to live and work freely. You can also say that you are a citizen of a city or state or town. Good citizens are people who are active. They vote and they help their communities. If they see something wrong, they try to fix it. In what ways were the Brownie Girl Scouts in the story good citizens? Can you think of some things that your community needs?

_____

_____

_____

_____

_____

_____

_____

_____

_____

_____

_____

_____

Doing a service project is one way to be a good citizen and to live by the Girl Scout Promise and Law. Service can be small. Reminding your friends not to litter is service. Recycling your aluminum cans and newspapers is service. Helping someone carry their packages home from the store is service. Service is catching! When you start doing things for other people, they often start doing things for others, too! If you keep your school playground clean, other kids won't be so quick to make it messy.

115

Tips

The concept of citizenship (that is, special rights to live and work freely) may be difficult for some girls to understand. You might want to highlight the idea that "good" citizenship is often "active" citizenship, and girls can think of ways that they can be active citizens. Page through magazines with girls to find pictures of people displaying active citizen-ship. Highlight articles from the local newspaper that demonstrate active citizenship.

Note: You may have girls who are not citizens of the United States or whose parents and relatives are not citizens. Include people who live in the community or who help in and contribute to the community in your discussion, regardless of whether or not they are citizens of this country.

Ask girls to close their eyes and think about services they provide for others. How is service catching? Can they think of a time when they saw this happen?

Try-Its and Other Resources

- Try-Its: Caring and Sharing; Citizen Near and Far; People of the World.
- Other Resources: _Earth Matters_.

Action Plans

Do you remember the Action Plan from the story?

Do you remember the steps to doing a service project?

Here are the steps written on a chart. You can copy the chart onto your own paper when you are making plans or if you are doing more projects. You can also try doing a mini-service project at home. What can you do for your family? What can be done in your home? Take a look around and see what you can do!

116

Name of Project _____

What problems do you see in your neighborhood or community? Try these steps:

1. Name the problem. Then get some information. _____
_____

2. Talk about actions and think of solutions.
_____
_____
_____
_____

3. Pick one that will work best.
_____

4. Decide how to do the project.
   a. Think carefully about the project.
   _____

   b. What will be done?
   _____

Tips

Action Plans: You may want to make photocopies or write out the steps on separate pages so that the chart included in the handbook can be used again. Welcome all ideas that girls offer. Using Step 4, help girls analyze their project ideas. This step should assist girls in weeding out ideas that have a prohibitive cost or are too complex.

You may want to contact your local Girl Scout council representative to see if other troops or groups in your area are working on a service project or would be interested in doing a service project with your troop or group. Some suggestions:

1. Planting flower or vegetable gardens.

2. Planting trees.

3. Adopting a "grandmother" as an ongoing project and visiting and running errands for her.

4. Finding and cleaning used toys and donating them to a homeless or battered women's shelter.

5. Assembling baskets of basic household supplies—soap, sponges, paper towels, etc.—in a bucket or laundry basket for emergency shelters or family assistance projects.

The steps in creating an action plan can also be applied to projects outside of Girl Scouting—school and home—and to decision-making. While making a decision may not require all of the steps of an action plan, the skills learned are transferable. Girls can think of times they needed to make a decision and discuss how these steps helped them.

More to Try: Making Up Your Mind—You have many choices to make every day. Some are easy ones—should I brush my teeth before I wash my face or after? Some are harder ones—should I take pi-

c. Will it cost money?

d. When will it be done?

e. Is it too hard to do? Can we divide the project into smaller parts?

f. Who will help us? Can we get other people in the community to help?

g. How much time will we need?

5. Do it!

6. Think about what we accomplished.

7. Share what we did with others.

When you plan a project, you are setting a goal. A goal is something you want to achieve. You can set a personal goal—a goal for yourself—or you can set group goals. Many times in Brownie Girl Scouts you will set group goals. You may want to set goals to do service projects or citizenship tasks. As you grow, you will also set many personal goals. Learning how to roller-skate could be a goal. Keeping your room cleaner is a goal. Getting along better with your younger sister is also a goal. In many countries people set goals for themselves at the beginning of the year. These goals are called New Year's Resolutions. Lots of times these resolutions are too difficult to do, like lose lots of weight very quickly or get up one hour early every day and run five miles. Then, the resolutions are broken because they were too hard to do in the first place.

117

ano lessons or acrobatics on Mondays? Some are very hard—should I tell my mother that I saw my older sister smoking a cigarette?

Try following these steps to help make up your mind:

1. Write down the question.

2. Think of all the good and bad points.

3. Decide which is the best thing to do.

4. Do it!

Try-Its and Other Resources

- Other Resources: *Earth Matters*; *Developing Health and Fitness*.

Tips

Goal setting is similar to making an action plan except that you would usually first decide on a goal and then make an action plan to achieve that goal. You might want to ask the girls what kinds of goals they set for themselves—learning how to do something? Doing something faster or better? You might also want to dis-

Have you ever made a resolution that was too hard to keep?

When you want to make goals that you can do, you can make a plan. First, decide on your goal. Maybe you want to learn how to

118

roller-skate. What would you do first? Maybe you would borrow some roller skates. Maybe you would buy some roller skates. Maybe you would talk to some people who roller-skate well.

What do you think you would do next?

Some goals are easier to achieve than others. "I will do better on my next spelling test" may mean you will study a little harder one night and not watch television. Some goals are easier for some people to do than for other people. Some people would find it easy to read one book a week. Other people may find that too hard to do. Each person has to set her own goals.

What goal would you like to achieve?

_____

_____

_____

What steps can you think of that will help you reach this goal? Make sure you write a time for each step to be completed.

_____

_____

_____

_____

How about a Brownie Girl Scout goal? What goal would you like to achieve in Brownie Girl Scouts this year?

_____

_____

_____

_____

cuss how people sometimes set goals that are too difficult to achieve. Sometimes big goals need to be broken into smaller goals. Girls can use the spaces in the handbook to record their goals or use a separate piece of paper for each year or set of goals. Girls can write in the dates by which they would like to accomplish a given goal. Girls can choose to keep their goals private or share them with family members or friends.

Try-Its and Other Resources

- Try-Its: Careers.
- Other Resources: *Into The World of Today and Tomorrow.*

Leadership and Troop Government

Brownie Girl Scouts have many chances to be leaders. Taking part in a service project is a good opportunity to be a leader. You can contribute good ideas for doing the project. That is one kind of leadership. You can help people decide what they want to do. That's another kind of leadership. You can help people work together and cooperate. That's also leadership. You may be in charge of a group of girls—and that is leadership, too. There are many different ways to be a leader. Can you think of some others?

_____

_____

_____

Brownie Girl Scout Ring

Round and round and round
  about
Take the hand of a Brownie
  Girl Scout!
Here we all are—
In a Brownie Girl Scout Ring—
Ready for almost anything!

In your Brownie Girl Scout troop or group, you may have a Brownie Girl Scout Ring. If your troop has lots of girls, or if you need to meet in smaller groups, you may also have circles. Both are ways to make plans and get things done in Girl Scouts. Both are ways that you can be a leader. A leader helps

119

Tips

Ask girls to complete the sentences:
  "A leader is a person who . . ."
  "I am a leader when I . . ."
  Girls can make a collage that shows the many different ways to be a leader or they can create a skit, puppet play, or group poem.
  The Brownie Girl Scout Ring is the basic method of troop government for this age level. Brownie circles are smaller-size groups that meet to plan or carry out troop business.

other people decide and make plans—and do what the group has planned.

In a Brownie Girl Scout Ring, all the girls in the troop or group sit in a circle and talk about what they would like to do. Girls should take turns being the Brownie Girl Scout Ring "leader." The leader makes

Talking Signal

120

sure that everyone gets a chance to speak, that no one person does most of the talking, and that the discussion is orderly. Sometimes your troop leader may need to help you in the beginning, when you are first learning how to make plans in a Brownie Girl Scout Ring.

The "talking signal" is a good way to show that you want to say something when you are meeting in a Brownie Girl Scout Ring. If you make this sign, the leader knows who wants to say something. It's a lot easier than shouting!

When you are making plans in a Brownie Girl Scout Ring, you may need to make notes about your plans and you may need to collect and keep track of money. The girl who writes notes can be called a recorder or a secretary, and the girl who keeps track of money can be called a treasurer or money recorder. Sometimes, your troop leader may do these jobs in the beginning and give you a chance to practice them before you take turns doing them.

Brownie Girl Scout Circles

In Brownie Girl Scout circles, the troop or group is divided into small groups with five to eight girls in each circle. Circles are a lot like the patrols that older Girl Scouts have. Some circles last a long time and some a short time. Sometimes, you are a part of a circle that is doing a special job. For example, you may be a part of a circle that is responsible for making posters to advertise a recycled toy collection day. When this job is finished, the circle no longer meets. A circle may have a leader. Girls take turns being the leader.

A circle leader may have special duties. She may take attendance. She may make sure everyone in the group has her chance to speak. She may keep track of the kaper chart and be sure the group does the jobs they have been assigned. She may get something special to wear to show that she is the circle leader.

Troop government is an ongoing, developing process. Girls need a lot of opportunities to practice making decisions. Older Brownie Girl Scouts can be excellent role models, but on the other hand they should not have all the "officer" or leader positions. Rotate jobs among the girls in the troop or group. More information on troop government is on pages 23–24 in Part I of this book. It may take a lot of effort and time before the Brownie Ring is running smoothly. In some cases it may never work perfectly, but it is still one of the best means for girls to develop and grow and be enthusiastic about the activities they have planned in Brownie Girl Scouts.

Leadership and Troop Money

You are also a leader when you make plans to earn money and spend money in your Brownie Girl Scout troop. Your Brownie Girl Scout troop or group gets money for activities in different ways—troop dues and money-earning projects like selling Girl Scout cookies. Sometimes you need more money because you want to do a special activity or trip. Then you need to earn some extra money. Decide how much money you will need. Make a plan. What if you want to go to the zoo? How will you get there and how much will it cost? Do you need to pay to get in? Will you need to buy lunch? Do you need money for extras, like souvenirs? Do you need to pay for people to come with you?

How does the treasurer keep track of the troop money? Here is a budget chart.

Date	Activity/Income	Add	Subtract	Sum

Here are some ideas for projects that will help you earn money. Can you think of some more?

- Try making printed notecards, stationery, and wrapping paper.
- Try washing cars.
- Try selling homegrown plants in decorated pots.
- Try fixing some old toys and selling them.
- Try making puppets, yarn dolls, knot bracelets, or jigsaw puzzles and selling them.
- Try baking loaves of bread and selling them.

- Try learning how to do some simple home repairs and offering to do them for your neighbors.
- Try making some of the crafts you learned about in the chapter "People Near and Far," and selling them.

Your leader can help you put your ideas into action. You might come up with many ideas. Decide on one as a group. Think of something that would be fun to do. You want to make money and have fun at the same time.

121

Tips

Before undertaking any troop money-earning ventures, review the program standards, guidelines, and activity checkpoints in *Safety-Wise*. More information is given on pages 32–34 in Part I of this book. You also need to be aware of the financial situations of the girls in the troop or group, as some girls may have difficulty contributing to trips and outings. Earning the money for these opportunities is often the fairest way to finance them.

You can do a lot of different types of activities with "play money" or with board games that use play money. Girls can practice balancing the troop budget. You might take them on an imaginary grocery shopping expedition or set up a banking activity. You might want to do the activities on money on handbook pages 131–132 in "How and Why?" either before or after the section on leadership and troop money.

Try-Its and Other Resources

- Try-Its: Math Fun; Numbers and Shapes.
- Other Resources: *Into The World of Today and Tomorrow*.

Girl Scout Cookies

Brownie Girl Scouts may decide to work on the Girl Scout cookie sale. You want to contribute to the activities of the group. Decide what part you can do best. You can sell cookies. Maybe you will want to sell cookies and help organize the money and the boxes. Maybe you will just help organize. All the girls and the leader can talk about what each person can do to help the troop.

Here are some ways to be a good salesperson:

* Learn about the cookies or whatever you are selling. How are the cookies special?
* Be able to tell the customer, the person who is buying, what you will do with the money. What special things do Girl Scouts do?
* Be able to tell the customer how much money she needs to pay, when you need to collect the money, and when she will get her cookies or other products.
* Make sure you give your customers the cookies and products on the day you promised.
* Always say thank you, even if a person decides not to buy anything. You are representing Girl Scouts and she'll remember that you had good manners.
* Practice what you will say and do before you see your

first customer. Practice will make you a better salesperson.

* Be sure to know all the ways to be safe when you are selling things or doing other money-earning projects.
* After your group has earned money, make a report on how much money you have earned and what you will do with it.

 Tips

Page 32 in Part I of this book contains information on selling cookies and other products. *Safety-Wise* has the standards, guidelines, and activity checkpoints that must be followed before the troop or group works on a cookie or product sale. Selling cookies is a program activity, and the process teaches useful skills. Sometimes, girls at this age level can get quite competitive as to who sells the most cookies. You will want to encourage all the girls in your troop or group to participate in some way. Emphasize the skills—selling, working with others, mathematics, goal setting, communications—rather than the quantity sold.

Before setting out to sell cookies, role-play some situations the girls may encounter.

Leadership and Group Planning

Leaders have special responsibilities. They do not always get to do what they want. They have to think about the members of the group. They have to find out the different ideas of the people in the group. They also have to encourage everyone to cooperate and to respect each other. They have to make sure that each person has a part in the activities. Sometimes that means letting other people do the things you wanted to do. Often it means letting other girls have the chance to be a leader.

In a Brownie Girl Scout Ring or in circles, you can use these four steps for planning things in a group. You can plan what service project you would like to do, what place you would like to visit, or which Try-It you would like to earn.

These steps will help you plan:

1. *Share your idea with others.* Speak up and let people know what you think. If you feel shy, practice what you want to say in your mind before you say it. Then, say it. Remember, there are often no "right" ideas—just a new way of looking at the same thing.

2. *Listen to others.* Listening to others is an important part of planning. Other people's ideas often help you think of some good ideas.

3. *Decide what you want to do as a group.* When you make group decisions, you should make sure that each person who wants to speak gets a chance and that only one person speaks at a time. No one should say anything that hurts someone's feelings. No one should keep talking too long. Everyone should have a say in the final decision.

4. *Look at the Action Plan chart on page 116.* Follow these steps. Having fun is also important when planning a project. Sometimes, things may not go the way you planned. Don't be upset if things aren't perfect. You can still learn a lot and still have fun.

Practice making decisions in a group. Practice deciding what steps you would need to plan.

123

Tips

This section is printed like an agenda book to emphasize the importance of group planning. The steps shown are similar to the action plan and to goal setting. An action plan is to carry out a project; goal setting is deciding what is a personal or group goal; group planning steps encourage communication among the girls in their circles and the Brownie Ring. Girls often welcome a structure that helps them when they work in groups. Encourage younger Brownie Girl Scouts to participate and speak up, and encourage all the girls to follow the "rules" listed on this page—such as no one says anything hurtful, only one person speaks at a time. Girls could create a troop or group behavior chart with which they all agree. The chart could be flexible so that as situations arise, more could be added or some could be taken away or changed.

What If . . .

- Your group decided to make the world more peaceful?
- Your group decided to help people get along better with each other?
- Your group decided to help others to have fun?
- Your group decided to help stop pollution?
- Your group decided to help every person have a place to live?
- Your group decided to stop all drug abuse?

These might seem to be very big things. But, thinking about what you can do and what your group can do may help make these very big things smaller. Each person has a lot of power to make things happen and to change things. Not only adults change things; kids can, too! What can you do to make things better for all the people who share this world with you? Where can you start? Look for the leader inside of you. She is there just waiting for you to give her a chance to make good things happen.

I am a leader because I _____

I am a leader because I _____

I am a leader because I _____

I am a leader because I _____

I am a leader because I _____

124

Tips

Girls can list one or two leadership qualities they would like to develop and enlist "peer support," pairing up with someone who identified the desired skill as a strength. Pairs or groups of girls could work together on developing leadership skills.

How and Why?

Kelsey's Computer Lesson

"I have a big problem. I have a super-duper kind of problem. And I don't know what to do." Kelsey had thought so much, her head felt like a giant water balloon ready to burst wide open. Her parents had just moved to Pittsford and she was the new girl in school. Kids were nice enough, but no one really paid her much attention, she thought. No one had invited her over yet. She really felt kind of invisible, so she did something really dumb. Her teacher, Mrs. Chee, had told the class that they were going to start writing stories on computers next week. All the kids thought that was great—computers were dynamite stuff. So, when Mrs. Chee asked who had worked on computers before, Kelsey's arm went right up

125

Tips

This chapter contains many activities about the sciences, mathematics, the outdoors, and the environment. Activities on these topics also appear in other parts of the handbook—for example, the measuring activities in "Taking Care of Yourself and Your Home" are mathematical activities. Since studies show that girls are often not encouraged to try experiences in math and science, you can play an important role by incorporating more of these opportunities into your meeting activities. Science and math are important aspects of everyday life skills—for example, budgeting, estimating, counting, experimenting, measuring, and problem-solving—and girls can practice them now. By doing these types of activities throughout the troop year, you are helping girls see the value of science and math. As girls learn new skills throughout this section, be positive with your praise for both successful and unsuccessful results of their experimentations.

in the air—she didn't even know she was waving her arm like a tree shaking in a hurricane until Mrs. Chee put her in charge of one of the computer learning groups.

And that is the problem. You see, the closest Kelsey had ever come to a computer was when her big sister, Denise, had taken her shopping at the mall and had told Kelsey she could type on the display computers while Denise looked at CD players! What was she going to do? All the kids in her group were depending on her. As they left school, they were all excited about next week. "Kelsey, I'm glad you're in my group," April had said. "My brother has a computer in his room and he won't let me touch it. Maybe once you show us how to use it, I can use my brother's and you can come over!"

As they were walking out the school door, Kelsey told the kids that she had to go back because she had left her sneakers in the classroom. Now, she sat, looking at the

126

row of shiny computers. Slowly, her eyes got watery. She knew she was going to start crying.

"Hey! What are you still doing here?"

Kelsey jumped half out of her chair and turned around.

"What's wrong, Kelsey?" Rick Beckwith asked. Mr. Beckwith was the school custodian. He knew every kid's name. He was always smiling.

He always had a funny story. "Did something happen today in class? Are you feeling homesick?"

He looked so sympathetic and Kelsey felt so miserable, that she told him everything—how she had felt, what she had said, what the other kids had said, and what could she possibly do now? Everyone was going to laugh at her and think she was awful because she had lied and she'd never make any friends here.

"Well, Kelsey, you really did do something wrong. You should never pretend you know something that you really don't. You'll always be found out and you'll look really foolish. Worst of all, people won't trust you." He looked at Kelsey's face. "But, I think you know that. I use a computer every day. I keep track of all the school supplies. I do the budgets. I write letters and purchase orders. Would you like me to show you how to use this one? I think if we spent some time practicing, you'd know enough to get

---

Tips

Girls can share times when they learned how to do something new or different and perhaps demonstrate their skills and talents to the group. Girls can guess why Kelsey volunteered to do something that she did not really know how to do. You might ask how it feels to be new to a group and ask why people sometimes do things that are wrong just to be accepted. When do girls in your troop feel that they might do something similar? Kelsey's story can also lead girls to talk about how to make friends when they join a new group and how to be a friend when someone new joins your group. You could look back to the "Friends" activities on pages 75–82 in the girls' handbook.

Although some girls may not have had experiences with computers, many girls will have used a computer at school and others may have a computer at home. You could schedule a field trip to a computer lab or other business or facility where computers are used extensively.

your group started. What do you say?"

Kelsey couldn't believe it. This was like a miracle! "Yes, please, I'd be really happy if you showed me. And, I know what I did was really wrong."

"Sure, but I have to tell the principal and you should tell Mrs. Chee before we get started— and your parents, too. Okay?"

"Okay, can we start tomorrow?" Kelsey replied.

Kelsey talked to her parents that night and to Mrs. Chee before school the next day. She said that she knew that pretending to know how to do something, especially when other people were depending on you, was wrong. And, after a lot of talking, her parents and Mrs. Chee said it was okay with them as long as Mr. Beckwith had the time.

(One week later)

Kelsey had finished showing the group how to save their stories on a disk. As they were leaving the

school, April said, "You know, I thought you didn't want to be friends with anyone. You never smiled and you always seemed to want to do things by yourself. I'm glad you're in charge of this group. I'm glad we're friends. I think you're really nice. Let's go to my house and practice on my brother's computer!" In the doorway, Kelsey saw Mr. Beckwith. He was smiling at her and gave her a long wink. She ran over and gave him a hug. "Thank you, thank you," she whispered. "You were my first true friend here."

127

Try-Its and Other Resources

■ Other Resources: *Into the World of Today and Tomorrow.*

The world is full of new things to learn. Think of all the new things you have learned in Brownie Girl Scouts. Can you write some of them here?

_____

_____

_____

_____

Part of the fun of learning new things is learning how things work and why things happen. In this chapter, you will learn some of the hows and whys of things.

Brain Power

You use your brain to figure many things. You think about how much time it will take you to get home after school if you walk instead of taking the bus. You think about how long a piece of ribbon you will need for your hair. You decide if you will have enough time to do your homework and watch television. When you don't actually measure these things, but think and guess, you are estimating.

Try this estimation game. Think and guess:

How many words are on this page?

How many steps is it from the front of this room to the back?

How many windows are there in your school?

How many times does one of the people in this room smile?

What is the average size in inches of all the people's feet in this room?

How will you know if you are right? Make up some more estimation questions for your friends.

Besides estimating, brain power helps you do many things, like measure, work on a computer, tell time, and count.

128

Tips

Making educated predictions or guesses is an important scientific skill. It is also something that everyone does in everyday life and an important part of problem-solving. To make an educated guess, you rely on known facts and past experiences. Making estimates is a form of educated guessing.

Encourage girls to predict what they think will be the answer to different questions or problems. For example, ask the troop members to predict what the sum of all the members' ages will be. Write their predictions where everyone can see them. Go around the room and ask each person how old she is. Use a calculator or pencil and paper to add up the ages. Compare the total with the totals the girls came up with. When your troop is traveling, you can play estimating games—for example, how many people are riding the bus? How many windows are there in an apartment building? How many cows are in the field? How long will it take to get to your destination?

Try-Its and Other Resources

- Try-Its: Math Fun.
- Other Resources: *Into the World of Today and Tomorrow.*

Tips

Around the world, the metric system is the most common form of measurement. It is really very simple! It is based on a system of tens. Each unit is ten times larger than the preceding unit. For example, ten millimeters make up one centimeter, ten centimeters equal one decimeter, and ten decimeters make up a meter. There are 1,000 meters in a kilometer.

The metric system is used widely in science and medicine, and lately in other fields as well. Many products that are bought in stores show both metric and English systems (that's still most common in the United States—not in England!). The same is true in liquid and dry measures.

- *Length:* Metric lengths are millimeters, centimeters, meters, and kilometers. In the English

Measuring

Different people in countries around the world found different ways to measure things. Some people measured distance using the length of their feet. Can you think of any problems that would happen if your foot was the only way you measured distance? Why do you think 12 inches are called one foot?

Today, most people use the metric system to measure, but in the United States, many people still use what is known as the English system of measurement. Many businesses, though, use the metric system.

Most rulers show the metric system and the English system. Do the following activities to practice measuring things with both the metric and English systems.

- Measure your height. How tall are you in inches? How tall are you in centimeters?
- Find a container that shows the amount in liters. Use the

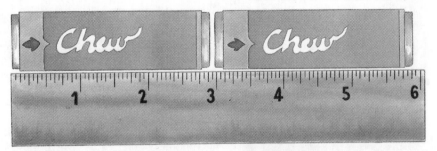

container to measure other liquids.

- Look through your groceries. Make a chart showing what something measures or weighs in the metric system compared to the English system.
- Try creating your own measurement system. How about using pieces of gum? Make your own gum ruler here. Now, how many gum sticks tall are you? If you don't want to use pieces of gum (or if you are chewing your ruler), try something else. What about peanuts or a favorite rock or seashell?

Computers

There are all kinds of computers. Some are very small and are used to make machines run better. Some very small computers are used in toys. Some are very big and keep track of millions of different things, like how much money is in the bank. Computers work very fast and use electricity. People make up instructions for computers. These instructions are called programs and tell computers what to do.

Each tiny instruction in a computer asks for a "yes" or "no" or "true" or "false" choice. You can get an idea about how a computer uses information to get an answer by playing the game "Twenty Ques-

129

system, length is in inches, feet, yards, and miles.
- *Volume:* Metric volumes are milliliters and liters. In the English system, volume is given in ounces, cups, pints, quarts, and gallons.
- *Weight:* Metric weights are milligrams, grams, and kilograms. In the English system, weight is in ounces, pounds, and tons.
- *Temperature:* In the metric system, temperature is meas-

ured in Celsius degrees; in the English system, temperature is measured in Fahrenheit degrees. **More to Try:** Find examples of products or measuring devices that show both metric and English. To start, look at food products, medicines, hardware supplies, and containers. You might make a chart showing what the same things measure in the metric and English systems. Do the measuring activities in "Your

Body Is One of a Kind" on handbook pages 36–37 in "Taking Care of Yourself and Your Home" using the metric system.

Try-Its and Other Resources

- Try-Its: Math Fun; Science in Action; Science Wonders.

YES
NO

tions." This is an example of the choices a computer is given.

The game goes like this: Other people will try to guess what you are thinking. Think of something that is an animal (including people) or made of something that comes from animals (like leather shoes); something that is a vegetable (plants) or made of vegetable (like paper); or something that is mineral (almost everything else!). Others try to guess by asking questions that can be

130

answered only with a "yes" or a "no." If you cannot answer the question with a "yes" or a "no," you should answer, "It does not compute," and the person who asked the question misses a turn.

Do you use a computer in school? Do you use a computer at home? in the library? Do you know someone who uses a computer at work? Find out about computers. Visit a place where they are used or sold and ask some questions. Practice using one yourself.

Telling Time

How long is a minute? 15 seconds? Can you tell without looking at a clock? With a buddy, get a watch or clock that has a second hand. When the buddy says "Start," close your eyes. Let her know when you think 15 seconds has passed. Take turns. Try 30 seconds and one minute. How good were you at estimating time? Now, try standing on one foot for 15 seconds. Can you do it?

How many times can you clap your hands in ten seconds? How many times can you stamp your foot in ten seconds? What other time challenges can you make up?

Hourglass

People have used different ways to tell time for thousands of years. One of the things people invented was an hourglass. Try making your own hourglass.

You will need:

* 2 one-liter clear plastic soda bottles with caps
* Heavy-duty package tape
* A nail

Tips

Computers: Girls might make a list of all the things they encounter on a daily basis that are run by computers or computer chips. Girls can go on a scavenger hunt at home, in the neighborhood, at a shopping mall, or at their school and see how many items they can find that contain a computer chip. A field trip might be made to a factory that uses robots or an engineering or graphics firm that uses computer-aided design.

Try-Its and Other Resources

* Try-Its: Science in Action.
* Other Resources: *Into the World of Today and Tomorrow.*

Tips

Telling Time: Ask the girls why time is so important to people. Write down some common time expressions, such as "I never have enough time," "Time flies when you're having fun," and "We'll save time if we take this road." What other expressions about time have the girls heard?

You may want to introduce the concept of time management in this

section. Brownie Girl Scouts may have very busy schedules with school, after-school activities, sports, and lessons. Also, some girls may have additional responsibilities at home, such as watching younger siblings or getting themselves ready for school, which can add to their pressures. Some activities in the "Taking Care of Yourself and Your Home" chapter apply to this section. The following activity is from *Developing Health and Fitness*:

Invite a consultant to discuss time management. Try budgeting your time for a day. Make a list of the things you must do during that day. Number them from most important to least important. If some of the tasks are large, break them down into smaller parts. Estimate the amount of time each task will take. Create a chart. Is it realistic? What things must you do? What things can be moved to the next day? Are there some things that you don't need to do?

- Sand or table salt
- A clock

Follow this diagram to make your hourglass:

1. Fill one of the bottles with sand.

2. Use the nail to make a small hole in each bottle cap. Ask an adult to help you with this part.

3. Screw the caps on the bottles.

4. Put the bottle full of sand on the bottom and attach the empty bottle on top.

5. Turn the bottle over. Look at your clock. How long does it take for all the sand to move from the top bottle to the bottom bottle? How can you change the amount of time that your "Hour Bottle" tells? Try putting more or less sand in your hourglass. How does this change the time the hourglass tells? Think of some games you can play using your hourglass as a timer.

The Moon

Watching the moon can help you measure time. The moon is brightest and roundest about once a month. This is a "full moon." Find a calendar or check a newspaper that tells you the phases of the moon. The moon looks round for about three nights, so the second night is the night of the full moon. Mark the full moon on your calendar. Try to count the number of nights until the next quarter moon, half moon, full

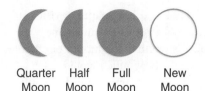

| Quarter Moon | Half Moon | Full Moon | New Moon |

moon, or new moon. Do you notice any other changes in the night sky when the moon is full?

Money

How is money measured? Pennies, nickels, dimes, quarters, one-dollar bills, five-dollar bills, and bigger bills are the kinds of money we use in the United States. Some other countries count their money in dollars, but only a few use dollars that look like United States dollars. Many countries have money that has its own special name and its own special look. Some countries have square coins. Some countries have coins with holes in them. Most countries have brightly colored bills with lots of pictures on them to make it easy to see the different amounts of bills that you have.

131

Tips

Hourglass: When making holes in the caps of the soda bottles, tap the nail lightly with a hammer while holding the nail in the center of each cap. Then hit it a little harder to make the hole. Put a piece of scrap wood or a pile of newspapers under the cap while doing this to avoid damaging any surface. Caution girls to avoid any sharp edges around the nail hole or the cap. Encourage girls to use the hourglass to time the things they do, such as jumping rope, taking a shower, or eating a snack.

Try-Its and Other Resources

- Try-Its: Science in Action.

Tips

The Moon: If you live near a very large body of water, girls can see how the tides change through the month.

Girls can also create their own calendars that show the phases of the moon or tides. With a ruler, mark off seven one- or two-inch boxes (horizontally) and five one- or two-inch boxes vertically. You will have 35 boxes. You can photocopy your master copy for girls who can then fill in the numbers, days of the week, and names of the months. Pictures from magazines and catalogs, greeting cards, drawings, or old calendars can be used for decoration.

Try-Its and Other Resources

- Try-Its: Space Explorer.

Look in a newspaper or visit a bank to find out how much one dollar is worth in the money of other countries. How much would your troop treasury money be worth in the currency of other countries?

Other Kinds of Money

Sometimes money doesn't look like money. Credit cards and checks are kinds of money people use to buy things without using coins or bills. If you put money in a bank account, you can use checks to pay for things with that money. You write the check. It is sent to the bank. The bank takes the money out of your checking account.

132

Credit cards can also be used like money. You use a credit card to charge what you want. The credit card company then sends you a bill once a month for all the things you have charged. If you do not pay the full amount, the credit card company adds extra money, called interest, to your bill. Credit cards can be more convenient (easy to use) than cash (bills and coins), but can also be more expensive.

Do you have a savings account? Some banks will let you open a savings account with an adult's permission. You can save money in a bank in a savings account. The bank will give you some extra money (interest), too, if you have a savings account. This is a good way to save money.

Talk to some adults about checks and credit cards. When do they use them? When do they use cash?

Visit a bank or credit union. What can you find out?

Science Is All Around You

Look around your world. Many of the things you see and many of the things you use every day depend on science and on technology.

Go on a science and technology hunt! Each of these things is an example of science or technology at work. How many can you find?

* Something made of plastic.
* Something made from oil.
* Something made from the forest.
* Something that moves in a circle.
* Something that comes from the earth.
* Something that uses a switch.
* Something made of metal.
* Something that uses electricity.
* Something that uses wheels.
* Something that measures.
* Something that uses metrics.
* Something made of glass.

Tips

Brownie Girl Scouts may have allowances and some may even have jobs, such as helping with younger children or paper routes. You can do the troop budgeting activities on handbook pages 121–122 in "Leadership in Girl Scouting and Beyond" or combine the food and nutrition activities from handbook pages 39–41 in "Taking Care of Yourself and Your Home" with a supermarket shopping trip. Girls can also look in a newspaper or visit a bank or stock brokerage firm to find out how much dollars are worth in the currencies of other countries. Or you could tell the girls to imagine that the President of the United States has asked them to design a new kind of money. They can share their designs with the group.

Try-Its and Other Resources

* Try-Its: Math Fun; Numbers and Shapes.

Tips

For the science and technology hunt, some items may be easier for younger girls to find, such as something that uses wheels or makes a sound. Other items, such as things made from oil, may be more difficult. Things made from oil include plastics, synthetic fibers, and polythenes. Girls can complete this science and technology hunt indoors, outdoors, or on a field trip.

Tips

Emphasize safety. Girls should:

* Never put chemicals into their mouths.
* Wash their hands after handling chemicals.
* Know how to contact the nearest poison control center listed in the telephone book.
* Follow the safety rules in this section.

- Something that makes or uses sound.
- Something from the ocean.
- Something made by people that can be recycled.
- Something run by computers.

Chemistry

Chemistry is the study of chemicals and how they mix and change.

Chemicals are all around you. Some may be right under your own kitchen sink or in your garden supplies. It is very important to handle certain chemicals with care. Some will react with others to make the air unbreathable, to burn your skin, or to poison you.

- Never handle chemicals unless an adult works with you.
- Don't touch any chemicals that say "Poison."
- If you have any doubt, always ask an adult whether a chemical is safe or not.
- Never mix household chemicals, like different cleaning solutions. This can be very dangerous.

One of the easiest places to learn about chemistry is in your own kitchen. When you make toast you are seeing chemistry in action. Heat is used to burn the bread and change it to toast.

Another chemical action that uses both heat and a combining of chemicals is bread making. You are using yeast to create air bubbles, and heat to make the yeast rise and bake the bread. Do the "Bread Making" activity in the Science in Action Try-It.

Matter: Solid, Liquid, Gas

Almost everything in the world is solid, liquid, or gas. Things can change from solid to liquid to gas. Water can be a liquid or a solid or a gas. What happens when water freezes into ice? It becomes a solid! And what happens when it boils and becomes steam? It becomes a gas.

- Try to find five things that are solid.
- Try to find five things that are liquid.
- What is air? The air you breathe is a gas.

Weird Glop

Make some weird glop. You will have something that isn't really a solid or a liquid.

You will need:

- 1/2 cup cornstarch
- 1/4 cup water
- Spoon
- Measuring cup
- Small pan

1. Pour the water into the pan.
2. Add the cornstarch a little at a time while stirring.

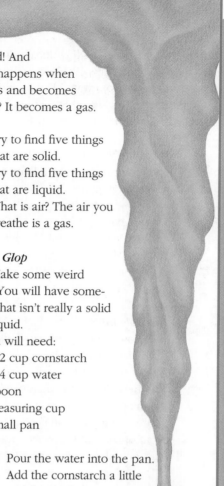

Tips

What is the difference between a solid, a liquid, and a gas? Sometimes all three states can be seen of the same substance. For example, ice, a solid, water, a liquid, and steam, a gas, are all the same substance. The temperature of each makes the difference. (Girls may be confused by the term "gas" since the term is also used for gasoline and it looks like a liquid.) Girls can think of other substances that change: rock can turn into liquid lava; butter melts and becomes a liquid; ammonia evaporates and becomes a gas that you can smell.

Tiny particles, atoms and molecules, make up all substances and act differently when the temperature or other conditions change. In a solid, the particles are close together and don't move around much. When a solid warms up, the bonds that hold the particles together become weaker and the solid becomes a liquid. The molecules now wander around and the substance can flow into any shape. When a liquid heats up, the molecules move even faster until some break the bonds that hold them together and break away. These particles become a gas. The substances you smell are gases, so as food cooks, for example, you know that some particles become gases and carry particles to your nose through the air.

Try-Its and Other Resources

- Try-Its: Science Wonders; Water Everywhere.

3. Keep mixing until your glop is one consistency. How is the glop different from water? How is it different from starch? Store the glop in a plastic bag. If it gets sticky, add a little starch. Do not eat the glop. What can you do with it? Try adding food coloring to make different colors of glop!

Dough Art

To create a chemical reaction, try the "Making Dough Shapes" activity in the Colors and Shapes Try-It.

Invisible Ink

You can make invisible ink from many different liquids. You cannot see what you write when you are writing, but when you heat the ink on the paper you can see your writing! You will need a cotton swab or paintbrush, paper, and at least one of the following liquids:

- Baking powder mixed with water
- Sugar mixed with water
- Lemon juice

Write on paper with one or more of the liquids and then let it dry. Your message is now invisible. Place your paper between two sheets of scrap paper and heat the paper with an iron. Get an adult to help you with the iron. What happens? Try leaving your invisible ink message in a sunny, warm window. What happens?

Blow Up a Balloon

Blow up a balloon without using your own breath.

You will need:

- 1/4 cup vinegar
- Small plastic soda bottle (with a neck that you can place a balloon over)
- 2 tablespoons baking soda
- A small balloon

You will need several people working together.

1. Pour the vinegar into the plastic bottle.
2. Stretch the balloon mouth open and carefully pour the soda into the balloon.
3. Place the balloon mouth over the soda bottle, holding the balloon to the side so that the soda does not fall into the bottle.
4. When the balloon is tightly around the neck of the soda bottle, shake the balloon so that the soda falls into the bottle.

What happened? Can you figure out why?

Chemical Butterfly

A black felt-tip pen is made up of many different colors of chemi-

134

Tips

Invisible Ink: You may be able to hold the paper near a lit light bulb. The heat from the bulb may be sufficient to make the ink visible.

Blow Up a Balloon: You are combining a solid with an acidic liquid. A chemical reaction takes place and a gas (carbon dioxide) is formed. The gas expands and fills up the balloon.

Chemical Butterfly: Some inks and dyes are made up of different-colored pigments. This experiment shows a way to separate the colors as the water is soaked up through the paper. The different pigments will travel different distances so that colored bands can be seen.

You will need to use water-soluble markers. Test the markers before trying the experiment with girls. Some markers bleed much more easily than others.

More to Try: Another simple experiment that girls can try is making pennies turn green! You will need a small dish, a piece of paper towel, pennies minted before 1975, and some vinegar. Fold the paper towel in half and then in half again to make a small square. Put it on the dish. Pour vinegar on the towel until it is wet. Place the pennies on top of the wet paper towel and put the dish somewhere where it won't be moved. Take a look at it the next day. What has happened to the pennies? The copper in the pennies and the acid in the vinegar have reacted to make the green coating on the pennies. It is best to use older pennies, which have a higher copper content. Newer pennies do not contain enough copper to make the experiment work as well.

cals. Mixed together, these colors look black. How can you see the different colors?

You will need:

- Black, water-soluble felt-tip pen (Try a variety of markers to see which works best.)
- Coffee filter
- Scissors
- Cup of water

1. Fold your filter in half and cut out a butterfly shape, like this.

2. Run a heavy black line down the fold, like this.

3. Dip the filter into the cup of water, like this.

Watch closely, but don't touch the filter. What happens?

Magnets

Magnets attract things made of iron. Go on a magnet hunt in your house. (Look at what else you can do on a magnet hunt in the Science Wonders Try-It.) How many things made of metal have iron in them?

Make Your Own Magnet

Make a temporary magnet by taking something that contains iron, like a pin or paper clip, and rubbing it in one direction many times across a magnet. Test your new magnet on another pin or paper clip.

Magnet Olympics

Have a Magnetic Olympics. Get a lot of different types and sizes of magnets and draw a line on a flat surface. Place different size objects at different distances away from the line to test which magnets are the strongest. See which magnet can hold the most paper clips. Make up some more Olympic events for your magnets and try to guess which magnets will be the winners.

Magnetic Attraction Box

You will need:

- Small cardboard or plastic box
- Steel wool
- Plastic wrap or a plastic lid for the box
- Magnet
- Tape

 1. Cut the steel wool into small pieces. Have an adult help you with this.

135

Tips

Magnets: The unique property of a magnet is that the atoms within it are all aligned in the same direction, giving it two poles or a different electrical charge at each end. The positive charge at one end of the magnet will attract the negative end of another magnet. Items like paper clips can become temporarily magnetized by stroking them along a magnet, but will lose their magnetic charge when dropped or shaken, because the atoms are no longer aligned in the same direction.

Girls can try making a compass. Magnetize a needle by rubbing it along a magnet in the same direction for 15 to 30 seconds. Then tape the needle to a broad, flat slice of cork and float the cork and needle in a saucer of water. The north pole of the needle will turn to the north. Girls can use their compasses with the mapping activities on handbook pages 84–85 in "Family, Friends, and Neighbors."

Magnet Olympics: Encourage girls to guess how many paper clips or other objects will be attracted to different sizes and shapes of magnets. After steel wool is cut up, discourage girls from handling it to avoid getting small pieces imbedded in the skin. Use a magnet to pick up any scraps.

Try-Its and Other Resources

- Try-Its: Science Wonders.
- Other Resources: *Into the World of Today and Tomorrow.*

2. Put the pieces in the bottom of the box so they cover the bottom completely.

3. Place a piece of plastic wrap or a plastic lid over the box and tape it shut. Use the magnet to make patterns on the bottom of the box.

What kind of patterns can you make? How far away can you hold the magnet and still make the steel wool move?

Light and Color

All colors are made from three basic colors: red, yellow, and blue. These are called primary colors. How do you make other colors?

Making Colors

You will need:

- 4 flashlights

- Red, blue, yellow, and green balloons
- White wall, ceiling, or white sheet of paper
- Dark room

1. Cut the necks off the balloons.

2. Stretch the balloons across the flashlights.

3. Turn off the lights in the room.

4. Shine the red light onto the white surface.

5. Shine the blue light onto the red.

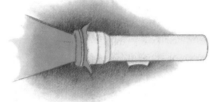

What happens? What color do you get?

Red plus blue =
Red plus yellow =
Yellow plus blue =

Combine the green with red, yellow, or blue. What happens when you shine all the colors together?

A Spectrum of Colors

The colors of a rainbow—red, orange, yellow, green, blue, and violet—are called the spectrum of colors. White light is made up of the spectrum of colors. A rainbow happens when sunlight, which looks white, is bent when it passes through raindrops. The bending light is a rainbow. On a sunny day, you can make your own spectrum of colors.

You will need:

- A straight-sided clear drinking glass
- A piece of card with a ½″ (1 centimeter) slit cut into it (See drawing.)
- A sheet of white paper
- Tape

1. Fill the glass with water.

136

Making Colors: In this experiment, girls will discover one way to combine colors. When combining red and blue they should see purple; red and yellow make orange; and yellow and blue make green. Encourage them to try other combinations. Putting all colors together results in white light, because white light is made up of all colors. In the next activity, a spectrum of colors, girls can see white light break into the different bands of colors.

Note: Mixing colors of light is different from mixing colors of paint, and different results are obtained.

A Spectrum of Colors: Sunlight is made up of light waves of seven different frequencies. The light is split as it passes through the water droplets into the different colors in a rainbow: violet, indigo, blue, green, yellow, orange, and red. Girls can make their own rainbows by allowing sunlight to pass through water and seeing how the colors are separated when the rays are bent.

Try-Its and Other Resources

- Try-Its: Colors and Shapes; Science in Action; Science Wonders.

2. Tape the card to the glass. (See drawing.)

3. Put the white paper close to a window.

4. Put the glass on the paper.

What happens when the sunlight passes through the slit in the paper and the water in the glass?

WEATHER

Weather is the way the air is at a certain time in a certain place. The weather can change from day to day and from month to month. Look in the puzzle at right. Can you find the "weather" words?

S	U	N	F	R	O	S	T
N	P	M	R	A	W	Y	H
O	L	X	E	I	C	E	U
W	C	W	E	N	J	M	N
B	L	I	Z	Z	A	R	D
S	O	N	E	G	G	O	E
Q	U	D	N	H	O	T	R
A	D	L	O	C	F	S	Z

Answers: wind, cloud, cold, hot, fog, ice, snow, sun, blizzard, thunder, storm, frost, freeze, rain, warm.

137

The words in the puzzle are wind, cloud, cold, hot, fog, ice, snow, sun, blizzard, thunder, storm, frost, freeze, rain, warm.

Sunny Days

The sun gives heat and light. It dries wet things and makes things grow. Sunlight helps your body make lots of Vitamin D, which your body needs to grow healthy bones and teeth. Sun can also be harmful to your skin. Have you ever gotten a sunburn? The sun was actually burning your skin! Even when you do not get sunburned, the sun can still hurt your skin. When you are in the sun, use sunblocks and sunscreens (lotion or cream that protects your skin from the sun). Don't forget to put more on after swimming or exercising. Can you think of some of the good things the sun does?

On a hot, sunny day, go outside and feel different objects in the sun and in the shade. Touch softly first to make sure you don't burn your hand. What kinds of things were hot? cold? warm? cool? Do the same with an outdoor thermometer. Measure the temperature in the sun, then in the shade to see the difference. You can also look for things that get energy from the sun. What can you find that is solar-powered?

Evaporation

The heat from the sun can turn water into invisible water vapor in the air. (Water vapor is very, very tiny drops of water in the air.) Evaporation means that heat is making water vapor rise in the air. The water cycle means that water evaporates into the air and then comes back to the earth in raindrops. You can see evaporation happen by trying the following experiments:

- Put two tablespoons of water in a dish and place it in a very sunny spot. Put another dish with two tablespoons of water next to your first dish, but put a book or other type of shade between the sun and this dish so that it is not in the sun. Look at the dishes again in four to six hours. What happened?

- Fill a dark cup or glass half full of water. Stretch some plastic wrap tightly over the top. Put the cup where it is sunny and leave it alone. Look at it again in an hour. What happened?

Wind

Wind is moving air. The wind moves around the earth, bringing different kinds of weather with it. The wind blows and moves things in its path.

Look outside on a windy day. What is moving in the wind? Which things move most easily?

What kinds of things can you make that will move in the wind? Try the "Wind Wheels" activity in

---

Tips

The human body uses sunlight to make vitamin D within the skin. This vitamin is also found in milk fortified with vitamin D, butter, egg yolks, and fish such as tuna. Vitamin D is needed in order to build strong bones and teeth from calcium.

Many people now have solar-powered calculators. Some people use sunlight to heat water in their homes or have a greenhouse or sun space that helps cut down on heating bills. Girls can draw or design their own solar-powered machines or solar-powered homes.

Try-Its and Other Resources

- Try-Its: Building Art; Earth and Sky; Earth Is Our Home; Plants.

Tips

Evaporation: Evaporation is a good example of a liquid (water) turning into a gas. The first experiment shows that evaporation can occur at different rates depending on the temperature. During the second one, girls should see water droplets forming under the plastic wrap. This is an example of water evaporating and then condensing (turning back into a liquid) when it touches the cooler surface of the plastic.

Try-Its and Other Resources

- Try-Its: Outdoor Happenings.

the Movers Try-It. Think of some ways to use wind power. What could you invent?

Clouds and Rain

Have you ever wondered what is inside a cloud? Clouds in the sky are made of water that is a gas. Fog is a cloud near the ground. Rain falls when the water mist in a cloud becomes drops that get bigger and heavier. What are some of the good things that rain does? Take a rain hike to see what changes are made by rain. Don't forget to dress properly.

Cloud Record

What can you notice about clouds? Try drawing the different shapes of clouds you see. What kind of weather followed what type of clouds? Do some kinds of clouds appear when it is rainy? Do some kinds of clouds appear when it is sunny? What patterns can you discover?

Tips

Wind: Girls can have fun drawing or cutting out pictures to make a wind chart. Make two headings: "Things to See" and "Wind Speed." Some examples for each wind speed are below:

- Lakes, puddles very still; no waves; smoke rises straight up: -01 m.p.h. = calm.
- Ripples on water; leaves rustle; breeze felt on face: 2–10 m.p.h. = slight breeze.
- Papers blow about; small flags wave; small waves on lakes: 10–20 m.p.h. = moderate breeze.
- Small trees sway; large flags wave; wind can be heard; rain falls sideways: 20–30 m.p.h. = strong breeze.
- Difficult to walk; twigs break off; large waves; snow and rain blow sideways: 30–45 m.p.h. = gale.

Girls can pantomime the "Things to See" on their charts. Others must guess how fast the wind is blowing.

Tips

There are three basic types of clouds:

- Cirrus—high, wispy clouds made of ice crystals.
- Cumulus—puffy, white clouds made of water vapor.
- Stratus—low-lying layers of clouds that usually bring rain.

There are other subvarieties of clouds within these three basic types.

Girls can keep a cloud book or cloud journal. A simple "I See" sort of game is also fun to play with cloud

Rain Gauge

Make a rain gauge to see how much rain falls during a rainstorm. You will need a clear glass jar with straight sides or a clear plastic container with the top cut off. Place your gauge outdoors in a clear area before the rain falls. After the rain has stopped, hold a ruler to the side of your gauge. Measure the height of the water. How many inches fell? How does your measurement compare with the inches of rainfall reported in the newspaper or on television or radio?

Rain can also move the soil. Try the "Going, Going, Gone" activity in the Earth and Sky Try-It.

Frost and Snow

When misty water on the ground freezes during a cold night, you can see frost the next morning.

Water freezes when the temperature is below 32° Fahrenheit or 0° Celsius. In the morning on cold days, you can see frost on windows and leaves. If you look at frost closely, you can see the ice crystals.

Snowflakes are ice crystals. When it is very cold, the misty water in clouds forms ice crystals instead of water drops. When these drops get big and heavy, they fall and you see snow. Each snowflake (and there are millions and millions) is different—just like people! Not every part of the world is cold enough to get snow. If you live someplace where it snows, try this experiment.

Catch some snowflakes on a piece of dark paper or cloth that has been cooled to the temperature outside. Look at the flakes with a magnifying glass. What do you see?

Storms, Blizzards, Hurricanes, and Tornadoes: Weather to Watch

A storm has very strong winds. Hurricanes have winds that move at 73 miles per hour or more! Blizzards are strong winds and snow. Tornadoes are winds moving very fast in a tall funnel shape. Thunderstorms have lightning—the flash of electricity you see—and thunder—the noise you hear when lightning heats up the air so much that the air swells and almost explodes.

All storms can be dangerous. Strong winds can knock down power lines, trees, even buildings, and make very tall waves. Lightning is a very powerful burst of electricity in the sky. Thunder is the sound made when lightning flashes. Thunder can't hurt you but lightning can. It is very important to know how to stay safe in a lightning storm. Weather reports can tell you that bad weather is coming. You can sometimes see bad weather

(continued on page 142)

140

---

shapes. The leader starts, for example, "I see a cloud shaped like an elephant" and the first person to find that exact cloud becomes the next person to play.

Look at the Arapaho story on handbook pages 106–108 in "People Near and Far."
Can girls make up their own stories about why each snowflake is unique? What other "weather tales" can they create?

Tips

Look carefully at snowflakes. Each is unique although each has six sides. You can have fun creating your own snowflakes by cutting snowflake shapes from paper.

Try-Its and Other Resources

- Try-Its: Earth and Sky; Outdoor Happenings.

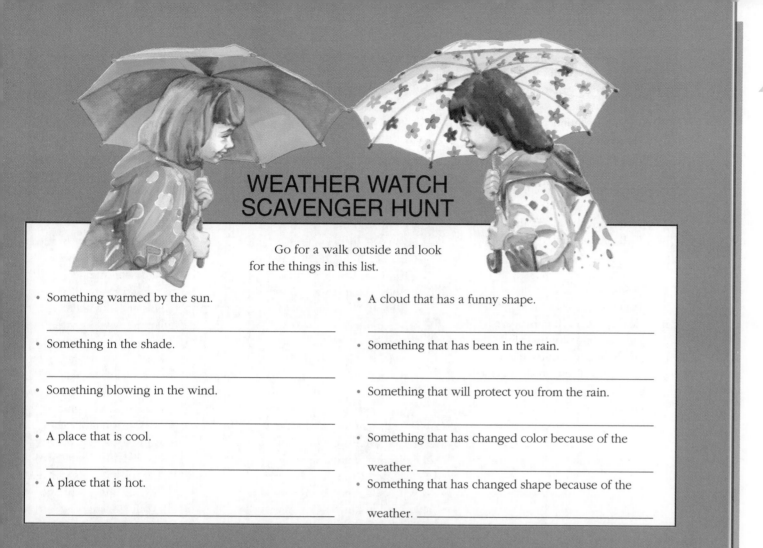

WEATHER WATCH
SCAVENGER HUNT

Go for a walk outside and look
for the things in this list.

- Something warmed by the sun.

_____

- Something in the shade.

_____

- Something blowing in the wind.

_____

- A place that is cool.

_____

- A place that is hot.

_____

- A cloud that has a funny shape.

_____

- Something that has been in the rain.

_____

- Something that will protect you from the rain.

_____

- Something that has changed color because of the

weather. _____

- Something that has changed shape because of the

weather. _____

Tips

Practice the safety rules for storms. Girls can pretend that different types of storms are occurring and then follow the precautions for each type of storm. More safety guidelines, on handbook pages 45–46 in "Taking Care of Yourself and Your Home," should also be reviewed. The safety rules for thunderstorms encourage you to stay away from pathways that may be traveled by the electricity discharged by the lightning. This includes staying away from tall objects like trees and telephone poles, telephone wires, and electrical appliances. If you are caught outside, you can crouch down on something dry or something that will not conduct electricity such as a sleeping bag or heavy jacket. A car is also a good place to be since its rubber tires provide insulation from electrical currents, but you should remember not to touch the metal parts during the storm.

(continued from page 140)

coming your way. You can tell when a thunderstorm is coming and how far away the storm is from you. When you hear thunder, count to five slowly and raise one finger. Then, count to five and raise the next finger. Keep counting in sets of five until you see the lightning. Each raised finger stands for one mile. If you have three fingers up, the lightning is three miles away.

Group Storm

Try making a "Group Storm." In a clear space, each person acts out one part of a storm—wind, thunder, lightning, clouds, rain, snow, hail, etc. Then, create a giant storm. How will each person's part be different as the "weather" changes?

142

Safety in Bad Weather

Thunderstorms

If you hear thunder or see dark clouds, you should follow these safety rules.

- Don't stand in an open field. Crouch down, don't lie down, on a sleeping bag or pile of clothes if you can. Try to put clothing or the bag between you and the ground.
- Don't stand under a tree. Lightning reaches for the tallest things to get to the ground. Lightning could hit the tree you are under!
- Get out of the water right away. Lightning can strike the water and hurt you.
- Stay out of ditches and arroyos. Storms can turn these ditches into big, fast rivers!
- Get inside a car or indoors. Once you are inside the car, do not touch the metal parts.
- If you are home, close all the windows.
- Don't use the telephone, air conditioner, television, or any other electrical appliance like a hairdryer.

Tornadoes

Tornado warnings are usually given on weather reports. If you hear that a tornado is expected where you live, you should follow these safety rules.

- Find shelter. The best places are storm shelters and basements, caves, tunnels, underground parking garages, or the inside hallways of buildings.
- Stay away from windows and outside doorways. Stay away from cars, trailers, tents, school gymnasiums, and auditoriums or stadiums.
- If you cannot find shelter, stay away from the tornado by moving to the side of its path or by lying flat in a ditch, culvert, or under a bridge. Put your arms over your head.

If you live in an area affected by tornadoes, develop a plan for what your troop would do during a meeting if tornado warnings were posted. Discuss with girls' parents the procedures that would be followed.

Big storms can stop the electricity into your home, knock down power lines, or knock down big trees. See the section "Taking Care of Your Home" in the chapter "Taking Care of Yourself and Your Home" for tips on indoor safety during storms.

When the Storm Is Over

- Be careful where you walk after a storm. Electricity from power lines that have fallen can travel through water and wet ground. If you step in a puddle or on ground that is wet, you can get a big shock!
- Do not go near streams or river banks where water is moving quickly. Stay out of ditches and low areas.
- Do not walk on the beach or grass near the ocean. Big waves can move quickly after a storm and come right up onto the beach.

More About Lightning and Static Electricity

Lightning happens when static electricity builds up in clouds. Have you ever taken clothes out of the clothes dryer and discovered that they stick together? That's an example of static electricity. On a dry day, walk across a rug shuffling your feet in a dark room. Touch a door knob or other metal object. The spark you see is static electricity. This spark is like the lightning that jumps from cloud to cloud or from a cloud to the ground.

Another way to see static electricity is to tear some paper into tiny pieces. Run or rub a comb through your hair. Put the comb near the paper. What happens?

Static Antics

Try this activity to see how static electricity can make things move.

You will need:
- Tissue paper
- Silk handkerchief or small silk scarf

- Plastic pen
- Metal plate or tray

1. Cut a large circle out of the tissue paper.

2. Cut the circle into a spiral. (See drawing.)

3. Put the tissue spiral on the metal plate.

4. Rub the plastic pen hard on the silk. If you don't have silk, rub the pen hard on your hair.

5. Hold the pen over the middle of the tissue spiral.

What happens? The paper will be pulled to the pen. Now keep lifting carefully into the air.

143

Tips

Static Antics: Experiments with static electricity work best when there is very little humidity in the air. In this experiment, the electrons jump from the silk and collect on the plastic pen. The electrons on the pen then act like a magnet to attract the tissue paper.

Try-Its and Other Resources

- Try-Its: Science Wonders.

MY NATURAL ENVIRONMENT

What is your environment? Your world is more than people and buildings. Your natural environment is the air, land, water, plants, and animals around you. The living and nonliving parts are so connected that it is sometimes hard to separate them. To find out more about these connections, try the "Food Chain" activity in the Plants Try-It.

A mini-environment helps you understand something bigger by looking at something smaller. Get a string about two feet long. Go outdoors and find a grassy area to study.

Lay the string in a circle. The inside of your circle is your mini-environment. Study what is happening inside. Look through a magnifying glass. What do you see now? Make a list of what you see here.

_____

_____

_____

_____

Imagine how it would feel to be a part of this environment. Can you draw a picture or write about how it would feel?

Pollution

Everything you do affects your environment. Pollution describes what people do that changes or hurts the environment. Pollution can harm the air, water, soil, and living things.

Your everyday actions can cause pollution. Your litter can make a clean place ugly and can hurt animals who try to eat it. The gum that you throw on the ground can kill a small animal or bird who cannot digest such stuff. The fire in your fireplace might cause smoke in the air. Or you might pour something down a storm drain that goes into a river or lake and pollutes it. These are all types of pollution.

What are some things you can do to stop polluting? How can your actions as a pollution fighter help others in your family and your community?

144

Tips

The natural environment includes everything around us: air, water, sun, soil, rocks, plants, animals, and people. Sometimes it is hard to see how all the different aspects of the environment interrelate. One of the important connections is the relationship between plants and animals and the food humans eat. A food chain is a model that shows the relationships between plants and the animals that consume them, and the predators, which eat the plant-eating animals. Plants use energy from the sun to grow. A plant eaten by an animal or a person is the first link in a food chain. The chain grows by showing each animal that can eat the one before. Studies show that eating more plant products than animal products is healthier; it also causes less pollution, takes less space, and saves energy. A food web is the complex set of interconnected food chains between the plants and animals in a particular habitat such as a pond, forest, estuary, or prairie.

The mini-environment activity can be done on a playground, in a backyard, in a park, at the beach, or at a campsite. Girls can look for relationships between the things they see—for example, grass grows from the soil; the roots of the grass hold the soil together; a bug walks along a stem or eats a leaf; a mushroom grows on a piece of old wood.

Try-Its and Other Resources

- Try-Its: Animals; Earth Is Our Home; Outdoor Fun; Plants.

- Other Resources: *Exploring Wildlife Communities With Children*; *Games for Girl Scouts*.

Tips

Pollution: Girls can become more aware of how their actions or lack of actions may affect their environment. Many service projects on

Oil Spills

An oil spill is a bad kind of pollution that can happen when a pipe, container, boat, or truck carrying something harmful leaks. Sometimes the leak is caused by an accident. Sometimes people dump the chemical or oil into the ground or water. The chemical or oil goes into the water or ground and harms the environment. It can make the water too dirty to use for drinking water or swimming. It can kill the fish, plants, animals, birds, and even people who need the water or land in order to live.

Try making your own oil spill so you can see what oil does to clean water.

You will need:

• Ground red pepper or paprika
• Cooking oil
• Small bowl
• Clean water
• A tablespoon
• Small pieces of paper, fluff, feathers, dandelion puffs, apple seeds, or other small, light things
• Cotton balls or pads
• Ice cream sticks, small twigs, spatula
• Dish detergent

1. Mix the red pepper or paprika with three tablespoons of oil.

2. Pour this oil into the small bowl of clean water. What does the oil do?

3. Drop the paper, feathers, fluff, seeds, and other small items in the bowl, then take them out. What has happened to the things you put in the bowl? Water birds and animals can get their feathers, fur, or gills coated with oil. The oil can prevent them from keeping warm, flying, or breathing. They can die.

4. Try cleaning up your oil spill. Real cleanup crews try to blot up the oil with straw or other materials. Try using cotton balls or pads.

5. Cleanup crews also use booms or logs to keep the oil all in one place. Try using small sticks or a spatula. How much of the oil can you clean up using the cotton pads? Do the sticks help you clean up the oil?

6. Cleanup crews also add detergent to an oil spill. Add some dish detergent. What happens to the oil? But now you have added a new kind of pollution to the water! You can see that oil spills are very hard to clean up!

145

environmental issues—recycling, taking care of a stream or pond, planting trees, making water and energy conservation efforts, or collecting batteries—are appropriate for Brownie Girl Scouts and get across the concept of environmental action. The Contemporary Issues booklet *Earth Matters* is an excellent resource for ideas and information.

Tips

Follow up the oil spill activity with a discussion of how oil spills and chemicals can be prevented from polluting the environment.

• Take any oil removed from a car or other engine to a service station for recycling.

• Don't dump pesticides, chemicals, or oil down storm drains.
• Use nontoxic chemicals to clean the house.
• Use batteries that are rechargeable if possible. Or find a way to recycle used ones.

Try-Its and Other Resources

• Try-Its: Earth Is Our Home; Water Everywhere.

breathe. Planting trees helps fight air pollution. Participate in tree planting in your community.

Using a car less often also helps fight air pollution. Can you think of some ways to use a car less often?

Do the "Our Air" activity in the Earth and Sky Try-It to discover more about the air you breathe.

Garbage: Reduce, Reuse, and Recycle

One of the biggest forms of pollution is garbage. There's just too much garbage! Where does garbage go? Many places have landfills— but they are getting full. Garbage does not go away once it is put in a landfill. You can burn it, which makes it smaller, but that often causes air pollution, and you still need a place for the ashes. You can bury it, and hope it rots away. But when you bury things, they usually don't go away because they need air in order to rot. So, some landfills have gotten so big that they look like giant mountains of garbage. Pheeew!!

Do the "How Long Does It Take?" activity in the Earth Is Our Home Try-It to find out how long it takes for your garbage to go away.

The best thing to do about garbage is not to make it. That means you have to reuse it in some way, or recycle it or pre-cycle it. Pre-

Air Pollution

Air pollution is another kind of pollution that hurts all living things. Perhaps you know someone who has trouble breathing when the air is bad, or you have seen plants dying because of the lack of clean air. The automobile is the biggest air polluter in the country. Factories can also pollute the air.

There are several things you can do about air pollution. Trees are a natural air cleaner. Trees breathe in the air you cannot breathe, and release oxygen, the air that you can

146

Garbage: Reduce, Reuse, and Recycle: Girls can walk through a supermarket to look at how products are packaged. Which kinds of packaging can be recycled in your area? What can be recycled at home and at school? How about newspapers, glass, plastics, old toys, books, or clothes? Sometimes new products can be made from the old. What are some old things that can be re-used or fixed up and then used? What skills did girls learn in "Taking Care of Yourself and Your Home" that they can use to fix and repair?

- Try-Its: Earth Is Our Home

cycling means buying the item that has the least amount of packaging or that is put into a container that is easy to recycle. For example, you can buy a hamburger wrapped in paper instead of a hamburger in a foam box. Choose a cereal in a box made from recycled cardboard. Buy a toy that doesn't have lots of extra plastic around it. Pre-cycling is smart!

Look for something that has too much packaging. Design a new package for it.

How do you know if something is made from recycled materials? Look for this sign:

Reduce. How much garbage does your family throw out every week? Keep track of a typical week's garbage. Can you think of ways to have less garbage? Try these with your family.

Reuse. Go on a recycling symbol scavenger hunt. See who can find the most items with a recycling symbol on them.

Reuse and recycle. Can you think of some things you can recycle or reuse at home? Wire hangers can often be returned to the dry cleaner to be reused. Funny papers can be used as wrapping paper or book covers. List ten things that you can recycle and do it.

_____

_____

_____

_____

_____

_____

Conservation

There are some things that cannot be recycled forever and ever. Some resources, like water or land, have only a certain amount. They can be used up. To conserve something means to save it or use it only a little.

Clean water is an important resource. In some places in the world, people must move from their homes because they have run out of water, or they must travel far distances to get water. As a young girl in many places of the world, you would have the job of getting water for your family. You might walk three miles or more to the closest well or stream and then walk home with a bucket full of water on your head. In some places, you might have one bucket of water or

147

Tips

Conservation: The Girl Scout Law states: ". . . to use resources wisely." Girls can talk about what they think this means to them and to their community and then discuss what they can do.

Try-Its and Other Resources

- Try-Its: Earth Is Our Home; Science in Action; Water Everywhere.

less to last you the entire day. You would need this one bucket for washing, cleaning, cooking, drinking, and maybe even farming! Do you know how much water you use in one day?

Here are some ways you can save water. Can you think of some more?

• Don't run the water when you are brushing your teeth.
• Don't let the water run when you are scraping and scrubbing the dishes.

• Run the dishwasher only when it is full.
• Run the clothes washer only for full loads, or use

148

the water-saver cycle.
• Take shorter showers.
• Install a shower head that uses less water.

Saving Electricity

One important kind of energy is electricity. People use electricity in many different things at home and at work. It is important to conserve energy. Here are some ways that you can do this. Can you think of some more?

• Turn off the lights when you leave a room.
• Turn off the radio and television when no one is using them.
• Think of what you want in the refrigerator before you open the door. Then open and shut it quickly.

Go on an electric hunt in your house. List or cut out pictures of all the things you find that need elec-

tricity to operate. Are there any you could live without?

Make a poster that shows ways to save water and energy. Put it up in a place where people can see it.

Outdoor Skills and Adventures

Becky's Camping Trip

Becky woke up an hour earlier than usual on Monday. She listened for a moment, holding her breath. "Fantastic! No rain." She jumped out of bed, almost tripping over her bright red backpack and duffel bag.

"I just have to finish packing and I'll be ready to go. It's supposed to be about 80 degrees. So, I'll have to decide on my clothing and my other things to bring. Think I'll do this before breakfast."

Just then Becky's father knocked on the door, opened it a little, and put his head around the corner.

"How are you doing? Your first

Tips

For many girls, Girl Scouting provides the opportunity to do outdoor activities and go camping. Preparation of your troop for any outdoor adventure starts with preparing yourself. Many Girl Scout councils provide training in outdoor activities that start at the door of your troop

meeting place, and progress over several months to include walks in the neighborhood, picnics, bike hikes, and outdoor games with other troops. You must feel comfortable in order to help girls prepare themselves properly and enjoy the activity with you. Read *Safety-Wise* and contact your local Girl Scout council representative for help and information.

Before attempting an overnight

experience far from home, girls should have a progressive series of experiences that teach them how to dress for the outdoors and how to prepare simple foods. They should know safety rules, how to be a buddy to another girl, and how to behave in a group. A slumber party or a backyard sleep-out close to home may provide some girls with their first night away from home, an opportu-

overnight camping trip! Are you almost ready? Mrs. Williams said to meet at the First Baptist Church at noon."

"I don't think I have too much more to do, Dad," Becky said. "Just finish packing. I can't wait to go."

"You mean you won't miss your dear old dad at all?" her father asked.

"We-e-elll," Becky said, "I guess I will—just a little bit, when we're not busy doing all our stuff at camp. Maybe I will be a little homesick, but Mrs. Williams told us to expect to feel homesick and she said we'll be so busy that we won't have too much time to think about it."

"Finish packing and I'll get you breakfast. What about my special pancakes for my special camper?"

"Great, Dad, I'll be downstairs soon."

Find out from your Brownie Girl Scout leader or older Girl Scout some of the things you can do on a camping trip. What things do you need to bring on a camping trip?

The outdoors is an especially good place for you to discover and observe the hows and whys of things in nature. Your outdoor adventure may be a nature walk, a picnic, an outside game, or a camping trip. Before you do anything in the outdoors, make sure you are ready. Always use this checklist to help you get ready.

☐ Plan ahead. Think about what

149

nity to care for their own belongings, and a learning experience that provides independence from one's family for a short time. Also, family involvement is important so that parents or guardians understand the types of clothing and equipment necessary for a girl's first overnight trip in the outdoors. A meeting with families to review the plans for the trip and the clothing and equipment list would be very helpful. In addition, parents can ask questions about the site you will be using and the activities that are planned. When families do not have the resources to provide the necessary equipment, check with your Girl Scout council for suggestions of other community resources.

Try-Its and Other Resources

- Other Resources: *Safety-Wise*; *Outdoor Education in Girl Scouting*; Girl Scout council outdoor training.

Look Out

What is it like where you are going? What do you need to know before going out? Here are some skills that will be important each time you go outdoors.

Plan Ahead

Your leader will help you plan where and when you go out. You will most likely work in your Brownie Girl Scout Ring to come up with ideas of where to go and what to do. Once you decide you are going out, you can discuss what you need to wear, what you need to take, and what will cost money. The best thing about most outdoor adventures is that they do not cost a lot of money. You only need to step out into your neighborhood, backyard, or schoolyard to enjoy the outdoors.

What to Wear

It is very important to learn about the best clothing to wear in different outdoor situations. It is

you will do. Talk about your plans with your friends, your parents, and the adults who will go with you.

☐ Learn skills. Learn and practice the skills you will need to enjoy the outdoors.

☐ Dress right. Make sure your clothes are right for the activities and the weather. Always be prepared!

☐ Keep safe. Learn the safety rules you need for the place you are going, and the safety rules for the equipment you will be using.

☐ Practice minimum impact in the outdoors. Leave a place better than when you found it. Be prepared to take out your garbage and practice conservation in the outdoors.

150

Tips

Becky's Camping Trip: Girls can brainstorm the types of things that Becky would pack in her duffel bag. You could also provide a long list of items and ask girls to choose just ten things that they "must bring." You could also "pack" for different

types of experiences and different lengths of trips.

The activities in the "Outdoor Skills and Adventures" section are organized progressively in the categories: Look Out, Meet Out, Move Out, Explore Out, and Sleep Out. Each set of activities builds on the skills and attitudes learned previously.

"Look Out" includes activities to prepare girls for their first experiences. Girls can also have a fashion show of the types of clothing to wear for different types of weather. Girls can draw cartoon do's and don'ts to show proper clothing. Try a relay game in which the girls pack and unpack a daypack.

always best to be prepared for the worst weather.

Some clothing hints:

- Remember that comfortable shoes and socks are a must for walking, whether in the city or the country. For long walks, always wear shoes that have been broken in.

- On hot days, loose clothing is good because it lets you move freely and lets the air in and out. On cold days, it is important to wear layers of clothing to hold your body heat and keep you warm.
- Cotton and other natural materials are much better than other fabrics to wear, especially in the summer. Wool is a good material to wear in the winter, especially when layering. Wool has air spaces and will keep you warmer than cotton.

- Wear a hat with a brim in the sun.
- In very sunny weather, wear a lightweight, cotton, long-sleeved shirt to avoid sunburn. Never wear a sun top or halter on a hike in the sun.
- Wear a wool hat in cold, windy weather to help you keep your body heat.

- Wear wool socks and wool mittens or gloves in cold weather.

Try this experiment. Take a strip of cotton material and a strip of wool material about four inches long. (You can also do this experiment with wool and cotton socks.) Hold each over a bowl of water and let the bottom of the material just touch the water. What happens? What would happen if the material was the bottom of your pant leg? Which material would be better to wear in the snow or cold rain?

On a sunny day, put a piece of dark cotton clothing and white cotton clothing in the sun. After a little while, feel the clothing. Which is better to wear in hot weather?

A Day Pack

Do you carry a day pack to school? Day packs are useful for trips in the outdoors. If you plan on going outdoors for several hours, a whole day, or even several days,

151

Try-Its and Other Resources

- Try-Its: Outdoor Adventurer.

what are some things to carry in your day pack?

• A **water bottle.** You can use a plastic soda bottle and fill it with water from home, or you can buy a plastic water bottle. You need to drink water because you perspire, even on a cold day.

• A **whistle.** This is to use if you become lost or separated from the group. It's better to spend your energy blowing a whistle than yelling or crying. You should not blow your whistle unless you are lost or in trouble.

• A **rain poncho or windbreaker.** This is part of being prepared.

• A **quarter for the phone.** This is in case of an emergency. It is also important to have emergency phone numbers written down, along with your name and address.

• A **high-energy snack.** Some hard candy will work, or, try some gorp. (See page 154.)

• **Sunscreen** and **lip protection.** These will protect your skin and lips from the sun.

• A **sit-upon.** Make one before going outdoors. See the "Sit-Upon" activity in the Girl Scout Ways Try-It.

Minimum Impact

Minimum impact is an important way of living for Girl Scouts. You think about the way you affect your environment before you act, and because you think first, you do the least possible amount of damage to the environment. When you are in the outdoors, you try to leave it just the way you found it or help to make it better.

Some ways of practicing minimum impact are:

• Don't pick the flowers or plants that you see on a hike.
• Take a garbage bag to collect litter when your group goes on a hike.
• Pick up all the garbage and either take it to a trash can or carry it out.
• Don't waste water when you are outdoors.
• Don't wash out dishes near a lake or stream.
• Take your own cup, forks, knives, and spoons on outings, instead of using paper, polystyrene, or plastic materials.
• Don't feed wild animals in the parks or forest.
• When hiking, stay on the trails. If you do not, you can cause soil erosion.

Meet Out

Your first adventures might be in the backyard, playground, or in your neighborhood with your troop. There are lots of fun activities in your Brownie Girl Scout Try-Its to do in the outdoors. Many activities in other chapters of this book can

152

Minimum Impact: Girls and adults should be aware of their impact on the environment. There are playgrounds and parks specially built for children's play. However, there are many other outdoor areas that can be severely disturbed by inappropriate behavior, such as leaving litter or unused food behind. It is best to leave no trace that you have been in a natural area. Your council may have a copy of the slide show *From Backyard to Backcountry: Camping Lightly on the Land*, which explains how Brownie Girl Scouts can start to learn outdoors skills without harming the environment.

• Try-Its: Animals; Outdoor Fun; Outdoor Adventurer.
• Other Resources: *From Backyard to Backcountry: Camping Lightly on the Land*; *Outdoor Education in Girl Scouting.*

be done in the outdoors.

Safety

Remember that you always go as buddies and that you are always prepared for the weather.

If you need to go to the bathroom in a strange place, you should let an adult know and use her as a buddy.

Before you meet out, find out where the nearest drinking water is. If there is none, be sure your group takes a supply or you take a water bottle.

You probably will see animals in the outdoors. Some of them are pets. They may be on a leash, or they may be running loose. What should you do if you see a strange dog? Do the "Meeting an Animal" activity in the Animals Try-It.

What about the wild animals you see in the parks, like birds, or squirrels, or even rats? You should never approach a wild or strange animal. Animals may carry diseases

that you can get from being scratched or bitten.

It is important not to leave food lying around that attracts wild animals like squirrels, raccoons, rats, and even bears. These animals have food in their environment and will become pests if you feed them. You may feed birds in the winter because food is hard for them to find.

Use Your Senses in the Outdoors

The following activities help you use your senses of touch, sight, smell, and hearing to explore the outdoors.

- Try the "Touch, Smell, Listen" activity in the Outdoor Fun Try-It.
- Use a magnifying glass to find the smallest living things you can.
- Have a cloud watch. Look for clouds of different shapes and colors.
- Look for different shapes in natural things— circles, squares, triangles, ovals, diamonds, and straight lines.
- Look for different colors in the outdoors. Cut out ten different color patches from a magazine and try to match them in the outdoors.
- Go on a listening hike in the woods or by the water. Listen carefully. You may hear many different sounds. Can you identify the sources of the sounds you are hearing?
- Sit in a spot very quietly with a piece of paper and pencil. Put an "X" in the middle of the paper that shows where

153

Tips

Meet Out: These activities are done outdoors. In many, girls use their senses to explore what is around them. Make sure girls know the appropriate safety rules before going outdoors. The area you choose for these activities should be examined ahead of time. Help girls learn to identify poison ivy, poison oak, or other, similar plants that may grow in your area. These are great activities to do during any outdoor adventure. However, you will not want to do them all at once. Girls need to be in the right frame of mind for careful observation and listening. Ask girls about the differences they find as they look at the bark, leaves, or stems of two different trees. Look for things that feel smooth, slippery, or velvety. Look for lots of different colors in nature: white, black, gray, purple, red, pink, yellow, silver. Many activities in other parts of the girls' handbook or in the Try-Its can just as easily be done outdoors— games, arts activities, and stories.

Try-Its and Other Resources

- Try-Its: Outdoor Fun.
- Other Resources: *Exploring Wildlife Communities With Children.*

you are. Listen for sounds and draw them on your map as you hear them. You can make symbols to show where the sound was, and how big a sound it was. Compare your map to the map of someone else listening at the same time. What was the loudest sound you heard? The softest? *Games for Girl Scouts* has many more

 154

outdoor games like this one.

• Learn many things through your sense of smell. Your nose can be a warning system for your body because things that smell bad might also be harmful. Smell as many different outdoor things as you can. Remember not to pick or cut any growing thing. Look for things already on the ground. Here are some ideas: a torn leaf, flowers, wet soil, a crushed blade of grass, recently snapped twigs, pond water, wet pieces of wood, pine cones, seashells, moss, evergreen needles.

• Go on a scent hike. Have a pair of girls or an adult lay out a simple scent trail that you can follow with your nose. Have them take an onion or cotton swabs dipped in oil of cloves or peppermint oil and rub it on things like trees or signs so that you can follow the trail with your nose.

• Try hugging a tree. How does your tree feel? How is it different from some other trees? Find out more about your tree. Try watching your tree throughout the year. What happens?

• Make a bark or leaf rubbing. Place a piece of paper over the bark of your tree, and with the side of a crayon rub in one direction to gently record your bark picture. Or use a leaf that has fallen on the ground. Place your leaf on a flat surface. With the paper over it, rub gently with a crayon to trace the outline of the leaf and its veins.

Move Out

Go beyond the backyard and playground to the neighborhood and nearby natural spots. Before you go, make some gorp to carry in your day pack. The ingredients are raisins, peanuts, dried cereal, dried fruit, dried coconut, and other dried nuts. Mix any and all of the ingredients and put them in a small container or plastic bag.

When you move out into the neighborhood and natural places, try these activities:

- Make a map of your neighborhood and do the "Street Safety" activity in the Safety Try-it.
- Learn to be a better observer in the outdoors. Practice describing the things you see and hear outdoors. Try this simple activity. Sit back-to-back with a friend. Pick up something or look at something and describe it carefully to your friend. Have your friend guess what you are describing.
- Make a record of a special spot. Take photographs, make a tape recording, draw a picture, or write a description. Share your special spot with others.

- Try a habitat hunt. Every plant and animal has a home or a place where it lives, called a "habitat." It may be a tree for a squirrel, the swamp for a frog, the forest for a deer, or the beach for a hermit crab. Look for a plant or animal in the outdoors. What things are part of its habitat? See how many animals you can find, and try to decide where each lives. Often a baby bird will fall out of the nest, or be hopping around on the ground waiting for the mother bird to come and feed it. It looks like it has been abandoned. What should you do? It is very important to leave the baby bird alone, so the parent can feed it. It is best to walk away.
- Try a seed hunt. Many plants start as seeds. Seeds differ in shapes and sizes and can travel, too! For example, dandelion seeds float as if they

Maple Seeds

Berries

Burrs

Dandelion

Violet Seeds

had parachutes. Maple seeds whirl like helicopter blades. Burrs ride piggyback on animals. Violet seeds pop like missiles. Berries are sometimes carried "air mail" by flying birds. Try to find as many different kinds of seeds as you can.

HANDBOOK Page 155

155

Move Out: In these activities, girls move beyond the troop or group meeting area. Again, reviewing safety rules is essential.

- Try-Its: Earth and Sky; Safety.

Explore Out

Plan a special outdoor activity. Learn some outdoor skills that will help you explore out beyond your neighborhood. You may still walk, take public transportation, or even car-pool to a special place. You will need some additional safety rules, and usually a permission slip from your parents.

Planning

When you begin planning, you may want to list some places to go. Have everyone list special places they would like to visit, or activities they would like to do. Your list might look like the one below.

PLACES TO GO:	THINGS TO DO:
The Mountains	Hike
The next town	Bike
An arboretum	Learn about trees
A forest	Plant trees
A national park	Visit with a ranger
The ocean	Study tide pools
An outdoor museum	Do a history walk
A lake resort	Swim
A pond	Study pond life
A stream	Clean up the stream

156

What other places would you like to visit? What other activities would you like to do?

Exploring out takes planning and preparation and you may spend meeting time making decisions about where you will be going, learning about the place you will be visiting, and practicing the skills you will need. Make sure you review the safety tips on page 153 and the sections on safety and first aid in the chapter "Taking Care of Yourself and Your Home."

Before You Go

Try making some no-cook snacks. Make a walking salad with carrots, celery sticks, raisins, and apple slices dipped in lemon juice. Stuff the celery sticks with peanut butter. Some other no-cook snacks that are good on a hike are cheese and crackers, fruit, energy bars, and dried fruit. If you are going to be traveling in hot weather, you should not take sandwiches with foods that can spoil. Peanut butter and jelly are two foods that won't spoil easily.

Tips

Explore Out: Proper planning is essential. Girls in the troop or group may have gone camping with their families and be able to show others the skills they possess. Girls should have an active role in the planning process, from choosing the place they will go to deciding what they need to bring.

Try-Its and Other Resources

- Try-Its: Food Fun; Good Food; Outdoor Adventurer; Outdoor Fun; Water Everywhere.
- Other Resources: *Exploring Wildlife Communities With Children; Safety-Wise.*

Before you explore out, learn how to make and use these trail signs:

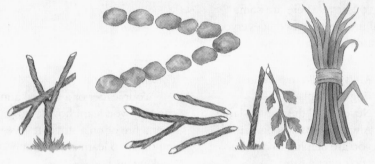

Turn to the right.

Keep going.

Warning:
Look for a message.

Turn to the left.

Turn around and go back.

You're Off!

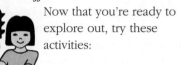

Now that you're ready to explore out, try these activities:

- Lay a trail for another group. Hide a nice surprise at the end.
- Visit a pond or stream and find out what creatures live in this habitat. Build a "Water Snooper" to use in your pond exploration from the Water Everywhere Try-It.
- Explore the city. Do some outdoor exploration from the Building Art Try-It.
- Do some activities from the Outdoor Adventurer Try-It, such as "A Hike" or "Camp."

Sleep Out

After you have explored out and felt comfortable being away from home and in the outdoors, you will probably want to

157

sleep out. You can get ready to sleep out in a camp cabin or tent by learning some new skills and going on a slumber party in someone's home or backyard. Sleeping out can be a lot of fun.

Staying overnight involves a lot of planning and learning some new skills. It is best to practice those skills in your meetings or when you are having your slumber party.

Fires

Campfires and cooking over a fire have always been a part of Girl Scout camping. Many people use cookstoves when they cook in the outdoors. To practice minimum impact, you should always have small fires. A fire that is too big uses too much wood and can get out of control.

You may be asked to help gather firewood. Look for small branches and sticks on the ground that have fallen from trees.

You may be asked to help start a fire. Your leader or an adult will show you how. There are some special fire safety rules that everyone needs to know.

- Always build the fire in a fire ring or fireplace.
- Never build the fire too large.
- Always tie back long hair if you are helping to build or cook over a fire.
- Never wear plastic or flammable clothing around a fire. Flammable clothing is clothing that burns easily.
- If you are cooking something over a fire on a stick, always be careful of the people around you.
- Do not play with sticks in the fire.
- Always wear shoes and long pants around a fire.
- A bucket of water or hose and a shovel should always be nearby.

Cooking

Your leader or a trained adult can help you learn how to cook over a fire or on a stove. It is very important to learn safety around the cooking area.

- You should never run or play around a stove or cooking area.
- You should always wash your hands.
- You should never play with matches.
- You should never turn the gas off or on unless an adult is watching you.

158

Tips

Sleep Out: Girls can attend an event sponsored by their Girl Scout council in which they stay overnight, or you may plan a slumber party at someone's home or in someone's backyard. You may have to assess the readiness of all the girls in your troop for an overnight experience. Some girls may not yet be ready to spend the night away from their families. All the activities in this section should be practiced in meetings. Most can easily be adapted into games.

Well before the group's first trip, conduct a meeting with parents to discuss what types of sleeping bags, bedrolls, and packing are needed for the trip. Therefore, girls and parents need information about the expected weather at the chosen site. The sleeping bag needs to be the right size for the child. One that is too big will not provide enough warmth when it is cold. Sleeping bags come with

Read the section called "Eating Right" in the chapter "Taking Care of Yourself and Your Home." With a group or troop, plan what you will need to eat. You might decide to cook a simple one-pot meal over the stove or fire. Look at the food pyramid on page 39. What foods could you mix in a pot to make a delicious and healthy outdoor soup or stew?

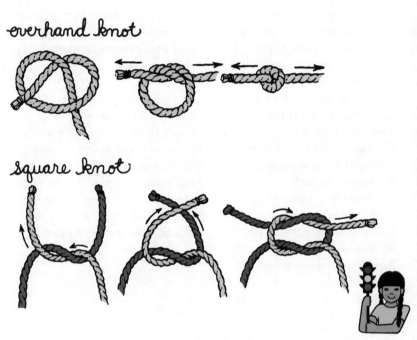

knots

You will need to learn how to tie a few knots in order to tie your sleeping bag and other camp gear.

An **overhand knot** is a knot in the end of a rope. This easy knot is made with one piece of rope. Follow the steps in the picture.

overhand knot

A **square knot** is used to tie two ropes together or to tie a package. It is also the knot used to tie a bandana around your neck.

square knot

1. Tie two pieces of rope together, following the steps in the picture. Remember this poem:
"Right over left and left over right Makes the knot neat and tidy and tight."

159

different amounts of filling, depending on the conditions in which they will be used. Girls who do not have a sleeping bag can make a bedroll with a sheet and two or more blankets.

Try-Its and Other Resources

- Try-Its: Food Fun; Outdoor Adventurer; Outdoor Fun.
- Other Resources: Council outdoor training; *Outdoor Education in Girl Scouting*; *Safety-Wise*.

Sleeping

Before you sleep out:

- Find out about sleeping bags or bedrolls.
- Learn how to roll and tie a sleeping bag or bedroll.
- Have a sleeping bag rolling relay. You need two sleeping bags. The first person runs with the sleeping bag to a line that has been set. She unrolls the bag and runs back to tag the second person. That person must run up to the bag, roll it up, and bring it back to the next person in line, and so forth.
- Try sleeping at home in a sleeping bag or bedroll.
- Plan a slumber party at a friend's house or backyard.
- Participate in an overnight sponsored by your Girl Scout council.
- Plan an overnight at a council-owned campsite. Stay in cabins or wall tents that have cooking and restroom facilities.
- Find out about day camp or resident camp in your council. Plan to attend and practice your skills.

The outdoor skills you learn in Brownie Girl Scouts are just a beginning to many more adventures in the out-of-doors in Girl Scouting. You may live in a big city or in a small town. You may live on a farm or in a suburb. Wherever you live, you can find a way to use your outdoor skills and learn more about the outdoor world.

160

Additional resources for this chapter:

Burnie, David, *How Nature Works: 100 Ways Parents and Kids Can Share the Secrets of Nature* (Pleasantville, N.Y.: The Reader's Digest Foundation, 1991).

Cassidy, John, *Explorabook: A Kids' Science Museum in a Book* (Palo Alto, Calif.: Klutz Press, 1991).

Downie, Diane, Twila Slesnick, and Jean Kerr Stenmark, *Math for Girls and Other Problem Solvers* (Berkeley, Calif.: Lawrence Hall of Science, University of California, 1981).

Farndon, John, *How the Earth Works: 100 Ways Parents and Kids Can Share the Secrets of the Earth* (Pleasantville, N.Y.: The Reader's Digest Foundation, 1992).

Flynn, Jennifer, Lisa Bucki, and Sherry Kinkoph, *MatheMagic, Computer Fun with Numbers*! (Carmel, Ind.: Alpha Books, Division of Prentice-Hall Computer Publishing, 1992).

Hann, Judith, *How Science Works: 100 Ways Parents and Kids Can Share the Secrets of Science* (Pleasantville, N.Y.: The Reader's Digest Foundation, 1991).

Salpeter, Judy, *Kids and Computers: A Parent's Handbook* (Carmel, Ind.: SAMS, Division of Prentice-Hall Computer Publishing, 1992).

Walpole, Brenda, *175 Science Experiments to Amuse and Amaze Your Friends* (New York: Random House, 1988).

Brownie Girl Scout Try-Its
and Bridge to Junior Girl Scouts Patch

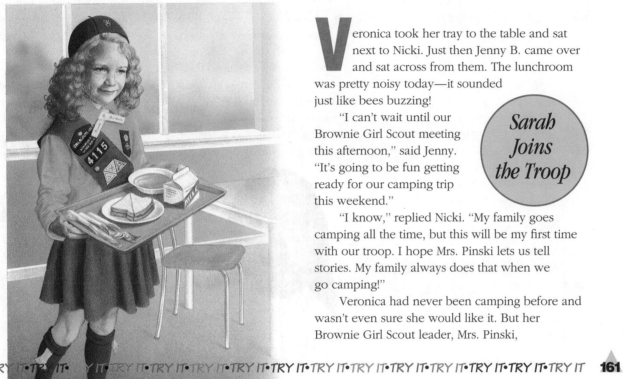

Veronica took her tray to the table and sat next to Nicki. Just then Jenny B. came over and sat across from them. The lunchroom was pretty noisy today—it sounded just like bees buzzing!

"I can't wait until our Brownie Girl Scout meeting this afternoon," said Jenny. "It's going to be fun getting ready for our camping trip this weekend."

"I know," replied Nicki. "My family goes camping all the time, but this will be my first time with our troop. I hope Mrs. Pinski lets us tell stories. My family always does that when we go camping!"

Veronica had never been camping before and wasn't even sure she would like it. But her Brownie Girl Scout leader, Mrs. Pinski,

Sarah Joins the Troop

TRY IT•TRY IT•TRY IT•TRY IT•TRY IT•TRY IT•TRY IT•**TRY IT**•TRY IT•TRY IT•TRY IT•TRY IT•**TRY IT**•TRY IT•TRY IT **161**

There are 40 Brownie Girl Scout Try-Its. Pages 10–11 in Part I of this book provide tips and information on the Try-Its activities.

Tips

This story covers some of the activities done by Brownie Girl Scouts. Some girls at the Brownie Girl Scout age level may become competitive about earning Try-Its. They begin to value the quantity of patches over the quality of their experiences. You can help guide girls to an understanding that "more doesn't equal better" and that there are other fun things to do: trips, service projects, activities in the handbook, games, songs, and the myriad of other activities the girls and you can plan together. Choices and variety are important for girls.

was really cool, and always helped them learn neat things. Everyone in the troop was really excited about the camping trip.

Just then, Sarah, a new girl in school, came and sat at their table. She was wearing her Brownie Girl Scout uniform. Nicki had heard Sarah was going to join their troop.

"We were just talking about our camping trip this weekend. Are you going?" asked Nicki.

"Yes, I think so," said Sarah. "I asked my mom and she said yes."

"I've never been camping before," said Veronica. "Mrs. Pinski has been teaching us lots of things to get us ready. Last week we practiced making a bedroll. Today we're going to use our mess kits and go over the safety rules again."

"Is there a Try-It for camping?" Sarah asked.

Jenny answered, "I don't really know. We don't do a lot of Try-Its in our troop"

"In my other Brownie troop, we got a lot of Try-Its," Sarah said

as she pointed to her sash.

Nicki got excited. "I remember! Mrs. Pinski said we would do some Try-It activities this weekend. But we're going to do lots of other things, too." Veronica also remembered. "We already did some other stuff for Try-Its, but we haven't finished everything yet. When we do, we'll have a special ceremony."

"Really?" Sarah said, "We got our Try-Its when we finished the activities. A special ceremony sounds like fun. What do you do?"

"A ceremony is like a special celebration. We had one when the other new girls joined our troop.

We took turns saying poems and we sang songs like 'Make New Friends.' Some of us are working on a special flag ceremony for our camping trip this weekend."

Sarah looked interested. "What else do you do?"

"We do lots of fun stuff all the time," said Veronica. "Last week we went to the Natural History Museum and saw dinosaur skeletons. It was fun!"

"Another time we planted flowers and plants in front of the nursing home," said Jenny B. "Then we had a party with the people who live there. We had a great time!"

162 *TRY IT•TRY IT•TRY IT•TRY IT•TRY IT•TRY IT•TRY IT•TRY IT•TRY IT•TRY IT•TRY IT•TRY IT•TRY IT•TRY IT•TRY IT•TRY IT*

163

"You know what I liked?" asked Nicki. "The time we had that spaghetti dinner for our families. We decided how much money we had to spend and then we shopped and then we cooked the whole dinner ourselves!"

"That sounds like fun, too!" Sarah said. "I like cooking. In our troop, we earned the Good Food Try-It. I even taught my mom some stuff about eating healthy food."

Sarah thought for a minute. "You really do a lot of fun things, trips, and projects. I thought getting a lot of Try-Its was fun and they are fun to do, but trips and other stuff you were talking about sound like fun, too!"

Just then the bell rang. Veronica, Nicki, Jenny, and Sarah all got up from the table.

"I think we'll have a lot of fun on our camping trip," said Sarah. "We sure will, even Veronica!" the others all said at once.

"Make New Friends" is a song that has been popular in Girl Scouts for decades. More songs can be found on pages 28–30 in Part I of this book and the "Brownie Girl Scout Smile Song," another traditional favorite, is on handbook page 24 in "Welcome to Girl Scouts."

About Try-Its

Brownie Girl Scout Try-Its are just one part of the whole Girl Scout program. Their name says it all—Try-It. You don't have to be perfect at an activity; you just have to try. Sometimes you may decide you don't want to finish a Try-It. That's okay. You can come back to it later. Or you can just go on to something else. You will want to do most of the activities with your troop or group anyway, and lots of things are more fun if you do them with others. The only requirement for Brownie Girl Scout activities is that they be fun!

You will probably work on Try-It activities as a group. Your whole troop or group may work together, or maybe just the girls in your Brownie Girl Scout circle. Before you start a Try-It, look at the section "Leadership and Group Planning" in the chapter "Leadership in Girl Scouting and Beyond" and read about working in a Brownie Girl Scout Ring or circle. Be sure to use the four steps as a guide to making decisions as a group.

For each Try-It, you have six activities to choose from. When you have finished four activities in one Try-It, you have done enough to complete it. You and the other girls can then plan a Court of Awards ceremony as a special way to receive your Try-Its. Sometimes you'll have one Court of Awards a year or you may have Court of Awards more often. Each troop is different.

Some of the Try-Its have a "More to Try" section. This section is extra and can be done if you really like a topic and want to learn more about it. You can also do more than four activities in a Try-It.

As Mrs. Pinski and the girls in her troop already know, Brownie Girl Scout Try-Its are a part of what you can look forward to as a Brownie Girl Scout. You don't have to earn all 40 Try-Its. In fact, if you do, you're missing out on a lot of the other things you could be doing, like camping or community service projects. And doing something just because it's fun!

Tips

The Try-Its are in alphabetical order. The color of the borders corresponds to one of the five worlds of interest.

Red = World of Well-Being
Blue = World of People
Orange = World of Today and Tomorrow
Purple = World of the Arts
Yellow = World of the Out-of-Doors

HERE IS A LIST OF THE BROWNIE GIRL SCOUT TRY-ITS:

A
Animals
Around the World
Art to Wear

B
Building Art

C
Careers
Caring and Sharing
Citizen Near and Far
Colors and Shapes
Creative Composing

D
Dancercize

E
Earth and Sky
Earth Is Our Home

F
Food Fun

G
Girl Scout Ways
Good Food

H
Her Story
Hobbies

L
Listening to the Past

M
Manners
Math Fun
Me and My Shadow
Movers
Music
My Body

N
Numbers and Shapes

O
Outdoor Adventurer
Outdoor Fun
Outdoor Happenings

P
People of the World
Plants
Play
Puppets, Dolls, and Plays

S
Safety
Science in Action
Science Wonders
Senses
Sounds of Music
Space Explorer
Sports and Games

W
Water Everywhere

TRY IT•TRY IT•TRY IT•TRY IT•TRY IT•TRY IT•TRY IT•TRY IT•TRY IT•TRY IT•TRY IT•TRY IT•TRY IT•TRY IT•TRY IT•TRY IT **165**

HANDBOOK
Page 166

Tips

Girls get an introduction to the animal kingdom. This is such a big topic that only portions are covered for girls to explore. Animals are divided into two groups: those with backbones and those without. Animals with backbones are found in five major groups: mammals, birds, reptiles, amphibians, and fish. Those without backbones and internal skeletons include everything from insects to worms to snails. If girls express interest in this topic, there are many great books about animals.

As girls learn more about animals, their level of sophistication will increase, and lead them to discover different ways to classify animals, beyond body types. Look for animals that eat meat (carnivores), those that eat plants (herbivores), or those that eat everything (omnivores). Discover animals that go about their lives in the dark (nocturnal), as opposed to the daylight (diurnal)? Are there animals that live only in salt water, instead of fresh? Which animals live only in cold climates, or which live in hot climates? As girls explore these differences, they can begin to see differences in habitat, a concept introduced in "Shelter for All" and "Animals in Danger." You might ask girls to design an animal to live in a particular habitat. This can be done either by drawing the creature or modeling it in clay after a habitat is described by the leader or chosen by the girls. Ask girls to describe the things that make up their own habitat.

Encourage girls to explore habitats in different ways. Take a night hike with flashlights and look for spiders and other small creatures, earthworms on top of the earth after a rain, or listen for sounds animals make at night (see the Listen List in the Outdoor Fun Try-It). Try the "Water Explorer" activity in the Water Everywhere Try-It.

Meeting an Animal. Girls might be interested in taking pets to visit adopted grandparents at a retirement home as a service project. See handbook pages 58–59 in "Taking Care of Yourself and Your Home" and handbook page 153 in "How and Why?" for more about animal safety.

TRY IT!

ANIMALS

There are many different kinds of animals. Insects, snakes, lizards, frogs, fish and snails, dogs, cats, and cows are animals. Explore the world of animals in this Try-It.

Meeting an Animal

How should you behave when meeting an animal for the first time? It depends upon whether it is someone's pet or an animal in the wild. Read about meeting an animal on page 153 in "How and Why?"

Visit a veterinarian or animal shelter and learn about the differences between animals that are pets and animals that are wild. Find out what the rules of conduct are around such animals. Find out what dangers there are in approaching wild or pet animals. Make a poster or play about how to treat animals in the neighborhood or in the wild.

How They Look

Animals are divided into groups by the kinds of bodies they have and how they live. Can you find animals that match the descriptions below by observing them in your habitat, at the zoo, or in a book?

- Animals that have 2 legs, 4 legs, 6 legs, and 8 legs.
- Animals with no legs.
- Animals that have fur.
- Animals that have lips.
- Animals that live in water.
- Animals that have antennae.
- Animals that have soft, squishy bodies.
- Animals with feathers.
- Animals with wings but no feathers.
- Animals with scales.
- Animals that have shells.
- Animals with paws, animals with claws, animals with flippers, animals with hooves.

How They Act

Observe animals at the zoo, in your neighborhood, or on TV. Find out how animals act. Find animals that:

- Eat meat.
- Dig.
- Fly.
- Hop.
- Crawl.
- Live underground.
- Live up in trees.
- Swim.
- Run.
- Live in groups.
- Live alone.
- Travel long distances.
- Stay close to home.

How can you keep a record of this information?

How does the type of bodies that animals have affect the way animals act?

Shelter for All

Every animal needs some sort of shelter to protect it from the weather and other animals. The place where a plant or animal lives is called its habitat. It includes space, food, shelter, and a place to raise young. Do the habitat hunt on page 155 of this book.

TRY IT•TRY IT•TRY IT•TRY IT•TRY IT•TRY IT•TRY IT•TRY IT•TRY IT•TRY IT•TRY IT•TRY IT•TRY IT•TRY IT•TRY IT **167**

How They Act. Girls might make a scrapbook of their animal observations, draw the animals they see, or describe animal actions in writing. You might brainstorm animal action words as a group before describing animal actions. Try the "Animal Moves" activity in the Dancercize Try-It as an introduction to this activity.

Shelter for All. The "Food Chain Lineup" and "Food Web Game" in *Games for Girl Scouts* are fun ways to learn about animals and how they interrelate. When doing these games, have the girls find out what each animal eats beforehand, or put information about each animal on the back of a picture of the animal to be used in the game.

Animal Sounds. Tapes of animal sounds may be available at your public library. Many girls may not have heard the many different sounds animals make. You might discuss the difference in sounds when an animal is communicating different things, such as when playing, when afraid, or when in danger. Girls might want to expand this activity to other forms of communication. Movements, such as thumping, strutting, grooming, posturing, fluttering, dancing, or spreading wings are animal acts that might be pantomimed after observation and/or discussion.

Animal Sounds

Animals communicate in many different ways. Some touch; some make noise; and some leave a smell. Play animal sounds charade. Have your friends guess what animal you are. Here are some animals to try.

Chicken	Lion	Parrot
Bee	Frog	Skunk
Cricket	Alligator	Elephant
Monkey	Horse	Donkey
Rattlesnake	Whale	Lizard
Cat	Squirrel	Robin
Dog	Fly	Bat

Write the name of each animal on a small piece of paper. Put the pieces of paper in a bag and shake well. Pull out an animal name and show others who you are by sounding like that animal.

Animals in Danger

Many animals need a special habitat to survive. Survival means that an animal can live and raise its young, while also having enough food, water, space, and shelter. When an animal group, called a species, loses animals because there is not enough food, water, space, or shelter, the animal species is said to be endangered. The group of animals can die if there are not enough of them to have families. Once a species disappears, it is extinct. Find out about an animal species that is endangered in your state or area. Find out what people are doing to save it and why. What can you do to help?

Animals in Danger. Your troop may wish to "adopt an animal" at your local zoo, help at a wildlife rehabilitation facility, construct bluebird, wood duck, or bat boxes, or plant an area for wildlife habitat. State wildlife agencies, local Audubon groups, and zoos are good resources to help with further discussion and activities.

Cautions: Many personal values and opinions are involved in any discussion of animal rights. It is important for girls to learn to care for animals and to respect animals in the wild. The guidelines for discussing contemporary issues found in *Safety-Wise* should be used when approaching the topic of animal rights.

Your troop may want to raise funds to assist animal shelters or wildlife causes. Review fund-raising guidelines in *Safety-Wise*. Girl Scouts cannot raise funds for other organizations, but they may decide to use troop funds for a specific purpose. Remember that you cannot write lobbying letters as Girl Scouts.

Try-Its and Other Resources

- Other Resources: *Exploring Wildlife Communities With Children* has excellent background material on animal habitats as well as many simple activities that can help girls learn about animals. *Earth Matters*; *Games for Girl Scouts*—"Animal Who Am I?," "Nature Lotto," and "Animal Call Out" are nature games that can be adapted for use with this Try-It. The following organizations are excellent resources for materials and activities: Defenders of Wildlife, National Wildlife Federation, National Association for Humane and Environmental Education, and World Wildlife Fund. Addresses can be found in the resource section of *Earth Matters*. *Ranger Rick's Nature Magazine* and *Ranger Rick's NatureScope* series from the National Wildlife Federation are also excellent sources for activities and information.

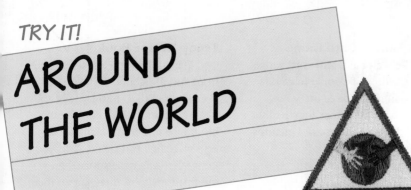

TRY IT!

AROUND THE WORLD

The world is made up of many different peoples and cultures.

Brownie Girl Scouts Around the World ✓

Look back at the chapter "People Near and Far." What did you

starts p. 87

learn about Brownie Girl Scouts in Ghana, Thailand, Peru, and Denmark? Pick one of the activities on these pages and do it. You could make Adinkra cloth or a kite or a woven belt or learn a game.

Look at the World

Here is a fun way to learn about the world.

1. Find the United States of America on a map or globe. Try to use one that is new. Names of countries change often.

2. Look at the other countries on the map or globe. Name two countries close to the United States and two countries far away.

3. The equator is an imaginary line around the world that is an equal distance from the North Pole and the South Pole. The countries farthest from the equator have a very cold climate. Find the equator and follow it around the world on a map or globe.

4. Name ten countries that you think would have a hot climate.

5. Name ten countries that you think would have a cold climate.

TRY IT•TRY IT•**TRY IT**•TRY IT•TRY IT•**TRY IT**•TRY IT•**TRY IT**•TRY IT•**TRY IT**•TRY IT•TRY IT•TRY IT•TRY IT•**TRY IT**•**TRY IT**•TRY IT **169**

Tips

Some girls may have been born in another country or have family members who are able to trace their heritage back to one or more countries. Other girls may not. The concepts of nation and country may be difficult for some girls to grasp, though many children by this age have a highly developed sense of political awareness and may be familiar with current global issues. You may want to note that Brownie Girl Scouts are sisters to Girl Guides and Girl Scouts in many nations around the world. Pages 63–65 in Part I of this book have more information on WAGGGS and the "People Near and Far" chapter complements the activities in this Try-It. You might also wish to use *Valuing Differences* when working on this Try-It.

Look at the World. More to Try: Trace a world map and make copies. Girls can color the map and then glue it to heavy cardboard and make a world map jigsaw puzzle.

Books

Many storybooks have been written about families from different countries. Visit a public library and ask the librarian to help you find a story about a family from another country. Read the story to a younger child (maybe a brother or sister), or have someone read it to you.

Global Family Card Game

Make a global family card game. Collect pictures of people from different countries. Make sure your pictures show people as they really live and dress. Don't use old pictures that may be out-of-date or inaccurate.

You will need:

* Magazines and newspapers (your public library may give you magazines it no longer needs)
* Glue
* Scissors
* Index cards or light cardboard cut into 3″ x 5″ shapes

Glue a picture onto one side of your card. Write the name of the country on the back of the card. Make up some games using your global family cards.

More to Try: Hang your cards from wire hangers/wood dowling and make a mobile.

Troop Recipe Book

Many foods you like to eat come from another country. Have you ever had noodles, tortillas, egg rolls, peanut butter, or quiche? Where did they come from? Many foods also were first eaten here. Did you know that American Indians grew the first tomatoes, then shared them with the rest of the world?

You can find out more information like this by making a "Troop Recipe Book." Bring in family recipes. Share information about your recipe. Where is it from? Who gave it to you? How do you make it? Put the recipes together in a book. Why not try them for a special lunch or supper?

170 TRY IT•TRY IT•**TRY IT**•TRY IT•TRY IT•TRY IT•TRY IT•TRY IT•**TRY IT**•TRY IT•TRY IT•TRY IT•TRY IT•**TRY IT**•TRY IT•TRY IT

Global Family Card Game. It is essential that the pictures used for this activity are accurate and current. If only old pictures are available, it is better to skip this activity. Using old photos can reinforce stereotypes and the concept of difference being "exotic" and strange, rather than valuable.

Try-Its and Other Resources

* Try-Its: People of the World.
* Other Resources: "People Near and Far" chapter; *Valuing Differences*; *The Wide World of Girl Guiding and Girl Scouting*; *World Games and Recipes*; *Games for Girl Scouts*.

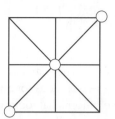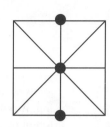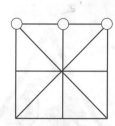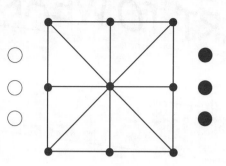

Tapatan

In countries all over the world, children play a game much like our tic-tac-toe. The game has other names. In England it is called Noughts and Crosses. In Sweden it is Tripp Trapp Trull. In Austria it is Ecke, Necke, Stecke. And in the Philippines it is called Tapatan. Like tic-tac-toe, the object is always to get "three in a row." Have fun playing Tapatan.

Each player needs three moving pieces. They can be pebbles, buttons, or checkers. Use the pictures to help you play.

1. Draw this diagram on paper or cardboard.

2. The game is played on the nine points where the lines meet. Players take turns putting their pieces on an empty point. This continues until all three pieces of each player are placed on the game board.

3. Player one moves one piece along a line to the next empty point. The pieces can be moved up or down or diagonally. Jumping over the pieces is not allowed. Player two does the same and they continue to take turns.

To win, a player must make a row of three across, up and down, or diagonally. If neither player can get three in a row, the game is called a draw.

TRY IT!

ART TO WEAR

Art can be many different things. It can be a painting or music or a poem. You can even wear works of art. Try these activities to see how.

T-Shirt Art

Show others your art by wearing it! Turn a plain T-shirt or sweatshirt into your own work of art.

You will need:

- A plain T-shirt or sweatshirt
- Paper
- A pencil
- Crayons or fabric paint

Decide what size design will fit on your shirt and draw it on a piece of paper. When you are satisfied with your design or picture sketch, you are ready to copy it onto the T-shirt. If you use paint, follow the directions that come with it. If you use crayons, color your design on a piece of white paper. Then put the design face down on the place where you want it. Put a paper towel on top. With the help of an adult, iron over the design. You may have to press down hard. It will soon show up on the shirt. Have a fashion show with the shirts you and your troop make.

OR

Hats can do more than keep your head warm. They can also show what a person does for a living. A police officer's hat looks different from a baseball player's cap. Sometimes people wear hats, like party hats, when they're celebrating. Make a special hat for yourself. Create your hat from paper, or find an old hat at home or in a secondhand store. You can also sew a hat from scraps of fabric. Decorate it with colored paper, fabric scraps, yarn, sequins, buttons, or natural materials.

Face Paint

Have a face-painting party. Make certain an adult is present. Be sure to use makeup and paints that are made just for the face. If you can't find enough face paint, or you just want to try something new, here

Tips

If you have the space available, even a bag or box in your car trunk, you might collect art supplies all year long so that you always have what you want at your fingertips. Parents and others in the community, including businesses, can save items for your troop or group. The following are some things you might collect: different kinds of paper, cardboard, tissue paper, white glue, crayons, markers, paper bags, shopping bags, yarn, fabric scraps, buttons, popsicle sticks, cardboard tubes, beads, costume jewelry, toothpicks, string, used greeting cards, wrapping paper, ribbons, wood scraps, paper clips, books and magazines, and other items.

are some face paints you can make right in your kitchen!

You will need:

* White shortening (or cold cream)
* Cornstarch (or baby powder)
* Unsweetened cocoa
* Food coloring
* Spoons
* Small bowls
* Cotton swabs to apply face paint

1. Mix the shortening and cornstarch together until they are creamy. Put some in each of the bowls.

2. Add the cocoa and more shortening to some bowls to make darker skin colors and shading.

3. Add food coloring to the rest of the bowls. Experiment with the colors.

4. Start painting each other's faces. Try different patterns, designs, and colors.

5. Clean up when you are

done. Use plenty of water on your face and don't rub hard with towels.

If possible, invite a makeup artist to your troop to demonstrate different kinds of face painting.

Papier-Mâché

Papier-mâché is a light material made from wastepaper and glue that can be easily molded. This is an easy way to make a new bracelet. It's lots of fun but really messy! Be sure to cover your clothes and your work surface.

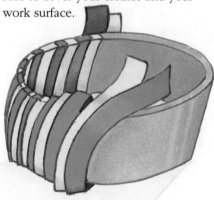

You will need:

* A cardboard tube that fits loosely over your wrist.
* Scrap paper for strips.
* Colored tissue paper, also used for strips.
* Scissors.
* Flour and water paste or liquid starch.
* A shallow pan (like the ones pies come in).

1. Cut the cardboard tube to the width you want for your bracelet.

2. Tear or cut the scrap paper and the tissue paper into strips. If you are doing this as a group, you can all do this at once.

3. Mix up a paste in the pan using flour and water. Make sure it is thin and runny without any lumps. Or, instead of flour and water, you can pour liquid starch in the pan and use it for paste.

4. Dip the scrap paper strips

TRY IT•TRY IT•TRY IT•TRY IT•TRY IT•TRY IT•TRY IT•TRY IT•TRY IT•TRY IT•TRY IT•TRY IT•TRY IT•TRY IT•TRY IT•TRY IT **173**

Papier Mâché. More to Try: Girls can experiment with different uses for papier mâché.

in the "People Near and Far" chapter can lead into this Try-It. *The Wide World of Girl Guiding and Girl Scouting.*

Try-Its and Other Resources

* Try-Its: Colors and Shapes.
* Other Resources: Art activities

into your paste, and pull them out one at a time. Layer the strips around the cardboard tube bracelet. Create an even surface or one with patterns and bumps. Use your fingers to mold and shape.

5. For the last layers, use strips of colored tissue paper. Create patterns or a solid surface. Place the bracelet in a warm, dry place. The thicker your bracelet is, the longer it will take to dry. Liquid starch may take longer to dry also.

Mask Making

Many people around the world make masks for ceremonies, holi-days, or dramatic events. Some masks are used to tell stories. Choose a holiday or special event and make a mask. Use a paper bag to create a new personality. Add bits of paper, yarn, or other materials to a paper bag. You can also draw on the bag with crayons or paint. Or use heavy cardboard as a base to create a mask that you hold to your face by a handle. (Chopsticks, popsicle sticks, or pencils make good handles.)

Beads

Create your own beads that you can use to make jewelry.

1. Follow the instructions for making the dough on page 186. You will need toothpicks to make the holes in the beads.

2. Take pieces of dough about the size of a grape, and roll or press them into beads with different sizes and shapes.

3. Use the toothpick to make the hole in the beads.

4. Let the beads dry. You can put them on string to make necklaces and bracelets.

More to Try: Decorate your beads with colored paints.

Knots

You can tie knots to make bracelets, necklaces, belts, and other things. On page 159 are some easy knots to tie. Find different kinds of string, ribbon, ropes, and cords. Look for a lot of colors.

Tie square knots until you have the right length. Then tie overhand knots at the end of each piece of rope.

More to Try: Try the finger-weaving activity on page 96. Make a belt, bracelet, or other things to wear.

174 *TRY IT•TRY IT•TRY IT•TRY IT•TRY IT•TRY IT•TRY IT•TRY IT•TRY IT•TRY IT•TRY IT•TRY IT•TRY IT•TRY IT•TRY IT•TRY IT*

TRY IT!
BUILDING ART

An architect (ar-ki-tekt) is someone who designs buildings and other spaces. You can have fun learning about architecture by doing this Try-It.

Your Home

Read pages 44–46 in "Taking Care of Yourself and Your Home." Learn how to do some of the things on the list.

Looking at Buildings and Spaces

Look at as many buildings as you can in one day. Look for different shapes, patterns, designs, sizes, colors, and materials. Look at play areas and how they are designed. Are the buildings and other spaces good for the people and other living things that use them? Share your ideas with another person.

The Best Neighborhood

Think of a neighborhood that would be a place where you would really like to live. Get a piece of cardboard or heavy paper at least 36 inches x 24 inches in measurement. Using that as a base, glue or paste cut-out pictures you find in old magazines that could go in your ideal neighborhood. Get crayons, markers, or paint to draw in other parts of your neighborhood that you think should be included. Show your ideal neighborhood to others and explain not only what it looks like, but how you would feel in your neighborhood, how people would act in it, what you could do there that you can't do in your neighborhood now.

Tips

Many girls at this age level love to manipulate materials and to build. Try to get an architect, an interior designer, or general contractor to visit your troop or group, or you can visit their offices. Make sure to provide some sort of activity for the girls rather than just a talk or discussion. Girls can look at the math and science concepts that are involved in designing buildings and spaces as well as the artistic sense of shapes and form.

Discovering the Strengths of Shapes

Architects have to know how strong building materials are and how different shapes can hold weight. Experiment with the strengths of designs and shapes by following these steps.

You will need:

- Paper
- A small stone or a coin or a button

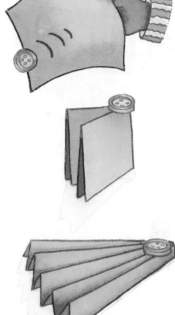

1. Sit on the floor. Take a single sheet of paper. Hold it by one edge in the air so the paper sticks out straight over the floor. Next, take a small stone, coin, or button and place it on the paper. (See the picture.) What happens? The flat piece of paper should be too thin and weak to hold up the stone, coin, or button. It does not have enough strength to hold the object.

2. Next, take that same piece of paper and fold it in quarters like a book. (See the picture.) Try to rest the stone, coin, or button on the edges of the paper. What happens? By changing the shape of the paper, there is more strength and the paper can hold up the object.

3. Make the fan shape and the curved shape out of your paper as in the picture and try to balance the objects on the paper. What happens? They should be able to support the objects.

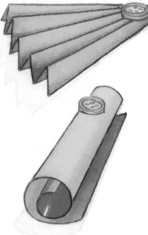

4. Experiment with other curved and folded shapes to see which ones can hold up the stone, coin, or button. Make a design sculpture with your shapes. Glue or tape may help put the shapes together. You can also make slits in the paper and fit the pieces together.

More to Try: Do this with friends. Using only tape, paper, and scissors, make a model of a house, a store, or some other kind of building. Make a bridge, too.

176 TRY IT•TRY IT•TRY IT•TRY IT•TRY IT•TRY IT•TRY IT•TRY IT•TRY IT•TRY IT•TRY IT•TRY IT•TRY IT•TRY IT•TRY IT•TRY IT

DESIGNING AN IDEAL GIRL SCOUT MEETING PLACE

Think about all the things you do and would do at your Girl Scout meeting place. Then imagine the perfect Girl Scout meeting place. Draw a picture or sketch or make a model that you can show others.

SCALE:	APPROVED BY	DRAWN BY
DATE:		
		DRAWING NUMBER

Designing Space for Someone with Special Needs

Read about people with disabilities on pages 75–79. Think about where you live or where you go to school. What would you change about those places to make them safer and more accessible (easy to get at, easy to get around in) for someone with a disability? Here are some ideas. You might make the doorways and halls wider. You could make a light flash when the telephone rings. You could make sure nothing is on the ground that could cause someone to trip. What else could you do? How could these ideas help someone with a disability? How could they also help someone without a disability?

Designing Space for Someone with Special Needs. New buildings are being built and old ones altered to accommodate the needs of people with disabilities. Architects have specific codes they must follow when designing or remodeling a building.

You can help girls determine the needs of people in their community by looking at a public building and doing a building analysis such as the one found on pages 10–11 in *Focus on Ability: Serving Girls with Special Needs*.

Try-Its and Other Resources

- Try-Its: Colors and Shapes; Numbers and Shapes.
- Other Resources: *Into the World of Today and Tomorrow*; *Focus on Ability: Serving Girls with Special Needs*.

TRY IT!

CAREERS

Future Jobs

Many jobs that people have today did not even exist many years ago. Interview some adults and ask what they wanted to grow up to be when they were young. Think about how the world will be when you are older. Make a list of the new kinds of jobs you think will be available when you grow up that don't exist now.

Today girls can look forward to more career choices than ever before. Have you thought about what you would like to do when you grow up?

Autobiography

Write or tape an autobiography. That's the story of your life. Find a book with blank pages, or make one of your own or use a cassette or videotape. Look at the time line you made on page 38 for some ideas. What else can you add?

What Am I Good At?

Read pages 66–67 about careers in "Taking Care of Yourself and Your Home." Some careers have more men in them than women. Find out about one of those careers. Try to interview a woman who is working in a career that more men used to do than women. What questions could you ask her?

Women Pioneers

Find out about famous women inventors or explorers. What were some of the things they did? Can you find women who were pioneers in other jobs? Share what you learn with your troop or group.

178 *TRY IT•TRY IT•TRY IT•TRY IT•TRY IT•TRY IT•TRY IT•TRY IT•TRY IT•TRY IT•TRY IT•TRY IT•TRY IT•TRY IT•TRY IT•TRY IT*

Tips

Many girls at this age level have dreams about what they would like to be when they are older. Girls can become familiar with the wide array of choices they will have and can begin to learn about the types of skills and education they will need to pursue a particular career path. A career can mean different things to different people. Some girls may want to grow up to be a teacher's aide, a veterinarian's assistant, a police officer, or a chef; others a singer, a ballet dancer, a banker, an astronaut, or a politician. Contact your local Girl Scout council representative to find neighborhood businesses that welcome Girl Scouts on visits or career shadowing trips. Find out if women in a variety of jobs can visit the troop or group.

Autobiography. Girls can create books or tapes of their lives so far or forecast their futures and create their autobiography as if they were 100 years old (or whatever age) and are looking back in time.

Career Charades

Divide the troop or group into two teams. Each team should take turns having a girl act out one of the jobs listed below. The other team has to guess what she is. You can also make up your own list or add to this list.

Bank teller	Scientist	Lifeguard
Coach	Bus driver	Potter
Youth counselor	Pharmacist	Chef
Physical therapist	Veterinarian	Farmer
Book illustrator	Musician	TV reporter
	Photographer	
	Plumber	
	Astronaut	

Learn to Earn

Learning how to handle money is important now and for when you get older. Read about money and budgets on page 121. With a group, plan one of the money-earning projects.

More to Try: You can learn business skills in your Girl Scout activities. There are tips on selling cookies on page 122. If you participate in this type of activity, practice these ideas.

TRY IT•TRY IT•TRY IT•TRY IT•TRY IT•TRY IT•TRY IT•TRY IT•TRY IT•TRY IT•TRY IT•TRY IT•TRY IT•TRY IT•TRY IT **179**

Career Charades. You can brainstorm a list of many more jobs, such as astronaut, police officer, doctor, construction worker, pilot, computer software designer, and athlete. You can also mention volunteer jobs.

Try-Its and Other Resources

- Try-Its: Hobbies.
- Other Resources: Career activities in "Taking Care of Yourself and Your Home," handbook pages 66–68. *Girls Are Great*; *Into the World of Today and Tomorrow.*

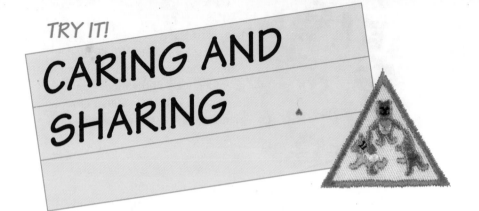

TRY IT!

CARING AND SHARING

No one in the world is exactly like you—or your friends! Show how you care about yourself and others with these activities.

I Care

Be a "secret pal" to someone. Think of nice things you can do for your secret pal. You may want to write a poem, make a friendship pin, send a card, or be a helper. Think of other things you can do.

Favorites

Everyone has some things that they like better than others. Make a list of some of your favorites—school subjects, books, places, things to do. Compare your list with your friends' lists. What things are the same? different? How much influence do your friends have on what you like? What about your family?

What If?

With your troop or group, talk about what makes a person a good friend. How can you be a good friend to another person? With your Brownie Girl Scout friends, role-play what you would do for each of these events.

- Your best friend is crying and you want to show you care.
- One of the girls in the troop has a birthday.
- Your mother has to finish a big project for work the next day.
- A neighbor falls and breaks her leg.
- Your friend is afraid she will fail a test.
- A classmate forgot her lunch.

You may want to think of other scenes to act out.

180 _TRY IT•TRY IT•TRY IT•TRY IT•TRY IT•TRY IT•TRY IT•TRY IT•TRY IT•TRY IT•TRY IT•TRY IT•TRY IT•TRY IT•TRY IT•TRY IT_

Tips

As a service project, girls can choose a number of ways to care and share. Several visits to a nursing home, a hospital, a rehabilitation center, or other facility can offer girls such opportunities. They may want to collect food, clothing, or make items, such as refurbished toys or simple blankets, for homeless and women's shelters. As you do such activities, it is important to avoid such phrases as "unfortunate," "crippled," "the poor," or others that stereotype people. Girls can begin to develop a sense of responsibility and concern for others in their communities and neighborhoods.

Feelings

What do you think of yourself? What do other people think of you? Do at least two of these activities.

- Write a story about your best friend. What do you like best about her?
- Write a story about one time when you were very happy.
- Draw or write about one time when you were very scared.
- Draw or write about one time you solved a problem that no one else could.
- Draw or write about one time when you were very mad.
- Draw or write about a time when you were very brave.
- Ask someone to draw a picture about what they think is best about you.

Differences Are Okay

Many people look different from you. Some have skin or hair that is another color. Some are taller or shorter. One person may see better and another not hear as well. All these people have similar feelings on the inside. They also have talents to share.

With your Girl Scout group, find out about ways that you are different from each other. Choose a partner and stand or sit facing her.

Write down three ways your partner is different from you. Write three ways you are the same. Change partners and do the same thing. Come together as a group and talk about some of the ways you are different and the same. Are these differences important?

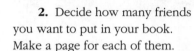

A Friend's Scrapbook

Make a scrapbook that tells about all of your friends.

You will need:

- Construction paper
- Writing paper
- A stapler
- Markers or crayons
- A pencil

1. Fold the construction paper in half. This will be the cover.

2. Decide how many friends you want to put in your book. Make a page for each of them.

3. Staple the pages and cover together.

4. Decorate the cover.

5. Make a page for each friend. You may want to put in pictures, phone numbers, birthdays, addresses, or other things you think would be fun.

TRY IT•TRY IT•**TRY IT**•TRY IT•TRY IT•TRY IT•TRY IT•TRY IT•TRY IT•TRY IT•TRY IT•TRY IT•**TRY IT**•TRY IT•TRY IT **181**

Try-Its and Other Resources

- Try-Its: Around the World; Citizen Near and Far; Earth is Our Home; People of the World.
- Other Resources: Activities in "Taking Care of Yourself and Your Home," handbook pages 62–65; "People Near and Far," 109–110; "Family, Friends, and Neighbors" chapter; *Caring and Coping*.

TRY IT!

CITIZEN NEAR AND FAR

When you remember not to litter or when you collect used books for the library, you are being a good citizen. When you take soda cans to be recycled or collect cans of food for a food drive, you are being a good citizen. A citizen is a person who tries to help out wherever she is needed. These activities will help get you on your way!

Television and Newspaper Reporter

Learn about a story reported on television or the radio, or in a newspaper that showed how someone acted like a good citizen. Share your story with your troop or group. Pick one story and take turns being the "good citizen" and "the reporter."

More to Try: Create a skit or puppet play on good citizenship.

It's the Law

Children and adults have laws to obey. Rules and laws help make things fair for people.

You are meeting for the first time as Brownie Girl Scouts. You want to talk about all the fun things you hope to do this year. What special rules would you need to follow during the meeting? What rules would you need to follow when you go on trips? What might happen if you or your friends did not follow the rules?

Share your ideas with your troop. Look at the ideas again before your next meeting begins.

What Do You Think?

People are often asked to make choices. Sometimes people vote to tell others how they feel about certain choices.

Think of a time when your troop had to make choices. How did you make a decision?

182 *TRY IT•TRY IT•TRY IT•TRY IT•TRY IT•TRY IT•TRY IT•TRY IT•TRY IT•TRY IT•TRY IT•TRY IT•TRY IT•TRY IT•TRY IT•TRY IT*

Tips

The full concept of citizenship may be difficult for girls to grasp at this age. Ask for their definitions and some of the ways they can practice being a good citizen. Some girls in your troop or group may not be citizens of the United States. Make sure the activities you do, apply to them as well. Refer also to the activities in the chapters "Welcome to Girl Scouts" and "Leadership in Girl Scouting and Beyond." **More to Try:** Provide girls with opportunities to see their local government in action. Town meetings, local courts, police or fire stations, government agencies or funded groups that help women, children, or the environment can give girls a better sense of active citizenship.

Voting is one way to make a decision. Voting can be public, like raising your hand, or private, like marking a piece of paper and putting it in a box. Think of some decisions your troop needs to make. When would voting be a good way to choose? When would voting not be a good way to choose?

Calling All Helpers

At the United Nations, people get together from many different countries to talk about problems they share.

1. Think of a problem that affects people all over the world like recycling, homelessness, or acid rain.

2. Go home and talk to your parents and neighbors to find out how they think the problem should be solved.

3. At your next meeting, hold your "United Nations" meeting. Tell how people in your area of the community feel about the problem.

4. As a troop, think about everything that you heard and decide how best to handle the problem.

5. Share your solution with your family and neighbors.

Lead the Way

Think of a problem in your neighborhood. Look at the chart on pages 116–117. Plan your project using the questions from the chart. Do the project and share what you did with others.

Reach Out

As a citizen of the world, you can help other people in other countries with their problems. With the help of an adult, find a group in your community that works to help people in other countries. Try to visit this group or ask someone to come to a group/troop meeting to learn more about what they are doing to help people in other countries.

TRY IT•TRY IT•TRY IT•TRY IT•TRY IT•TRY IT•TRY IT•TRY IT•TRY IT•TRY IT•TRY IT•TRY IT•TRY IT•TRY IT•TRY IT•TRY IT   **183**

Try-Its and Other Resources

- Try-Its: Caring and Sharing; Girl Scout Ways; People of the World.

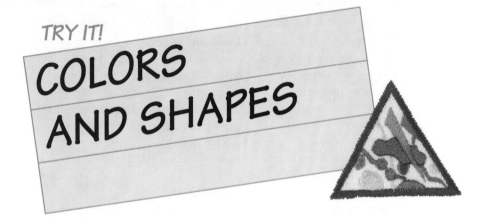

TRY IT!

COLORS AND SHAPES

3. Dip a sponge shape into one of the pans. Place it where you want on the paper and press. You can use this same shape over and over or you can add other shapes. Try other colors, too.

Artists use colors, lines, and shapes to make art. How would you like to make your own? Try out your own creativity with these activities.

Stencil Stampers

You can make your own stamps to use over and over. Use these designs to create your own greeting cards or wrapping paper.

You will need:

- Old sponges
- Scissors
- Tempera paint
- Pans to hold the paint (old pie tins or baking pans are good)
- Paper to paint on
- Water (for cleanup)
- Construction paper
- Shelf paper

1. Cut the sponges into a shape you want.

2. Pour small amounts of paint into each pan.

184 TRY IT•TRY IT•**TRY IT**•TRY IT•TRY IT•TRY IT•**TRY IT**•TRY IT•TRY IT•TRY IT•TRY IT•TRY IT•**TRY IT**•TRY IT•TRY IT

Tips

See "Tips," page 234 in this book, under the Art to Wear Try-It. If materials are difficult to come by for any of these activities, you and the girls can brainstorm other ways to do them. You can find other ways to mix colors, such as with food coloring, natural dyes, or chalks and crayons.

Try-Its and Other Resources

- Try-Its: Art to Wear; Numbers and Shapes; Puppets, Dolls, and Plays.
- Other Resources: Activities in "People Near and Far" chapter; *Into the World of Today and Tomorrow.*

More to Try: Try the Adinkra cloth activity on pages 91–92.

STENCIL STAMPER

Colors and Shapes Mobile

A mobile is a work of art that can move. Try making your own simple mobile.

You will need:

- Long plastic drinking straws
- Large needle
- Thick thread
- Cardboard
- Paints
- Crayons or markers

1. Thread the needle and tie a knot at the end of the thread. (Take care in using the needle. Be sure an adult or older person is around to help.)

2. Poke the needle through the straws to attach them. Use three, four, or five straws.

3. Tie a knot in the thread near the straws.

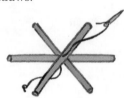

4. Cut the thread, leaving enough for you to hang the mobile.

5. Add colored shapes, which you can cut from the cardboard and paint, to your mobile by attaching them to the straws with a needle and thread. Hang them at different lengths.

6. Your mobile may tell a story or be on a subject that interests you. See the illustration for ideas.

7. Have someone help you balance your mobile.

Making Dough Shapes

You can mold and shape dough you make yourself.

You will need:

- 1 cup cornstarch
- 1 cup salt
- 1½ cups flour
- Water
- A mixing bowl
- A spoon

1. Put one cup of cornstarch, one cup of salt, and one and one-half cups of flour in the bowl.

2. Stir.

3. Add one-half cup of water and stir.

4. If the dough is still too stiff and dry, add one or two spoonfuls of water and mix with your hands.

5. You can make something with your dough after it is mixed, or you can save it for about two days in a plastic bag. Close the bag and keep it in a refrigerator until you are ready to use it.

6. Make something with your dough. Here are some ideas. Roll pieces of the dough into little balls of different sizes. Put the balls together to make things. Rub a little water on the balls to make them stick.

OR

Start with a ball the size of a lemon, and pull and pinch the clay to make a shape—an animal or a building, for example.

OR

Roll the dough into a ball that fits into your hand. Press your thumbs into the middle of the ball. Press the hole to make it bigger with one thumb while you turn the dough with the other hand. Keep doing this until the dough forms a pot or bowl shape.

Weaving Color Patterns

You will need:

- Sheets of different-colored paper
- Scissors
- Ruler
- Clear tape
- A pencil

1. Use the ruler to draw lines on the colored paper.

2. Make spaces between the lines the width of the ruler.

3. Cut the paper on the lines to make strips.

4. Lay eight or more strips of the same color next to each other evenly.

186 *TRY IT•TRY IT•TRY IT•TRY IT•TRY IT•TRY IT•TRY IT•TRY IT•TRY IT•TRY IT•TRY IT•TRY IT•TRY IT•TRY IT•TRY IT•TRY IT•TRY IT*

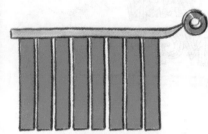

5. Tape them together very close to the top.

6. Take eight strips of another color.

7. One at a time, weave the strips in and out, as the picture shows.

8. If you started on the top for the first row of weaving, start at the bottom for the next one. See the picture.

9. After you have woven all the strips, cut the extra edges and tape them together.

10. Turn your finished weaving over to see how it looks without the tape showing.

A Rainbow of Colors

You can mix your own colors. To learn how, try making your own painting. Start with only three colors. These three colors (red, blue, and yellow) are called "primary colors."

You will need:

- Poster paint or tempera in red, blue, and yellow
- Paper cups
- A paintbrush
- Paper
- A teaspoon

1. Mix your three primary colors to form other colors. Follow this guide when you are ready to mix a color.

red + blue = purple
blue + yellow = green
yellow + red = orange
red + blue + yellow = brown

2. Put two teaspoons of each of the colors you need in a cup and stir.

3. After you have mixed the colors, you are ready to paint.

4. Paint a picture.

More to Try: Use black and white paint to make more colors.

red + white = pink
blue + black = dark blue

Try some more combinations. What colors can you make?

TRY IT•TRY IT•TRY IT•TRY IT•TRY IT•TRY IT•TRY IT•TRY IT•TRY IT•TRY IT•TRY IT•TRY IT•TRY IT•TRY IT•TRY IT•TRY IT **187**

Yarn paintings are a beautiful way to combine colors and shapes. Most yarn paintings are of animals or flowers.

You will need:

- Piece of cardboard
- Fine-tip pen
- Different colors of yarn or string
- Scissors
- White glue

1. Make an outline of your painting on the cardboard.

2. Cover the border with white glue.

3. Press a piece of yarn into the glue on the outline.

4. Fill in small areas with glue and then the yarn, using your fingers and scissors to press the yarn pieces tightly together. Always work from the outside in winding your yarn so it fills in all the spaces.

5. Let the glue dry and display your painting!

MEXICAN YARN PAINTING

1 2 3 5

188 TRY IT•TRY IT•**TRY IT**•TRY IT•TRY IT•TRY IT•TRY IT•TRY IT•TRY IT•TRY IT•TRY IT•TRY IT•TRY IT•TRY IT•TRY IT•TRY IT

CREATIVE COMPOSING

We must take care
And be sure to share,
Our world is our home.
(Can you think of any more
   lines?)

Sometimes the words create a design.

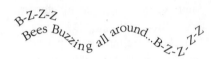

B-Z-Z-Z
Bees Buzzing all around...B-Z-Z-Z-Z-Z

Sometimes each line has the same rhythm.

When **I** grow **up**,
I'll **be** a **Queen**,
And **never** have
To eat **stringbeans**.

When **I** ride **my** bike,
I move **so** quickly,
I **can't** see **the** world.

Follow these examples or try your own ideas. Share your poem with your family and friends.

Compose means "to put together," "to make up," "to create." Every person has creative abilities that she can use to compose something. You can learn about your own abilities by taking time to listen, to look, to hear, and to do. In this Try-It, you can have fun exploring creative composing.

Composing a Song
Read about Girl Scout ceremonies on pages 23–24 in the chapter "Welcome to Girls Scouts." Then compose or make up a song for a Girl Scout ceremony. Sing it alone or with your friends.

Composing a Poem
Compose a poem. Poems use words in special ways. Sometimes the words rhyme, which means they sound alike—scout and shout, sing and ring.

TRY IT•TRY IT•**TRY IT**•TRY IT•TRY IT•**TRY IT**•TRY IT•**TRY IT**•TRY IT•**TRY IT**•TRY IT•TRY IT•**TRY IT**•TRY IT•**TRY IT**•**TRY IT**•TRY IT   **189**

Tips

There are many different ways girls can compose. Girls can work as a large group, in smaller groups, in pairs, or individually on any or all of the activities. Girls can follow the model given for composing a poem or painting or do something very different. Some girls may be eager to share their work; others may not and should be allowed to keep their work private.

Composing a Song. A special occasion or favorite topic could be the inspiration for a song.

Composing a Poem. Poetry books can help with ideas on how to develop poems.

Composing a Play. If girls aren't able to decide on a storyline, many of the stories in the handbook could be rewritten as plays or skits. Girls could base their plays on the characters introduced in the stories but make up new situations or "what happens next?" situations.

Composing Music for Instruments. Girls learn how to make some simple instruments in the Sounds of Music Try-It.

Composing a Painting

Think of a special place. It can be a real place that you've seen or a make-believe place. Draw it lightly on a piece of paper in pencil. Look at where things are placed in your sketch. Should anything be moved? Should some things be made smaller? Should some be made larger? In a painting, the things that are closest to you are usually drawn bigger. Things that are farther away are usually smaller. Next, think of colors for your painting. You can use tempera, water-color, poster paints, felttip pens, chalk, crayons, or colored pencils. Hang your painting for others to see.

Composing a Message

Read about sign language on pages 77–78. Compose a sign message and sign it to someone.

Composing a Play

Make up a play about a person you admire or about one of the stories in this book. Work with friends or create a one-person play. Make invitations and perform your play.

Composing Music
for Instruments

Compose a piece of music for an instrument. It can be an instrument you have made. Share the music with others.

190 TRY IT•TRY IT•**TRY IT**•TRY IT•TRY IT•TRY IT•TRY IT•**TRY IT**•TRY IT•TRY IT•TRY IT•TRY IT•**TRY IT**•TRY IT•TRY IT

Try-Its and Other Resources

- Try-Its: Colors and Shapes; Dancerize; Listening to the Past; Me and My Shadow; Music; Puppets, Dolls, and Plays; Sounds of Music.
- Other Resources: *Brownies' Own Songbook*; *Sing-Along Songbook and Cassette*.

TRY IT!
DANCERCIZE

Physical exercise helps keep our bodies healthy. Some exercises can be done to music.

Aerobics

Exercise is a way to keep fit and have fun. Aerobic (air-row-bic) activity means you keep moving while your heart pumps harder. This makes your heart and lungs stronger.

You will need:

• A record or tape
• Record player or tape player
• Shorts and T-shirt or leotards and tights
• Sneakers

Note: Always do a warm-up activity before aerobic exercise. This one is from the Contemporary Issues book *Developing Health and Fitness: Be Your Best!*

Practice these movements to your favorite music.

• March in place.
• Step forward and backward and swing your arms to the sides.
• Step sideways and swing your arms in circles.
• Put your hands on your hips and move from side to side.
• Walk in a circle, lifting your knees very high while clapping your hands.

Make up some of your own moves. Do them for at least 10–15 minutes.

Always cool down after aerobic exercise. You can try some of these for your cool-down.

• Sit on the floor and make your legs into a "V." Reach over and try to touch your right toes. (Your knees can be slightly bent up.) Then try to reach your left toes. Be careful not to bounce.

Tips

You can be a role model for these activities by leading girls through the exercises. Make sure everyone is dressed comfortably, with appropriate shoes for active movement. All girls will not participate the same way. Some girls who are overweight, asthmatic, or who have heart problems or other medical conditions may need to modify their level of activity. This can be done by letting them move more slowly, walking in place for some activities, or moving the upper body while standing in place. Girls with physical disabilities may also need adaptations or special equipment to participate. Ask their parents, teachers, or therapists for specific suggestions on proper body positioning and movement.

- Keep your legs in a "V." Lean forward and stretch your arms out. Again, be careful not to bounce.
- Lie on your back. Bend your knees and bring them to your chest.

More to Try: Make up your own tape of music for exercising.

Dance on Stage

Watch a dance performance at a theater, outdoor stage, community center, or on television. What parts of the dance can you imitate? Describe this dance to others without using any words.

My Own Dance

Make up a dance to your favorite song or choose a song from this book and create a dance.

Dance Party

Have a dance party with a group of friends.

You will need:

- Records, tapes, or CDs
- A record player, tape player, or radio
- Snacks

1. Pick a time and place for a get-together with your friends.

2. Decide on the music. Each person can bring her favorite dance music.

3. Teach each other dance steps.

4. Have a healthy snack for energy.

Follow the Leader

Take turns with other girls in being the leader in your troop. The leader should call out a movement and show everyone how to follow it. You can do these movements to start: climbing a ladder, reaching for the sun on tiptoes, moving like a windmill, touching toes with knees slightly bent. Think of others you can do. Warm up for about five minutes.

Animal Moves

Play music while you make these animal moves. You can even match the music to the animal!

Rabbit jump: Bend your knees and jump forward.

Seal crawl: Pull yourself forward with your hands at your side while dragging your body and feet.

Dance on Stage. You may be able to rent a video of a dance or ballet performance. Some girls may be taking dance lessons and may be able to demonstrate their warm-up or basic movements to the group.

Animal Moves. Girls can watch how animals move. Help them see how limbs and bodies change position. Using different types of music can help them think of moves that are fast or slow or represent the movement of particular animals.

Elephant walk: Bend forward. Extend your arms and place one hand over the other, fingers pointed toward the ground, to form a trunk. Walk slowly with legs straight and trunk swinging from side to side.

Inchworm: Place both hands on the floor. Try to keep your knees stiff and legs straight, but bend your knees if you have to. Walk forward with your hands as far as you can, and then walk forward with your feet to your hands.

Crab walk: Sit on the floor with your hands behind you. Lift up your body with your hands and feet. Walk on all fours. Walk forward and backward in this position.

Frog jump: Squat on the floor with hands in front of feet. Jump forward and land on both hands and feet.

Make up your own animal moves and try them.

Inchworm

Seal Crawl

Frog Jump

Crab Walk

Elephant Walk

Rabbit Jump

TRY IT•TRY IT•TRY IT•TRY IT•TRY IT•TRY IT•TRY IT•TRY IT•TRY IT•TRY IT•TRY IT•TRY IT•TRY IT•TRY IT **193**

Try-Its and Other Resources

- Try-Its: Creative Composing.
- Other Resources: *Developing Health and Fitness.* Fitness activities in the "Taking Care of Yourself and Your Home" chapter.

Tips

These activities focus on leading girls to an increased awareness of their surroundings.

The Soil. Soil is made up of materials that have decomposed or broken down, such as rock and plant and animal matter, along with air and water. Girls can describe soil in terms of color, how it feels, and how it smells. They can rub a bit between their fingers. Does it feel sandy (gritty), clay-like (sticky, smooth, plastic), or silty (silky-smooth, slick, or flour-like)? This activity can be done in the backyard, a forested area, a beach area, or anywhere there is vegetation and soil. Watch out for poison ivy or other natural hazards.

Going, Going, Gone. A public park, camp, or area near a construction site are perfect places to observe soil erosion. Look for areas that people have used as "short-cuts" off trails or between two points. Stress the importance of staying on walks and paths, by asking girls what they can observe about the vegetation and soil where there has been erosion. With the watering activity, you

---

TRY IT!

EARTH AND SKY

L ook down. Look up. What do you see? Earth below and sky above!

The Soil

Find a special spot in an outdoor area.

You will need:

- A magnifying glass
- A spoon or small trowel
- A pencil or tweezers
- White paper or a plastic dish
- A yard of string

1. Make a circle on the ground with your string. Look on the surface inside your circle. What do you find? Do you find plants? What about animals? Is there anything else?

2. Next, dig three small holes in your circle so that you can look below the surface of the top layer of soil or forest litter. Can you find differences in plants and animals as you dig down one inch, three inches, and six inches? Is there a difference in how the soil feels or in its color as you go deeper? Use your white paper or plastic dish to help you study soil critters as you find them.

3. Share your findings with someone or the group. Carefully fill the holes and leave your circle as you found it.

Going, Going, Gone

On a walk or hike, examine the edge of a stream or a place where the ground is bare on a hillside or slope. Look for places where soil has been worn down or disappeared.

Find out what causes soil erosion. In the backyard or in a sandbox, build a mound of soil about two feet high or knee-high. Pretend that this is a hill or mountainside in your community. Wet the hill with a watering can or a slow, steady stream of water from a hose. What happens to your hill? Find a slope that is covered with grass or plants. Water it with your watering can. What happens? Is the result different from what happens on your mountain of soil?

---

should be able to observe a dramatic difference between the site with no vegetation and the site with vegetation. After, girls might want to do some planting in areas that suffer erosion. If the soil is compacted, you may need to add some mulch or topsoil after loosening it. If you are working on a slope, you may need to do some terracing or put in water bars, or watch your work wash away! (Straw placed over seeds on a slope will often check erosion as well.)

Check with local resources to find out what is best to plant and how.

More to Try: Test how compacted soil is. Take a soup can with both ends removed. Insert the can into the ground so that about one-quarter inch is buried. Fill the can with water and measure the time it takes for the can to drain. If the water takes a long time, there are no air holes, and the soil is compacted (or water in the ground has filled up existing air spaces so that no more wa-

ter can enter). Girls can do this test easily in more than one place and compare the drainage time. Try in the middle of a trail, and off the trail, for a real contrast.

The Sky's My Home! The best site for this activity is a place where there is open sky and plant life. A field trip to a park or wildlife refuge would be just the thing, but you can do it in the schoolyard or in a backyard as well. Girls should see a variety of insects and birds, and possi-

The Sky's My Home!

Find a place outside where you can sit and be a "sky watcher." Observe the types of creatures in the air. Also observe the ways these creatures move. Share what you observe with others by acting out the movements.

More to Try: Build a feeder for a creature of the sky. Be alert for what comes to visit your feeder.

Our Air

Can you see the air? Be an air quality inspector.

You will need:
• A roll of tape
• Some string about 2 feet long

1. Find a spot out-of-doors protected from rain and strong winds where you can tie your string. Tie it about chest-high. You can use thumbtacks to tack down the ends.

2. Each day for three weeks, take a strip of tape about three inches long and write the date on the non-

stick side. Put a piece of tape on the string so that the sticky side is on the outside. At the end of three weeks, you should have a record of particles from the air. Which tape strip is the cleanest? On what day did you notice a change? What do you think is in the particles in the air that you can see?

Rooting Around

Trees and most plants send roots into the ground to take in water and minerals. Plants have different kinds of roots. Some roots go deep for water way underground. Some spread wide to catch rainwater as it falls. Start a plant and see some roots grow.

① Carrot

② Avocado

③ Stem with leaves

Hot and Cold

Learn how to use a thermometer safely. What temperature makes water freeze? What point makes it boil? What is your normal body temperature? Try the activities about the sun on page 138 in "How and Why."

1. Cut the top of a carrot. Push four toothpicks on the sides. Rest on top of a jar or glass filled with water.

2. Do the same thing with an avocado seed.

3. Take a stem with leaves from a plant. Put it into water.

TRY IT•TRY IT•**TRY IT**•TRY IT•TRY IT•TRY IT•TRY IT•TRY IT•TRY IT•TRY IT•TRY IT•TRY IT•**TRY IT**•TRY IT•TRY IT **195**

that happens, the good air becomes more polluted and can make people sick.

Rooting Around. Another plant that roots very well in water is a sweet potato. Visit a nursery or arboretum and look for plants that grow in the air without soil and plants that grow in water only. Also look for different kinds of soils needed for different types of plants.

Hot and Cold. Refer to handbook page 138 in "How and Why?" Have girls measure and compare temperatures at ground level and chest level in different spots. Is there a difference? You can also compare temperature between water and air.

bly an aircraft. Gliding, soaring, fluttering, diving, and flapping are movements girls might observe. Ask the girls if they have ever felt a bird bone. Is it heavy or light? If you decide to build a feeder for a sky creature, you might consider planting plants that birds can feed on, planting a butterfly garden, or hanging a hummingbird feeder. Bird feeders can be made from recycled plastic jugs, milk cartons, wood scraps, or pine cones. Don't forget the night sky! Look around lights at night or

set out your own light with a white sheet hanging behind it to find out what kind of insects fly at night. Look in the night sky for bats and late flying birds. (Bats are great for eating mosquitos and other insects that fly at night.)

Our Air. This project will take some patience; it may be done at home with parental supervision or as a school project. A follow-up field trip for this activity might be a visit to an auto-emission test center or to an agency that provides information on

lung disease or smoking. Girls can find out how smoking hurts their lungs. Have them think about how they might help someone they know stop smoking. An excellent service project is planting trees. Make the link between trees taking in carbon dioxide (what people breath out) and giving off oxygen (the part of the air that people can breathe). The more healthy trees and vegetation there are, the cleaner and better the air is. Pollution from car exhausts and factories can harm trees and plants. If

Try-Its and Other Resources

■ Other Resources: *Exploring Wildlife Communities With Children; Developing Health and Fitness.* Your local Audubon chapter, Cooperative Extension Service, or Soil Conservation Service can provide additional information and resources.

TRY IT!

EARTH IS OUR HOME

You, all other people, and plants and animals share the earth. How can you make your home a better place?

How Long Does It Take?

Collect a sample of trash and garbage to create your own landfill. Include plastic, glass, aluminum, fast-food containers, soda straws, plant clippings, grass, an apple core, some orange rind, a stick of gum, a candy wrapper, and some newspaper.

1. Put the trash into an old nylon stocking. Make a list and a drawing of what goes into the stocking as a record.

2. Bury the stocking completely in the earth and mark the location. Don't bury it near water because it might make the water polluted.

3. Wait two or three months. Dig up the stocking and the trash. What do you discover? Be sure to wear gloves and avoid touching items in your landfill. You might use a stick or a small trowel to look at the items in your stocking. Have any of the items changed? How have

they changed? Are there some things in your stocking that will keep a lifetime? What happens to garbage that leaves your house? Does it get buried like your stocking? Is any of it recycled? Does it get hauled to a dump far away from your town?

More to Try: Keep track of how many bags of trash your family throws out each day, week, or month.

Recycling

Read about recycling on pages 145–147. Then recycle something.

Trash Busters

Participate in a community cleanup day or adopt a special place for the troop year. Care for your place and let others know about your efforts. Remember to wear clothing and gloves that protect you if you help clean up.

Oil Spill

Try the "Oil Spill" activity on page 145.

Tips

With direction, this activity can help girls become conscious of their roles as caretakers of the earth. You can encourage them by making sure that what they learn here is carried out in future activities. Girls might make a list or booklet of environmental tips, then use it to plan camping trips, cookouts, local events, or family outings.

How Long Does It Take? Help girls not to become disappointed when there is not much change. Explain that garbage does not go away. Many things don't rot or decompose at all, but some things rot away when they are exposed to air. Since most garbage is buried in landfills, it is not exposed to air and it does not rot away, even if it is considered to be "biodegradable." The problem is not what is buried, but how much is buried. Everyone needs to consider reducing the amount of garbage created. For example, the biggest reason for using recycled paper is not to save trees (most of the trees used in paper production are a renewable resource grown on tree farms), but to reduce the amount of paper that goes to landfills.

Recycling. See handbook pages 144–148 in "How and Why?"

SOLAR COOKER

You can use the sun's energy to cook your food in the outdoors. Follow the chart at right to build a solar oven. You will need to ask an adult to help you measure and cut. Building hints: Appliance boxes make good ovens. Place the shiny side of the foil so that it faces out when glueing onto cardboard. Foil should not be on the outside of your oven because you want the box to soak up the sun's heat. Foil is on the inside of the box to bounce heat onto the black cooking pans.

HERE'S WHAT YOU WILL NEED: Single plate of glass; corrugated cardboard for two large boxes with one lid and four "toppers"; aluminum foil; glue; insulation (crumpled newspaper); a dark metal tray; string; and a stick or wire.

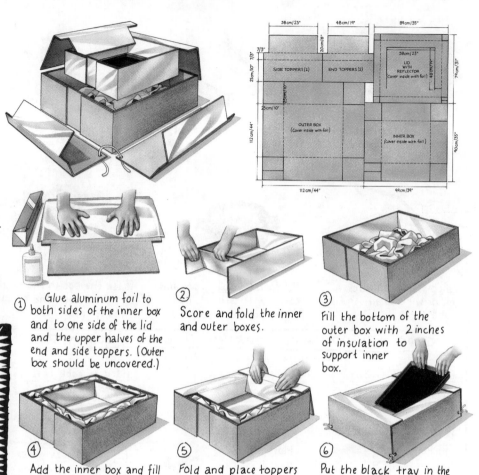

① Glue aluminum foil to both sides of the inner box and to one side of the lid and the upper halves of the end and side toppers. (Outer box should be uncovered.)

② Score and fold the inner and outer boxes.

③ Fill the bottom of the outer box with 2 inches of insulation to support inner box.

④ Add the inner box and fill the sides with more insulation.

⑤ Fold and place toppers over the edges of the boxes.

⑥ Put the black tray in the bottom of the inner box. Tie or glue the outer flaps.

TRY IT•TRY IT•TRY IT•TRY IT•TRY IT•TRY IT•TRY IT•TRY IT•TRY IT•TRY IT•TRY IT•TRY IT•TRY IT•TRY IT•TRY IT•TRY IT **197**

You can model good environmental behavior. Encourage the troop to use cups labeled with girls' names, washed, and reused. Encourage healthy snacks, like fruit that comes without packaging. Use reusable bags when shopping. Use recycled materials in craft projects. Avoid juice that comes in multiple packaging, so that the containers can be easily recycled. Plan meals that girls will eat when traveling or camping. Have girls keep track of how much waste the troop produces.

Trash Busters. "Let others know about your efforts" does not mean crediting your troop as adoptees of a specific site. Posters and flyers about needed behavior, like "Help Keep This Place Clean," are fine. Ownership of a site can imply legal responsibility, which a troop does not want to assume. Actions should be undertaken in the Girl Scout tradition of service, not to seek recognition. *Cautions:* Remember that Girl Scouts cannot lobby or raise money for other causes. This Try-It will often lead to discussion of changes needed in your community and the world, and girls will want to write letters and protest environmental practices. A leader can show girls how to write letters, but girls must send letters as individuals, not as Girl Scouts. Help girls explore all sides of an issue and avoid value judgments.

⑦ Score and fold reflector lid over the finished box. Glue the corners.

⑧ Make three measured cuts inside the lid to make the reflector flap.

⑨ Spread glue or caulk around edge of glass.

⑩ Press glass to inside of lid until glue is dry.

⑪ Fold up flap and attach a stick or wire to adjust the height.

⑫ Put food into <u>black</u> pot and cover with a <u>black</u> lid. (Shiny pots cook poorly.)

⑬ Place the pot in the center of the cooker and replace the reflector lid.

⑭ Face your cooker toward the sun. Adjust the flap so that light reflects onto the pot. Leave closed until cooked (see chart). No need to stir, food will not burn. Rotate box if necessary to capture sunlight.

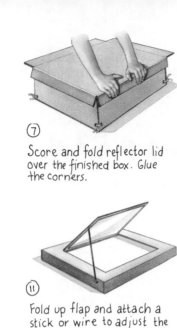

TYPE OF FOOD AND COOKING TIME ON A SUNNY DAY

For 10 pounds (4 kilos) of food

Easy to cook (1-2 hours)	Medium (3-4 hours)	Hard to cook (5 hours)
Eggs	· Potatoes	Most dried beans
Rice	Pastry	Large roast (all meats get more tender)
Fish	Some beans, lentils	
Chicken	Most meats	
Fruit	Bread	
Vegetables (above ground)	Vegetables (roots)	

TO PASTEURIZE WATER:
Small jar : 2 hours
Large jar : 4 hours

COOKING TIME IS LONGER:
• With larger amounts of food
• If partly cloudy
• When the sun is lower in the sky

198 TRY IT·TRY IT·TRY IT·TRY IT·TRY IT·TRY IT·TRY IT·TRY IT·TRY IT·TRY IT·TRY IT·TRY IT·TRY IT·TRY IT·TRY IT·TRY IT

Solar Cooker. This activity is in this Try-It to emphasize the need for energy-saving forms of power. In many countries, women must walk miles to gather firewood to cook the daily meal or forms of fuel are burned that pollute the air. There is a worldwide shortage of firewood, particularly in countries with large populations and little industrialization. When trees are used for firewood, soil erosion occurs, and air pollution is worsened (see Earth and Sky Try-It). The solar cooker cannot only be used to cook, it can also be used to sterilize water. Making the solar cooker requires lots of adult assistance! It is best to start out with large pieces of cardboard, like those taken from refrigerator or stove boxes. You will need markers, yardsticks, and a hand-held cardboard cutter. Girls can help with lay-out, assembling, and glueing, but it is strongly advised that an adult do the final cutting. Glass can be cut to size when purchased. A liquid glue that works on both wood and paper is recommended. To increase the life of the cooker, wrap duct tape around glass edges before and/or after glueing and on corners of the cardboard. When using the cooker, start out with something simple, like the recipe shown.

Recipe for a Miniworld. Refer to handbook page 138 for information about evaporation. When your lid is on your terrarium, you will have your own "water cycle." You might want to construct a large terrarium as a group or troop. A one-gallon or five-gallon plastic water jug works well.

Sun Pretzels

2¼ cups baking mix   2 tablespoons vegetable oil

⅔ cup lowfat milk   1 egg   salt

Combine baking mix, milk and oil. Stir 20 times. Form dough gently into a ball. Knead 5 times. Form dough into 32 strips the size of a pencil. Bend into pretzel shape. Beat egg. Brush pretzels with egg and sprinkle them with salt. Bake in solar oven on dark baking sheet for 20-30 minutes or until done.

Recipe for a Miniworld

A terrarium is a small world in an enclosure and is made up of living things, soil, water, and air. It is surrounded by a covering that lets in light. The earth we live on is covered by air and is like a huge terrarium. Plants and animals need soil, air, water, and light in order to survive in both a terrarium and on the earth. If any of these things are missing or are damaged by pollution, the plants and animals will suffer.

Have someone help you make your own healthy terrarium. Here are some things to use:

- A clear wide-mouthed jar (like a peanut butter jar)
- 2 handfuls of small rocks or sand
- 2 handfuls of soil
- 1 handful of dead leaves
- Some moss from a forest, a vacant lot, or elsewhere
- Several small ferns or plants from a forest, a vacant lot, or a plant store

(Do not pick protected plants or overpick an area. Ask permission to gather materials if you are not on your own property.)

Follow these steps to make your terrarium.

1. Put the sand in first, then the soil, and layer them evenly. Place the dead leaves on top.

2. Using a pencil, tongs, or a chopstick, make holes. Then plant your plants. Use the moss to fill in around the plants after you have tapped the soil down gently.

3. Water your world with a squeeze bottle or sprinkle water with your hands, but do not drench your world.

4. Place the lid on your jar. Keep the lid closed, as your world should have everything it needs to survive. Place the jar in good light, but not directly in the sunlight.

Observe your terrarium daily. You might want to keep a diary of what you see or make some sketches. Watch for changes. Are there any new plants or animals? How do you think they got there? What do you think would happen if you removed your terrarium from light? What do you think would happen if you put it in direct sunlight?

TRY IT•TRY IT•TRY IT•TRY IT•TRY IT•TRY IT•TRY IT•TRY IT•TRY IT•TRY IT•TRY IT•TRY IT•TRY IT•TRY IT•TRY IT **199**

Try-its and Other Resources

- Try-Its: Citizen Near and Far; Earth and Sky; Outdoor Fun; Water Everywhere.
- Other Resources: *Safety-Wise*; *Exploring Wildlife Communities With Children*; *Earth Matters*.

Solar Box Cookers International is a good resource for information and recipes. Write or call SBCI, 17 11th St., Sacramento, Calif. 95814, (916) 444–6116. *Ranger Rick's NatureScope* magazine, published by the National Wildlife Federation, and *Zillions*, published by the Consumers Union, have frequent articles on recycling, conservation, and good buying practices for kids. Children's Television Workshop ("3-2-1 Contact") has an excellent video called *The Rotten Truth* that focuses on garbage and recycling.

TRY IT!
FOOD FUN

Eating the right foods is very important for your health.

Baked Apples

You will need:

- 1 tart baking apple for each person
- 1/4 cup unsweetened apple juice for each apple
- 2 tablespoonfuls of raisins for each apple
- 1 marshmallow for each apple
- Some ground cinnamon

1. Have an adult help you peel the apples halfway down. Core the apples almost to their bottoms.

2. Stuff the core with raisins.

3. Put apples in baking or microwave pan. Pour juice over apples. Sprinkle each with cinnamon.

4. Bake in microwave on high for 8–10 minutes. Melt marshmallow on each apple for last minute/30 seconds.

OR

Bake in 375° F. oven for 40–45 minutes. Put marshmallow on top of each apple for last 2–5 minutes, until melted.

5. Apples should be tender, but not mushy.

6. Enjoy hot or cold!

Recipe Fun

Try this activity from *Developing Health and Fitness: Be Your Best!*, the Contemporary Issues booklet. Collect recipes from different cultures that include grains and starches, like rice, noodles, quinoa, kasha, polenta, cous-cous, and many others. Try some in your troop or group.

Snacks for Girl Scouts

Here are two snacks to try at Girl Scout get-togethers.

1. Vegetable snacks. Make the "walking salad" on page 156 in the chapter "How and Why?"

Tips

These activities give girls ideas on ways to make food fun, flavorful, and healthy. A cookbook or magazine that concentrates on low-cholesterol, low-fat recipes can provide some more ideas. A shopping trip or visit from a dietician or nutritionist could also be fun.

Baked Apples. If you do not have access to a microwave or regular oven, try making an apple salad instead. Mix apple slices, orange or grapefruit slices and their juice (to prevent the apples from turning brown), raisins, green seedless grapes, and a sprinkling of brown sugar or a few mini-marshmallows for each serving.

Recipe Fun. Many supermarkets carry quinoa, kasha, couscous, and polenta. Try to use brown rice and whole wheat noodles if you are using those in your recipes.

2. Fruit juice fizz.

You will need:

- 1 orange or lemon
- Orange juice
- Pineapple juice
- Cranberry juice
- Seltzer or club soda
- A bowl
  or pitcher
- A knife

1. Cut the orange or lemon into slices.

2. Put one or two cups of each juice into the pitcher.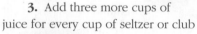

3. Add three more cups of juice for every cup of seltzer or club soda.

4. Chill the juice.

5. Serve.

Sloppy Joes

Here is a fun recipe you can make with your Girl Scout friends or your family. It is especially good when you make it outdoors! The Girl Guides of Canada submitted it to *World Games and Recipes.* The recipe will serve 4–6 people.

You will need:

- 1 pound of ground beef or chicken
- 1 can of tomato or chicken soup, or half of each
- Ketchup
- Prepared mustard
- Hamburger buns or French bread
- Skillet
- Container to hold excess fat
- Strainer
- Stove top, hot plate, or outdoor oven

1. Brown the meat in the skillet.

2. Hold the strainer over the container for fat. Pour everything in the skillet into the strainer. It will catch the meat and let the fat run through. You can also rinse the meat in the strainer under hot water to get off more fat.

3. Put the meat back in the skillet. Add the soup, ketchup, and mustard. Heat until thoroughly cooked.

4. Serve on the buns or French bread. Yum!

Food for a Day

Make your own breakfast, lunch, and dinner for a day. Use your favorite recipes. Ask an adult to help you plan.

Food Pyramid

Read about the food pyramid on page 39 in "Taking Care of Yourself and Your Home" and try the activities on these pages.

Try-Its and Other Resources

- Try-Its: Good Food.
- Other Resources: *Developing Health and Fitness*; *The Wide World of Girl Guiding and Girl Scouting. World Games and Recipes* contains recipes from many different countries that are members of the World Association of Girl Guides and

Girl Scouts. Here is a healthy recipe from France.

Tuna Rice Salad

1 can of tuna fish packed in water
1 cup of rice
small can of small pitted black olives
1 large tomato
1 small head romaine lettuce
1 small green pepper

Boil the rice and cool. Make a dressing by mixing together 2 table-spoons of wine vinegar, 1 teaspoon olive oil, ½ teaspoon dry mustard, and a sprinkle of black pepper. Stir the dressing into the rice. Add flaked tuna fish, black olives, chopped green peppers, and chopped tomatoes. Layer lettuce leaves on a plate and scoop the salad on the lettuce to serve. Serves 4.

TRY IT!

GIRL SCOUT WAYS

Being a Girl Scout makes you part of a very special group of people! Here are some activities that show some of the things Girl Scouts everywhere know.

About Girl Scouting

In the chapter "Welcome to Girl Scouts" you learned about many of the things that make Girl Scouting special. This activity is about some of those things you learned.

Reread the section on "The Girl Scout Promise and Law" in the chapter "Welcome to Girl Scouts." Try the activities in that section.

OR

Make up a puppet show or play that tells about the Girl Scout Law. Show it to some new Girl Scouts or to girls who want to become Girl Scouts.

Special Girl Scout Ways

Reread the section about "Special Girl Scout Ways." Practice the hand signs listed below and show them to someone who is new to Girl Scouting.

- Girl Scout handshake
- Girl Scout sign
- Quiet sign
- Friendship circle
- Friendship squeeze
- Girl Scout sayings

Ceremonies

Ceremonies are a very special part of Girl Scouting. You can learn about them and practice doing them with this activity. Be sure to read pages 23–24 to find out all about ceremonies. Plan a ceremony for one of Girl Scouting's special days.

Girl Scout Birthday

Juliette Low started the first Girl Scout troop on March 12, 1912. This day is the Girl Scout birthday. Plan a party for this day. See page 25 for more ideas on ways to celebrate.

202   TRY IT•TRY IT•TRY IT•TRY IT•TRY IT•TRY IT•TRY IT•TRY IT•TRY IT•TRY IT•TRY IT•TRY IT•TRY IT•TRY IT•TRY IT

Tips

These activities introduce girls to some of the traditions of Girl Scouting. Women who were Brownie and Junior Girl Scouts can share some of their experiences— maybe even display their old uniforms or badge sashes. Some Girl Scout councils have space set aside in their offices for a display of Girl Scout memorabilia which the girls in your troop can visit.

Some activities once popular in Girl Scouting are no longer considered good for girls to learn. Some examples of these are lashing (which involves chopping trees), lighting large bonfires (which pollutes the air), picking wildflowers for projects, or singing graces or hymns very specific to one religion. You may have participated in such activities, but, as Brownie Girl Scouts learn about their responsibilities as stewards of the environment and as sisters to every other Girl Scout, the activities they do must reflect these principles.

S'mores

This is a special sweet treat that is not an everyday snack. You'll probably want to try it on a camping trip or at a cookout. Find out why it's called "S'mores."

You will need:

- Graham crackers
- Large marshmallows
- Milk chocolate bars
- A long stick or roasting wire to hold over the fire

1. Break the graham crackers into a square shape (see the picture).

2. Break the chocolate bar into a square the same size as the cracker or smaller. Put this square on top of the graham cracker (see the picture).

3. Put one or two marshmallows on the end of the stick.

4. Use the stick to hold the marshmallows over the fire, but not too close (see the picture).

5. When the marshmallows start to melt just a little, take them off the stick and put them on top of the chocolate bar square (see the picture).

6. Put another graham cracker square on top of the marshmallows.

7. Eat it! Now do you know why they're called S'mores?

(Be careful that your marshmallow and/or stick do not catch on fire. If they do, do not wave them around. Carefully blow them out or let them burn. Always be careful with your stick and never play near or in the fire.)

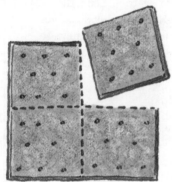

TRY IT•TRY IT•**TRY IT**•TRY IT•TRY IT•TRY IT•TRY IT•TRY IT•**TRY IT**•TRY IT•TRY IT•TRY IT•TRY IT•TRY IT•**TRY IT**•TRY IT•TRY IT   **203**

The "Welcome to Girl Scouts" chapter contains photographs and information depicting some history of the Girl Scout Movement and explains some ways that Girl Scouting is a unique organization. Girls can think of some of the special things they do as Brownie Girl Scouts. Girls can make banners or posters completing the sentence: Girls Are Special Because . . . or Girl Scouts Are . . . You might want to start the activities in this Try-It during Girl Scout Week, the week in which the Girl Scout birthday, March 12th, falls.

Girl Scouts make sit-upons to use when the ground is damp or too hot or cold and they want to keep their clothes clean. You can make your own to use at troop meetings, camping events, or other Girl Scout get-togethers. Follow these steps and look at the pictures for help.

You will need:

- A large piece of waterproof material (like an old plastic tablecloth or shower curtain or a plastic garbage bag)
- Newspapers or other stuffing
- A yarn needle
- Yarn or string

1. Cut the waterproof material into two large squares big enough for you to sit on.

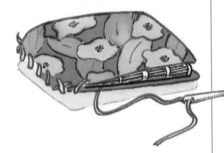

2. Put newspapers or old rags between the two squares to form a cushion.

3. Sew the two squares together with yarn or string, using the yarn needle. Have an adult show you how to use the needle safely. Be sure to sew completely around the edges of the sit-upon.

204 TRY IT•TRY IT•**TRY IT**•TRY IT•TRY IT•TRY IT•TRY IT•TRY IT•**TRY IT**•TRY IT•TRY IT•TRY IT•TRY IT•TRY IT•**TRY IT**•TRY IT•TRY IT

Try-Its and Other Resources

- Other Resources: *Brownies' Own Songbook*; *Ceremonies in Girl Scouting*; *Games for Girl Scouts*; *Outdoor Education in Girl Scouting*; *Sing-Along Songbook and Cassette*; *The Wide World of Girl Guiding and Girl Scouting*; *World Games and Recipes*.

TRY IT!

GOOD FOOD

In "Taking Care of Yourself and Your Home," you read about good nutrition. Here are some good food activities.

Smart Shopper

Labels list the ingredients in a food product, starting with the largest amount down to the smallest amounts. Cut out or remove lists of ingredients from cereal cartons, cake-mix boxes, and canned and frozen foods. Check the labels to see if sugar or salt is in the list of ingredients. Many times, sugar or salt is added to food as a flavoring. Too much sugar or salt is not good for you. Sugar is sometimes called corn syrup, sucrose, glucose, or fructose. Salt may be listed as sodium. Find three labels that have little or no salt. Try to eat these or other foods with little or no salt.

Great Groceries

Help your family make up a grocery list. Write down foods your family likes to eat during the week. Look at the list with the person who does the food shopping in your home. Go with her or him to the grocery store to help choose good foods. Then plan at least one meal using what you have learned from the food pyramid.

Dairy Foods

1. Many kinds of foods come from milk, such as yogurt, butter, and ice cream. Bring several kinds of these foods to your meeting for a taste test. Which one is your favorite?

2. Try making some new flavors of yogurt. Get some plain, low-fat or no-fat yogurt. Then, set out small bowls of different toppings: crunchy cereal, strawberries, bananas, peanut butter, blueberries, apple slices, nuts, honey, and other fruits. Have fun eating your unique dessert.

TRY IT•TRY IT•TRY IT•TRY IT•TRY IT•TRY IT•TRY IT•TRY IT•TRY IT•TRY IT•TRY IT•TRY IT•TRY IT•TRY IT•TRY IT•TRY IT **205**

Tips

Girls can learn to read the nutritional information on food and drink labels. These labels give information on carbohydrates, proteins, and fats, as well as vitamins, minerals, and fiber content. You can go on a field trip to a supermarket or grocery store or girls can bring in boxes and cans. **More to Try:** This activity is from *Developing Health and Fitness*: Compare several different brands of the same canned or packaged food. How do nutritional contents compare? Which is the healthiest? Why?

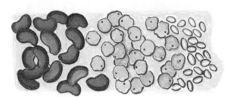

Proteins

Protein helps your body while you are growing. Beans are an inexpensive and healthy way to get protein. Find out about beans!

1. Bring in samples of dry beans.

2. Find three recipes for cooked dry beans.

3. In your troop meeting, or with an adult at home, make a bean recipe. Try to mix two or three kinds of beans with some vegetables, sauce, or salad dressing.

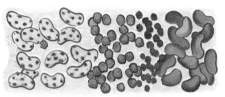

Plenty of Pasta

You learned from the food pyramid that you need to eat a lot of food from the bread, cereal, rice, or pasta group every day. Pasta (like spaghetti or other noodles) is easy and quick to cook and tastes good too. It comes in many shapes and sizes and colors. Find out about pasta that is made from spinach, whole wheat, or other foods.

You and your Brownie Girl Scout friends can make your own healthy and colorful pasta.

You will need:

- All kinds of pasta, in different shapes and colors
- A large pot for boiling water
- Colander or strainer
- Individual plates
- Forks
- Stove
- Two kinds of sauce (see at right)

Sauce One

- 1 small onion chopped
- Package of frozen broccoli
- Package of frozen carrots (pieces)
- Package of frozen chopped zucchini or yellow squash
- Package of frozen peas
- 1 can low-salt chicken broth (or make with chicken bouillon cubes)
- 1 tablespoon olive oil

Thaw vegetables. In large frying pan, heat olive oil. Carefully cook onion until yellow and soft. Add broth and vegetables. Cook until firm. Serve over pasta.

Sauce Two

- 1 can of puréed tomatoes
- Dried oregano
- Dried basil
- 1 bunch parsley
- Grated Parmesan or Romano cheese

206 *TRY IT•TRY IT•TRY IT•TRY IT•TRY IT•TRY IT•TRY IT•TRY IT•TRY IT•TRY IT•TRY IT•TRY IT•TRY IT•TRY IT•TRY IT•TRY IT*

In addition to the pasta recipes, girls can try making tortillas. This recipe is also from *Developing Health and Fitness*.

Mexican Tortillas

2 cups flour
1 cup cornmeal
2 eggs
½ tsp. salt
water

Mix ingredients together, adding water until you have a thin paste. Heat an ungreased griddle. Spread batter thinly to form a 2- to 3-inch cake. Cook on both sides until done—about 2 minutes.

Girls can eat the tortillas with butter or margarine or fill with cooked chicken, raw or cooked vegetables—peppers, tomatoes, lettuce, cucumbers, squash, black olives—or low-fat/low-salt cheese. Girls can make or add salsa. Look for one without additives.

Girls can also try making vegetable chili.

Heat tomatoes in pan, stirring them slowly. Break off bits of parsley and add to tomatoes. Add dried spices to taste. Add two tablespoons grated cheese to sauce. Heat until almost bubbling. Pour over pasta and serve. Add more cheese if you like.

Cooking Pasta

1. Fill the pot with water until it is almost full. Put it on the stove to boil.

2. When the water is boiling, add the pasta.

3. Put the lid on the pot and turn down the temperature on the stove.

4. After about ten minutes, the pasta should be done. With an adult, carefully take the pot to the sink. Pour everything into the colander.

5. Serve a little bit of pasta on each girl's plate.

6. Add sauce and cheese; serve.

Brownie Soup

You can make Brownie Soup. This recipe should get bigger with each girl who adds to it. Use what you learned in the "Smart Shopper" activity to help you choose the ingredients. Remember, an adult must be with you to be sure you're safe when cooking.

You will need:

- A can opener
- A large spoon
- A large pot
- Bowls
- Spoons
- Ladle
- 4 cups of broth (low-sodium is best)
- 3 cups of different kinds of vegetables
- 1 cup of beans
- ½ cup of rice or ½ cup of small noodles (*Everybody should help decide on an ingredient*).

1. Put the vegetables and one cup of water into the pot. Stir.

2. Heat until hot.

3. Serve.

4. Clean up.

TRY IT•TRY IT•TRY IT•TRY IT•TRY IT•TRY IT•TRY IT•TRY IT•TRY IT•TRY IT•TRY IT•TRY IT•TRY IT•TRY IT•TRY IT•TRY IT **207**

Vegetable Chili

28 oz. can pureed or chopped tomatoes
1 green pepper, chopped
16 oz. can of kidney beans
1 small onion
1 tsp. oil or cooking spray
chili powder
½ cup uncooked brown rice
a combination of chopped vegetables—carrots, celery, zucchini, yellow squash, broccoli, peas, etc.

In a large pot, cook the onion and the green pepper in 1 tsp. oil or a light spritz of cooking spray. Add the tomatoes, beans, and chopped vegetables. Add the rice. Add chili powder to taste. Cook until the rice and vegetables are soft. Serves 4.

Note: If you make this in the microwave, you might use cooked rice. This will shorten the amount of cooking time.

If you do not have access to a stove or microwave, try making a chili salad. Mix beans, chopped vegetables, and cooked rice. Make a dressing by combining 1/2 cup tomato juice, 1 tsp. olive or corn oil, and chili powder, to taste. Pour over salad. Mix and serve on lettuce leaves or in tortillas.

Try-Its and Other Resources

- Try-Its: Food Fun; My Body.
- Other Resources: *Developing Health and Fitness*; *The Wide World of Girl Guiding and Girl Scouting.* See handbook pages 39–41 in "Taking Care of Yourself and Your Home."

TRY IT!

HER STORY

An issue is a subject or topic that people may have strong feelings about and want to discuss. How can you learn about issues important to women and children?

A Girl Scout's Story

Read the Juliette Gordon Low story on pages 8–12 in the chapter "Welcome to Girl Scouts." Then try to find a woman in your community who has been a member of Girl Scouting for a long time. Invite her to speak to your troop, if possible. Think of some questions you can ask her. Find out about her memories of being a Girl Scout.

Talk to Women

This activity is a requirement. Ask at least three women of different ages (from teenagers to women over 55 years old) what are the five most important issues facing women today. Include at least two women from a race or ethnic group different from your own. Tell others what you learned from the women.

More to Try: Make a chart to show what you found. Which issue was named most often? What does this tell you about the important issues in your community?

Create Tales

What are some of your favorite fables and fairy tales? Would these stories be different if they were written today? How would the women in the story be different? be the same? Modernize some stories. How can you share your "modern" stories with others?

208 TRY IT•TRY IT•*TRY IT*•TRY IT•TRY IT•TRY IT•TRY IT•*TRY IT*•TRY IT•TRY IT•TRY IT•TRY IT•TRY IT•*TRY IT*•TRY IT•TRY IT

Tips

Having positive female role models for girls is a very important element in Girl Scouting. As girls meet and talk with women in their community, they can focus on a particular aspect of these women's lives or ask more general questions. Review with girls the questions they might ask. In your troop or group meeting, role-play doing an interview. You might also want to make a chart, poster, or mural that records the information the girls discover.

If the girls choose to plan a ceremony, you may want to distribute copies of a simple worksheet for girls to complete. Or, you can write the information on a flip chart or butcher paper.

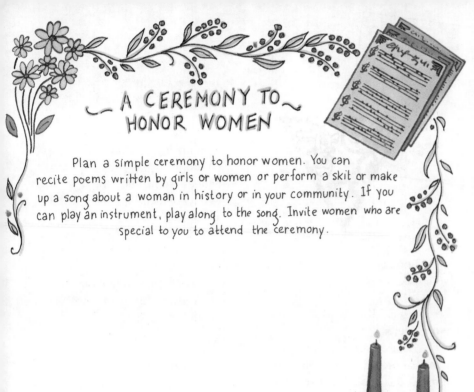

A CEREMONY TO HONOR WOMEN

Plan a simple ceremony to honor women. You can recite poems written by girls or women or perform a skit or make up a song about a woman in history or in your community. If you can play an instrument, play along to the song. Invite women who are special to you to attend the ceremony.

Help in Your Community

Read the story starting on page 111 in the chapter "Leadership in Girl Scouting and Beyond." What did the girls find out? Service is an important part of being a Girl Scout. Look at the section on service that follows the story. Choose a service project you would like to do, and follow the action steps given.

Your Story

Think about where you will be when you are a grownup. Create a time line like the one on page 38, but write in what you would like to do or to have happen in your future.

TRY IT•TRY IT•TRY IT•TRY IT•TRY IT•TRY IT•TRY IT•TRY IT•TRY IT•TRY IT•TRY IT•TRY IT•TRY IT•TRY IT•TRY IT•TRY IT **209**

Your worksheet could include:

Name of ceremony _____
Date and time _____
Place _____
Who will attend? _____
Outline of activities for the opening, middle, and closing parts of the ceremony _____
List of songs, poems, and skits _____
Names of those responsible for bringing props, refreshments, and other items _____
_____
Rehearsal schedule _____

Try-Its and Other Resources

- Try-Its: Careers; Citizen Near and Far; Girl Scout Ways.
- Other Resources: "Leadership in Girl Scouting and Beyond" chapter; "Family, Friends, and Neighbors," pages 74–75; "Taking Care of Yourself and Your Home," pages 67–68; *Girls Are Great*; *Ceremonies in Girl Scouting*.

TRY IT!
HOBBIES

	YES	NO
Is this hobby fun?	___	___
Will this hobby be too expensive?	___	___
Do I have enough room in my home to do this hobby?	___	___
Will this hobby hurt the environment?	___	___
Is this hobby safe?	___	___
Do I have enough time for this hobby?	___	___

A hobby is something that you like to do when you have some free time. Hobbies can be collecting things, like shells or rocks, making things, like knitting or drawing, or doing things, like reading or playing a sport.

Your Talents, Interests, and Hobbies

Most people start a hobby because they are interested in something or because they are good at doing something. On pages 66–67, you listed your interests and talents.

What hobby ideas can you get from your lists?

New Ideas

You are exploring many new things in Brownie Girl Scouts. Look through this book. What activities do you like the most? Make a list. Would these make good hobbies?

Getting Started

Before starting any hobby, you should ask yourself these questions. Then, talk about starting a hobby with your family.

How can you find out the right answers to these questions? Whom should you ask?

Types of Hobbies

What are some things you can collect? Make a list here.

_____

_____

_____

210 *TRY IT•TRY IT•TRY IT•TRY IT•TRY IT•TRY IT•TRY IT•TRY IT•TRY IT•TRY IT•TRY IT•TRY IT•TRY IT•TRY IT•TRY IT•TRY IT•TRY IT*

Tips

You might want to try a "Hobby Day," when girls bring in and/or demonstrate their hobbies. They can set up exhibit tables or booths, and invite family members or other Girl Scouts in the community to participate.

Many of the activities in the handbook and Try-Its can be the beginning of a hobby. Ask the girls to point out which Try-Its would make good hobbies.

You could also look at the Careers Try-It or handbook pages 66–68 in "Taking Care of Yourself and Your Home." Point out the hobbies that could become these careers. Or, when girls are interviewing women, they could ask about their hobbies and interests.

Maybe you have already begun a collection and don't even know it! Look around your home. Do you already have two or three or more things that can make a collection?

What are some hobbies that you can do? Make a list here.

_____

_____

_____

_____

What are some hobbies that you can make? Make a list here.

_____

_____

_____

_____

Organizing Your Hobby

If you are starting a collection, try organizing it. When you organize a collection, you give each thing a label with its special name and write other special information on the label. You also make an arrangement of your collection. Your collection should be easy and attractive to see. What ideas can you get to arrange your own collection?

Practicing Your Hobby

Hobbies, like sports, need practice. Make some time every week to practice your hobby. Here's a chart. Fill in the time you spend on your hobby. Once you have practiced your hobby, try teaching it to others.

Monday _____

Tuesday _____

Wednesday _____

Thursday _____

Friday _____

Saturday _____

Sunday _____

Try doing your hobby with some other people who practice your hobby.

Making an Example

If your hobby is making things, like knitting, drawing, or making models, make an example. Show some other people how you make it.

Make a way of displaying your hobby. Make a label that describes the work you did.

Find someone who has the same hobby. What more about your hobby can you learn from this person?

TRY IT•TRY IT•TRY IT•TRY IT•TRY IT•TRY IT•TRY IT•TRY IT•TRY IT•TRY IT•TRY IT•TRY IT•TRY IT•TRY IT•TRY IT **211**

Try-Its and Other Resources

- Try-Its: Any of the Try-Its activities can lead to hobbies.
- Other Resources: *Games for Girl Scouts*.

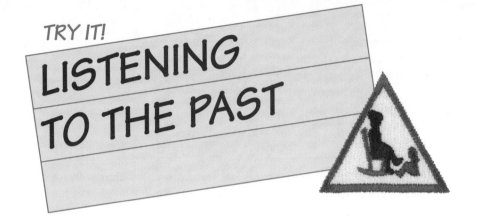

TRY IT!
LISTENING TO THE PAST

Everybody has a story to tell, a story about her family, her special interests, and her life in general. When you listen to someone talk about his or her life, you are participating in oral history.

Listen to the Stories
Read pages 74–75 about family history and try the activities.

Community Stories
Get to know the stories of some of the oldest people in your community. You might get someone in your family to introduce you. Or, contact a senior citizens' group for help. Find some way to share these stories with the community.

Know Your Town
Visit an old cemetery in your area. Do the following activities.

1. Look for the oldest dates on the tombstones you see. Write them down. How old were these people when they died?
2. Write down the most unusual names.
3. Take pictures of the most unusual tombstones.
4. Find out the most common name there.

Become a Storyteller
Choose three stories written in the past or about the past and tell them to others.

OR

Act out the three stories you choose.

212 TRY IT•TRY IT•**TRY IT**•TRY IT•TRY IT•TRY IT•**TRY IT**•TRY IT•TRY IT•TRY IT•**TRY IT**•TRY IT•TRY IT•TRY IT•**TRY IT**•TRY IT•TRY IT

Tips

If you live in an area that has an archivist, a town historian, a local museum, or historical society, you could invite someone to meet with your troop or group. Especially interesting would be artifacts, old toys or game pieces, and photographs or drawings, which the girls could handle.

Most of the developed areas of this country were once part of American Indian lands. Find out about the people native to the area where you live. Do any of them still live there? Find out about some of their traditions.

In addition to jacks, girls could make simple pick-up stick games from twigs or straws, practice double-dutch jump-rope or hopscotch, learn how to twirl a hula hoop, spin a yo-yo, or set up a game of stickball or stoopball. *Games for Girl Scouts* contains directions for jump-rope, string, and hopscotch games. Girls can develop a wide

Games of Yesteryear

Hopscotch, paddleball, jacks, and stickball are some favorite games from long ago. Try playing jacks. You can use ten small shells, pebbles, or beans if you can't find jacks. You also need a small ball that fits in the palm of your hand. Bounce the ball, try to pick up as many jacks as you can, and catch the ball before it bounces again. You can try picking up one jack, then two, then three without touching any others. You can try picking up jacks with the jacks you've already picked up still in your hand. How else can you play jacks?

Community Record

Try the activity "Explore Your Neighborhood," on page 85.

TRY IT•TRY IT•TRY IT•TRY IT•TRY IT•TRY IT•TRY IT•TRY IT•TRY IT•TRY IT•TRY IT•TRY IT•TRY IT•TRY IT•TRY IT•TRY IT **213**

---

game, in which each station has a game that the girls play before moving on. Girls can teach other Girl Scouts the games they have learned. You could invite some women from the community or neighborhood to teach games that were their childhood favorites.

Girls can make a booklet of family or community stories or a videotape or collection of photographs of community historical sites.

Try-Its and Other Resources

- Try-Its: Citizen Near and Far; Puppets, Dolls, and Plays; Sports and Games.

- Other Resources: The National Women's History Project, 7738 Bell Road, Windsor, Calif. 95492, has an extensive catalog of inexpensive storybooks and activity books appropriate for this age level. *Games for Girl Scouts*; *Right to Read*; *Valuing Differences*.

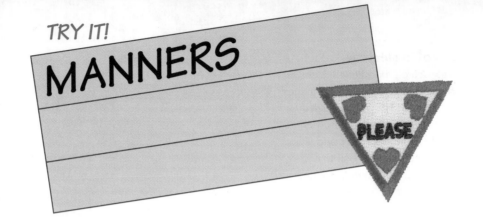

TRY IT!

MANNERS

When you meet new people or when you're with your family and friends, good manners show that you are considerate.

Table Manners

Pretend you are at a restaurant. Take turns being the server and the customer. Talk about polite and impolite ways to act in a restaurant. You can have even more fun by using sample menus from restaurants in the community and a place setting (plates, cups, silverware) for each person.

More to Try: Many cultures use tableware different from a knife and fork and spoon. You could use chopsticks, a special spoon, or just your right hand. You might also have different table settings or one large bowl for the family. Learn about some other ways to eat.

Happy Helper

Good manners can mean helping at home. Think of a job you could do that an adult does now. Offer to do the job for one week. Could you keep doing this job?

Respect for Others

Showing respect for others means treating them the way you want to be treated. The Girl Scout Law states, "I will do my best to show respect for myself and others through my words and actions."

Repeat the Girl Scout Law. Think of as many ways as you can to show respect for others. Talk about things you can do when people are not respectful to you and others. Create a song, skit, or group poem.

Phone Fun

Practice the right way to use the telephone. In pairs, act out some conversations.

1. Someone in the house needs help.
2. Someone from your mother's workplace wants to leave a message.
3. Your grandmother calls you to chat.

214 TRY IT•TRY IT•TRY IT•TRY IT•TRY IT•TRY IT•TRY IT•TRY IT•TRY IT•TRY IT•TRY IT•TRY IT•TRY IT•TRY IT•TRY IT•TRY IT•TRY IT

Tips

People have different expectations for manners. What is considered to be "good" manners depends on the traditions of a particular culture. Be sure that you respect the cultural norms for each girl in your troop or group. For example, in some cultures, direct eye contact is considered rude, while in the United States, avoiding eye contact is often seen as a sign of lying or extreme shyness. If you do have girls in your troop from different cultural groups, religions, or geographic regions, you may want the girls and their families to share some of their beliefs of good and bad manners. **More to Try:** Girls can practice writing thank-you notes and discussing the occasions when thank-you notes would be appropriate.

Meeting People

Good manners include knowing how to introduce yourself and others. Introductions are different in different cultures. Meeting someone new may be the first step in making a new friend.

Try the following activity on introductions at home and away from home.

1. Practice introducing yourself to others in your troop, at home, and in school. Include a smile, a handshake, and a friendly hello. Say something like "Hi, my name is. . . ."

2. Practice introducing other people. Introductions are made in a certain order. The common rule is that you say a woman's or older person's name first, as well as the name of people with important positions or titles. For example, you would say, "Ms. Lewis, I'd like you to meet Alexis Smith. Alexis, this is Ms. Lewis." The following list contains ideas for practicing introductions:

- A new girl in your troop
- A friend to a parent
- A girl to a boy
- A person with a special title or degree, such as father, rabbi, doctor, or judge. Try using a person's job title—for example, "Hello, Dr. Jones, I am. . . ."

Practice these greetings used in different parts of the world:

- In Japan, a bow is a traditional greeting.
- In Chile, a handshake and a kiss to the right cheek are customary.
- In Fiji, a smile and an upward movement of the eyebrows are how people greet one another.

More to Try: Learn titles that are used in other languages and cultures. For example, "Señora" is the Spanish title for a married woman. In Japan, "San" is used after someone's name to show respect for the person. In Turkey, an older woman calls a younger woman "Canim," which means "dear" or "beloved." In this country, Navajo people use the term "Hosteen," which means uncle, for older men they admire. Can you find some others?

Parties

Pretend you are a party host. What should a host do so that her guests have a good time? Pretend you are a party guest. How is a good guest considerate?

TRY IT•TRY IT•TRY IT•TRY IT•TRY IT•TRY IT•TRY IT•TRY IT•TRY IT•TRY IT•TRY IT•TRY IT•TRY IT•TRY IT•TRY IT•TRY IT **215**

Try-Its Other Resources

- Try-Its: Around the World; Caring and Sharing; People of the World.
- Other Resources: *Valuing Differences.*

TRY IT!
MATH FUN

Did you know that you use math every day? When you count money, or measure your height and weight, or tell time, you are using math.

My Numbers

Numbers are used to tell many things about you. For instance, you use numbers to tell how old you are. Think of the many things about yourself that can be described with numbers. How many toes do you have? Make a "My Numbers" poster that tells all your important numbers facts.

Can You Guess?

Find out how well your friends and family can guess amounts. Find a large jar with a lid. Fill it with something like seeds, beans, or marbles. Count each one as you fill the jar. Have at least five people guess the number of objects that are in the jar. Ask family and friends to record their guesses and how they made them. Let them pick up the jar if they wish. Did anyone make a close guess?

Math and Me

Read page 38 and do the time line activity about yourself. Share it with other girls in your troop or group. How are you alike? How are you different?

Measure Up

Read page 129 in the "How and Why?" chapter. Try the stick of gum measuring activities.

Working Together

Read about planning a budget on page 121. Think of three activities your troop would like to do and plan a budget for each one.

Tips

Girls use many types of math skills in their daily activities. When they count by two's for teams, count out snacks, collect and record dues, measure for cooking or art activities, they are using math skills. Playing board games, such as Checkers or Go, requires calculations and problem-solving skills. Girls can challenge each other with math problems, or use calculators to create word games. For example, when you turn a calculator upside down the number 07734 looks like the word "hello." In addition to the mathematics activities in the "How and Why?" chapter, math activities can be found throughout the handbook and in many of the Try-Its. See how many you and the girls can discover.

My Numbers. See handbook pages 36–38 in "Taking Care of Yourself and Your Home" for related activities.

Can You Guess? Before you try the "Can You Guess?" activity, look at the estimating activities on handbook page 128 and the stick of gum measuring activities on page 129 in "How and Why?" To help girls estimate in a more visual way, fill a bag of candy-coated chocolate or fruit chews, or similar things that come in different colors—beans, marbles. Make a line graph, with a space for each candy color. Ask the girls to guess which color most of the candies will be. Choose a girl to help, or let each girl have a turn picking a candy from the bag. One by one, fill in the space for each candy picked from the bag. When the bag is empty, the girls tally the results. Which color appeared the most? Try this procedure again or have each

Alphabet Code

Make up your own secret code. Write down the letters of the alphabet. Next to each letter put a different number from 1 to 26. You don't have to write the numbers in order.

Use your code to send a secret message.

More to Try: Give a dollar value to each letter of the alphabet. For example, A = $1.00, B = $2.00, C = $3.00, and so on. Then add up the dollars that are in the letters of your first name. You may use pencil and paper or a calculator if you have one. Find the most expensive word or name you can.

TRY IT•TRY IT•TRY IT•TRY IT•TRY IT•TRY IT•TRY IT•TRY IT•TRY IT•TRY IT•TRY IT•TRY IT•TRY IT•TRY IT•TRY IT **217**

girl work with her own chart and bag of candy.

"Measure Up." Girls might enjoy measuring distances too. Girls could count how many steps it is from their bedroom to the kitchen at home, how many streets from their home to their school, or how many traffic lights from their home to their Girl Scout meeting place. They could try measuring in the metric and English systems of measurement (see pages 190–191 in this book for comparison of English and metric systems).

Try-Its and Other Resources

- Other Resources: *Into the World of Today and Tomorrow;* try this activity from the booklet:

Probability is a number prediction of whether something might happen. It is more accurate than a guess, but may not always be true. Try it for yourself: If you flip a penny 20 times, how often will it land on its head? Flip a penny 10 times and tally how many times it lands on its head and on its tail. Do this 10 more times. Compare the results after 20 flips. What patterns emerge? **More to Try:**

Try playing tic-tac-toe. Can the girls figure out different winning strategies? Look at "Make a Box" on handbook page 81 in "Family, Friends, and Neighbors." What strategies can girls discover to help them win the game?

TRY IT!

ME AND MY SHADOW

A shadow is formed when a body or object blocks light. Artists study how light falls on things to create shadows, and use this knowledge in their paintings, photographs, and other artwork.

Making Shadow Bags

You will need:
- A paper shopping bag with handles
- Scissors
- Tape or glue
- Colored construction paper
- Colored cellophane paper

Cut out designs on the sides of your shopping bag. Tape the colored paper and the colored cellophane paper from the inside over parts of your design. Leave some parts of the design open so light can come through. Use the bag to carry things, as a decoration, or give it to someone as a gift.

Tracing Your Shadow

With a partner, stand so your shadow falls on a big piece of paper taped to a wall or the floor. Stand still while your partner traces your shadow. Then do the same for your partner. Try creating some different shadow shapes.

Making Shadow-and-Light Plaques

Read about tools in the section "Home Repairs" in the chapter "Taking Care of Yourself and Your Home." Collect some lightweight aluminum pans (like the ones frozen pies come in). With a felt marker, draw a design on a pan. Place the pan on a table or counter. Put lots of newspaper between the pan and the table so you don't damage the surface. Punch holes in the aluminum with a hammer and nails of different sizes. Place your pan plaque against a window or lamp so that light can pass through the nail holes and highlight your design.

218 *TRY IT•TRY IT•TRY IT•TRY IT•TRY IT•TRY IT•TRY IT•TRY IT•TRY IT•TRY IT•TRY IT•TRY IT•TRY IT•TRY IT•TRY IT*

Tips

Tracing Your Shadow. Try this activity outdoors. Use chalk to trace each girl's shadow on the concrete. Girls can do this at different times of the day to compare the length of their shadows.

Making Shadow and Light Plaques. This can also be done using paper plates, shirt cardboard, or foam plates.

Keeping Shadows

Take some pictures of interesting shadows that you see outdoors. You may need an adult to help you. You can use black-and-white film. Notice how things look in light, in shade, and in the dark. Make a display of your photos of interesting shadows.

OR

You will need some light-sensitive paper from an art supply store or clean fresh newspaper or newsprint. Place an object on the shiny side of the paper or on the newspaper in bright sunlight. After a few minutes for the paper or a half-hour for the newspaper, you should be able to see a shadow image.

Shadow Box

Tell a favorite story in a shadow box. Get a shoe box or other small box, paper and cardboard, glue, tape, scissors, and scraps of wood, ribbon, fabric, and other materials. Decorate the inside of your box to tell a scene from your story.

DOING A SHADOW PLAY

Make a shadow theater with a bright light bulb and some white sheets. Choose a play with lots of action and invite an audience to your performance.

TRY IT•TRY IT•TRY IT•TRY IT•TRY IT•TRY IT•TRY IT•TRY IT•TRY IT•TRY IT•TRY IT•TRY IT•TRY IT•TRY IT•TRY IT **219**

Doing a Shadow Play. How to make a shadow theater: You will need a bare, bright light bulb and some old bed sheets. Hang the sheets over a rope, or tack them to the walls and ceilings. The play is acted out behind the sheet while the audience watches the shadows on the front of the sheet.

Try-Its and Other Resources

- Try-Its: Building Art; Colors and Shapes; My Body.

TRY IT!

MOVERS

How many ways do things move? These activities will help you find out.

Wind Wheels

Try this experiment to see how moving air has energy to move things.

You will need:

- Square sheets of stiff paper
- Straight pins
- Straws or thin wooden sticks, 8″ or more long

1. Cut paper squares, following the dotted lines on the diagram.

2. Fold the bottom right-hand corner up to the center, but don't press to make a crease.

3. Then go around to the other three corners and fold them the same way.

4. Poke the pin through the middle of the paper and then into the end of the straw or stick.

5. If the point comes through the straw or stick, cover the point with clay, glue, or other material. Or bend the end down and cover with tape.

220 TRY IT•TRY IT•**TRY IT**•TRY IT•TRY IT•TRY IT•TRY IT•TRY IT•**TRY IT**•TRY IT•TRY IT•TRY IT•TRY IT•TRY IT•**TRY IT**•TRY IT•TRY IT

You can refer girls to the illustration of the astronaut Dr. Tamara Jernigan, on handbook page 70 in "Family, Friends, and Neighbors," as a person who moves through space. Since several of the activities in the Movers Try-It involve air as a mover, challenge girls to show that air exists. A good way to do this is to provide them with soda straws, balloons, and a tub of water. Ask girls to demonstrate that air is something that is there. They will come up with variations on blowing, capturing, and releasing, to demonstrate the existence of air. Refer girls to the illustrations in the Try-It when making items. These activities lend themselves to asking "what if?" As a leader, do not try to give all the answers. Let girls ask questions and then try to discover the answers by designing a way to find out.

Wind Wheels. The obvious safety precaution here is to work carefully with straight pins and long wooden sticks. (You might use Girl Scout pencils for the sticks.) Caution girls to stand apart when testing their wind wheels.

Windmills are used to convert wind energy into mechanical energy. Believed to have originated in Iran, they are most frequently associated with the Netherlands, where they were used to grind grain and pump water to drain land. In the United States, windmills can be found pumping water from wells, generating electricity, and grinding grain. Scientists and power companies are experimenting with wind turbines, capable of converting wind energy into electricity.

Water is also used to propel machinery. Look for a water wheel in your community, or challenge girls to create one. Turbines found in dams are run by water to create electricity.

You can decorate the paper before making the wind wheel. Find out the different ways you can make the machine spin. Hold it over a lighted bulb. Blow on it. Run with it. What happens? Your wind wheel is a pinwheel.

Find out about windmills—where they are, what they are used for, and how they work.

Energy Saver

In the chapter "How and Why?" you read about ways to save energy. Did you know some machines can store energy, too? Try this simple experiment to find out that something can move and save energy at the same time.

You will need:

- A coffee can
- 2 plastic coffee can lids
- 2 rubber bands
- String
- Nuts or bolts

1. With an adult, cut off the ends of the coffee can so that you have a cylinder (sil-un-der).

2. Punch two holes about two inches apart, on each lid. Make sure they are an equal distance from the center of the lid.

3. Cut open each rubber band. Thread each one through the holes of the lids, and retie the ends.

4. Join the two rubber bands inside the coffee can by tying them together with a piece of string. Tie a weight, such as a nut or bolt, onto the string.

5. Snap the lids onto the can. Try to roll the can across the floor. What happens?

Wind, Clouds, and Rain

Read about "Wind" and "Clouds and Rain" on pages 138–140 in the chapter "How and Why?" and try one of the activities on those pages.

TRY IT•TRY IT•TRY IT•TRY IT•TRY IT•TRY IT•TRY IT•TRY IT•TRY IT•TRY IT•TRY IT•TRY IT•TRY IT•TRY IT•TRY IT•TRY IT **221**

The problem with a simple windmill or a water wheel is that energy is not stored. If the wind isn't blowing or the water isn't running, the wheels cannot go around to move the machinery. This "Energy Saver" activity introduces girls to a simple mechanism for storing kinetic energy (energy produced by a moving object). In constructing the energy saver (refer to illustrations), it is best: to use strong, thick rubber bands; to make large knots so the tension does not pull the string through the plastic lids; and to use a washer for the most effective results. As a safety precaution, cover the inside edges of the can with tape so girls cannot cut themselves. Tie your washer to the middle of the string, then tie your two rubber pieces to the string ends. Adjust the tension when you tie the knots so that the rubber bands and string are taut, but not tight. To roll the can, choose a place with lots of room, like a gymnasium or sidewalk.

When rolling the can, girls should stay to the side, as the can may roll back into them. Girls can mark the start point and measure the distance that the can is rolled forward. As the can is rolled, the rubber bands twist because of the weight of the washer, and energy is stored in the twists. When the can is let go, the rubber bands unwind, and the can should roll back past the point of starting, build up additional kinetic energy, then roll back and forth until the energy is used up. Have the girls compare the distance the can is rolled, storing up energy, and the distance the can rolls back on its own. Are they equal? Is the rolling can losing energy? Girls might want to experiment by varying size of cans, length of rubber bands, and other factors to see if they can change the distance rolled.

Go Fly a Kite

When a kite is held into the wind, air pushes the kite upward so it can fly. Make your own kite.

You will need:

- Thin paper (like newspaper), 3 feet by 2½ feet
- Thin sticks (like bamboo, cane, or balsa)
- A ball of string
- Tape
- Glue
- Scissors

1. Pick two sticks for the frame. One stick must be twice as long as the other one.

2. Cross the sticks and tie them with the string. Run string around the edges to make a diamond shape.

3. Lay the frame on the paper. Cut around the frame so that you have about one and one-half inches all around.

4. Fold the paper over the frame and glue it down. Let it dry.

5. Make a tail for your kite with a piece of string about twice as long as the kite. Tie the tail onto the kite.

6. Tie two short strings to the long stick of the frame, above and below the cross. Tie the two ends together. Then tie them to the ball of string.

7. On a breezy day (but not too windy), take your kite and let the wind carry it up into the air. Unwind the string a little to let it go higher. You can run into the wind to get off to a good start.

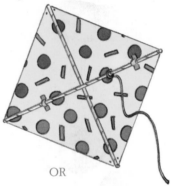

OR

Read pages 92–93 about kite-flying in Thailand. Try making a kite.

Fliers

Try making these paper fliers. The air holds them up and their shape makes them fly in different patterns.

You will need:

- Sheets of paper the size of this book (construction paper or magazine covers work well)
- Scissors
- A drinking straw
- Tape
- Paper clips

Helicopter

1. Cut the paper in half the long way. You'll only need one of those halves.

2. Fold the paper in half the long way, then fold in half the long way again.

3. Fold the paper in the middle.

4. Fold the ends, as the diagram shows.

Go Fly a Kite. Read about the kite festival in Thailand on handbook page 93 in "People Near and Far." Your group might want to hold its own kite festival. Visit a kite shop and see the variety of shapes and materials used in kite making. Have someone who is a master kite flier demonstrate kite flying and different kinds of kites in the air.

Fliers. Have the girls experiment with the design of their fliers. Girls can make simple predictions and test them. Does the size of the flier affect flight? What happens if you vary the weight of the paper used in construction? Vary the length, width, and shape of the plane wings and see what happens. Does the angle of the wings affect flight? Have the girls measure distance or time the length of flight and record the results. Girls might like to visit an airport or a science museum that has an exhibit on flight.

5. Weight the bottom with a paper clip.

6. Drop your helicopter from a high point to see it fly.

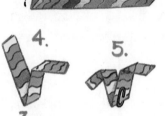

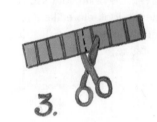

Circle Glider

1. Fold a piece of paper in half the long way. Fold it in half the long way again.

2. Make two strips by cutting along the folds. Give a friend the other strips for her glider.

3. Cut the width of one of your strips in half.

4. Make a loop with the long strip, and paper clip it to the straw. Put the small loop of the clip into the straw.

5. Loop the half-strip and paper clip it to the other end of the straw.

6. With the short loop facing forward, give your glider a quick toss to send it flying.

Have the girls find out about women who have been famous aviators or visit with a woman pilot. Girls can do the "Space Sleuth" activity in the Space Explorer Try-It. How is the source of energy different in the rocket and in a glider? Girls can look for animals and plants that fly or glide through the air. The Seed Hunt on handbook page 155 in "How and Why?" is a good start for investigating natural movers.

Try-Its and Other Resources

- Try-Its: Science in Action; Science Wonders; Space Explorer.
- Other Resources: *Into the World of Today and Tomorrow* has more activities on science and a list of science museums.

Twig Rafts

These small rafts are like the bigger ones that used to cross rivers and streams years ago. You can sail them in the bathtub or pool or on a waterway.

You will need:

- 14 straight twigs, or sticks 10″ long
- String
- White glue
- Stiff paper or cellophane

1. Follow the drawing. Line up seven sticks on the wax paper.
2. Squeeze glue between the sticks.
3. Let the glue dry.
4. Lay down two sticks on each end and glue.
5. After the glue dries, turn over the raft and glue down two more sticks.
6. Make a sail by pushing the paper onto the last stick. These will be the mast and sail for sailing.
7. Glue the mast down between one of the cross-sticks and put the last one next to it.
8. Tie the string to one end of the raft so you can keep it from floating away.

More to Try: Decorate your sail. To make the raft look more like a real one, bind the raft sticks with string instead of glue.

224   *TRY IT•TRY IT•TRY IT•TRY IT•TRY IT•TRY IT•TRY IT•TRY IT•TRY IT•TRY IT•TRY IT•TRY IT•TRY IT•TRY IT•TRY IT•TRY IT•TRY IT*

TRY IT!
MUSIC

 **M**usic is the art of making sounds. Different cultures find different sounds pleasing to the ear. Some sounds in nature, like birdcalls, are musical. You can make your own music.

Move to the Music

Listen to different kinds of music—fast, slow, lots of instruments or voices, one instrument or one voice. Think of a story that goes with the music. Make up movements to tell the story.

Rhythm Instruments

Look at pages 266–268 for directions to make some instruments. Play in your own troop band.

Singing in Rounds

To sing in rounds, groups start singing a song at different times. Practice singing "Make New Friends," page 168. Split into two groups. Group A sings first. When Group A reaches the second line of the song, Group B starts singing. What other songs can be sung in rounds?

Action Songs

Practice the action song on page 24. The "Brownie Smile Song" is an action song. "Bingo," found in the *Sing-Along Songbook*, is another. Do you know any action songs you can share with your friends?

TRY IT•TRY IT•TRY IT•TRY IT•TRY IT•TRY IT•TRY IT•TRY IT•TRY IT•TRY IT•TRY IT•TRY IT•TRY IT•TRY IT•TRY IT **225**

Tips

Many Brownie Girl Scouts love to sing and move. Even if you feel that singing is not one of your talents, most girls are not yet self-conscious about singing and your enthusiasm will certainly counteract a few sour notes here and there. Some girls may have memorized songs they may be eager to teach the group.

Caution: Older sisters, brothers, and even adults at home may be listening to music with lyrics quite suggestive and inappropriate for this age level. Also, girls are exposed to videos and music on television more suited to older girls. While the girls may not understand the meanings (or double entendres) of what they are singing, they may still be eager to sing the most current popular songs. Showing discomfort or stopping the singing may make the songs even more desirable to some girls. With two or three active, fun songs in reserve, you can easily lead the girls into singing songs more appopriate to their age level.

Move to the Music. More to Try: Find music about seasons, animals, weather, emotions, or celebrations. Make up movements to go with the music.

Melody Glasses

Drinking glasses filled with different amounts of water can become a musical instrument. This activity and many other fun ones are in the Contemporary Issues book, *Into the World of Today and Tomorrow: Leading Girls into Mathematics, Science, and Technology*.

Twinkle, twinkle, little star,
 1   1   5   5   6 6   5
How I wonder what you are
 4   4   3 3   2   2   1
Up above the world so high
 5   5   4   4   3   3   2
Like a diamond in the sky.
 5   5   4   4   3   3   2
Twinkle, twinkle, little star
 1   1   5   5   6 6   5
How I wonder what you are.
 4   4   3 3   2   2   1

You will need:

• 8 same-size drinking glasses
• Water
• Spoon

1. Number the glasses from one through eight.
2. Fill each glass with the amount of water shown in the picture.
3. Play "Twinkle, Twinkle, Little Star" on your melody glasses. The numbers tell which glasses to tap. If a note doesn't sound just right, try adding or taking away a little water. Tap fast or slow in different places to follow the rhythm.

Music Around the World

Try singing The "Brownie Friend-Maker Song" from the *Sing-Along Songbook* and cassette. The tune is from Israel. Do you know any songs from different countries you can choose?

Try-Its and Other Resources

- Try-Its: Creative Composing; Sounds of Music.
- Other Resources: These activities are from *Developing Health and Fitness*:

Circle Romp: To the beat of music, form a circle and begin marching in place, slowly at first, then pick up the pace with more vigorous movements. Move around the circle formation; change movements as the leader calls them out: skipping, hopping, and galloping. Vary the music.

Jumping Rope to Music: Jumping rope increases coordination, rhythm, and timing while it tones up circulatory and respiratory systems. There are many variations to try, and girls can make their own: jump with both feet together, cross arms forward, slightly swing the foot and leg forward as you jump.

Brownie Friend-Maker Song

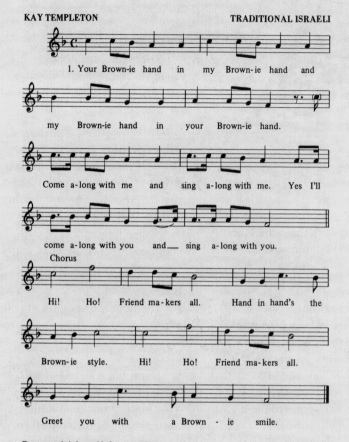

KAY TEMPLETON   TRADITIONAL ISRAELI

1. Your Brown-ie hand in my Brown-ie hand and

my Brown-ie hand in your Brown-ie hand.

Come a-long with me and sing a-long with me. Yes I'll

come a-long with you and__ sing a-long with you.

Chorus

Hi! Ho! Friend ma-kers all. Hand in hand's the

Brown-ie style. Hi! Ho! Friend ma-kers all.

Greet you with a Brown - ie smile.

Do a grand right and left as you sing.

2. Your Brownie hand in my Brownie hand,
   And my Brownie hand in your Brownie hand.
   We have Brownie friends in many lands
   Across the seven seas, the mountains and the sands.

   Chorus:
   Hi! Ho! Friend ma-kers all.
   Hand in hand's the Brown-ie style.
   Hi! Ho! Friend ma-kers all.
   Greet you with a Brown-ie smile.

3. Your Brownie hand in my Brownie hand,
   And my Brownie hand in your Brownie hand.
   On Thinking Day our love goes forth to ev'ry friend,
   A chain of Brownie hands reaching out, their help to lend.

   Chorus:
   Hi! Ho! Friend ma-kers all.
   Hand in hand's the Brown-ie style.
   Hi! Ho! Friend ma-kers all.
   Greet you with a Brown-ie smile.

TRY IT!

MY BODY

Try these activities to find out more about your body.

Brain Power

Try these activities to see how your brain works.

Different Muscles

Sit at a table and write your name. Then take one of your feet and move it in a circle on the floor.

Now try doing both things together. Sometimes it's hard for your brain to do two things at once.

Eye to Brain to Hand

Cut a piece of paper the size of a dollar bill. Hold it in front of a friend who has her fingers ready to catch it. Drop it and ask her to try to catch it before it falls to the floor. The eyes send messages to the brain that then tell the hands what to do. But sometimes an object falls faster

than messages travel. Try to improve through practice.

Dreams

Your brain works even while you're sleeping—that's why you have dreams. In a circle with friends, tell about one of your dreams.

Fingerprints

Your fingerprints are not like anyone else's. Even identical twins have different fingerprints. Do the fingerprinting activity on page 37. Then make fingerprints of three other people on clean white paper.

Reflexes

Try these activities to test your reflexes.

Eye Changes

In a room with lots of light, sit facing a friend. Watch what happens to the black center part of the eye called the pupil. The colored part of the eye, the iris, is changing with

Tips

Brain Power. Your brain and nervous system control all the things your body does. This includes actions you think about before doing and actions you do without thinking (automatically or by reflex). To help girls understand about the brain's messages to the body, girls can try spinning. In a wide, clear space, stand with arms straight out and spin around 10 times. Ask girls how they feel when they stop. Eyes and ears help your brain keep your body balanced. Your brain is not sent messages when you spin and you feel dizzy.

Different Muscles. Writing your name and moving your foot in a circle involves two different kinds of motions, thus two different messages being sent from your brain to different parts of your body. Most people are either right-handed or left-handed. Most also have a dominant foot, eye, thumb, ear, and leg. Some people have mixed dominance. Have

the girls think up ways to test for dominance. (For checking foot dominance, have a girl roll a ball to another to kick. Which foot was used?)

Eye to Brain to Hand. This activity demonstrates the time it takes for a message to travel from eye to brain, and then to the hand. If the paper flutters as it falls, not falling in a straight trajectory, the brain takes longer to estimate where the paper will be when the hand goes out to catch it. A person who plays Ping-

Pong or basketball improves with practice, because the response time improves as the messages for certain acts become part of the brain's response pattern. A person who practices piano or learns multiplication tables repeats actions stored in the brain as memory.

Dreams. The experiences being stored by the brain are very different for each person. The way each person thinks, feels, and acts is different. That's what makes people

unique. No two people are totally alike—not even twins. In talking about dreams, do not attempt to analyze them for girls. Instead, question girls about how dreams are alike or different, such as: did they dream in black and white or color? Were the people in the dreams familiar or were they strangers? Were the dreams full of action or were they in slow motion? Did they seem real or did they seem fake? Were they scary or were they friendly?

the light. Your body does this automatically.

Knee Jerk

Sit on something that is high enough so that your feet don't touch the floor. Cross your legs. On the top leg, feel your kneecap. Just below your kneecap is a soft spot. Have a friend gently tap this spot with the back of this book.

Muscle Reaction

Make one of your arms very straight. Ask a friend to hold your arm down while you try as hard as you can to lift it. Your friend can use both hands. Count to 20, trying as hard as you can to lift your arm. After you have counted to 20, your friend can let go. Stand still and let your arm relax. What does your arm do?

Pulse

Your heart pumps blood through the body. Every time your heart beats, it pushes a new supply of blood into your arteries (ar-tuh-reez). Arteries are the tubes that carry blood away from your heart. You can feel this as your pulse. The blood then goes into your veins, the tubes that carry the blood back to your heart.

Take your pulse by placing three fingers of the hand you write with on the flat side of your neck. (See the picture.) Hold them still until you feel a slight beating. Now try to feel your pulse in your wrist. Hold your fingers as the diagram shows. You can even watch your pulse. Try this: Put a thumbtack through one end of a wooden match. Rest your arm on a table. Rest the thumbtack with the match on the spot on your wrist where you found your pulse. Watch closely. What happens?

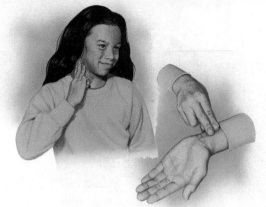

More to Try: Try to find a different spot on your body where you can feel your pulse. Practice taking someone else's pulse.

A Fit Body

Try making a fitness wheel like in the picture and do some of the exercises.

You will need:

* Heavy cardboard
* Scissors
* Crayons or markers

1. Cut a piece of heavy cardboard into a circle.

TRY IT•TRY IT•TRY IT•TRY IT•TRY IT•TRY IT•TRY IT•TRY IT•TRY IT•TRY IT•TRY IT•TRY IT•TRY IT•TRY IT•TRY IT **229**

Reflexes. Reflexes are actions your body does automatically in response to a stimulus, or message sent by your senses. They are actions that muscles take before the thinking part of your brain gets involved. In each of the activities, have girls decide what the outside stimulus is (light, touch, smell, movement) and what the reflex is. Can they think of any other reflexes, such as eyes blinking, hands jerking away from something hot, mouth watering?

Pulse. Take the pulse of someone before and after she has exercised and compare the heart rate. Blood is moved through your heart about 1,000 times a day. If you squeeze a tennis ball 10 times a minute, it gives you an idea how hard your heart (a giant muscle) works to pump blood throughout your body. Invite a medical professional to demonstrate the taking of blood pressure and explain what it means. Listen to the heart using a stethoscope. You

can make a simple stethoscope using rubber tubing (from a hardware or aquarium store), a small funnel, and glue. Glue the tubing and funnel together. Listen through the tube with the funnel held over the heart. Someone who has taken a certified course in CPR can show girls how to do mouth-to-mouth resuscitation and CPR using a doll. (Girls should not practice on each other or a sibling.)

A Fit Body. The fitness wheel is a great activity for wide games or

group fitness breaks. The Individual and Partner Minichallenges found in *Games for Girl Scouts* would be good activities for the wheel as well. Girls might like to select music for each activity on the wheel. A simple arrow can be made out of cardboard and affixed with a pin or a brad to make a spinner. Be sure to stress the importance of drinking water to replace water lost during exercise.

2. Draw four straight lines through the middle of the circle. Color them different colors, if you want. These will be your eight places to write the names of exercises. Here are some ideas:

- Jumping jacks
- Marching
- Skipping
- Side leg raises
- Hopping
- Sit-ups
- Push-ups
- Waist twists

3. Close your eyes and point to the wheel and do the exercise you picked.

Body Parts

Your body has many parts that work together. Most people have the same parts, but none are just alike. Try this activity to see how you are alike and how you are different.

You will need:

- Butcher paper or other long pieces of paper
- Pencils
- 13 paper fasteners for each girl
- Scissors

1. Choose a partner. Take turns tracing each other's bodies on the paper.

2. Cut around the body that was drawn.

3. Cut the body apart at the neck, shoulders, elbows, wrists, thighs, knees, and ankles (see the picture).

4. Fasten the body parts back together with the paper fasteners. You now have moving body parts, like parts of a puppet.

5. Label the different body parts.

6. Display your "body puppets" around the room.

Body Parts. These bodies might be pretty floppy unless reinforced with a piece of cardboard or tagboard on either side of each cut. Use glue to add the strips to the top of the arm, the shoulder, etc., before punching holes for movement. Besides labeling body parts, girls can label joints, such as elbow, shoulder, knee, or ankle. Have girls write their favorite actions associated with each body part, such as running, skipping, walking, on the feet; thinking, singing, and talking, on the head. A similar activity might be to cut out pictures from magazines, mount them on cardboard, and make body parts jointed.

Try-Its and Other Resources

- Try-Its: Dancercize; Good Food; Play; Safety.
- Other Resources: *Developing Health and Fitness*, *Growing Up Female*, and *Tune In to Well-Being* have health and self-esteem activities appropriate for Brownie Girl Scouts. *Games for Girl Scouts* has the chapter "Active Games for Indoors and Outdoors." *Blood and Guts, A Working Guide to Your Own Insides* by Linda Allison (Little Brown and Co., 1976) is an excellent resource for activities and information on the body.

NUMBERS AND SHAPES

Sailboat at dock

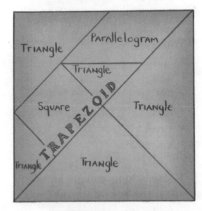
Triangle · Parallelogram · Triangle · Square · TRAPEZOID · Triangle · Triangle · Triangle

Have some fun with numbers and shapes.

Math Shapes

Try to make different patterns from the same shapes.

You will need:

- Paper
- Scissors
- A ruler
- A pencil

1. Have someone help you trace or draw the different shapes inside the square.

2. Cut the paper on the lines.

3. Try to put your shapes back into the same square.

4. Try to make other patterns and designs. You will find out more about shapes, like triangles and rectangles, when you study geometry (gee-om-eh-tree).

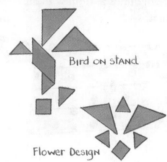
Bird on stand

Flower Design

Tips

Girls can explore the geometrical concepts of numbers, space, and shapes. Geometry skills are used in mapping, giving directions, understanding diagrams, and other aspects of our daily lives. Proportion and symmetry are present in nature, in design, in concepts of art and beauty, and in fashion. Manipulating shapes and other hands-on experiences help make learning about geometry fun.

Books on origami and folding paper are available in most public and school libraries. These resources can provide diagrams for more fun things to fold, such as boats, drinking cups, hats, other animals, and decorations. Girls can fold their paper into zoos, farms, towns, or other wacky collections of things.

Mobius Strips

Simple paper magic can happen with Mobius (mo-bee-us) strips. These paper strips are named after the German mathematician August F. Mobius.

You will need:

- Sheets of newspaper
- Scissors
- Tape
- A ruler
- A pencil

1. Draw long, straight lines on the paper. Use the ruler to help you space the lines and draw them straight.

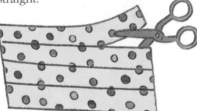

2. Cut the paper into strips along the lines.

3. Make the three different kinds of loops, as shown.

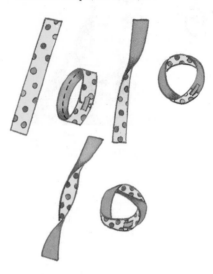

4. Tape the ends.
5. Cut the loops in half.

More twist fun: Make the same kinds of loops as above, but do not cut them in half. Cut one-third of the way in and keep on cutting.

Origami

Origami (ore-ee-gahm-ee) is the Japanese art of folding paper. Try making an origami cat.

You will need a square sheet of paper (you can make a paper rectangle into a square by copying these pictures).

Cat

1. Fold the square to make a triangle. See the picture.

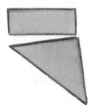

2. Fold the bottom part of the triangle up. This is called a trapezoid (trap-uh-zoyd). See the picture.

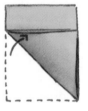

The origami "cat" shape is a geometric figure called a "pentagon."

Girls can cut shapes out of paper and try constructing 3-D sculptures, animals, or greeting cards and decorations. Girls can make symmetrical "inkblot" pictures by folding a piece of paper in half, opening it, and putting some paint on one side, folding it again and pressing on the reverse side, and then opening it to see the symmetrical design. Girls can also cut into the fold of paper folded in half to make symmetrical designs. When girls are looking at shapes in natures, they can look for those that are symmetrical.

3. Fold the right and left points up and to the front. See the picture.

4. What do you have? You can draw a cat's face. Do you know what the shape of the face is called? Hint: It has five sides. What other animals or things can you make by folding paper?

More to Try: Find a book on origami and try making art with other shapes.

Jigsaw Puzzles

Try making your own puzzle. You will need:

- Scissors
- Heavy paper
- Glue or paste
- Newspaper or wax paper
- Books or other heavy things
- A pen
- A picture of something you like
- An envelope

1. Spread a thin coat of glue on the heavy paper.

2. Put your picture on the gluey paper and press it smooth.

3. Dry the paper flat by covering it with newspaper or wax paper and laying books on top. Let the papers dry for one day or more.

4. Trim the edges of your paper.

5. Draw four or five lines over the back of your paper.

6. Cut the paper apart.

7. Try to put your puzzle back together.

8. Store the pieces of your puzzle in an envelope for safekeeping.

More to Try: Trade puzzles with friends. Are some easier to put together than others? What makes a jigsaw puzzle hard to complete?

Time and Money

Read pages 130–132 about time and money in "How and Why?" Try some of the activities.

Nature Shapes

Read pages 153–154 in "How and Why?" Do the activity about looking for different shapes in natural things.

TRY IT•TRY IT•TRY IT•TRY IT•TRY IT•TRY IT•TRY IT•TRY IT•TRY IT•TRY IT•TRY IT•TRY IT•TRY IT•TRY IT•TRY IT•TRY IT   **233**

Try-Its and Other Resources

- Try-Its: Colors and Shapes; Math Fun.
- Other Resources: Activities in the "How and Why?" chapter. *Into the World of Today and Tomorrow.*

Tips

This Try-It contains an overnight activity along with opportunities for girls to venture out. Parents who accompany girls on hikes and overnights as chaperones need to understand the concept of girl/adult partnership and girl/adult planning. You will want to meet with chaperones and other parents/guardians before the overnight trip. Pages 34–35 in Part I of this book contain more information on trips. Girls need the opportunity and space to grow and learn from their mistakes and successes. The outdoors acts as a great vehicle for these learnings.

Neighborhood Map. Girls might need to first map their meeting room and more immediate areas to develop the concept of mapping. They can use pace distances (measuring distance by number of steps taken) to get a feel for relative size. Older girls might use graph paper to make maps that represent scale in a room (one square equals one pace). This

---

TRY IT!

OUTDOOR ADVENTURER

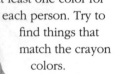

Doing activities outside is a special part of being a Brownie Girl Scout. Before you do any of the activities below, review the outdoor skills checklist on pages 149–150.

Neighborhood Map

Pretend that you are a bird looking down on the earth. Draw a map of your meeting place, backyard, or a neighborhood park as you might see it from above. Put in buildings, pathways, plants growing, and other things of interest.

Sleep Out!

Plan for and go on an overnight with your troop in someone's backyard, a troop camping facility, or a council camp area.

Review your outdoor skills on pages 149–150. Pick an activity from this book to do and a recipe to make.

Camp

Visit your council camp or day-camp area.

A Hike

Plan a day hike in a forest, park, or nature preserve. Your plan should include clothing, a snack or sack lunch, and safety measures. Use a map of the area when making your plan. Do one of the following activities:

1. Try following a nature trail that leads you on a guided exploration of the area.

2. Try a color hike. Take a box of crayons with you on your hike with at least one color for each person. Try to find things that match the crayon colors.

3. Try one of the hiking activities on pages 153–154.

---

is a good activity to do when exploring your neighborhood. See handbook pages 84–85 in "Family, Friends, and Neighbors." Have the girls make a map key on the lower corner of their maps. A map key uses symbols or colors to represent things put on your map. For example, a star-shaped symbol may represent a tree, or the color blue may represent water. You might share some different kinds of maps with girls and look at symbols used. Have

girls try their maps out on a buddy. They can hide a colored piece of paper somewhere in the area represented by their map. Then ask them to place an "X" on their map to mark the hiding place. They can give the map to their buddy and see if she can find the hidden paper.

Sleep Out! The story on handbook pages 148–149 is an excellent introduction to this activity. Refer to handbook pages 157–160 for more information on sleeping out. The

sleep out activities in the "Outdoor Skills and Adventures" section in "How and Why?" are placed last to emphasize the importance of progression in Girl Scout program. Pages 34–35 in Part I discuss the importance of readiness in skills, planning, and equipment. Practice girl/adult planning by brainstorming possibilities, giving lists of suggestions, or having patrols plan segments. Plan some activities to do while on your overnight. Activities

Using a Pocket Knife

When using a pocket knife, always be very careful. Always carry the knife closed. Always close the knife before giving it to someone else. You can learn to use a pocket knife by practicing these safety tips:

1. Use both hands to hold the knife.

2. Keep fingers behind the cutting blade edge when opening and closing.

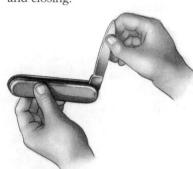

3. Hold the knife like this.

4. Always cut away from your body.

5. Put the knife in a safe place when you are not using it.

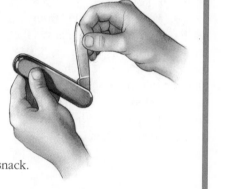

Try to peel and cut a carrot into sticks for an outdoor snack.

TRY IT•TRY IT•TRY IT•TRY IT•TRY IT•TRY IT•TRY IT•TRY IT•TRY IT•TRY IT•TRY IT•TRY IT•TRY IT•TRY IT•TRY IT **235**

---

from the World of the Arts, Out-of-Doors, and Today and Tomorrow offer many appropriate choices. Plan an evening, complete with campfire, songs, skits, and s'mores, a talent show, or a starwatching expedition. Evaluate the overnight with the girls after it is over. What did they enjoy the most? What would they change? Sometimes the greatest learning comes from discussion of things that did not go as anticipated. Often overnights allow girls to learn more

about themselves and living and working with others than regular activities do.

Camp. Arrange for a camp tour if you are not familiar with the site. Perhaps you could get an older Girl Scout who is a program aide or Counselor-in-Training to do this. Use a map of camp to determine where girls stay overnight, eat meals, and do different activities. This activity might take place during a council-wide event held at camp, or during

parents' day prior to the start of resident camp. Ask your Girl Scout council for information on summer camp activities. At the least, an adult in your troop should be trained to prepare for troop camping. Your council can be a great resource for activities and campcraft skills.

A Hike. Go over hiking safety with girls and check footwear and clothing before venturing forth. If girls have the proper clothing, inclement weather shouldn't be a problem. You

should pre-visit the hiking area so you can answer questions about bathrooms, safety, accessibility, and transportation. Hiking can be done in an urban setting, too. Look at the city as an ecosystem. What kinds of activities do you see? What can you observe using different senses? Can you observe any wildlife?

Using a Pocket Knife. For practice, you might suggest girls construct a simple knife out of heavy cardboard. The knife has a blade and a handle, attached by a brad in the middle so the knife can be folded. Girls can practice safety techniques before handling the real thing. Many girls may not have had cooking experiences and may not have used simple tools like paring knives or peelers. When cutting a carrot with a paring knife, provide a plastic cutting board and a work surface that each girl can reach comfortably. Knife safety should extend to dishwashing. Wash knives separately and do not leave them in the dishwater for someone else to discover.

Dress for the Weather Relay

Play this game with your troop before you go on an outdoor trip. You will need:

- 2 paper bags
- 2 sets of clothes, adult size and for different types of weather

1. Divide into two teams. Pick a starting point and a turnaround point.

2. Have each team form a line behind the starting line. Give each team a bag of clothes.

3. At a signal, one girl from each team puts on the clothes in the bag. She moves as quickly as possible to the turnaround point. She then returns to the starting line, and takes the clothes off and puts them into the bag. She then hands the bag to the next girl in line.

4. This continues until each girl on the team has done the same thing as the first girl. The first team to finish sits down and the members raise their hands.

To make the game even more fun, place clothes for different kinds of weather in one bag. The team has to pick the right clothes for the kind of weather the group decides on.

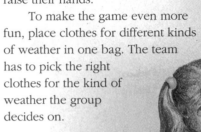

 236 TRY IT•TRY IT•TRY IT•TRY IT•TRY IT•TRY IT•TRY IT•TRY IT•TRY IT•TRY IT•TRY IT•TRY IT•TRY IT•TRY IT•TRY IT

Dress for the Weather Relay. A variation of this game can be played by placing clothes for different kinds of weather in one bag for each group. Then ask the group to dress one girl for a specific kind of weather. This can be assigned or drawn out of a hat. You might also want to add some incidentals like dark glasses, sunscreen, water bottle, and lip balm.

Try-Its and Other Resources

- Other Resources: *Developing Health and Fitness*; *Exploring Wildlife Communities With Children*; *Games for Girl Scouts*; *Outdoor Education in Girl Scouting*.

TRY IT!
OUTDOOR FUN

Girl Scouts have always been learning and doing things in the out-of-doors. These activities will help you learn and practice new skills and become an outdoor discoverer.

Trail Signs

Trail signs form shapes that show you which way to go and what to do on a trail. Learn how to make and use the trail signs that are on page 157.

Knots

Knots are very useful in the out-of-doors. Learn how to make the knots on page 159. Read the directions carefully.

Ecology Hunt

"Ecology" (ee-kol-o-gee) is the study of living things—plants and animals—and their environment, their place on earth.

Try to find the things on the list below. Go on a look-and-see hunt. Keep a record of what you find without disturbing anything.

☐ 3 kinds of leaves

☐ 3 kinds of rocks

☐ 3 kinds of plants

☐ 3 kinds of insects

☐ 3 animals that live in the air

☐ 3 animals that live under the ground

☐ 3 animals that live in plants or trees

☐ 3 things that show an animal has been here

TRY IT•TRY IT•TRY IT•TRY IT•TRY IT•TRY IT•TRY IT•TRY IT•TRY IT•TRY IT•TRY IT•TRY IT•TRY IT•TRY IT•TRY IT•TRY IT **237**

Tips

These activities can all be done in the outdoors and are excellent on overnights or hikes. Most take little knowledge on the part of the leader, but call for enthusiasm and a sense of adventure.

Trail Signs. This is an activity that Juliette Gordon Low might have done as a Girl Scout. Be sure to remove signs after your hike. Look for other kinds of signs when walking. Are there directional signs, highway signs, tree blazes (made by foresters on trees above snow line), or interpretive signs?

Knots. Knowing how to tie knots is useful for many things from tying sleeping bags and tent flaps to everyday chores and arts and crafts projects, like macramé. A favorite way for Brownie Girl Scouts to learn knot tying is to use shoestring licorice. Start out using rope, though, so adults can guide hands if needed. Use the licorice for girls to demonstrate their mastery of the knot. As each knot is tied successfully, a bite can be taken!

Ecology Hunt. See the Plants Try-It for information on how to construct a food chain. Then use the living items found on the ecology hunt to construct a food chain of the ecosystem you are exploring. As you find the items on the list, you might ask girls to describe the "habitat" (see page 155 in "How and Why?") of each found item. Do this hunt at different times of the year. Have girls make up their own ecology-hunt lists, then trade with friends. You can even make up a nighttime ecology hunt. Although it is dark, you can look for night creatures using a flashlight. (By covering a flashlight with red cellophane, you can observe without blinding or startling wildlife.) Girls might be interested in meeting people whose work involves them in the

Touch, Smell, Listen

You can learn about the outside world with all your senses. In this hunt, you will use more than your eyes to learn about the out-of-doors. You will need this book and a pencil.

Find the things in the out-of-doors that match the descriptions on this list. Try to find more than one. Try to find things that are not on the list. After you find something, touch it and smell it to find out more about it.

Touch List
☐ Something rough
☐ Something smooth
☐ Something dull
☐ Something pointy
☐ Something soft
☐ Something hard
☐ Something bumpy
☐ Something squishy
☐ Something crumbly
☐ Something wet

Smell List
☐ Something sweet-smelling
☐ Something sour-smelling
☐ Something flowery
☐ Something minty
☐ Something bad-smelling
☐ Something pinelike
☐ Something lemony
☐ Something fruity

Listen List
☐ Leaves rustling
☐ Birds singing
☐ Birds flying
☐ Animals moving
☐ Water running
☐ Insects chirping
☐ Wind moving things

238 *TRY IT•TRY IT•TRY IT•TRY IT•TRY IT•TRY IT•TRY IT•TRY IT•TRY IT•TRY IT•TRY IT•TRY IT•TRY IT•TRY IT•TRY IT•TRY IT*

---

ecology of an area. Botanists, environmental scientists, wildlife biologists, or foresters might be approached. Look for people who are able to explain their jobs to this age level.

Touch, Smell, Listen. Safety needs to be discussed with girls before starting this activity. Identify any natural hazards, such as poison oak or ivy, water, or stinging nettles. Girls can work in pairs or as a group. Use judgment in what is touched, and wash hands afterwards. Have girls select and complete some of the sensory activities on handbook pages 153–154 in "How and Why?" Another activity that might follow is making a wind chime. Girls will need fishing line, a coathanger or stick, scissors, and glue. They also need something like old silverware, bottle caps, old keys, or something else that can be strung up to chime in the wind. Length of line and number of chimes can be varied for different sounds.

Rubbings

A rubbing is one way to bring home something from the out-of-doors without disturbing nature. Check the lists at right to see which are good and not good to use for rubbings:

You will need:
- Crayons
- Plain white paper

1. Lay your paper against the thing you want to rub.

2. Gently rub a crayon back and forth until a pattern starts to show.

3. Do any of your rubbing patterns look alike? Try to collect many different patterns.

4. Show your rubbings to others. See if they can guess what your rubbings are.

Good

☐ Tree bark ☐ Flat stones

☐ Leaves ☐ Pine needles

☐ Sand ☐ Large rocks

Not Good

☐ Living creatures

☐ Flowers

☐ Very soft things

Outdoor Snacks

On pages 154–155 and 156 in "How and Why?" you learned to make a fruit-and-nut mix and a walking salad. Find a cookbook that has other healthy recipes for foods that can be kept safe without a cooler. Make one to take on your next outdoor trip.

TRY IT•TRY IT•TRY IT•TRY IT•TRY IT•TRY IT•TRY IT•TRY IT•TRY IT•TRY IT•TRY IT•TRY IT•TRY IT•TRY IT•TRY IT **239**

Rubbings. Rubbings can be made into notecards, framed as wall hangings, or become part of a collage. Rubbings can also be made from manufactured things, such as building signs and surfaces. The best technique for rubbing is to use the crayon lengthwise with its paper removed. Charcoal and chalk work as well, but may smear unless set with an artist's fixative. If you decide to apply a fixative, spray outdoors. See page 26 in Part I for more about working with artist materials safely.

Outdoor Snacks. Solar ovens can be used to dry fruit (use a rack so air circulates), or you can prepare fruit for drying in a real food dryer. See the Earth is Our Home Try-It to learn how to make a solar cooker.

A favorite Brownie Girl Scout snack is called "Ants on a Log." Put peanut butter in celery sticks and sprinkle with raisins. Since this is a snack that's easier to make at the destination than to prepare beforehand, carry the peanut butter in a plastic container; celery sticks can be cut ahead of time. You might take along jelly and crackers in plastic containers, too.

Try-Its and Other Resources

- Try Its: Art to Wear (macramé); Food Fun; Good Food; Outdoor Adventurer; Outdoor Happenings.
- Other Resources: *Earth Matters*; *Exploring Wildlife Communities With Children*; *Developing Health and Fitness*; *Games for Girl Scouts*.

TRY IT! ✓

OUTDOOR HAPPENINGS

It is fun to see how and why things happen outdoors. Try these activities to learn more about outdoor happenings like seed sprouts in the spring and morning dew.

Water Evaporator

Read page 138 and try the water evaporation activity.

Watching Rain and What it Does

Read the section on clouds and rain on page 139. Make a rain gauge using the directions on page 140.

Fossil Prints

Fossils are the prints that animals and plants left in soft mud a very long time ago.

Try this to see how prints that are made on soft, wet mud can harden.

You will need:

- Plaster of Paris
- A 2″ deep tray made from the bottom of a milk carton
- Something to imprint (leaf, feather, piece of bark, etc., you can even use your hand!)

1. Have someone help you mix the plaster and fill the container. Be careful not to make the plaster too wet.

2. Lay the thing that you are going to imprint on the moist plaster.

3. Gently press on the whole piece and leave it for one and a half minutes.

4. Lift it carefully and leave the plaster to dry.

5. Compare your imprint with others.

240 TRY IT•TRY IT•TRY IT•TRY IT•TRY IT•TRY IT•TRY IT•TRY IT•TRY IT•TRY IT•TRY IT•TRY IT•TRY IT•TRY IT•TRY IT•TRY IT

Tips

Challenge girls to open their eyes and find out why things happen the way they do in the natural environment. "What if's" can be posed by the girls, and often answered by them using observation, trial and error, and simple research.

Water Evaporator. Here is another activity that shows water evaporation.

Dew Maker

Water is in the air, but you can't see it. When the air cools, this water will sometimes settle on the ground. These drops of water are called "dew." If it is very dry where you live, there may not be enough water in the air for dew to form. You can make some of this water form by following these directions.

You will need: a dry metal can without the label, ice cubes, cold water.

1. Fill the can with ice cubes.
2. Add cold water.
3. Let the can sit for 30 minutes.
4. Check for dew on the outside of the can.

Watching Rain and What It Does.
Many parts of the world suffer from inadequate rainfall. Areas with inadequate rainfall all the time are deserts. Areas where rainfall is irregular can experience drought. Explore with girls ways to conserve water.

See handbook pages 147–148 in "How and Why?" and learn about the effects of drought in countries around the world.

Too much water also brings problems. Do this simple activity to observe how quickly splashing rain can erode sand or soil. You need a shallow plastic dish, a cup of sand, and several coins. Make a pile of sand in the dish. Place the coins on the sand. Place the dish outside in the rain and observe. What hap-

Seed Race

Seeds take different amounts of time to grow. Try this experiment to see which seed wins a sprout race.

You will need:

- Potting soil
- 6 kinds of seeds
- 1/2 of an egg carton
- Spoon
- Water

Fill each section of the egg carton with about two tablespoons of potting soil. Put one kind of seed in each section. Label each section. Cover the seeds with soil and sprinkle with water. Add some water every day. Which seed sprouts first? Try planting your sprouted seeds outside.

Which Way Does the Wind Blow?

Read about the wind and what it does on page 138. Go out on three different days and watch the wind. You can do it more easily by making your own weather vane. Here is a simple one you can try.

You will need:

- Large paper cup
- Clay
- Pencil with eraser
- Pin
- Straw
- Heavy cardboard
- Index cards or construction paper
- Tape
- Compass (optional)

1. Make a hole in the middle of the bottom of the cup and push the pencil in.

2. Use the clay to make the cup stick to the heavy cardboard.

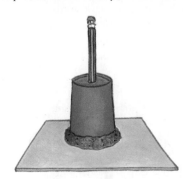

3. Cut two small triangles from the index card or construction paper. Connect one to each end of the straw.

4. Push the pin through the middle of the straw and into the eraser.

---

pens? The sand erodes and pillars of sand are left under the coins. The coins have slowed erosion.

Fossil Prints. This activity can get messy, so it is a good one to do outside. Make plaster casts of real animal tracks outdoors by cutting off the top and bottom of a milk carton or tuna can to make a form. Place the form around the track. Pour the plaster into the form and wait for it to harden. Look for tracks on trails and near watering areas. Look for tracks at different times of the year, in dry, wet, or snowy conditions. Visit the library and look for books on dinosaurs, fossils, and animal tracks.

Seed Race. Girls can graph the growth of their seeds with graph paper and different colored pencils, or keep a pictorial or written record of the process. This project is a good one for home or school. Your troop or group might like to participate in a community garden project or plant flower boxes to brighten up their neighborhood. Potted bulbs make wonderful plants for the elderly in rest homes.

Which Way Does the Wind Blow? If the weathervane were hooked to a machine that measured its speed when blown by the wind, the weather vane would be called an anemometer. Try to estimate how fast the wind is moving by using the list on page 201 in this book.

5. Take the weather vane outside and put it on a flat surface. Use the compass to mark north, south, east, and west on the cup. If you do not have a compass, use the sun as your guide. It rises in the east and sets in the west.

Rocks

In the out-of-doors, you can find many kinds of rocks. Some are formed by mud and sand and other hardening things. They are "sedimentary" (said-ah-men-ta-ree) rocks. Try this experiment to see how they form.

You will need:

- Pebbles
- Sand
- Pieces of rock
- Dirt
- Plaster of Paris
- Water
- A paper cup

1. Have someone help you mix the plaster in the paper cup. Make one-half cup.

2. Measure one teaspoon of pebbles, sand, dirt, and rock pieces.

3. Stir these into the plaster.

4. Let the plaster mix dry.
5. Peel away the paper cup.

6. See if you can find a natural rock that looks like the one you made.

242 *TRY IT•TRY IT•TRY IT•TRY IT•TRY IT•TRY IT•TRY IT•TRY IT•TRY IT•TRY IT•TRY IT•TRY IT•TRY IT•TRY IT•TRY IT•TRY IT•TRY IT*

Rocks. Sedimentary rocks were formed when layers of sand, silt, and broken-down rock hardened over millions of years. Sandstone, siltstone, limestone, clay, coal, shale, and conglomerate are common sedimentary rocks. This activity makes a type of conglomerate, a rock probably created by pebbles formed from beaches or river shores. Rock formed by the cooling of molten lava from the earth is called igneous rock.

Igneous rocks are the oldest of all. Granite, a very common rock, is an igneous rock. Igneous or sedimentary rock that has been changed over millions of years by pressure and heat is metamorphic rock. Marble is igneous rock changed over time from limestone. Start a rock collection with girls, or visit a rock shop, museum, or have someone take you on a tour of buildings made from different kinds of rock.

Try-Its and other Other Resources

- Try-Its: Earth and Sky; Hobbies (rock collecting); Outdoor Adventurer; Outdoor Fun; Plants.
- Other Resources: *Earth Matters*; *Exploring Wildlife Communities With Children*. The National Gardening Assoc., 180 Flynn Ave., Burlington,

Vt. 05401, has excellent resources for doing gardening projects with girls. Community resources could include a weather station, a government agency such as the U.S. Forest Service, which has a small weather station, the Cooperative Extension Service for information on growing things, science museums, rock shops, and local hobby clubs for rock collectors.

PEOPLE OF THE WORLD

Try these activities to learn more about people.

Language Hunt

Look through this book. How many different languages can you find in this book? Hint: Not all the languages in this book are spoken. How many languages are spoken in your community?

Brownie Girl Scouts in Other Countries

Learn about Brownie Girl Scouts in different countries. Read the chapter "People Near and Far" and do two of the activities.

Games of the World

Look through this book. Find some games from other countries. Learn them well enough to teach them to others.

Songs

Look in your school or local library for some tapes or books of songs from other countries. Try learning a new song.

Prejudice Fighter

Read pages 109–110 about prejudice and do the role-play activities.

World Stories

Close your eyes and put your finger on a globe or world map. Use your imagination and tell a story about a girl your age who lives there.

PAPUA NEW GUINEA

TRY IT•TRY IT•TRY IT•TRY IT•TRY IT•TRY IT•TRY IT•TRY IT•TRY IT•TRY IT•TRY IT•TRY IT•TRY IT•TRY IT•TRY IT•TRY IT **243**

dance or a story to fit the music, learn an authentic folk dance or learn the songs in the original languages.

Try-Its and Other Resources

- Try-Its: Around the World; Citizen Near and Far.
- Other Resources: *Creative Conflict Resolution*, by William J. Kreidler, Good Year Books, Glenview, Illinois, 1984, is an excellent resource for activities that teach cooperation, tolerance, and peacemaking. *Cooperative Learning, Cooperative Lives* by Nancy Schniedewind and Ellen Davidson, Circle Books, Somerville, Massachusetts, 1987, and *Open Minds to Equality: A Sourcebook of Learning Activities to Promote Race, Sex, Class, and Age Equity* (same authors), Prentice-Hall, Englewood Cliffs, New Jersey, 1983, are also good resources. Activities in "People Near and Far," handbook pages 87–110. *Trefoil Round the World; Valuing Differences; World Games and Recipes; The Wide World of Girl Guiding and Girl Scouting.*

Tips

The concept of nations and the world may be a bit abstract for many Brownie Girl Scouts. A globe or world map (a current one) can help. An equal-area projection map shows the world and relative size of nations most accurately and should be used if available. The Mercator projection, which appears in many schoolbooks, actually distorts the size of many of the world's land masses, making Africa and South America appear much smaller than they really are.

Some picture books or atlases that show children from different countries could be a help. Make sure the books you choose are recent publications—the ways people are depicted, the types of photographs used, and the information written may be more culturally sensitive and factual than older publications. The "Day in the Life" books are good choices to show the variety of people who live in a particular country.

Girls can go on a "world" hunt at a local supermarket, mall, or even in their homes. Individually or in pairs, they can see who can find the most things made or grown in countries other than the United States. This is a good way of showing how interrelated the world is.

Check local or school libraries for records and tapes of music from other countries. Girls can create a

Tips

Seed Sprout. Girls can record daily growth of the sprouts by observing and measuring. Girls should notice a difference in the color of the sprouts as well. The ones in the dark will be yellowish, while those in the sunlight will be green. Ask girls which plants they think will live the longest, those in the dark or those in the light. Why? Plants use a substance called chlorophyll (found in green plant cells) in a process called photosynthesis to make food. Chlorophyll helps a plant use sunlight (a form of energy), water, and carbon dioxide (the air we breathe out) to manufacture food (sugars) and oxygen (the important gas that we need to breathe). Food is stored in plants in the form of such substances as starch and glucose sugar. Chlorophyll is dependent upon sunlight, and without chlorophyll, food is not manufactured. You can also take a leafed plant and cover one leaf so that light cannot reach it. Observe what happens. Although plants cannot move from where they are rooted, they can grow towards sunlight. This is called phototropism. Move a plant from a sunny window

---

TRY IT!

PLANTS

Plants have many uses—lumber, paper, medicine, food— and plants make oxygen part of the air you breathe.

Seed Sprout
Sprinkle some alfalfa seeds on two damp sponges. Put one in a dark place and one in a sunny place.

Keep them damp. What happens to the seeds?

Supermarket Plant Hunt
Plants are the beginning of the food chain, even for people. Visit a market or grocery store. Find at least five different plants or plant products that you normally do not eat. Find out how to prepare them and try them. Try preparing an all-plant meal with your Brownie Girl Scout troop or group.

Adopt a Tree ✓
Adopt a tree by choosing a tree to care for near your home or in your neighborhood. Keep a record of the tree's growth, if possible, and observe how it changes during the seasons. What did you learn about your tree? Share this with other girls in your troop.

Leaf Hunt

Look for different types of leaves that have fallen to the ground. (Don't put your hands in your mouth after touching leaves and never put any leaves in your mouth. Be sure to wash your hands when you are done.) Pick one leaf that you like a lot. Describe it by drawing it or writing about it. You and your friends can put all your leaves in a pile. Describe your leaf to someone. Can she find it?

TRY IT•TRY IT•**TRY IT**•TRY IT•TRY IT•TRY IT•TRY IT•TRY IT•**TRY IT**•TRY IT•TRY IT•TRY IT•TRY IT•TRY IT•**TRY IT**•TRY IT•TRY IT

---

and observe how it grows for a week, or place a plant in a box with a lid, cutting a hole for light on one side, near the top of the box.

Supermarket Plant Hunt. Help girls decide whether foods that they find—such as meat, spaghetti, pizza, and fish sticks—come directly or indirectly from the sun's energy. You might also look for plant products other than food, such as matches, packaging, rope, dishcloths, and cotton T-shirts to discuss how they

have come from the sun's energy.

Adopt a Tree. Find out about Arbor Day, celebrated in many communities. You might ask someone who works with trees to come speak to the group. Ask a forester to show you and the girls, or go on a hike and find, a tree stump or log with rings. Or visit a natural history or science museum that has an exhibit showing a tree's rings. Girls can count the rings. Each year is represented by a dark and light ring. Dis-

cuss with girls theories about why there's a difference in the width of tree rings. (Trees grow at different rates due to environmental conditions.)

Leaf Hunt. Have girls look for different characteristics of leaves. How are they shaped (round, oval, long, short, skinny, fat)? What is the tip like (sharp, blunt)? What are the edges like (smooth, rough, jagged, toothed, lobed)? Are they simple (one leaf per stem) like a maple leaf,

Food Chain

Plants make food for all living things and use the sun's energy to grow. When animals eat plants, they get energy. You get energy from eating food. Your food may be from plants or animals. A food chain shows how food energy is passed from one living thing to another. All food chains start with plant life. You can make your own food chain with this activity.

You will need:

* Paper the size of this page, cut in half the long way
* Crayons or markers
* Pencils
* Tape
* Pictures of plants and animals

1. Find a picture of a plant, or draw one. Tape it to a strip of paper.

2. With a piece of tape, loop the ends of the paper together. You now have the first link in your food chain.

3. Find or draw a picture of something that can eat your plant. Tape this to a new strip of paper. Loop the strip through the first link and tape the ends. Now your food chain has two links.

4. Find or draw a picture of something that can eat your second link, and make a third loop as in Step 3.

5. Keep going. Here are some food chain ideas for you to start with:

Corn—insect—small bird— fox.
Acorn—squirrel—hawk.
Flower—beetle—skunk—great horned owl.
Plankton—water insect— frog—fish—bigger fish— heron.

Simple Plants

Mold is a very simple plant that makes spores. Spores are like very small seeds. They are in the air and in dust. Try making some mold.

Wet a folded paper towel with water. Wave some bread in the air or sprinkle it with dust. Put the bread on the towel, wrap it in foil, and put it in a dark spot. Check the bread every day. Rewrap it after checking. Use a toothpic to move the bread and wash your hands each time. Keep a record of what you see. A magnifying glass can help.

hands after handling the mushrooms. Place the mushroom cap onto the paper so the gills face downward. Cover the paper and mushroom cap for a day. Carefully lift the mushroom cap. If the cap left no spores, leave it for another day. You may have a mushroom that did not have mature spores to fall onto the paper, so don't be disappointed if nothing was found. If you do this with different kinds of mushrooms, you might get different colors of spore prints.

Try-Its and Other Resources

or compound (many leaves on one stem) like an English walnut? Have girls sort leaves by common characteristics. Do the "Ecology Hunt" in the Outdoor Fun Try-it.

Food Chain. See page 206 in this book for a definition of the food chain.

Simple Plants. All fungi reproduce from spores, a very simple kind of seed. Girls should be able to observe the parts of the mold that produce spores. Spores usually look like small, dark dust-like spots and are often at the end of very thin stalks. Spores are so small that they can drift through the air. There are many important uses of fungi. Besides mushrooms that may be eaten, fungi are used in cheese-making. Some medicines, like penicillin, are made from mold.

Fungi are grouped with plants, but many consider them to be in their own category, neither plant nor animal. They live off other plants and animals, and decaying matter, and play an important part in the ecosystem by helping things decay. Some fungi do feed off living plants and animals and can cause disease. Many fungi, like mushrooms, are poisonous. Girls can make spore prints from mushrooms. Look for mushrooms with gills, the thin layers found under the mushroom cap. You will need white paper, a bowl or box to cover the mushroom, and artist's fixative spray. Be sure to wash your

* Try-Its: Earth and Sky; Outdoor Happenings.
* Other Resources: *Exploring Wildlife Communities With Children*; *Games for Girl Scouts*; *Earth Matters*. Public libraries, the Cooperative Extension Service, gardening clubs, greenhouses, nurseries, and parks can be very helpful with this activity and in creating program trails (see pages 48–51 in Part I of this book).

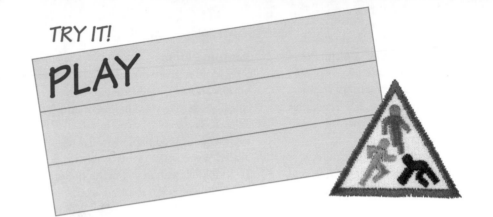

TRY IT!

PLAY

People all over the world have ways to relax and play. Here are some games for you to try that children in many countries play. Look in *Games for Girl Scouts* for more ideas.

Kim's Game (England)

Girl Scouts and Girl Guides all over the world play this game. You and your Brownie Girl Scout friends can have fun playing it too!

You will need:

- 1 or more friends
- At least 10 small things
- A scarf

1. Put ten things on a table. Be sure you can cover all of them with the scarf.

2. Show the players the ten things for one minute. Then cover them with the scarf.

3. Ask the players what was on the table. See if they can list all ten things.

Red Light, Green Light (United States of America)

Here is one of many ways to play this game.

1. Choose someone to be It. The person who is It stands at one end of the playing field, far away from all the other players.

2. The others line up along the starting line at the other end of the field.

3. It turns her back to the group and yells "green light." The players may now run toward It.

4. When It yells "red light," everyone must stop running and freeze. It turns around right after she yells "red light." If It catches anyone moving, that person has to go back to the starting line.

5. The game continues until someone has been able to reach and touch It while It has her back turned to the group.

6. That person becomes It.

246 *TRY IT•TRY IT•TRY IT•TRY IT•TRY IT•TRY IT•TRY IT•TRY IT•TRY IT•TRY IT•TRY IT•TRY IT•TRY IT•TRY IT•TRY IT•TRY IT*

Tips

Tips on adapting activities are on pages 57–58 in Part I of this book. Many Brownie Girl Scouts have lots of energy, and games are a good way to release it; however, make sure you do keep control of games and other active experiences so that no one gets hurt through too energetic play. Plan your activities so the last game or exercise is done at a slower, more relaxing pace. This allows the girls to mellow a bit before returning to other troop or group activities. Also, you may find that some girls do not wish to participate in group games. Make sure that alternate activities are available—books, experiments, magazines, paper and crayons—and that girls are able to join the game if they change their minds about participating.

Help all girls understand the rules of a game before playing. You could have a practice round or have the rules written out ahead of time on a flip chart or poster paper. You could make a "rules game" in which you pop around the circle in a quick, random pattern asking girls to repeat a section of the rules you have just stated.

Try-Its and Other Resources

- Try-Its: Around the World; People of the World; Sports and Games.
- Other Resources: *Games for Girl Scouts*; *World Games and Recipes*. The following games are adapted from *World Games and Recipes*.
   From Colombia, **Juan**

Palmada— Johnny Clap Hands—is a game played by Brownie Girl Scouts. Brownie Girl Scouts make a circle, leaving one empty place in it. Two girls stand by the space, back to back, outside the circle. At a signal, these two girls run in opposite directions around the circle. When they meet, each jumps in the air and claps her hands over her head. Then they continue run-

Sheep and Hyena (Sudan)

See if you can keep the sheep away from the hungry hyena! Get at least ten people to play—more are even better!

1. Players join hands and form a tight circle.

2. One player stays outside the circle. She is the hyena.

3. Another player stays inside the circle. She is the sheep.

4. The players in the circle have to try to keep the hyena from breaking through the circle to get to the sheep. The game ends when the hyena gets the sheep or gets too tired to go after the sheep anymore.

5. Two other people become the sheep and hyena.

Jan-Ken-Pon (Japan)

This is a fun game played in Japan. Look on page 101 to find out how to play it. Teach it to someone else.

Mr. Bear (Sweden)

The moral of this game is "Watch out for sleeping bears!" Look on page 101 to find out how to play this game.

Hawk and Hens (Zimbabwe)

This is a great chasing game for times when you have lots of energy and want to run. See page 101 to learn how to play. Try teaching it to some younger children.

TRY IT•TRY IT•TRY IT•TRY IT•TRY IT•TRY IT•TRY IT•TRY IT•TRY IT•TRY IT•TRY IT•TRY IT•TRY IT•TRY IT•TRY IT **247**

---

ning to see who reaches the empty space first. The girl to the right of the empty space takes the place of the one who reached the empty space first.

Kwa-Kwa—The Blindfolded Crow—is played by Girl Scouts in Ghana. Girls form a circle. One girl remains in the middle of the circle. She is the blindfolded crow. She is blindfolded and moves slowly around flapping her arms like wings. Meanwhile, the players in the circle change places. They cannot, however, go outside the circle. The first girl touched by the "wings" is the new blindfolded crow.

The **Egg Game** is a game Brownie Girl Scouts play in Iceland. Girls stand in a circle, facing inwards with their feet apart. One girl has a ball about the size of a basketball. She tries to roll the ball through someone's legs. Girls cannot put their feet together to stop the ball. They can only use their hands. Whoever stops the ball tries to roll it between someone else's legs but she cannot move from her place.

Ducks and Fish is a game that can be played by girls with varying levels of ability. Two girls are ducks and the rest are fish. The ducks are blindfolded and sit at one end of the room, facing each other with about a yard (one meter) between them. The fish start at the other end of the room and must "swim" up and pass between the ducks without being heard. If a duck hears a sound, she points directly to it and makes a duck noise. If a fish is there, she must sit down on the spot and say "caught." The game continues until all the fish have been caught.

TRY IT!

PUPPETS, DOLLS, AND PLAYS

You know about many kinds of art. Did you know that making puppets and dolls is an art? You can use them in plays or stories.

Finger Puppets

Turn the fingers of the gloves into little puppets. Then put on a play.

You will need:

• An old cloth or knitted glove
• Piece of ribbon
• String
• Thread
• Yarn
• Glue
• Scraps of old material
• Markers
• Small buttons
• Beads
• Tissue paper

1. Make five grape-sized balls with the tissue paper, and stuff one into each finger of the glove.

2. Tie a piece of ribbon or yarn under the tissue ball.

3. Put a face on the fingertip with the markers, or sew or glue on buttons or beads.

4. Glue threads or yarn on the tip of the finger for hair.

5. Use yarn and scraps of cloth to dress your puppet.

6. Play with your finger puppets.

248 TRY IT•TRY IT•**TRY IT**•TRY IT•TRY IT•TRY IT•TRY IT•TRY IT•**TRY IT**•TRY IT•TRY IT•TRY IT•TRY IT•**TRY IT**•TRY IT•TRY IT

Tips

Girls may like to introduce their favorite doll to their Brownie Girl Scout friends. Each girl could write a play about her doll and bring the doll in to perform it.

Your troop could write a play, then perform it for a Daisy Girl Scout troop or another Brownie Girl Scout troop or group. Practice the play or puppet show. Then take the show on the road!

Puppet stages can be made from most anything. (See "Tips," page 234 in this book, under the Art to Wear Try-It, for tips on collecting materials for puppets and stages.) It's best to have three sections—the stage, the curtain, and scenery. Girls can even use their bodies to make a stage by crouching on their hands and knees, while two other girls become the curtain, standing in front and moving to each side. Other girls become scenery—trees, flowers, machines, etc.—and other girls work

Yarn Doll

These dolls are easy to make. You can add your own ideas.

You will need:

- Yarn or heavy thread
- A small Ping-Pong ball, a small round pebble, or a small ball of yarn
- Ribbons
- Cloth scraps
- Buttons
- Other materials you like

1. Cut yarn into strips the length of this page.

2. Make enough strips to fill your hand.

3. Tie all the strips together at the top.

4. Insert a Ping-Pong ball, pebble, or small ball of yarn to give shape to the head.

5. Tie another string to the bottom of the ball, pebble, or ball of yarn to make a neck.

6. Make arms and legs and a waist, like in the drawing.

7. Use cloth and ribbons to dress the doll.

TRY IT•TRY IT•TRY IT•TRY IT•TRY IT•TRY IT•TRY IT•TRY IT•TRY IT•TRY IT•TRY IT•TRY IT•TRY IT•TRY IT•TRY IT•TRY IT **249**

the puppets. A cardboard box, a table on its side, a doorway, or two chairs could all be stages. You could make scenery out of cardboard. The scenery can stand upright by taping circular strips of cardboard to the bottoms or by cutting slits into the bottoms and then sliding another piece with a slit perpendicularly to make an x-shaped stand.

Paper-Bag Puppet

These puppets are easy to make. They are especially good if you want to make an animal puppet.

You will need:

- Small paper bags
- Pieces of paper
- Crayons
- Markers or paint
- Scissors
- Glue

1. Place the paper bag flat on a table with the bottom fold on top.

2. Draw and color designs on the bottom fold of the bag. This will be the head of your puppet. You can add eyes, ears, and hair.

3. Decorate the rest of the bag. What did you make?

Safety Play

Read about safety on pages 48–57. Create a puppet show about safety do's and don'ts.

A Puppet Stage

A stage will make a puppet show much more fun. A puppet stage will have three parts—the stage itself, a curtain, and scenery.

Try using a box, a table, chairs, and a sheet, a towel, or tablecloth for the stage and curtain. What can you use for scenery? Look around your home or meeting place, or cut out some shapes from heavy cardboard.

250 TRY IT•TRY IT•TRY IT•TRY IT•TRY IT•TRY IT•TRY IT•TRY IT•TRY IT•TRY IT•TRY IT•TRY IT•TRY IT•TRY IT•TRY IT•TRY IT

Try-Its and Other Resources

- Try-Its: Colors and Shapes; Creative Composing; Her Story; Listening to the Past; Me and My Shadow; My Body.
- Other Resources: The handbook contains many stories and activities that can be acted out by puppets. Girls can make a puppet of themselves, their families and friends, the characters in the stories, or people in their communities.

Marionette

There are string puppets as well as hand puppets. String puppets are called "marionettes." You can make them move around just like you do! Try making this marionette.

You will need:

- Cardboard
- String
- Beads or buttons
- A stick or dowel
- Crayons or paints
- Paper
- Glue
- A big needle
- Heavy thread

1. Cut the cardboard into an animal or human shape. Make a head, body, arms, and legs.

2. Color the pieces.

3. With the needle, poke four holes in the body for the arms and legs. Then poke a hole at the top of each arm and leg.

4. Thread the needle and use it to tie together each leg and arm to the body.

5. Make a hole for the head at the top of the body.

6. Attach the head to the body by threading the hole. Tie a knot and cut the string.

7. Tie another string to the top of the head. To make your puppet move, raise and lower it by holding the string.

OR

8. Tie a string to each arm and leg. Then tie these strings to two sticks tied in a cross.

9. Make your marionette walk and dance by moving the sticks.

TRY IT•TRY IT•**TRY IT**•TRY IT•TRY IT•**TRY IT**•TRY IT•**TRY IT**•TRY IT•TRY IT•TRY IT•TRY IT•**TRY IT**•TRY IT•TRY IT **251**

TRY IT!

SAFETY

Every Girl Scout knows the motto, "Be Prepared." Read pages 48–57 about safety and try these activities.

Street Safety

Being safe on the street is just as important as keeping yourself safe at home. To be safe on the street, you should get to know your neighborhood. Try these two activities to learn more about your neighborhood.

1. Take a walk through your neighborhood with an adult you trust. Look for street names, the firehouse, and the police station. Look at the people around you.

2. Make a map of your neighborhood and mark the places you need to know about to stay safe.

Fire Safety

Read the section on fire safety on pages 54–56. Find out about the fire escape plan for your Brownie Girl Scout meeting place and practice it.

A fire escape plan is important, but it is not the only part of fire safety. A fire can start at night or during the day, and being alert to the danger is the first step to help get you and your family out alive. Try this fire safety activity.

1. Learn what a smoke alarm is and how it works. If there is no smoke alarm in your home, go with an adult in your family to a hardware store. Have an employee explain why smoke alarms are necessary in everyone's home.

2. Have an adult test the smoke alarm so you can hear what it sounds like.

Playground Safety

A playground should be a place where you can enjoy good and healthy fun and exercise. But if you don't use playground equipment correctly, it can be dangerous. Learn the rules of playground safety and share them with others before you have an accident.

252 TRY IT•TRY IT•TRY IT•TRY IT•TRY IT•TRY IT•TRY IT•TRY IT•TRY IT•TRY IT•TRY IT•TRY IT•TRY IT•TRY IT•TRY IT•TRY IT

Tips

Many Brownie Girl Scouts enjoy learning about safety and many older Girl Scouts remember safety activities as some of the most important and interesting activities they had done. Before starting this Try-It, you should do the activities on safety, handbook pages 48–62 in "Taking Care of Yourself and Your Home," and review the safety rules in *Safety-Wise*.

1. Make up some rules for playgrounds. Use these rules to make safety posters to put up in your playground and troop meeting place.

2. Look at the equipment in the playground at your school or in your neighborhood. With an adult, give the equipment a safety check. Are the swings anchored well? Is the slide stable? Make notes about unsafe equipment and show them to the proper officials.

First Aid

Sometimes you may be the only one around when somebody needs help. Learn a skill that could save a life in an emergency. One skill that is good to know is how to save a person who is choking. Many people do choke while eating. You can tell if a person is in trouble if she can't talk, if she points to her mouth, or if she is turning blue. With an adult, try this exercise on first aid for choking.

1. To find your rib cage, use your left hand, make a fist, and place it over your belly button. Then, using your right hand, make a fist and place it on top of your left fist. This spot is just below the rib cage and is important to find when you are doing first aid on a person who is choking.

2. With a partner, practice the following, but be sure when you're practicing not to push hard on the person's stomach.

Pretend your partner is choking. Keep her calm. Ask if she is all right. Ask her to cough. If she cannot breathe, cough, or speak:

- Stand behind her.
- Use your left hand to make a fist and place it over her belly button.
- Use your right hand to make a fist and place it on top of the left fist. Remove your left hand. Then cover your right fist with your left hand.
- Then push your fist in and up quickly.
- Keep doing this until she can cough, breathe, or speak.

More to Try: Practice first aid for choking on yourself in case there is a time when no one can help you. See the pictures in the center column.

More to Try: Practice the other first-aid skills on pages 58–62.

TRY IT•TRY IT•TRY IT•TRY IT•TRY IT•TRY IT•TRY IT•TRY IT•TRY IT•TRY IT•TRY IT•TRY IT•TRY IT•TRY IT•TRY IT•TRY IT **253**

Introduce the first aid for choking activity by the name "Heimlich maneuver." Many girls may know this already, but others may need to know it by this name in case of an emergency.

Help girls sharpen their memory skills by playing "Kim's Game" in the Play Try-It. (Good memory skills are important for personal safety.) Try a variation of this game by cutting out pictures of various people from magazines. Give girls a little while to study them. Ask them to describe the person in the picture. How many details could they remember?

Review with girls other safety issues they may encounter each day, such as car safety (seat belts) or bicycle safety (helmets). Remind them that they may need to help their families and friends remember how to stay safe.

Safety Center

Make a place to keep information you'll need in an emergency. You will need:

- A hanger
- A large piece of fabric
- Scissors
- A stapler or a needle and thread
- Markers
- At least 4 legal-sized envelopes

1. Cut the fabric into a large square.

2. Wrap one end of the fabric around the hanger and staple or sew it with a needle and thread as shown.

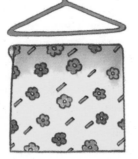

3. With a marker, label the envelopes. A few ideas are:

- Small change
- Emergency phone numbers
- Reminder notes

Include an envelope in which to keep paper and a pencil for taking messages.

4. Staple or sew each envelope to the fabric as shown. Have someone hang it near the phone for you to reach easily.

Suzy Safety Says

Can you find all the Suzy Safety pictures in this handbook? Suzy Safety is asking you to do things the safe way. Every time you see her picture, remember the safety rules you have learned.

254 TRY IT•TRY IT•**TRY IT**•TRY IT•TRY IT•**TRY IT**•TRY IT•TRY IT•**TRY IT**•TRY IT•TRY IT•**TRY IT**•TRY IT•TRY IT•**TRY IT**•TRY IT•TRY IT

More to Try: Girls can make and play a "safety" card game. Girls make the cards by pasting magazine pictures that demonstrate safety messages onto index cards. Girls pick from a pile of face-down cards and try to identify the safety message shown on the card. If correct, she can keep the card. The one with the most cards wins.

You can set up a troop or group wide game with different safety and first-aid stations. Girls move to each station and do a safety activity.

Designate a "safety month," during which the troop or group does safety activities. Use the resources in your community by inviting a police officer or firefighter, for example, to come and talk. (Make sure the speakers have some "hands-on" activities planned for the girls.) Schedule field trips, speakers, and activities on the safety theme.

Try-Its and Other Resources

- Other Resources: Safety and first-aid activities in "Taking Care of Yourself and Your Home," handbook pages 48–62. *Staying Safe*; *Developing Health and Fitness*; *Tune In to Well-Being, Say No to Drugs*. The following activity is from *Tune In to Well-Being, Say No to Drugs*:

Act out what you would do if:
- Someone in your friend's family leaves a can of beer on the table.
- Your younger sister drinks a bottle of cough syrup.

What other situations can you make up?

TRY IT!
SCIENCE IN ACTION

Science is a part of our daily life. Science is in action when you use machines, tell time, go to the doctor, or grow a plant. Did you know that even making bread uses science? It uses chemistry (kem-is-tree). This Try-It will help you see science in action.

Computer Fun Fair

Organize or participate in a computer fun fair. Find a computer that you and your friends can use. Have people in your troop bring computer games to a meeting and try them, or visit a store that carries computer games and have an employee give you a demonstration. Decide what to look for in a good computer game.

Energy Sleuth

Think of the kinds of energy that you use daily. Do you use electricity? Do you use gas or oil? Do you use solar energy or thermal power? Keep a record of the times you use some form of energy, other than your own power, for a full day. Look closely at your list. Are there any ways that you can save energy each day? Find at least three ways and try them for a week.

More to Try: Create a poster or sign to help family members or friends at school conserve energy in some way.

Make a Color Spectrum

Try the color spectrum activity on pages 136–137.

Tips

Introduce these Try-It activities by doing the science and technology hunt activity, handbook pages 132–133 in "How and Why?"

Computer Fun Fair. You might want to have girls make a list of what they like most about using a computer or a computer game, and what makes it "user friendly." If girls are unable to visit a computer store, you might provide them with some catalogs and computer magazines. Have them cut out or list the kinds of computers and programs they see.

Energy Sleuth. Girls can put on a play or make up a song about energy conservation. Instead of posters, they can make post-it reminders to affix at specific energy conservation sites, such as light switches. Model energy conservation with your troop by walking instead of driving, car pooling, or using public transportation.

Make a Color Spectrum. Here's another way to create a rainbow, like the ones seen outside. Set up your equipment on a counter or table in a room that can be made dark. You will need: a clear plastic cup, water, a flashlight, food coloring (red, green, blue), a stiff piece of white paper (folded), paper to draw on, crayons, and a ruler.

1. Have girls fill the cup with water halfway and place it near the table edge. Place the folded paper about three inches behind the glass to make a screen.

2. Turn off the lights while holding the flashlight against the edge of the table, shining the light up through the water so that the light hits the screen behind the cup. Experiment with the angle of light until a band of colors appears on the screen. Have a girl copy the color band on another

Computers in Your Life

Use a computer at home or at school to solve a problem, check your spelling, write a story, or learn something new.

OR

Talk to three people who use computers at work. Find out what they do and what kind of help and information they get from their computers. Ask them how they learned to use a computer. Tell others what you learned.

Time Check

Read about time on page 130. Look for different ways of telling time. Try making the hourglass on pages 130–131 in "How and Why?"

Bread Making

All sorts of things happen when you make a loaf of yeast bread. Yeast is really millions of tiny one-celled plants that start to grow when you add water or milk. Without the yeast, your bread would not have all those wonderful air spaces that make it light and fluffy. Many of the things we cook depend on chemistry between ingredients to get to the finished product.

 This is a great activity for a rainy day. Be sure to do it with an adult. Make sure you measure carefully.

You will need:

• A kitchen with an oven and these items:
• 1 package or cake of yeast
• 2 cups of lukewarm milk
• 2 tablespoons of sugar
• 1 tablespoon of salt
• 6 cups of flour
• 5 tablespoons of butter or margarine, melted
• A large mixing bowl
• A wooden spoon
• 2 loaf pans
• A small pan for melting butter
• A kitchen towel
• A pot holder

1. Wash your hands. Put all of your materials out so that you can get to them easily.

2. Place the two cups of lukewarm milk into your bowl. Warm the milk slightly if it has

piece of paper and label the colors. Ask them what has been created.

3. Experiment by changing the angle of the flashlight. What happens if you move the flashlight toward the table, or away from the table, while still shining the light through the water onto the screen? What is the water doing to the light beam to create the colors?

4. Drop three drops of red food coloring into the water. Shine the light through the water. Is anything different when the color band is made? Ask girls to guess what would happen if you used blue or green water, then let them experiment to see if their guess is correct. (They will have to change water each time.) Refer to handbook pages 136–137 in "How and Why?" for another rainbow experiment. As a follow-up, have the girls write a recipe or equation for an outdoor rainbow.

Computers in Your Life. As an introduction to this activity, girls can read about Kelsey and her computer on handbook pages 125–127 in "How and Why?" You might want to send a questionnaire to parents to find out how many of them use computers in their job or at home.

Time Check. Girls can do the "Shadow Time" activity in the Space Explorer Try-It. Time activities can be used to introduce simple graphing and comparisons. Questions like "Which activity takes longer?" can be answered by recording times and then comparing them. Have girls list how many ways time affects their lives. Help girls learn to read movie or bus schedules or suggest they go on a time hunt in a newspaper. (How often does the word or concept of time appear?) Compare a grandfather clock or old-fashioned pocket watch to a digital clock or watch. How are they alike? How are they different? Try making the hourglass on handbook pages 130–131 in "How and Why?"

been in the refrigerator.

3. Add the yeast and sugar and salt. Stir with the wooden spoon so the yeast dissolves.

4. Add the flour a little bit at a time, and stir it with the wooden spoon. When it gets too hard to stir with the spoon, add the melted butter or margarine. Use the spoon to mix it in. Keep adding the flour until it is used up. By this time you may want to use your hands (be sure they are clean) to mix the dough.

5. The dough should look smooth and be stretchable. Now you get to knead the dough. Sprinkle flour on a wooden breadboard or on your kitchen counter. Then pour the dough onto this surface. This is called "turning it out." Fold the dough toward you, then push away in a rocking motion with the heels of your hands, eight to ten times. Turn the dough a one-quarter turn and do it again. Take turns if you are doing this as a group. Knead for about five to ten minutes.

6. When you are finished kneading, shape your dough into a nice big ball and put it in the mixing bowl again. Cover it with a towel and place it in a warm spot in the kitchen, away from drafts.

7. Now comes the easy part. You have to wait for an hour and a half to two hours for the chemical reaction to take place. You should let the dough grow until it is double its original size. What is happening here? The yeast plants are reacting with the sugar and produce carbon dioxide, which is a gas. When the bread dough is warmed, the carbon dioxide gas bubbles grow larger and cause the dough to rise.

8. After your dough has grown to twice its size, it is time to punch it. What happens when you punch it hard two or three times? Sprinkle some flour on your breadboard or table and take your dough out to knead it for about three or four minutes.

9. Divide your dough into two equal parts. Coat the inside of your loaf pans with butter or vegetable oil. Mold each portion of dough into the shape of the pan and put it in the loaf pan. Cover the loaf pans with the towel and put them in a warm place. The loaves should double in size again.

10. When your loaves are doubled in size, pop them in the oven at a temperature of 375° F. Bake for around 45 minutes or until the loaves are a nice golden brown. Remove the loaves from the oven with a pot holder. Cool the loaves before removing them from the pan. Eat the bread while it is still warm.

When you cut the bread, look at the texture. During the baking, the carbon dioxide bubbles have continued to grow and have made those air spaces. All the better for butter and jam!

TRY IT•TRY IT•TRY IT•TRY IT•TRY IT•TRY IT•TRY IT•TRY IT•TRY IT•TRY IT•TRY IT•TRY IT•TRY IT•TRY IT•TRY IT•TRY IT **257**

Bread Making. Help girls recognize that what they are doing is a scientific process, as well as a food-making activity. You might want to make chocolate milk to go with your bread. Again, point out science in action by having girls taste each ingredient separately, then mix sugar, unsweetened cocoa, and milk to make chocolate milk. Challenge them to make up a recipe or use directions found on the cocoa container.

Try-Its and Other Resources

- Try-Its: Science Wonders.
- Other Resources: See handbook pages 132–137 in "How and Why?" *Into the World of Today and Tomorrow* is an excellent resource. The centerfold has additional activities on computers and math. Your local power and light company may provide materials about energy conservation.

TRY IT!

SCIENCE WONDERS

Try these activities to see how wonderful science is. The changes seem like magic, but a scientist can make them happen. And you get to be the scientist!

Home-Grown Crystals

Crystals are minerals that are clear and sparkly. Some crystals have colors, too! Ice, salt, and diamonds are all crystals. So is rock candy! Try growing some of your own crystals with this experiment.

You will need:
- Jar
- Hot water
- 1 cup of sugar
- Clean string
- Pencil
- Paper clip

1. Fill the jar with one-half cup of hot water.

2. Add the cup of sugar.

3. Wrap one end of a piece of string around the pencil. Knot it.

4. Put the pencil across the top of the jar and let the other end of the string hang almost to the bottom.

Use the paper clip to keep it down.

5. Let it sit for a few days. Then you can eat your experiment!

More to Try: Look for crystals outdoors. Many rocks have crystals. A magnifying glass will help you see them.

Bubbles

You can make some special bubbles. Try this mix.

- 1 gallon water
- 40 drops of glycerine
- ½ cup dishwashing liquid

Mix together in a large flat pan. Stir slowly. If you can, let it set for at least one day. The glycerine can make stronger bubbles.

For your bubble maker, have an adult help you shape a metal hanger. Dip your bubble maker into the pan and then gently wave it in the air. Try other shapes for your bubble makers.

258 *TRY IT•TRY IT•TRY IT•TRY IT•TRY IT•TRY IT•TRY IT•TRY IT•TRY IT•TRY IT•TRY IT•TRY IT•TRY IT•TRY IT•TRY IT•TRY IT*

Tips

These activities should inspire some questions. Let girls explore those "What if's" or "Why does this do this?" by asking how they might find the answers. Some answers can be discovered by observation and measurement, while finding answers to others might mean a library trip

and possibly more experimentation. Encourage girls to pursue answers to their questions and remind them that no question is "dumb."

Home-Grown Crystals. Crystals form when minerals dissolved in a liquid begin to solidify and crystallize. In this instance, a solid (sugar) is dissolved in a liquid (water) to make a solution. The trick to crystal-making is to keep adding solid to

your liquid until no more will dissolve. Sugar is a crystal before it is dissolved. Let the girls observe it closely with a magnifying glass before the experiment. When the crystals form on the string, have girls observe if they are different from the original sugar granules. Crystal-making can be done with salt, alum, or washing soda as well. (Do not eat any of these crystals!) Each kind of

crystal is shaped differently. Experiment with growing time and amounts of solid and liquid needed. Girls might also like to visit a geologist or rock collector, or take a trip to a museum to look at crystals.

Bubbles. This is a great activity for outdoors, although it can be done indoors on tabletops. Just have plenty of dry sponges or old rags and use trays if you have them. The

Homemade Recycled Paper

A fun recycling activity is making your own paper. You can make paper for books, posters, newsletters, paintings, and many other things.

You will need:

- A large mixing bowl
- An eggbeater
- A cup
- A big spoon
- An old newspaper
- Water
- A screen about 3" square or bigger
- A flat pan a little larger than the screen
- Starch

1. Tear a half-page of news-

paper into very small pieces. Put the paper in a large mixing bowl full of water.

2. Let the paper soak for one hour.

3. Beat the paper with an eggbeater for ten minutes. The paper should be soft and mushy. It is now called "pulp."

4. Mix two tablespoons of starch in one cup of water. Add this to the pulp. Stir well. The starch makes the paper pulp strong.

5. Pour the pulp into the flat pan.

6. Place the screen in the bottom of the pan. It will become evenly covered with pulp.

7. Put the rest of the newspaper on a table. Pick up the screen covered with pulp and put it on one half of the newspaper.

TRY IT•TRY IT•TRY IT•TRY IT•TRY IT•TRY IT•TRY IT•TRY IT•TRY IT•TRY IT•TRY IT•TRY IT•TRY IT•TRY IT•TRY IT•TRY IT **259**

---

bubble mixture works better if made up the night before or even several days in advance. You might make up two mixtures, one with a cheap liquid soap, the other with a more expensive one, and have the girls compare the two solutions. Bubble-blowing tools can be made from coat hangers, canning rings, plastic straws, plastic straws cut and strung on string to form shapes, and plastic

berry baskets. Divide girls into teams and challenge them with the following: What is the average size of bubbles blown on your team? How many bubbles within bubbles can you make? Can you make a square bubble? What happens when two bubbles meet? Does that always happen? What factors limit the size of a bubble? Is it possible to put the straw back in after you've drawn it

completely out of a bubble? What color sequence occurs at the top of the bubble? Using that knowledge, can you predict when a bubble will pop? Is there a difference between brands of soap used? Give girls plastic rulers and pencil and paper to record their findings.

Homemade Recycled Paper.
Dried flowers or grass can be sprinkled onto the recycled paper pulp

just before pressing it out to add a decorative touch to notecards. Refer to handbook pages 146–147 in "How and Why?" for information on "Garbage: Reduce, Reuse, and Recycle." Look for the recycling sign, shown on handbook page 147, and go on a recycled paper hunt in your local shopping mall or grocery store. How many paper products are made from recycled paper?

10. When it is dry, peel your recycled paper from the screen.

8. Fold the other half of the newspaper over the top of the screen. Press down very hard.

9. Fold back the newspaper so you can see the pulp. Let it dry overnight.

Chemistry Magic

Try this experiment to see how new things are formed through chemical reactions.

You will need:

- 5 tablespoons pure laundry soap
- 2 cups warm tap water
- 4 tablespoons salt
- A large glass
- A large spoon for stirring
- 2 one-cup measuring cups

1. Put the laundry soap into one cup of water. Stir until the soap has dissolved.

2. Next, put the salt into another cup of water and stir until the salt is dissolved as much as possible.

3. Pour the soap solution into a large glass. Then pour the salt solution on top of it. Mix well.

260 *TRY IT•TRY IT•TRY IT•TRY IT•TRY IT•TRY IT•TRY IT•TRY IT•TRY IT•TRY IT•TRY IT•TRY IT•TRY IT•TRY IT•TRY IT*

Chemistry Magic. This activity is related to the "Water Layers" activity in the Water Everywhere Try-It. As each chemical is added to water, it creates a solution. The soap solution is lighter than salt water, so it floats on the salt water. The soap particles are attracted to each other, like dust in a dustball.

Magnet Hunt. In this activity, girls are encouraged to use observation and testing skills to draw conclusions about what things stick to magnets. Read about magnets on handbook pages 135–136 in "How and Why?" and do several of the activities suggested. Challenge girls to come up with a way to measure and compare the strength of different magnets. Provide them with several kinds of magnets and a box of steel paper clips.

Static Electricity. Read the section on handbook page 143 in "How and Why?" about static electricity and try some of the activities. Static electricity is produced by two things rubbing together. This produces a "charge." "Opposites attract" is a

What happens? You should see the soap harden and turn into a ball right away. If you let the mixture stand still for a few minutes, the soap will rise to the top and the bottom will stay clear.

Magnet Hunt

Magnets can pull things to them. Most magnets are made of iron and come in many different shapes. Not everything will stick to a magnet. Get a magnet and find out what will stick to it.

1. Take your magnet and touch it to as many different things as you can find.

2. Write down all the things that are pulled to the magnet and all those that are not.

Static Electricity

A special kind of electricity, called static electricity, can be made by rubbing some things together. Lightning is a kind of static electricity in the clouds. The spark you sometimes feel when you touch something after walking on a rug is static electricity. You can try making it now with these activities.

You will need:

- Balloons
- String
- Very small pieces of paper
- Wool cloth

A. **1.** Blow up the balloons and tie the ends.

2. Make static electricity by rubbing a balloon very quickly on the wool cloth. You can use your hair instead of the wool cloth.

3. Hold the balloon over the very small pieces of paper to see static electricity in action.

B. **1.** Take two more balloons and tie a piece of string to each one.

2. Rub the balloons on the wool cloth.

3. Hold the balloons by the string and try to make them touch.

C. **1.** Rub another balloon on the wool cloth.

2. Hold the balloon next to a thin stream of water from a faucet. What happens?

3. Hold this balloon to the wall. If it has enough static electricity, it will stick. Rub the balloon to give it more static charges.

term borrowed from science. When two charges are unlike, they attract each other; when two charges are alike, they repel each other. For example, when you rub a comb briskly through your hair, the comb picks up a negative charge. If you hold the comb over tiny bits of paper, the paper will stick to the comb because the paper is neutral or has no charge. When hair with no hairspray or other additives is brushed briskly, the hair strands become "flyaway" because the strands have a positive charge and repel each other.

Try-Its and Other Resources

- Try-Its: Senses; Science in Action; Water Everywhere.
- Other Resources: *Into the World of Today and Tomorrow*; *How Science Works*, by Judith Hann, Reader's Digest, Pleasantville, N.Y., 1991, illustrates additional fun scientific activities.

TRY IT!

SENSES

You learn about your world in many ways. Seeing, hearing, feeling, smelling, and tasting are the five senses that send messages to your brain about the world around you. You use your senses almost all the time, even when you don't know it!

Only the Nose Knows

Your sense of smell can be very helpful. For example, if food smells bad you probably won't eat it. How is your sense of smell?

You will need:
- A paper or foam egg carton
- A bandanna for a blindfold
- Some paper and tape
- Some "smelly" items

You might start with the following: cinnamon powder, lemon peel, pepper, clove powder, nutmeg, chili powder, garlic powder, soap, toothpaste, or baby powder. You might ask an adult to help you find more spices from the kitchen or other things with strong smells.

1. Break apart the egg carton into separate little cups.

2. Put a small amount of different things to smell in each cup. Write on a small piece of paper what each smell is and attach it to a cup.

3. Blindfold a friend. Have her guess what each smell is, using only her nose. Check her answers by reading the papers.

Making a Better Ear

Many animals depend upon their sense of hearing to find dinner or avoid being eaten for dinner. Do you ever wish that you could hear better? Let's see if you can make a better ear.

For this activity you are going to need:
- A loud ticking clock
- Paper plates
- Construction paper
- Newspaper
- Paper cups
- Cardboard rolls from the middle of paper towels
- Scissors
- String
- Glue

Only the Nose Knows. Discuss how the sense of smell is developed in many wild animals so that they can find food, identify their young in a crowd, or be alerted to danger. Even the family dog can use its nose to follow a scent, if it leads to food or a pat on the head.

Girls can go on an onion hike or a sensory hike by following a scented trail laid out for them on trees next to a trail.

Find out about flowers, like marigolds, which are planted in vegetable gardens because their scent repels insects. These plants can be used in place of harmful chemicals. Observe plants, such as the Venus flytrap, that use scent to capture insects.

Making a Better Ear. Sound travels in waves and bounces off hard surfaces. Is there a difference in sound when this activity is done in a carpeted room than when it is done in a room with a wood or tile floor? Is the sound different in different-sized rooms? Is there a difference in the hearing distance if one ear is larger than the other? Girls might enjoy doing the sound mapping activity on handbook page 154 in "How and Why?" If they combine this listening activity with "Making a Better Ear," do they notice a difference in the number of sounds they hear?

If girls would like to "see" sound, have them do this simple experiment.

(If you want to decorate your ears you will need crayons, markers, or paints.)

Design a pair of ears that will hear the ticking of the clock before anyone else. Should they be small or should they be large? Should they be long or should they be short? Try it!

When you are ready to test your ears, have someone take the ticking clock across the room. Close your eyes and listen with your ears. You might want to turn your body so that your ears face the direction of the clock. The person with the clock will move closer to you. As soon as you hear the clock ticking, raise your hand and sit down. May the best ears win! Talk about what you have learned from this activity with the rest of the group. Can you find some pictures of animals that have ears like the ones that you made?

Now You See It

Do you always see what is really there? Try this activity that can fool your senses. Make a toy that uses your eyes to trick you. If you close your eyes tight, what do you see? You will see the last thing you were looking at.

You will need:

• A piece of heavy paper or light cardboard that is cut into a 2″ square
• Markers or crayons
• A pencil
• Some tape

1. Hold the paper so that it looks like a diamond, not a square. On one side draw a fishbowl, without the fish, in the middle of the paper.

2. On the other side of the paper, draw a fish. Place your fish on the paper so that if you hold your paper up to the light, the fish would be swimming in the fishbowl. (See illustration.)

3. Tape your paper onto the pencil point, with the bottom of the diamond on the top of the pencil tip.

4. Hold the pencil between your hands in an upright position. Roll the pencil back and forth so the paper flips back and forth. Look at the paper. Where is the fish? Why do you think it is there?

Take a large metal bowl and stretch plastic wrap to fit tightly across the top. Make sure it is taut. Place a large rubber band around the plastic so it remains in place. Sprinkle some brown sugar crystals on the plastic wrap. Take a cookie sheet and hold it above the bowl several feet. Bang the cookie sheet with a wooden spoon. What happens? The sugar should jump on the plastic as sound vibrations from the cookie sheet move through the air hitting the plastic wrap. Vary the distance between the cookie sheet and covered bowl.

Now You See It. This is a simple optical illusion based on the brain's ability to retain images. Girls can try making other illusions, such as a bird in a cage or a face in a window. Have girls play Kim's Game in the Play Try-It. This game is based upon observation, not optical illusion.

Girls might want to make a moving picture or a simple animated cartoon. Girls start by creating a small, blank book with at least 12 pages in it. They should think of a simple movement, such as raising a hand, throwing a ball, or jumping rope. Girls break the movement into 12 steps; they then draw the sequence of steps—one to a page. Girls staple the pages so they can be flipped by a viewer. When the pages are flipped, the drawing appears to be moving. Cartoons and motion pictures use much the same principle, capturing movement on film frames, then running the frames through a projector.

Can You Feel It?

Your sense of touch helps you find things in the dark, tell hot from cold, and enjoy warm hugs. Insects have antennae to help them feel their way around. You have hands. For this activity you will need two large paper bags and two of everything else. Pick objects that are the same, or identical, like two sponges, two dried beans, two mittens, two pennies, two rubber bands, two

spoons. Make sure you do not pick anything sharp. Put one of each thing into each of the paper bags. Shake the bags up, then reach into each bag without looking. Can you find the matching objects using only your sense of touch?

Mapping the Tongue

Think about the different kinds of tastes there are when you eat. Mmmmmmm. Tastes can be sweet, salty, sour, or bitter. When you taste something, does your whole tongue taste it? Find out how and where you taste things by making a map of your tongue.

You will need (for each person doing the activity):

- 4 small dishes or plastic film canisters
- Sugar, vinegar, salt
- Unsweetened grapefruit juice
- 4 cotton-tipped swabs
- Sheet of paper
- 4 different-colored crayons or colored pencils
- A cup of water for each person to rinse her mouth with

Safety tip: Do not share the dishes or the cotton swabs.

1. Place one teaspoon of each of the substances,

sugar (sweet), vinegar (sour), salt, and grapefruit juice (bitter) into a different dish or canister. Add a little water to each of the first three.

2. Draw a big letter "U" onto your paper. This is your tongue map.

3. Dip a cotton swab into the sweet solution. Touch it to at least four different parts of your tongue. Wherever you taste sweet, mark it on your tongue map in one color of crayon.

Can You Feel It? Have the girls do the "hug a tree" activity on handbook page 154 in "How and Why?" Ask girls to work as partners, one partner blindfolded. The sighted partner leads the blindfolded one to a tree. The blindfolded girl must feel the tree and describe it to her partner. The sighted partner leads her blindfolded friend back to the starting point, and asks the girl to find her tree after the blindfold is removed.

Mapping the Tongue. Have girls work as partners in this activity, but caution them about not sharing cotton swabs or solutions. These tastes (salty, sweet, sour, and bitter) are actually the only tastes that can be distinguished. Taste is sensed by organs on the tongue called taste buds. The many flavors detected in food are actually a combination of taste and smell. That is why when a person has a cold, food loses its taste (because she can't smell). Different tastes are actually in different places on the tongue. Taste buds are concentrated more on the edges and back of the tongue, than in the middle.

4. Rinse out your mouth very well with water. Use a different cotton swab and a different solution to do the next parts of your map for salty, bitter, and sour. Rinse between each solution.

5. You now have a map of your tongue's taste buds. Does your tongue taste the same flavors in the same spot? Where does your tongue taste sweetness, saltiness, sourness, bitterness?

6. Compare your map with another girl's map. Are they the same?

What's It Like?

What is it like to be missing one of your senses? How do you communicate if you cannot hear? People who cannot hear often use sign language to communicate with others. Learn how to sign your name using the sign alphabet on page 78 or learn how to say the Girl Scout Promise in American Sign Language (see pictures at right).

Girl Scout Promise

On my honor I will try

to serve God country help people

at all times and live Girl Scout Law

TRY IT•TRY IT•TRY IT•TRY IT•TRY IT•TRY IT•TRY IT•TRY IT•TRY IT•TRY IT•TRY IT•TRY IT•TRY IT•TRY IT•TRY IT•TRY IT **265**

What's It Like? Often when one sense is missing, a person is able to compensate for its loss by concentrating on the other senses. A blind person will often seem to be able to hear or smell better, a person without hearing will learn to feel vibrations so she can dance to the beat of music. Girls can visit a sensory garden, a barrier-free trail or building, or experience an activity that simulates the loss of one of their senses. (See handbook pages 75–79 in "Family, Friends, and Neighbors.")

Try-Its and Other Resources

- Try-Its: My Body; Outdoor Fun.
- Other Resources: *Focus on Ability: Serving Girls with Special Needs* has an excellent chapter on disability simulations that will help with the "What's It Like?" activity. *Games for Girl Scouts.*

TRY IT!

SOUNDS OF MUSIC

What makes music different from any other noise? If you think about it, some noises, such as the drip, drip, drip of a faucet, can sound like music. What other noises inside or outside can sound like music? Count one-and-two-and-three-and-four. Or one-one-two-two-three-three-four-four, or one-and-two and one-and-two. Music is different from noise because it usually has a regular sound, or rhythm. Can you make some instruments to make your own rhythms?

Make Your Own

Percussion instruments make a sound when hit or shaken. They can be drums, rattles, gongs, tambourines, or shakers. Try making a shaker, using a paper plate, dry beans, or other small things that rattle, and a stapler. Place the beans on the paper plate, fold in half and staple plate halves to close. Make one for each hand. See page 226 for some other ideas.

Single String Swing

Can one string make music? It can if it's a one-stringed bass fiddle. Try your hand at this one:
You will need:

• A large empty can (#10 size or 48 ounces) that is open at one end
• A nail
• A hammer
• A heavy string
• A pencil

1. Ask an adult to help you use the hammer and nail to punch a hole in the middle of the can bottom.

2. Measure and cut a length of string that goes from the floor to the middle of your thigh.

3. Knot the end of your string. Pull the other end through the inside of the can and through the hole you made. Make sure the knot is big enough so that it keeps the string from pulling all the way through.

266 *TRY IT•TRY IT•TRY IT•TRY IT•TRY IT•TRY IT•TRY IT•TRY IT•TRY IT•TRY IT•TRY IT•TRY IT•TRY IT•TRY IT•TRY IT*

Tips

This Try-It contains a lot of math and science. Notice how rhythm is actually based upon numbered repetition in a set time sequence. And, musical instruments create vibrations that can be manipulated by movement, and the size and shape of the instruments. Before doing individual activities, listen to music and have girls try to identify the different instruments. For example, girls can learn to distinguish between percussion (drums, xylophone) and string (guitar, violin) instruments.

Make Your Own. Percussion instruments are found in almost all cultures of the world. Compare sounds of percussion instruments from at least three different countries. What makes them different? Girls can make a simple drum by stretching heavy plastic across a coffee can. Make the plastic taut by securing with heavy, tight-fitting rubber bands.

Single String Swing. Listen to music that has a bass fiddle, guitar, violin, or other stringed instruments. Vibrations are created by plucking or rubbing the string. The sound can be changed by varying the length of the string, the amount of tension, where the string is stroked, and how the string is moved, by fingers or bow.

Invite someone who plays a guitar to attend your meeting. Ask her to tune the guitar and point out to the girls as she tightens or loosens the strings the difference in sound. Do the strings vibrate—move back and forth more quickly—when tight or when loose?

4. Tie the other end around the middle of a pencil.

5. To play your instrument, place one foot firmly on the floor and the other foot on the top of the can. Pull the string straight up from the floor so that it is stretched tight with one hand. Now, pluck or jerk the string with the forefinger of the other hand. Experiment with your fiddle sound by plucking in different places on the string. Try holding the string tighter or looser. How does the sound change? Can you get different sounds by changing the length of the string?

Sliding Air

What does wind have to do with music? Different sounds, or notes, are made by changing the amount of air in a tube. If you haven't seen a slide trombone, find a picture of one before doing this activity.

You will need:

- A straw
- Water
- A plastic soda bottle

1. Fill the soda bottle about three-fourths full with water.

2. Place the straw in the water and blow across the straw.

3. Lower the bottle or lift the straw and continue to blow. What happens? What is happening to the air in the straw as you slide it up in the water and as you slide it down? How does that affect the sound? When is the sound the highest? When is it lowest?

Blowing Air

Make a simple wind instrument with a straw. This instrument will have two wedges at one end, called reeds, which lie inside your mouth. The reeds open and close allowing air into the straw. The moving air makes the sound.

You will need:

- A paper straw
- Scissors

You may need an adult's help to cut the triangles.

1. Pinch and flatten a straw about one-half inch to three-fourths inch to the end. Cut off triangles as shown in the diagram. (If you use a plastic straw, you need to flatten the end carefully.)

2. Cut small holes that can be covered by your fingers about one

Sliding Air. A sliding whistle kazoo is a simple version of a slide trombone. The length of the tube can be changed to create different sounds.

The trick to the "Sliding Air" instrument is to blow evenly across the straw, not into it.

Blowing Air. When any wind instrument is blown, the air inside vibrates. With woodwinds (such as a flute or oboe), the musician blows over a reed to get the air blowing. With brass instruments (such as a trumpet or saxophone), a mouthpiece is used. The speed of vibration (and the note sounded) depends upon the length of the column of air inside the pipe. If it is short, the note is high, because the air vibrates fast. If it is long, a low note is sounded, because the vibration is slow. Notes can be changed by fingering holes, closing keys, or shortening or lengthening the length of the column (see "Sliding Air" activity). If possible, get someone to demonstrate a reed instrument, and remove the reed so girls can see it. Some girls may know how to make a simple whistle, using their thumbs and a blade of grass. A piece of cellophane can be made to vibrate if held the right way between fingers and mouth.

inch apart, about two inches from the other end of the straw, as shown.

3. Put the straw into your mouth so that your lips do not touch the corners of the straw.

4. Blow hard. Do not crunch the straw. Cover one, then two, then three of the small holes. You can play simple tunes by covering the different holes.

Do not march or run with the straw in your mouth!

More to Try: Create a horn by putting a funnel in the end of a length of rubber hose. (Do not cut your garden hose up!) Put your lips tightly together and blow through them into the hose. Guess what moves?

Yahoo, a Kazoo

A kazoo is another instrument that works by moving air. Your mouth can help make the sound. You will need:

- A cardboard tube from paper or aluminum foil
- A piece of wax paper
- Some tape

1. Stretch the wax paper tightly over one end of the tube. While holding it tight, get someone to help you tape the wax paper to the end, as shown at right.

2. Near the end of the tube with no wax paper, poke a small hole with a pencil so that air can escape.

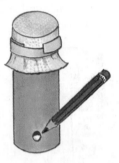

3. Play your kazoo by humming your tune into the tube. Do not sing, but hum "du-du-du."

Strike Up the Band

Try making your own band with your new instruments. Can you make up your own songs? Can you play a song you already know? Try giving a performance for others.

More to Try: Attend a concert put on by a band or orchestra, or view a video of a concert. Can you find instruments that are like the ones you made?

268 *TRY IT•TRY IT•TRY IT•TRY IT•TRY IT•TRY IT•TRY IT•TRY IT•TRY IT•TRY IT•TRY IT•TRY IT•TRY IT•TRY IT•TRY IT•TRY IT*

Yahoo, a Kazoo. Kazoos can be purchased inexpensively. Girls might find it fun to compare a store-bought kazoo with a homemade one. There are also many varieties of kazoo, including the sliding one. Have a kazoo band and practice along with a tape or video.

Strike Up the Band. For leader sanity, do not do this in a small room! It is probably best to settle on a song that everyone knows and to proceed from there, although girls might have a lot of fun composing their own song or rap.

Try-Its and Other Resources

- Try-its: Senses; Music.
- Other Resources: The *Sing-Along Songbook and Cassette*; *Brownies' Own Songbook*.

Attend a local concert (check for children's concerts) to see various instruments at work. Or visit a music store and arrange for a demonstration of different instruments.

TRY IT!

SPACE EXPLORER

Learning about what you see in the sky can be fun. It may be your first step in exploring space. Scientists, astronomers, and astronauts use telescopes, satellites, spaceships, and other scientific equipment to study space.

The Night Sky

Go stargazing with someone who knows the planets and the stars, or have someone help you read a star map. Try to find the North Star, the Big Dipper, the Milky Way, or other constellations. Look for planets and satellites overhead. Perhaps you will even see a meteor or a meteor shower.

The Moon

Why does the moon look like it changes shape? The moonlight you see is the sun shining on one side of the moon. When the earth and moon move around the sun, you see the moon in different places. You also see the parts of the moon that get sunlight. Draw the moon on the same day of the week for four weeks. What did you see?

Ready, Set, Jet!

Pretend that you are on a journey to a Girl Scout center on the moon. How would you dress for space? How would you move in space? Find a way to show what you would wear on your journey. Show your drawing to others. Be ready to answer questions about your space outfit.

Shadow Time

Did you know that the earth rotates? It turns around much like a top. Have you seen the sun in different places in the sky? It looks like the sun is moving, but the earth is moving. Try this activity to mark the earth's movement.

Dr. Tamara Jernigan, the astronaut whose photo is on handbook page 70 in "Family, Friends, and Neighbors," is one of many women now involved in the space program. Girls can find out about other famous women of flight and space (Amelia Earhart, Sally Ride, Mae Jemison).

Tips

The Night Sky. Binoculars or a telescope to view the night sky can add a lot to a stargazing party. The best times for stargazing are when the moon is a small crescent or during a new moon (no moon visible). If you want to study the moon, the best time for viewing is during the full moon. Girls might even pick out their own constellation patterns.

The Moon. This activity can be divided up among girls in a group or troop, by assigning specific nights for each girl to observe the moon. Have each draw what she sees and date her observations. Bring the drawings together and arrange them in sequence. (See the illustration of phases of the moon on handbook page 131 in "How and Why?") Girls can observe a full moon and make drawings of the darker sections. These are usually shadows caused by mountains, valleys, and other surfaces of the moon. Have girls find a calendar that shows the phases of the moon and determine how many days a lunar cycle is (29). Explain that the light seen on the moon is actually reflected light from the sun. The moon revolves around the earth, just like the earth revolves around the sun. (*Note*: Rotating is spinning in place; revolving is movement around an object.) Many people think the earth blocks the light of the sun and

1. Take a stick or stake and put it in the ground. Notice that it casts a shadow. Find the very end of the shadow and mark it with another stick or rock.

2. Leave your markers in the ground and return in an hour. Has something changed? Mark where your shadow is now. Do this once more in another hour. Which way did your shadow move? Did the stick move? What do you think moved to make your shadow move?

More to Try: Keep track of the shadow's movement over several hours. Is there a way you could use this movement to tell time? Visit a sundial in a park or learn how to make one to tell time. Learn how to find which way is north by where the sun is in the sky.

Space Sleuth

Make a model rocket. You can make a very simple rocket that will give you an understanding of rockets that are used to explore space. Try making this balloon rocket to see how.

You will need:

- A large balloon
- Tape
- A plastic straw
- 6 feet or more of string

1. Wet the string and pull it straight.

2. Tie each end of the string to something—a chair, for example.
3. Stretch the string straight.
4. Blow up the balloon and hold the opening closed.

270 TRY IT•TRY IT•**TRY IT**•TRY IT•TRY IT•TRY IT•TRY IT•TRY IT•TRY IT•**TRY IT**•TRY IT•TRY IT•TRY IT•**TRY IT**•TRY IT•TRY IT

---

casts a shadow on the moon, creating the phases of the moon. This only happens in a lunar eclipse. The sun is always shining on the moon, except during an eclipse. On earth, different portions of the lighted side of the moon are seen, depending on where the earth, sun, and moon are in relation to each other. The moon is a satellite of the earth. Have the girls find out if there are other planets that have moons.

Ready, Set, Jet! Have the girls try space-food snacks, such as instant orange drink, freeze-dried ice cream, or energy bars and discuss why food in space needs to be light and compact.

Shadow Time. Shadows occur when light is blocked. Use a flashlight and shine it on a girl's hand against a wall. Have girls observe shadow changes with distance and angle of the light.

More to Try: Girls can measure shadows outdoors at different times of the day. As the earth spins on its axis, that is, rotates, locations on the earth turn towards or away from the sun. When the sun is overhead, midday, shadows are very short. The longest shadows are in the early morning as that part of the earth is turning towards the sun, and in the late afternoon as that part of the earth is turning away from the sun.

Space Sleuth. Rockets need a lot of power to escape the gravitational pull of the earth. The balloon simulates a rocket engine, while the straw is the rocket. The air that escapes propels the rocket forward.

Look at some pictures of rockets. How are they shaped? The top of the rocket is designed so there is little resistance, which helps the rocket move through the air better. Compare pictures of race cars with regular cars. How are they designed differently?

5. Tape the balloon to the straw.

6. Let go of the balloon.

7. Air leaving the balloon pushes against the air in the room, and the balloon moves forward.

OR

Visit a museum or planetarium that has an exhibit or program on space or the stars. If there are none in your community, visit a library to find books on stars and space. Share something you have learned with another person.

Star Maker

Learn about several constellations in the night sky. Pick one and find out how it got its name. Use the pattern of your constellation to make your own indoor star show!

You will need:

- A cylinder-shaped oatmeal or grits container
- A flashlight
- A large safety pin

1. Draw your constellation on the bottom of the cylinder-shaped container on the inside (or draw it backwards on the outside of the box). Mark where the stars are in the constellation. Punch holes in the box very carefully to form your constellation.

2. At night or in a darkened room, place the flashlight in the box and shine it on a blank wall or on the ceiling.

3. Show your constellation to others. Tell them about your constellation. Put on a star show with friends who have made their own constellation boxes.

More to Try: Learn American Indian or native Hawaiian stories about the movement of the stars. Share what you learn with your group.

TRY IT•TRY IT•TRY IT•TRY IT•TRY IT•TRY IT•TRY IT•TRY IT•TRY IT•TRY IT•TRY IT•TRY IT•TRY IT•TRY IT•TRY IT•TRY IT **271**

Star Maker. Patterns of constellations can also be poked into the bottom of plastic film cannisters and viewed individually. Make constellation bingo boards with nine common constellations.

Try-Its and Other Resources

- Try-Its: Me and My Shadow; Movers; Science in Action.
- Other Resources: *Keepers of the Earth: Native American Stories, with Environmental Activities for Children* by Michael J. Caduto and Joseph Bruchac (Fulcrum, Inc., 1988) is an excellent resource for American Indian legends about the stars. *Ranger Rick's NatureScope: Astronomy Adventures* (National Wildlife Federation, Washington, D.C.) has many activities for this age group, as well as clear explanations for leaders. For information on space exploration, write to NASA Headquarters, Code FEP, Publications, 300 E Street S.W., Washington, D.C. 20546.

TRY IT!

SPORTS AND GAMES

Skating

Ice skating and roller skating are fun sports and are good for fitness. Always skate with a buddy and follow safety rules. You will need:

- A pair of skates
- Comfortable clothes
- Safety items—knee pads, wrist guards, etc.

1. Practice falling. Stand in your skates and bend your knees so that you are squatting. Bend backward a little and fall on your bottom. Extend your arms in front of you.

2. Skate forward, to your left, to your right, around corners, and stop.

3. Skate backwards, to your left, to your right, around corners, and stop.

4. Skate forward and backward to music with a partner.

Ball Games

Many sports are played with balls. Try these exercises with at least two kinds of round balls, such as a baseball and a basketball. You'll also need this book. Practice each of these steps.

1. Toss the ball back and forth from your right hand to your left hand.

2. Bounce the ball with your right hand, then with your left hand.

3. Throw the ball in the air and catch it with two hands.

272 TRY IT•TRY IT•**TRY IT**•TRY IT•TRY IT•TRY IT•TRY IT•TRY IT•**TRY IT**•TRY IT•TRY IT•TRY IT•TRY IT•**TRY IT**•TRY IT•TRY IT

Tips

See page 308 in this book under the Play Try-It for tips on playing games with Brownie Girl Scouts. You will also want to read the Activity Checkpoints in *Safety-Wise* to see if you must follow any special guidelines for these sports. Tips for adapting activities appear on pages 57–58 in Part I of this book.

Skating. If possible, take your Brownie Girl Scout troop to a local-ice- or roller-skating rink. They will have the opportunity to see older skaters in action. Many rinks have group discounts. Girls can decide whether to spend troop or group dues on this activity, or raise the money through other means. Tips on managing troop or group money are on handbook page 121 in "Leadership in Girl Scouting and Beyond," pages 32–34 in Part I of this book, and in *Safety-Wise*.

Ball Games. Explore with girls the types of games that are played with balls. Make a chart and discuss the different aspects of each game (number of players, shape of ball, rules, etc.). Which games use just a ball, and which games use a ball and some other equipment? Try playing at least three different ball games.

Bicycling

Bicycling is fun and good exercise. If you have a bicycle, try these bicycling skills.

1. Ride as slowly as you can without stopping.
2. Ride in circles. Try to make the circles as small as you can.
3. Ride in a long, straight line.
4. Practice turning, using hand signals. To turn left, put your left arm straight out with the palm forward. To turn right, put your left arm out and bent upwards at the elbow, with fingers pointing up. To stop, put your left arm out and bent down at the elbow, with fingers pointing down.
5. Set up a bicycling practice course. Place 10–20 large metal cans in a wide play area. Try to ride around the course without touching the cans.

Swimming

Have an adult teach you how to swim. Always remember the following rules:

* Have an adult watch you.
* Swim with a buddy.
* Swim where there are a lifeguard and rescue equipment.
* Leave the water before you get tired or cold.

You will need:

* A swimsuit
* Water (pool, beach, or lake)
* An adult to watch

Ask the adult to help you practice these swimming skills.

1. Sit down in knee-deep water with feet and legs in front of you and hands behind you on the

TRY IT•TRY IT•TRY IT•TRY IT•TRY IT•TRY IT•TRY IT•TRY IT•TRY IT•TRY IT•TRY IT•TRY IT•TRY IT•TRY IT•TRY IT•TRY IT   **273**

Bicycling. Find out if your state or local government has approved bicycle-helmet and/or safety-pad laws. If so, get acquainted with the laws and discuss them with the girls. Check with your local council representative to see if there are resources or community groups to offer help on bicycle safety. If not, you and the girls might plan your own safety meeting and invite others to attend. Discuss with girls how to keep their bicycles maintained.

If girls express an interest, you may wish to plan a field trip to a sporting event, such as a baseball or basketball game, or an equestrian or ice-skating show. Remember that some sporting events can be quite lengthy and some Brownie Girl Scouts may have a difficult time sitting through a long event.

bottom. Move your head back slightly. Straighten your legs and raise your feet.

2. Kneel in water up to your knees. Hold your friend's hand for balance. Put your head into the water and see if you can hold your breath while you count to ten. See if you can keep your eyes open when underwater.

3. See how long you can tread water. Move your arms and legs underwater. Keep your head above the water and your body straight.

Games

Look through this book and find some games you'd like to teach others. Find at least two and teach them to someone else.

Paper Kick Ball

Your feet are very important for many sports and games. Try this football game with your friends.

You will need:

• 1 large brown paper bag
• 4 or more players

1. Press the brown paper bag into a ball.

2. All the players stand in a circle.

3. Choose one player to be the first kicker.

4. The first kicker kicks the paper ball to someone she names in the circle.

5. The ball keeps getting kicked until someone misses it and it goes outside the circle.

6. The person who missed the ball gets a point. She then kicks the ball to someone else.

7. The winner is the player with the lowest number of points.

274 TRY IT•TRY IT•TRY IT•TRY IT•TRY IT•TRY IT•TRY IT•TRY IT•TRY IT•TRY IT•TRY IT•TRY IT•TRY IT•TRY IT•TRY IT•TRY IT

Try-Its and Other Resources

■ Try-Its: Dancercize; Listening to the Past; Me and My Shadow; My Body; Play.

■ Other Resources: See pages 56–57 in "Taking Care of Yourself and Your Home." *Developing Health and Fitness*; *Games for Girl Scouts*.

TRY IT!

WATER EVERYWHERE

Find out about water without getting wet.

Made of Water

Water is part of more things than you may think. It's even part of you! Your body has more water in it than any other substance.

Water mixes with other things so that it often doesn't look like water—milk and orange juice are two examples. Try to find food containers that list water as an ingredient. Make a list. Work with friends.

Drip Drop

Read the section called "Conservation" on pages 147–148. Find a faucet that leaks around your house, school, camp, or neighborhood park. Put a measure under it and time how long it takes to fill up. How many cups or even gallons are wasted in a day at this site? See if you can get someone to fix the faucet or learn how to fix it with someone who knows how to make the repair.

Clean, Clear Water

Do a taste test using water from the tap, distilled water, and bottled spring water. Can you taste a difference? Where does the tap water come from in your home, at your school, and at your camp?

Try this, *but no taste tests!*

1. Do some simple tests using coffee filters and a funnel. Gather some water samples from mud puddles, standing water, a lake or a stream, the tap, and other sources.

2. Write in pencil on the edge of each filter the name of your water source. Strain that water through the filter.

3. Compare filter papers. Are there differences among them?

TRY IT•TRY IT•TRY IT•TRY IT•TRY IT•TRY IT•TRY IT•TRY IT•TRY IT•TRY IT•TRY IT•TRY IT•TRY IT•TRY IT•TRY IT•TRY IT **275**

Tips

Made of Water. Have girls look for foods that are made by adding water (freeze dried) or foods that have had water removed (dehydrated). Plan a refreshment break with the foods. Dehydrate foods using the solar cooker (see Earth Is Our Home Try-It). People can go as long as three weeks without food, but they can go only three days without water before becoming deathly ill. Girls and adults should drink six to eight glasses of water a day to keep their bodies functioning well. Water can be obtained through liquids like juice and milk. Try the "Evaporation" activities on handbook page 138 in "How and Why?"

Drip Drop. Show girls how to brush teeth using only one cup of water, as opposed to letting the water run. Water conservation is a very serious issue in many parts of the world, including the United States. Contact your local water district office to obtain pamphlets on water conservation and to get samples of water-saving devices to install in showerheads and toilets.

Clean, Clear Water. You may need to contact your local water district office to trace the source of your drinking water. You can use a contour map to determine your watershed (the drainage basin of a river or lake). Polluted water and water-borne diseases are responsible for over 25 million deaths a year worldwide.

The filter tests will not tell you if the water contains bacteria or pollutants because most are microscopic. The tests will show you sediments that are too large to go through the filter. Look for color differences in the sediment. Girls can do simple water testing—to test for chemicals or minerals—with kits available for home use. Invite someone to visit your

Water Snooper

To build a water snooper, you will need:

- A large can
- Clear plastic wrap
- Rubber bands

1. Have someone help you remove both ends of the large can.

2. Take the plastic wrap and put it on one end of the can.

3. Hold it in place with the rubber bands.

4. Use the snooper to look into a pond or tide pool, or an aquarium or puddle, by submerging the end with the plastic into your water.

More to Try: Make a water-drop magnifying lens. Take a piece of clear plastic wrap and put two or three drops of water in the middle of it. Hold the plastic over the letters in this book. Are they larger? Hold the plastic over other objects.

Water Explorer

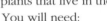

Visit a pond, lake, small stream, or a protected tide pool with your troop or with an organized group. Look for creatures and plants that live in the water.

You will need:
- A strainer
- A white plastic bowl with water in it

1. Dip the strainer in the water and empty what you find into the white plastic bowl that has water in it.

2. If you find living things, how do they move?

3. Look under rocks in the water. Do creatures hide under them or cling to them?

4. Remember to leave the area as you found it. Just use the water snooper to see into the water.

More to Try: Visit an aquarium. Create an aquarium with pond water and draw the changes that take place over several weeks.

276 TRY IT•TRY IT•TRY IT•TRY IT•TRY IT•TRY IT•TRY IT•TRY IT•TRY IT•TRY IT•TRY IT•TRY IT•TRY IT•TRY IT•TRY IT

---

group and demonstrate the use of a portable water filter (your council may have some for backpacking groups) or construct your own water filter using a ceramic flowerpot lined with water filter paper, four inches of washed charcoal, and two inches of washed sand. Pour murky water through the flowerpot and compare the colors before and after. (Do not drink water from the flowerpot.) You might also try using a coffee filter.

Water Snooper. You can make a simple water-viewing box with a milk carton, plastic wrap, and rubber bands. Cut the top off the milk carton, and cut a hole in the side of the carton large enough to put your fingers through. Stretch plastic wrap tightly across the top, and secure it with a rubber band. Place the object to be viewed on the bottom of the carton. Place a drop of water on top

of the plastic wrap. Look through the drop of water and your object should appear larger.

Water Explorer. *Cautions:* Be sure to read *Safety-Wise* before taking a field trip to a water habitat. Make a site visit yourself before leading a group. If girls are working at the edge of a stream or pond, you may not need a lifeguard. If they are wading, exploring ocean tidepools,

or traveling in moving water, you should have one. Do not choose a site that has crumbly banks or swift water. If doing tidepool studies, know your tides and find out about the area's safety.

Have girls do a food-chain activity (see the Plants Try-It and page 206 in this book) using animals and plants found in their water study. Be sure to make observations about

plants and animals out of the water, as well as in the water. Ask girls what would happen if a drought occurred in the area. Discuss photosynthesis (see page 306 in this book under the Plants Try-It) taking place in the water. Plants like seaweed and microscopic algae are the basic food source in the food chain in water as well as on land. Girls could draw a picture of their water ecosystem.

Water Layers

You can see that salt water is different than fresh water in more ways than taste.

You will need:

- 2 glasses
- Warm water
- Container of salt
- Food coloring or ink
- Spoon
- Measuring cup

1. Put one cup of water in a glass. Slowly add salt. Keep stirring. Stop when salt won't dissolve and stays at the bottom.

2. Add some food coloring or ink to the salty water.

3. Hold the spoon to the top of the water and very slowly pour one cup of fresh water onto the spoon. The fresh water will stay on top, because it is not as heavy as salt water.

More to Try: Do this experiment in reverse. Add salt water to fresh water. Try adding cold salty water to warm fresh water.

HANDBOOK Page 277

TRY IT•TRY IT•TRY IT•TRY IT•TRY IT•TRY IT•TRY IT•TRY IT•TRY IT•TRY IT•TRY IT•TRY IT•TRY IT•TRY IT•TRY IT•TRY IT **277**

Water Layers. Salt water is heavier and more dense than fresh water, and that is why it goes to the bottom. A cup of salt water is heavier than a cup of fresh water. Temperature makes a difference, too. Cold water is heavier than warm water, so cold salt water is heavier than warm fresh water. Boats and people float higher on salt water than on fresh water because of the density. (Try it with a paper boat!) Most oils are lighter than water. Try layering cooking oil and rubbing alcohol with the water. (Pour each slowly and carefully into the side of your container.)

How can you make a substance heavier than water float? Take a ball of modeling clay and drop it into a tub of water. It sinks because it is more dense than water. It also makes the water rise in your container. How can you make it float? (Shape it into a boat.) Try different shapes to see which floats best. Test the floatability of the "boats" by adding weights like marbles or paper clips. Girls could see who makes the boat shape that can hold the most weight and compare what makes this boat so good at floating.

Try-Its and Other Resources

- Try-Its: Earth and Sky; Outdoor Happenings; Plants; Science Wonders.

- Other Resources: *Exploring Wildlife Communities With Children*; *Earth Matters*; *Pond Life* by George K. Reid, edited by Herbert S. Zim, Golden Nature Guide Series, Western Publishing Co., 1967.

BRIDGE TO JUNIOR GIRL SCOUTS PATCH

- Invite an adult who works with Junior Girl Scouts to tell you about Junior Girl Scouting. Find out how you can become a Junior Girl Scout.
- Find a Junior Girl Scout to be your "big sister" and help you with bridging activities.
- Look at the uniform and recognitions for Junior Girl Scouts.

Bridging Step 2:
Do a Junior Girl Scout Activity

- Do a Junior Girl Scout badge activity from a badge with a green background in *Girl Scout Badges and Signs.*
- Do an activity from the *Junior Girl Scout Handbook.* (You may do a badge activity from the badges at the back of the handbook.)
- Make something described in the *Junior Girl Scout Handbook.*

As a Brownie Girl Scout, you have fun, make friends, and learn new things. At the end of your last year in Brownie Girl Scouting, you can look forward to Junior Girl Scouting! To help you become a Junior Girl Scout, you may take part in bridging activities that will help you learn all about Junior Girl Scouting.

To earn the Bridge to Junior Girl Scouts patch, you must do at least one activity from each of the seven bridging steps in the order that they are numbered. You and your leader can also decide on special things to do for each step.

Seven Bridging Steps

Bridging Step 1:
Find Out About Junior Girl Scouting

- Invite a Junior Girl Scout to tell you about Junior Girl Scouting.

Tips

At the beginning of the Girl Scout troop year, ask your local Girl Scout representative to introduce you to the Junior Girl Scout leader of the troop or group your Brownie Girl Scouts could join as Junior Girl Scouts. If no Junior Girl Scout troop is available, she could suggest an alternative approach. Together, plan a fun activity or event at which both troops can mix. Maybe the Junior Girl Scouts can put on a skit or play for the Brownie Girl Scouts. The Brownie Girl Scouts could demonstrate something they have learned to do. By meeting early in the year, Brownie Girl Scouts will feel more comfortable when approaching a Junior Girl Scout later when they are doing their bridging steps.

You will also want to become knowledgeable of the types of activities and experiences available to Junior Girl Scouts. This helps girls look ahead. If, during the troop year

Bridging Step 3:
Do Something with a Junior
Girl Scout

- Go on a field trip.
- Do a service project.
- Make something, using your camping skills.

- Make some food to share with other girls.
- Find and write to a Junior Girl Scout pen pal who lives in your area or another state. Ask your local Girl Scout council representative for help.

Bridging Step 4:
Share What You Learn About
Junior Girl Scouting with
Brownie or Daisy Girl Scouts

- Make a collage about Junior Girl Scouting for your Brownie or Daisy Girl Scout friends.
- Show them a Junior Girl Scout activity.
- Tell them about a field trip or service project that you did with a Junior Girl Scout.
- Teach them a song or game that you learned from a Junior Girl Scout.

TRY IT•*TRY IT*•*TRY IT*•TRY IT•TRY IT•*TRY IT*•TRY IT•TRY IT•*TRY IT*•TRY IT•TRY IT•*TRY IT*•TRY IT•*TRY IT*•TRY IT•TRY IT   **279**

you can mention, "You can go _____ when you are a Junior Girl Scout" or "I heard that some Junior Girl Scouts went _____ ," you are helping girls stay in Girl Scouting. Studies have shown that self-esteem and feelings of competence of many girls drop when they are at the Junior and Ca-

dette Girl Scout age levels. Activities that give girls opportunities to learn and grow in an all-girl setting help counteract this negative trend.

Girls only need do one activity from each of the seven steps. They should be done in sequence. You may substitute activities you and the

girls create for the activities within the steps as long as the activities are equivalent. For example, for Bridging Step One, the girls could read the *Junior Girl Scout Handbook* and *Girl Scout Badges and Signs* to become familiar with the Junior Girl Scout age level. They would not have to actually

do any of the activities in those books, as that is a requirement for Bridging Step Two.

For Bridging Step Three, you could substitute learning some games from a Junior Girl Scout.

Bridging Step 5:
Do Junior Girl Scout Recognitions Activities

- Earn a Dabbler badge from one of the worlds of interest in *Girl Scout Badges and Signs.*
- Earn a badge with a green background from *Girl Scout Badges and Signs.*

- Do a badge activity from each world of interest in *Girl Scout Badges and Signs.*
- Do one activity from five different badges in the *Junior Girl Scout Handbook.*

Bridging Step 6:
Help Plan Your Bridging (Fly-Up) Ceremony

- Learn how to do an opening or closing for a ceremony that is different from any opening or closing you have done before.

- Write a poem about Brownie or Junior Girl Scouting.
- Make up a song for the ceremony.
- Design and make invitations for the ceremony.
- Make decorations to be used at the ceremony.

280   TRY IT•TRY IT•**TRY IT**•TRY IT•TRY IT•TRY IT•TRY IT•TRY IT•TRY IT•TRY IT•TRY IT•TRY IT•TRY IT•**TRY IT**•TRY IT•TRY IT

For Bridging Step Five, the Dabbler badges and the green-backed badges are the Junior Girl Scout badges easier than others to do. Bridging Step Six involves planning the actual bridging ceremony. This is a very special occasion for a Brownie Girl Scout. The girls should be the active planners of the ceremony. They can use some of the songs, recipes, and other activities they have learned in Brownie Girl Scouts. The book *Ceremonies in Girl Scouting* is an excellent resource.

Find sample ceremonies on pages 27–28 in Part I of this book. Girls may wish to invite relatives or friends to their ceremony. Brownie Girl Scouts who are not ready to bridge should also be included in the ceremony.

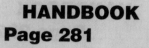

Bridging Step 7:
Plan and Do a Summer
Girl Scout Activity

If your Girl Scout group has its Court of Awards before summer, you may be able to get your Bridge to Junior Girl Scouts patch then. Remember to promise to do Step 7 over the summer.

* Go to Girl Scout camp.
* Plan and go on a picnic with some other Girl Scouts.
* Have a campfire or cookout with other Girl Scouts.
* Make a summer scrapbook to share with your new Junior Girl Scout friends.
* Have a sports day with other Girl Scouts.
* Plan a get-acquainted activity that you can do in the fall with your new Junior Girl Scout friends.
* Write a summer newsletter to send to other Girl Scouts.
* Do a service project.

Looking Back and Looking Ahead

Brownie Girl Scouts who become Junior Girl Scouts receive Brownie Girl Scout wings that they can wear as Junior Girl Scouts. Girls who join Junior Girl Scouting without first being Brownie Girl Scouts do not receive Brownie Girl Scout wings. They may ask you about your wings. Do you know how they got their name?

A long time ago, Brownie Girl Scout leaders were called "Brown Owls." Remember the Wise Owl in the Brownie story? At the fly-up ceremony, the Brown Owl gave wings to those girls in her troop who were ready to go to the next age level in Girl Scouting.

At a fly-up ceremony, you receive your wings and renew your Girl Scout Promise and you get the membership pin that is worn by Junior, Cadette, Senior, and adult

TRY IT•TRY IT•TRY IT•TRY IT•TRY IT•TRY IT•TRY IT•TRY IT•TRY IT•TRY IT•TRY IT•TRY IT•TRY IT•TRY IT•TRY IT **281**

Girls may ask about the Brownie Girl Scout wings. If you remember the Brownie Story, handbook pages 17–21 in "Welcome to Girl Scouts," the Brown Owl was the wise character who helped the children. Girl Scout leaders used to be called "Brown Owls" and still are in many WAGGGS countries. The Brown Owls gave wings to girls who had completed their bridging steps and were ready to move (or fly up) to the next age level.

Helping Others Learn About Girl Scouting

Now that you know how much fun Girl Scouting can be, why not tell your friends about it! You can help others learn about Girl Scouting by:

- Making a poster for Girl Scout Week showing things you do as a Brownie Girl Scout.
- Helping in a flag ceremony at a neighborhood or council event.
- Bringing a friend to a Girl Scouting event.
- Helping to get a Girl Scout camp ready for a summer season.

Girl Scouts. You will have a chance to plan your fly-up ceremony with the girls in your troop and with the Junior Girl Scouts in the troop you will be joining.

Each step of Junior Girl Scouting can be filled with fun and adventure. There are badges and signs you can work on as a Junior Girl Scout, or you can invent your own badge and develop an "Our Own Troop's" badge. You can also earn the Junior Aide patch by helping Brownie Girl Scouts bridge to Junior Girl Scouting. The *Junior Girl Scout Handbook* has a lot of information and fun activities for you and your Junior Girl Scout friends. The possibilities are many!

Not every girl may be going into Junior Girl Scouts. Some girls may be moving to a new community. You will want to let your local council representative know about any girl who is moving so the Girl Scout council in her new community may contact her. At year's end, Brownie Girl Scouts will appreciate an opportunity to share memories.

Brownie Girl Scout Memories

Your copy of the *Brownie Girl Scout Handbook* can be a record of all the fun times you had and of all the new things you learned as a Brownie Girl Scout. Think of the new friends you made. What will you remember most about being a Brownie Girl Scout? Use this space for friends' autographs, special memories, or your own special thoughts.

283

Girls have a place for autographs and addresses in their handbook. You may want to send each girl a postcard or note over the summer just to let her know she is in your thoughts. You can encourage the girls to write or phone each other over the summer. If your Girl Scout council has planned some summertime wider opportunities, make sure girls know the dates and other details. Girl Scout camp is another summer activity many girls enjoy. Find out about camp activities offered by your council.

Try-Its and Other Resources

- Other Resources: *Ceremonies in Girl Scouting*; *Girl Scout Badges and Signs*; *Junior Girl Scout Handbook*; *Junior Girl Scout Activity Book*.

Index